Nature Behind Barbed Wire

Nature Behind Barbed Wire

*An Environmental History of
the Japanese American Incarceration*

CONNIE Y. CHIANG

OXFORD
UNIVERSITY PRESS

OXFORD

UNIVERSITY PRESS

Oxford University Press is a department of the University of Oxford. It furthers
the University's objective of excellence in research, scholarship, and education
by publishing worldwide. Oxford is a registered trade mark of Oxford University
Press in the UK and certain other countries.

Published in the United States of America by Oxford University Press
198 Madison Avenue, New York, NY 10016, United States of America.

Library of Congress Cataloging-in-Publication Data
Names: Chiang, Connie Y., author.
Title: Nature behind barbed wire : an environmental history of the
Japanese American incarceration / Connie Y. Chiang.
Description: New York, NY : Oxford University Press, [2018] |
Includes bibliographical references and index.
Identifiers: LCCN 2018003904 (print) | LCCN 2018028938 (ebook) |
ISBN 9780190842079 (Updf) | ISBN 9780190842086 (Epub) |
ISBN 9780190842062 (hardcover : alk. paper)
Subjects: LCSH: Japanese Americans—Evacuation and relocation, 1942-1945. |
Concentration camps—United States—History—20th century. |
World War, 1939–1945—Environmental aspects. | Human ecology—United States—History.
Classification: LCC D769.8.A6 (ebook) | LCC D769.8.A6 C35 2018 (print) |
DDC 940.53/1773089956—dc23
LC record available at https://lccn.loc.gov/2018003904

For Anna Klingle and Jollin Chiang
and
in memory of Augustine Young

Contents

Acknowledgments

IT TOOK ME a decade to complete this book. Many debts have accrued over the course of ten years, and I'm delighted (and relieved) to finally have the opportunity to extend my heartfelt gratitude to a long list of friends, colleagues, and institutions.

This book would not have been possible without Bowdoin College, the National Endowment for the Humanities, and the American Society for Environmental History. They all provided critical financial support for archival research. Bowdoin also funded two sabbatical leaves that gave me time to conduct research and write. I am deeply grateful to work at an institution that provides such generous support for faculty scholarship.

I am indebted to the staffs of several libraries and archives, all of whom provided invaluable assistance. Thanks to the Denver Public Library, the Huntington Library, the Idaho State Historical Society, the National Archives and Records Administration in Washington, DC, Special Collections at the Charles E. Young Research Library at the University of California, Los Angeles, Special Collections at the J. Willard Marriott Library at the University of Utah, and Special Collections at the University of Washington. Bowdoin's librarians are also outstanding. Special thanks to Guy Saldanha for securing dozens of microfilm reels and Barbara Levergood for teaching me to navigate government documents. During the course of my research, many institutions also began to digitize records related to the Japanese American incarceration. My ability to remotely access thousands of documents and images facilitated the completion of this book. I would especially like to thank the Densho Project for recording the memories of hundreds of Japanese Americans and making a treasure trove of sources available to the public.

I had the pleasure of presenting my research at several colleges and universities, where engaged audiences asked smart questions and helped me refine my claims. Many thanks to my gracious hosts at these institutions: Jen

Seltz and Niall O'Murchu at Western Washington University and Fairhaven College; Melanie Kiechle, Kara Schlichting, and Adam Zalma then at Rutgers University; Liz Escobedo at the University of Denver; Tamara Venit-Shelton then at Reed College; Louis Warren at the University of California, Davis; Scott Wong at Williams College; and Jay Turner at Wellesley College. I also thank Peggy Shaffer and Phoebe Young for inviting me to participate in the Third Nature Symposium at Miami University of Ohio. The feedback that I received from them and the other participants transformed chapter 5.

Many friends and colleagues offered thoughtful suggestions and encouragement over the years. My deepest thanks to Matthew Booker, Kathy Brosnan, Kate Brown, Lizzie Grennan Browning, Bill Cronon, Jared Farmer, Mark Fiege, Drew Isenberg, Karl Jacoby, Karen Leong, Neil Maher, Mary Mendoza, Tom Okie, Rachel St. John, Paul Sutter, Julie Sze, Elena Tajima-Creef, Jay Taylor, Cecilia Tsu, Richard White, and Bob Wilson. Andrea Geiger offered sage advice at a key moment of the revising process. Kathy Morse not only helped me think about the bigger argument of this book, she also photographed sources for me in the archives while she was doing research on her own book. Kendra Smith-Howard did the same thing, long before we actually met in person. Liz Escobedo carefully read and critiqued several chapters of the manuscript. I am beyond grateful for her keen insights and, most importantly, her unwavering friendship and support for over two decades.

My Bowdoin colleagues also shaped this project in many ways. Laura Henry, Jill Smith, and Krista VanVleet provided incisive comments on an early version of chapter 6. I spent several summers and holiday breaks writing in an empty classroom alongside Natasha Goldman and Jayanthi Selinger, both of whom offered camaraderie and friendship. Jayanthi, along with Sakura Christmas, fielded my numerous questions about Japanese language, culture, and history as well. I am also indebted to Dharni Vasudevan, who, in addition to being a wonderful mentor, explained basic soil chemistry and helped me make sense of the pipeline corrosion story that unfolds in chapter 3. Thanks also to Belinda Kong and Nancy Riley, whose insights into the Asian American experience informed this project in many ways, and to Chuck Dorn, Brian Purnell, Susan Tananbaum, and Allen Wells for cheering me on throughout.

I am fortunate to teach excellent students, who humored my frequent discussions of this project and always asked terrific questions. In particular, students in my US home front seminar helped me grapple with the messiness of the war years; their influence pervades this book. Students in my North

American environmental history and Asian American history surveys also reminded me of the vibrancy of these fields and helped me think about their connections. Two students provided research assistance. Andrew Raisner helped to compile the bibliography, and Paul Landsberg dug up sources for me in eastern California.

As I was finishing the final revisions on the book, I had the pleasure and honor of participating in the Densho Scholars Roundtable alongside Tom Ikeda, Karen Inouye, Lon Kurashige, Eric Muller, Brian Niiya, Greg Robinson, and Alice Yang. Their comments, questions, and deep knowledge shaped my eleventh-hour tweaks in critical ways. I was also inspired by their warmth, passion, and generosity. Special thanks to Eric Muller for extending the invitation and for providing perceptive comments on the entire manuscript. His feedback proved to be indispensable.

Susan Ferber expressed interest in this project long ago, and I'm enormously grateful that she stuck with me for so many years. She has been a superb editor. She helped me think through the argument and narrative of the manuscript, then edited every single page, demanding precision and clarity throughout. Her professionalism, sense of humor, and encouragement also made this process a true pleasure.

Family and friends, near and far, provided much support. For their hospitality during my research trips, I thank my cousins Angela Kwan, Carl Potts, Jeff Young, and Stephanie Young. A million thanks to my remarkable mom, Jollin Chiang, whose presence nourished me in so many ways during her visits to Maine. Scott Chiang is everything an older sibling ought to be, and his resilience and wisdom are inspiring. Closer to home, I am grateful to Seth Ramus, Michael Kolster, and Christy Shake for showering my family with meals, drinks, and endless good cheer. I would be remiss if I didn't also thank the Mackey family, my extraordinary neighbors who kept me laughing and always offered a helping hand.

My immediate family supported and encouraged me at every turn. Matt Klingle has been much more than my spouse and colleague throughout this process. He has also been the most loyal and loving friend. He always knows just the right things to say, and his unfailing confidence in my abilities and great enthusiasm for my work have sustained me for many years now. As I toiled on this book, I also had the immense joy of watching our children grow up into such beautiful and amazing human beings. Between Ben's insatiable curiosity and strong sense of justice and Anna's tender heart and enormous empathy, I had constant reminders of why this story matters. My love for and pride in them have no bounds.

This book tells a story that spans several generations of Japanese American families and speaks to their remarkable resilience. It thus seems fitting that my dedication is also multigenerational. This book is for my daughter, my mom, and my late grandfather, Augustine Young. Models of human decency, all three have enriched my life with their kindness and generosity.

Note on Terminology

THE WORDS USED to describe the wartime experiences of people of Japanese ancestry are controversial. "Internment" has been the most commonly used term, but many scholars have rejected its use because it refers to the detention of enemy aliens during war. The federal government did intern some German, Italian, and Japanese enemy aliens in army and Department of Justice camps, but roughly two-thirds of the people of Japanese ancestry expelled from the Pacific Coast were US citizens by birth. Thus, I do not use the term "internment" and instead use "incarceration," "confinement," and "detention."[1]

My choices are not without problems. Some scholars rebuff "detention" because it implies a short-term period of confinement, but I maintain that it adequately captures the lack of freedom that people of Japanese ancestry experienced. Others reject "incarceration" because it implies that the camps were penitentiaries and that those confined therein had committed crimes.[2] My use of "incarceration" is not meant to question their innocence. Rather, it highlights the harsh conditions under which they lived. It is true that the facilities were not actual prisons; they did not have cells with steel bars that were unlocked only at certain times of the day. Nonetheless, they were surrounded by barbed wire fences and guarded by armed men. They shared enough characteristics with penitentiaries for "incarceration" to be an appropriate term.

To describe the facilities where people of Japanese ancestry were confined, I reject "internment camp" and "relocation center," the government's term, except when I am quoting from or referring to documents from the war years. What, then, is a more appropriate term? Some scholars have adopted "concentration camp," but many question its close association with the Nazi death camps. Using this term in conjunction with the confinement of people of Japanese ancestry, they argue, diminishes the atrocities that Jews faced. Historian Alice Yang Murray adds that "concentration camp" and Nazi "extermination camp" have become "inextricably linked in the popular imagination. During World War II, officials and commentators could say Japanese Americans were confined in 'concentration camps' without evoking images of Nazi atrocities. I don't think that this is true today."[3] Sympathetic to Murray's argument, I avoid "concentration camp" and employ "incarceration camp" or just "camp."

In addition to "relocation center," the federal government used the euphemistic terms "evacuation" and "relocation" to describe the rounding up and removal of people of Japanese ancestry from their homes. According to the leaders at Densho: The Japanese American Legacy Project, a nonprofit organization dedicated to preserving and disseminating Japanese Americans' wartime stories, "evacuation" is closely associated with a natural disaster and thus suggests that their removal was a safety precaution.[4] While some federal officials believed that this was the case in 1942, numerous scholars have rejected that justification since. "Relocation," likewise, has a benign connotation and does not suggest the compulsory nature of expulsion. Thus, I use "forced removal," "mass removal," and "expulsion."

The last dilemma involves what to collectively call the thousands of people of Japanese ancestry who were confined at the camps. To this end, I have adopted "Japanese American." While this term typically refers to Nisei—those who were born on American soil to immigrant parents and were US citizens—I apply it to Issei, the immigrant generation, as well. Because many Issei had lived in the United States for four decades at the start of the war, had no intention of returning to Japan, and would have become naturalized citizens had immigration law allowed, I think it is appropriate to call them "Japanese Americans."[5] Generational divides were certainly relevant, however, and I make the distinction when necessary. More generally, I also refer to them as "detainees" and "incarcerees."

---

1. "Terminology," http://www.densho.org/terminology/ (accessed July 27, 2015); Roger Daniels, "Words Do Matter: A Note on Inappropriate Terminology and the Incarceration of Japanese Americans," in *Nikkei in the Pacific Northwest: Japanese Americans and Japanese Canadians in the Twentieth Century*, ed. Louis Fiset and Gail M. Nomura (Seattle: University of Washington Press, 2005), 190–214. See also Civil Liberties Public Education Fund, "Resolution Regarding Terminology," http://www.momomedia.com/CLPEF/backgrnd.html#Link%20to%20terminology.

2. "Terminology," http://www.densho.org/terminology/; Greg Robinson, *A Tragedy of Democracy: Japanese Confinement in North America* (New York: Columbia University Press, 2010), vii–viii; Cherstin Lyon, *Prisons and Patriots: Japanese*

American Wartime Citizenship, Civil Disobedience, and Historical Memory (Philadelphia: Temple University Press, 2011), xi–xiii.

3. Daniels, "Words Do Matter," 204–205; Alice Yang Murray, *Historical Memories of the Japanese American Internment and the Struggle for Redress* (Stanford, CA: Stanford University Press, 2008), 7; Edward Schumacher Matos and Lori Grisham, "Euphemisms, Concentration Camps, and the Japanese Internment," National Public Radio, February 10, 2012, http://www.npr.org/sections/ombudsman/2012/02/10/146691773/euphemisms-concentration-camps-and-the-japanese-internment (accessed July 27, 2015).

4. "Terminology," http://www.densho.org/terminology/.

5. "Terminology," http://www.densho.org/terminology/. It was not until the passage of the McCarran-Walter Act in 1952 that people of Japanese ancestry could become naturalized US citizens.

Introduction

THE NATURE OF CONFINEMENT

WHEN DILLON S. MYER became director of the War Relocation Authority (WRA) on June 17, 1942, he faced an enormous job: to oversee the confinement of over 110,000 people of Japanese ancestry.[1] Many seemingly minor details also demanded his attention, such as choosing a name for the post office at the Central Utah Relocation Center, one of the ten camps that detained his charges. Seeking advice, he dashed off a letter to Utah governor Herbert Maw on July 2. "It seems to us that the name of the new post office should originate within the state," he commented. Myer went on to note that detainees would be engaged in reclamation and conservation projects, so he wanted to honor a Utahan "actively identified" with this type of work.[2] For Myer, a name embedded in local land uses was fitting, given plans for Japanese Americans to continue natural resource work in camp.

Maw's secretary, Elias J. Strong, replied to Myer a month later. After conducting a telephone survey of nearby residents, he explained that there were "not any real old time settlers whose names could be used for this purpose." The most prominent local resident involved with conservation work was R. J. Law, "who [was] still alive and very active." Strong recognized that adopting the name "Law, Utah" "in conjunction with what many will refer to as a concentration camp hardly sounds appropriate."[3] Given the massive violation of civil liberties that was at the heart of the wartime incarceration of Japanese Americans, "Law" would be completely incongruous—an ironic name at best, insulting and demeaning at worst.

Instead, Strong looked to the surrounding environment for inspiration. One possibility was nearby Drum Mountain, so named because "when the wind blows a noise comes from this mountain very similar to the noise of beating drums." According to Strong, this was the "favorite choice of the citizens." The other possibility was Topaz, the name of another nearby mountain that "glistens in the sunlight" like the orange-hued gemstone.[4] Both "Drum Mountain" and "Topaz" pointed to notable environmental features, whether sonorous wind or dazzling color. Neither name had problematic connotations. In the end, "Topaz" stuck and became the colloquial name for the camp. Embracing the gemstone idea, the masthead for the first issue of the *Topaz Times*—the camp newspaper produced by Japanese Americans but under WRA supervision—was even emblazoned with the slogan "JEWEL OF THE DESERT."[5]

At first glance, this discussion may appear unremarkable, even inconsequential, but the act of naming can be an exercise of power.[6] For Myer and Strong, the post office name asserted how Japanese Americans might interact with the environment. Myer, who had worked for the Soil Conservation Service, saw the detainees as following in the footsteps of earlier white settlers and thus wanted a name to reflect that continuity. As they toiled to make the Sevier Desert productive, detainees would also contribute to a progressive narrative surrounding the WRA's program. Their labor would make the camps self-sufficient and "fill gaps in the wartime economy of the Nation," including food production, the development of "raw lands," and "other essential public works."[7] For his part, Strong preferred to focus on Utah's geographic features and draw attention away from the inherent injustices of the camp. In short, these men believed that the environment would be a site of productive labor or a source of inspiring scenery.

In practice, the environment played a more complicated and often contradictory role in the Japanese American incarceration. While detainees did clear marginal land and grow crops and did come to enjoy and find inspiration in their surroundings, the environment also proved profoundly vexing and oppressive. As illustrated by Japanese Americans' wartime memoirs, social isolation and psychological distress were tied to the harsh environmental conditions of the camps. For example, Yoshiko Uchida associated "exile" and "uprooting" with the desert. In recounting her journey to Topaz, she recalled her dismay as the environment became "as bleak as a bleached bone," with barracks "sitting sullenly in the white, chalky sand."[8]

Artwork from the camps reinforces this point. *Sevier Desert*, a sumi-e (ink painting) by Chiura Obata, is explicit about nature's toll:

The spring has come, but here in Topaz there is not even one green,
   growing plant.

Everything is like it is drawn with a grey brushstroke.
Yellow dust blows into eyes, mouth and skin.
It is not known how long we will stay in this desert.[9]

Obata was clearly discouraged by the harsh desert, but he also drew strength from nature. In *Nagare no Tabi* (Stream's Journey), he chronicled Japanese Americans' time in Utah. One panel shows the silhouette of Topaz Mountain looming over the barracks along with the text, "Four months of hardship have passed. Our strong hopes and iron will to succeed have never wavered. At last, we see the beautiful dawn as reflected in the morning sun bright against snow-covered Mt. Topaz!" After their first long winter, stunning vistas restored Japanese Americans' spirits.[10]

Japanese American photographers also depicted the environment as a source of both hope and hardship. While detainees were initially not allowed to bring cameras to the camps, the government eased this restriction by the spring of 1943. At the Heart Mountain Relocation Center, several detainees, including Bill Manbo, subsequently retrieved their cameras and formed a camera club.[11] While Manbo often featured camp events in his photographs, he also captured the pleasure and disquiet brought by the natural world. In one image, his family enjoys an outing to the Shoshone River. With the sun shining brightly, three women, pants rolled up to their calves, wade into the water, one with a broad smile on her face. In another image, his son, Billy, walks alone on a dirt road edged with tarpaper-covered barracks and piles of coal. He appears as a small figure against the gray skies and sage-colored earth, Heart Mountain looming in the distance. Even in this color photograph, the landscape is almost colorless, and the mood is somber. For Manbo, then, the natural world brought joy and sorrow.[12]

While these sources suggest that the natural world was an important, if not central, part of the confinement experience, most scholars of the Japanese American incarceration have not adopted an explicit environmental focus.[13] They invariably mention the bleak and harsh conditions of the camps, but then focus on other themes. Many have explored the political and legal aspects of incarceration, such as the federal government's justifications for removal and confinement, Japanese Americans' efforts to resist and challenge their incarceration, and the movement for redress.[14] Some have taken a social and cultural approach and examined the impact of confinement on Japanese American families and communities during and after the war.[15] To illuminate these topics, still other scholars have edited the correspondence, memoirs, and oral histories of former detainees.[16] Collectively, this scholarship highlights the multiple factors that shaped incarceration policy and the resilience and creativity of Japanese Americans, but the environment remains mostly an unexamined backdrop rather than an integral part of this wartime program.

Among those scholars who have embraced an environmental perspective, some have grappled with the paradox of the wide-open spaces of the American West—long associated with freedom, democracy, and unfettered opportunities—as the site of confinement. WRA officials equated the camps with "pioneer communities" and suggested that Japanese Americans were following in the footsteps of their white predecessors, but western lands were undeniably the site of their oppression.[17] Others have explored detainees' material changes to nature, whether as agricultural laborers outside the camps or as farmers and gardeners within the camps.[18] The work on gardening has been especially enlightening, as this endeavor helped to ameliorate the hardships of incarceration while allowing Japanese Americans to resist state power.[19]

Nature Behind Barbed Wire provides a more comprehensive environmental history of the Japanese American incarceration, from the early debates about removal in 1941 to the postwar resettlement years. It embraces the "core tasks" of the field, offering thick descriptions of the environment's influence on detainees and analyzing their interactions with and transformations of the natural world.[20] With the environment placed squarely at the center of the story, it explores several facets of camp life, from outdoor recreation to agricultural production, and analyzes how natural forces shaped them.[21] Agriculture is particularly important because it was central to many Japanese Americans' lives before, during, and after the war. Like other agroenvironmental studies, this book examines how various environmental factors—soil, weather, insects, to name a few—affected crop output and social interactions on the farms.[22]

In addition to reorienting the scholarship on the Japanese American incarceration, this book contributes to Asian American history and environmental history. Few studies in either field have analyzed the environmental practices of Asian Americans and how the shifting political and racial climate shaped their changes to and attitudes toward nature.[23] Given Asian Americans' diverse interactions with the natural world since the nineteenth century, the wartime experiences of Japanese Americans must be understood as part of a longer environmental history. Their time in the camps, moreover, demonstrates how racial identities and the dynamics of race relations have intertwined with the environment through time. Indeed, this book expands discussions about environmental inequalities and further illuminates how the natural world has helped to both define and challenge racial divisions.[24]

Ultimately, the book asks: how does the lens of environmental history alter our understandings of Japanese Americans' wartime incarceration? It argues that the confinement of Japanese Americans was an environmental process, deeply embedded in the lands and waters along the coast and the camps further inland. Each step in the process was shaped by the natural world, whether its physical properties and fluctuations or humans' shifting understandings of and interactions with it. For example, building camps in undeveloped areas required the clearing of large swaths of land, which often contributed to dust storms. These blinding squalls wreaked havoc on the infrastructure, but they also intensified Japanese Americans' feelings of outrage and despondency. Throughout the war years, the environment operated as a material reality and a cultural force, molding the camps' physical contours and influencing how both WRA officials and Japanese Americans perceived the incarceration.

The environmental process of incarceration was simultaneously a social process, shaped by confrontations and compromises between and among Japanese Americans and WRA officials. Once at the camps, they engaged in constant negotiations with the environment—and with each other. For WRA officials, their ability to keep the camps running smoothly depended, in part, on favorable environmental conditions as well as the cooperation of detainees. Neither was a given, and state power was never absolute.[25] Of course, Japanese Americans faced the most constraints. The WRA restricted their ability to work and checked their access to the resources with which they could feed and shelter themselves. Their state of relative dependence and their overall vulnerability compounded the environmental limitations that they already faced. Nonetheless, they found many ways to harness nature and assert some control over the terms and conditions of their confinement. In doing so, they often proclaimed their Americanness.

These negotiations and adaptations took place during a time of global war, which had widespread environmental implications.[26] As natural resources were funneled to soldiers fighting abroad, Americans at home had to make do with less and abide by federal rationing strictures.[27] Japanese Americans and WRA officials were not exempt from these mandates, but confinement in desolate locales made their plight far more challenging. Food was rationed so as to provide meals for the troops overseas. Construction materials were often second-rate. Coal for heat and wallboard for insulation were in short supply. The war stymied efforts to make the camps habitable and hospitable.

Japanese Americans and WRA officials also had to navigate the complex ideological terrain of the war. With the United States waging a war, in part, against Nazism, many American intellectuals and activists continued their long-standing attacks against racial prejudices and pushed for antidiscrimination measures. This principle of racial liberalism—that "government could and should play a role in promoting racial equality"— received legitimacy when President Franklin Delano Roosevelt issued Executive Order 8802, which created the Fair Employment Practices Committee to combat inequalities in the workplace.[28] However, as historian Nikhil Pal Singh argues, World War II was also "a war in which a discourse of antifascism, freedom and democracy was counter-poised with clashes along the color-line."[29] The incarceration of Japanese Americans was a glaring example of how racial liberalism fell short of its idealistic goals. This book expands on this point by highlighting how the suffering and indignities wrought by the natural world made the government's empty words even more galling.

To illustrate the environment's pervasive and vital role in the incarceration process, *Nature Behind Barbed Wire* focuses on four of the ten WRA "relocation centers": Gila River, Manzanar, Minidoka, and Topaz. Gila River was about fifty miles south of Phoenix, Arizona, on the Gila River Indian Reservation, home to the Akimel O'otham (Pima) and Maricopa Indians since 1859. Located in southern Idaho, Minidoka was a US Bureau of Reclamation project, established in 1904 to control the flow of the Snake River in order to support farming in the region. In contrast, Topaz was a conglomeration of private, county, and federal property in central Utah, mostly used for grazing and agriculture. Meanwhile, Manzanar, a former ranching and farming town known for its lush apple orchards, was on Owens Valley land acquired by the City of Los Angeles in the 1920s to provide water for metropolitan growth.[30] These camps represent a range of ownership and land use arrangements. They also highlight key themes in the history of the American West—the prevalence of public lands, the influence of aridity, and an enduring record of displacement and social inequality—that connect the Japanese American incarceration to the region's development.[31]

Detainees at these four camps came from a wide swath of rural and urban locales up and down the Pacific Coast. Gila River was inhabited by many rural residents of California's Central Valley, along with individuals from Los Angeles and the southern California coast; Manzanar was populated by metropolitan Los Angeles residents, a diverse mix of urban professionals, nursery owners, and Terminal Island fishermen; Minidoka was occupied by urbanites from Seattle and Portland and farmers from outlying areas; and Topaz pulled a predominantly urban populace from the San Francisco Bay Area.[32] Japanese Americans from these communities had developed strong ties to nearby lands and waters, often through their labor in natural resource industries. These prewar environmental experiences undoubtedly shaped their reactions to their incarceration.

Concentrating on Gila River, Manzanar, Minidoka, and Topaz comes at the expense of exploring Jerome and Rohwer in southeastern Arkansas. This is a notable absence given their distinct environmental features. Located on Farm Security Administration land in the marshy delta of the Mississippi River floodplain, these two camps contained bayous and swamps and were surrounded by forests, which Japanese Americans logged for heating fuel.[33] While juxtaposing the southern and western camps could yield some intriguing points of comparison, it is beyond the scope of this book. Moreover, all of the camps, whether in the interior West or Arkansas, represented an environmental contrast from the Pacific Coast and required considerable adaptation on the part of detainees. The exact location of their confinement was, in some respects, less important than the larger process in which they participated.

The first step in the incarceration process was displacement, the topic of the opening two chapters. Chapter 1 examines how Japanese Americans' prewar involvement in natural resource industries along the Pacific Coast— especially agriculture—shaped the campaign for their removal. Given the heightened need for foodstuffs during the war, federal officials struggled with how to address the elimination of Japanese American cultivators. Chapter 2 turns to the site selection and construction process for the ten "relocation centers," concentrating on the WRA's environmental and geographic criteria and local responses to their placement in particular locations. It also analyzes detainees' initial reactions to these facilities and how they, along with WRA officials, addressed their first environmental challenges: the dust and heat. This chapter does not examine the temporary assembly centers, which housed Japanese Americans for an average of three months while the camps were being built.[34] Because these centers were located in close proximity to Japanese Americans' homes on the West Coast, the displacement experienced was both short-lived and not as dramatic as in the permanent camps.

The next four chapters delve into the subsequent step in the incarceration process: segregation and confinement. Chapters 3 and 4 focus on the use of Japanese American labor to maintain the camps and make them self-sufficient. As they toiled on the land, the camps became workscapes, places transformed by "the interplay of human labor and natural processes."[35] Chapter 3 demonstrates how harsh environmental conditions structured detainees' labor protests, while chapter 4 turns to agriculture, another important arena for Japanese American work. The WRA wanted to develop viable farms to keep costs in check, but poor soil, short growing seasons, resistance from local municipalities, and wartime mandates made this challenging. Labor shortages were also an ongoing problem, despite the fact that both detainees and WRA officials couched farming as a noble endeavor that aided the war effort and displayed loyalty.

Japanese Americans engaged in many other activities that likewise carried symbolic or personal meaning. At a time when many Americans were suspicious of people of Japanese ancestry, participation in certain environmental activities was framed as an expression of patriotism. Chapter 5 focuses on these pursuits—from tending victory gardens to cultivating a plant-based rubber substitute—that purportedly helped detainees prove their loyalty. Chapter 6 shifts away from politicized activities and analyzes leisure—hiking, fishing, swimming, and gardening—which provided joy, freedom, and a sense of personal fulfillment and renewal. These activities sometimes took detainees beyond the guard towers and fences, demonstrating the permeability of the camp boundaries and Japanese Americans' willingness to challenge their physical and social restrictions.

In the immediate postwar years, the environmental process of incarceration continued where it began: with displacement. Chapter 7 examines the closing of the camps and Japanese American farmers' efforts to establish operations inland or back on the Pacific Coast. Neither destination provided an easy entrée back into agriculture, given hostile neighbors and neglected property on the Pacific Coast or unfamiliar crops and weather patterns in the western interior. Newly freed Japanese Americans simply could not resume their previous lives and were forced to adapt and readjust once again.

For WRA officials, President Harry S. Truman's termination of the WRA on June 26, 1946, and the final liquidation of the camps marked the end of the incarceration process, but it continues to this day for former detainees and their descendants.[36] While many Japanese Americans tried to put the war years behind them and never spoke of their confinement, they began to break their silence by the 1960s. The epilogue explores how the natural world has become a critical element of Japanese Americans' wartime memories and the public commemoration of the incarceration. Diverse acts of remembrance are firmly embedded in the environments of the Pacific Coast and the former incarceration camps.

To narrate these years, this book draws on a variety of sources. The voluminous records of the WRA figure prominently, as they provide a detailed portrait of the camps' daily operations from the perspectives of government officials. Japanese American experiences are elucidated in their wartime correspondence, essays, and newspapers and their postwar testimonies, memoirs, and oral histories. Postwar sources can be skewed by the problems of memory, the passage of time, and the context of their creation, whether before a congressional committee or at the request of an academic scholar. Despite these shortcomings, they shed important light on how Japanese Americans responded to confinement.

Social scientists also studied the incarceration as it was experienced during the war years. The WRA Community Analysis Section employed twenty-one non-Japanese American "community analysts," mostly anthropologists, who researched "camp life" and advised administrators.[37] In addition, the Japanese American Evacuation and Resettlement Study (JERS), an academic investigation of the removal, confinement, and resettlement of Japanese Americans, dispatched over two dozen Japanese American and non–Japanese American fieldworkers to four assembly centers, six WRA camps, and several postwar resettlement areas between 1942 and 1946. Directed by sociologist Dorothy Swaine Thomas, a professor at the University of California, Berkeley, the study delved into this "extremely important social experiment" in order to test social science theories and to offer principles for future forced mass migrations.[38] Many have criticized these social scientists' failure to critique the morality of incarceration, their inexperience, their ethical lapses, and their "lack of explicit direction and theoretical orientation."[39] Nonetheless, when combined with other sources, their records allow for the reconstruction of a nuanced environmental history of the incarceration process.[40]

For most Japanese Americans, wartime incarceration was part of an ongoing experience of exclusion and discrimination. Long before they boarded trains and buses for the camps in 1942, inequalities had become inscribed on the West Coast streets and fields where they had lived and worked since Japanese immigration began in the 1890s. In the urban West, they developed their own ethnic enclaves—Little Tokyos or *Nihonmachi*—or settled in multi-ethnic neighborhoods because restrictive covenants and racist attitudes often prevented them from living elsewhere.[41] Discrimination also pushed them to develop their own ethnic economy of restaurants, hotels, boarding houses, laundries, barbershops, and pool halls, and their own cultural institutions of Japanese-language schools, baseball leagues, and churches.[42] What emerged were vibrant communities serving people of Japanese ancestry throughout the urban West.

Japanese American agriculture was central to this ethnic economy. Since many immigrants had previously farmed in Japan, they often pursued agriculture when they arrived in the United States. As their presence and success in farming grew, they also had to navigate restrictions. Some white farmers and business interests saw them as unfair competition, leading the California legislature to pass an alien land act in 1913 that barred "aliens ineligible for citizenship"—a euphemism for Asian immigrants, who could not be naturalized—from owning agricultural land and leasing it for more than three years. Several other states followed suit. Farmers circumvented these laws by buying land in the names of their American-born children or through corporations. After California closed such loopholes in 1920, they negotiated unwritten agreements with white landlords or asked citizens to buy land as "nominal owners." Enforcement of alien land laws was uneven and often lax, but these statutes still etched inequalities on rural lands.[43] The stakes were not just economic. According to historian Cecilia Tsu, some white farmers believed that the "control of California farmland defined white racial and national identity." Restrictive legislation was thus intended to limit the social and cultural threat posed by farmers of Japanese ancestry.[44]

In addition to formal restrictions on landownership, Japanese Americans also faced informal restrictions. White farmers in California's Santa Clara Valley retained control over the cultivation of deciduous fruits, while Chinese and Japanese farmers grew berries, vegetables, and garden seed.[45] The region's social hierarchies were literally growing in the orchards and fields, and farmers knew their status based on the crops they loaded into their crates and trucks. Nonetheless, such restrictions were neither universal nor uniformly negative. In Oregon's Hood River Valley and California's Livingston colony, for example, Japanese farmers did not face the same restrictions and were successful orchardists. Berry-growing, moreover, became a lucrative ethnic enterprise up and down the Pacific Coast.[46] Although their agricultural activities were circumscribed, farmers found ways to wrest livelihoods and support their families.

Similar challenges awaited Japanese Americans in the wartime camps. Once again, they were restricted to particular environments, which, in turn, reinforced their racial status. Once again, they learned to adapt to new social and environmental conditions. But incarceration also marked a dramatic disjuncture that demanded distinct strategies for Japanese Americans and government officials alike. *Nature Behind Barbed Wire* shows that their efforts were not divorced from the environments where their confinement unfolded. Indeed, the Japanese American incarceration was an environmental story as much as it was a social, political, and legal one. At the most fundamental level, the natural world provided space and resources essential to detaining thousands of people. But it was much more than just a source of material goods. For Japanese Americans, the inequalities and injustices that they endured were inextricably linked to the environment. Their interactions with nature also helped them to challenge, reconfigure, and even dismantle the constraints placed upon them. Thus, Japanese Americans' efforts to understand and negotiate their tenuous wartime status—and to assert their American identities—became entangled with the natural world behind and beyond barbed wire.

I
_____

Removal and Displacement

AS TOYO SUYEMOTO and her family prepared for their forced removal from Berkeley in April 1942, she was surrounded by the flowering blossoms of the California spring. The vibrant and fragrant blooms—signs of growth and rebirth—seemed at odds with the uprooting that lay ahead of her. She explained, "Certain natural events like the punctuality of the changing seasons disregard the way people treat one another, and they enchant the observer with the perfection of the moment. So the wisteria bloomed again and purpled the exterior of an old church near the campus, and the new grass turned the winter-drab ground to a brisk green."[1] Even as Suyemoto was packing her belongings, she recognized the beauty of the landscape around her. Perhaps the season of rebirth gave her some comfort, but she also recognized that the imminence of her departure paralleled the onset of the new season. Neither could be stopped.

Suyemoto alluded to the environmental displacement that was at the heart of the wartime removal of over 110,000 Japanese Americans from the Pacific Coast. While they were leaving behind their houses, businesses, schools, and churches, they were also being torn away from familiar natural surroundings. Some Japanese Americans had forged intimate ties to these places by tilling the soil or plying the ocean as agricultural or fisheries workers. Others, like Suyemoto, simply found pleasure in the local flora and fauna, temperate climate, and picturesque scenery. For instance, the Seattle Camera Club, a group of Issei photographers active in the mid-1920s, took excursions to Mount Rainier, Mount Baker, Snoqualmie Falls, and other nearby destinations, where they captured "various forms of beauty according to the change of season all year round."[2] Whether in the Pacific Northwest or California, many Japanese Americans were disheartened by their expulsion from these well-known, beloved environments.

Environmental displacement also had serious economic ramifications. Despite alien land laws, Japanese Americans were firmly established in western agriculture on the eve of World War II. They also had a strong presence in the Pacific fisheries, both as fishermen and cannery workers.[3] In 1940, nearly twenty-three thousand people of Japanese ancestry were employed in agriculture, forestry, and fisheries in the three far western states, which constituted almost 47 percent of Japanese Americans employed that year.[4] Mass removal thus meant emptying the region of skilled fishermen, farmers, and laborers. Among the farmers, many stood to lose valuable farm equipment and land, not to mention crops planted and awaiting harvest.

As a result, calls for forced removal sparked debates that centered on Japanese Americans' involvement in natural resource industries. Those who supported removal warned that farming and fishing provided a cover for suspicious activities and insisted that Japanese American laborers could be easily replaced. In the process, they put forth a vision of whites cultivating the rich soil of the Far West. Others rejected these claims and called attention to Japanese Americans' expertise cultivating specialized crops. Because this broader environmental knowledge had been acquired over the course of several years, it could not be quickly transmitted to others. For government officials, removal ran counter to increased wartime demands for food. One of their goals was to ensure that Japanese American farms—encompassing over 250,000 acres in California, Oregon, and Washington in 1940—did not lie fallow at a time when food was vital to the war effort.[5]

Japanese Americans, then, were actively displaced, wrested from lands and waters they knew well. This environmental displacement concerned many individuals involved in and affected by incarceration. What would happen to the nature left behind, from the oyster beds of Puget Sound to the peat islands of the San Joaquin Delta? Japanese Americans' enduring environmental ties to and knowledge of the Far West shaped the discourse surrounding removal and prompted direct action by the federal government.

"I Do Hope They Will Be Run out of This State": Campaigns for Mass Removal

Calls for the mass removal of Japanese Americans from the Pacific Coast emerged in the wake of Japan's attack on Pearl Harbor on December 7, 1941.[6] Within hours, the Federal Bureau of Investigation (FBI) began to round up and arrest many enemy aliens. Agents targeted individuals who were community leaders or officials in ethnic organizations, owned property in their homeland, or made frequent visits there. Race also clearly factored into their decisions, as a disproportionate number of Japanese immigrants were arrested in relation to their total population in the United States. More Germans aliens were eventually detained in Department of Justice internment camps, but Japanese aliens were, according to a Western Defense Command (WDC) officer, held on "far slimmer evidence."[7]

Less than two weeks after Pearl Harbor, limited incarceration turned into calls for more widespread removal. The first formal military proposal came from the office of Lieutenant General John L. DeWitt, head of the WDC. Since the WDC was a designated "Theater of Operation," DeWitt's charge was to defend the entire West Coast. On December 19, 1941, his office proposed that all "alien subjects" of enemy nations over fourteen years of age be removed to the nation's interior and held "under restraint after removal." This proposal would have affected forty thousand Japanese nationals, as well as Italian and German nationals. Major General Allen W. Gullion, the army's provost marshal general, learned of the proposal and urged DeWitt to recommend that all people of Japanese ancestry, both citizen and alien, be rounded up. He also requested warrantless raids on homes inhabited by at least one Japanese alien, which US Attorney General Francis Biddle authorized on December 30, 1941.[8]

Most Pacific Coast residents stayed composed during this time, but some individuals and groups began to fan the flames for mass removal.[9] John B. Hughes, a radio broadcast journalist for the Mutual Broadcasting Company, was one such person. In early January 1942, he lobbied Los Angeles mayor Fletcher Bowron and California attorney general Earl Warren to remove people of Japanese ancestry from strategic areas.[10] Meanwhile, he tried to educate his listeners. During his January 16, 1942, radio broadcast, *News and Views by John B. Hughes*, which was distributed to eighty stations across the nation, he explained the "menace inherent in the larger Japanese population, especially in California where aliens are permitted control over vital factors of the economic order, and are permitted almost complete freedom of movement, despite the evidence which proves the widespread enemy organization among those U.S. residents and many so-called U.S. citizens." In particular, he questioned the loyalty of "American born Japanese," who were beholden to their alien parents and grandparents and sometimes held dual citizenship. He concluded, "There can be no divided allegiance in such time as this."[11]

Hughes went on to criticize California officials, who seemed "completely cowed by the political pressure that is bein[g] brought to bear in behalf of the alien enemy-influence minority, and contrary to the welfare of the nation as a whole." He attributed this lack of action to Japanese American involvement in fishing and agriculture. Although some observers insisted that the fishing industry could not survive without people of Japanese ancestry, Hughes countered that "Japanese have always been in the minority in California commercial fishing." As for agriculture, he disputed the assertion that the nation's supply of vegetables would decline without them. He concluded, "There is surely no basis for the apologist claim that moving the Japanese would rob the state and deplete the nation of fresh vegetables."[12]

After the broadcast, Hughes received numerous letters in which many of his correspondents seemed to relish the possible expulsion of Japanese Americans from agriculture and the advent of a white-dominated landscape.[13] Agnes McAllister, a self-described housewife from Los Angeles, bristled at their dominance of the retail produce trade; one study estimated that they operated between 670 and 880 markets in Los Angeles in 1941, in addition to many roadside stands. She elaborated, "We are obliged to purchase our green food from the Japs, and at times take much of their insolence. I do hope they will be run out of this state."[14] For Alice Fuller of Santa Monica, the major issue was ensuring that the void left by farmers of Japanese ancestry would be filled by "American farmers." She noted, "We do not want the Jews to step in and take over the farm and truck business. . . . Surely the Government should be willing to help farmers from the Middle West. Could not they become established in this lovely, sunny California?"[15]

Frustration with the Japanese American presence in Pacific Coast agriculture was inflected with racial antipathy. Mrs. O. Rickeer, a "farm woman" from Davis, California, explained, "Too many of us have tried to sell vegetables, plants and in short make a living and the blasted old skunks always move in next door and undersell us until we have to go out of business." But Rickeer also believed that "their ways of life are not ours and the sooner we mop up the quicker."[16] Edward Jucksch of Fresno, California, explained how he had watched "with alarm" for twenty years "the trend in Japanese land holdings and the transition from American operators or owners and from raw land into Jap hands." He concluded, "Any time that I can be of any service of any kind to any agency working in any way against even the American born Japanese, please turn my name over to that agency. . . . More power to your exposition of the yellow peril within our borders."[17]

In contrast, C. L. Conrow of the Arroyo Grande Truck Company noted that "all my dealing with the Japs have been very good." However, he lamented that "they are too strong here because they have aid from the Jap Government and by their Associations." If one farmer failed, he was refinanced immediately, whereas "an American farmer as a rule when he has a failure is all washed up." It was true that Japanese American farmers had established agricultural cooperatives, but their intent was to mitigate discriminatory practices and provide economic security, not to deliberately drive their competitors out of business. Nonetheless, Conrow ultimately expressed his support for another nonwhite, non-"American" group: Filipino farmers, who "say that if they could have the same backing as the Japs they could raise all the vegetables we need."[18]

Other correspondents helped corroborate Hughes's claims about the questionable loyalty of Japanese Americans. Mrs. Paul Hollie of McFarland, California, had worked for a "Jap farmer" for almost ten years and witnessed suspicious activities. For instance, she had seen farmers with frequent crop failures, "yet they always have the money to re-plant. They always drive fine automobiles and live just as good as those who have made money on their crops. How can they do this? Do they print their own money?" She also related incidents in which families boasted about their American-educated sons who served in the Japanese army, and she noticed many Japanese American farmers living near California airports.[19] Alan Reveil of the Music Department at Santa Ana Junior College added, "I know it to be a fact that upon a recent investigation of a landing place for airplanes in the foothills of Orange County, that the best and most satisfactory location is at present being leased by Japanese for truck gardening."[20]

Reports of suspicious activities also extended into the Pacific Ocean. Based on regular trips to the Gulf of California since 1908, George Farnsworth of Catalina Island, California, blamed Japanese American fishermen for overharvesting numerous species, including abalone, oysters, and tuna. He also contended that their fishing activities—such as a short-lived sea cucumber operation—coincided with the gathering of sounding data to determine "the exact character of the bottom of these bays." In other words, the fisheries served as a cover for seditious operations. He concluded by offering Hughes his "pages and pages of data" that showed "the distruction [sic] of our food fish along this coast by all alien fisherman [sic]."[21]

Farnsworth's accusations aligned with those of Miller Freeman, publisher of the *Pacific Fisherman*, a fishing industry journal, and longtime adversary of Japanese immigrants. In January 1942, Freeman asserted that the Pearl Harbor attack was "verification" of his consistent warnings about the "dangers to the American nation as well as the American fisheries" posed by people of Japanese descent.[22] When the United States entered the war, new fishing rules were instituted to address this perceived threat. Most significantly, all boat crew members had to be American citizens with Coast Guard–issued identification.[23] This restriction had dramatic consequences. In California, 699 Japanese aliens with commercial fishing licenses lost their livelihoods.[24]

In January 1942, plans for removal accelerated and solidified. California congressman Leland Ford urged Secretary of War Henry L. Stimson to place all people of Japanese ancestry in "inland concentration camps." Stimson eventually responded and agreed with Ford, pledging his commitment to providing "internment facilities." However, he also explained that it was ultimately Biddle's responsibility and told him to direct his request to him. Meanwhile, DeWitt asserted that Japanese spies had "a conspiracy not to commit sabotage until America dropped its guard." As historian Roger Daniels explains, the logic was to "evacuate the potential saboteurs before they could do any damage." DeWitt recommended that removal begin with both citizen and foreign-born Japanese, followed by German and Italian aliens.[25]

On February 11, Stimson recommended mass removal to President Roosevelt, who later gave him the go-ahead to "do anything you think necessary," even if it involved American citizens. Some federal officials, however, wanted to put on the brakes. General George Marshall, chief of staff of the US Army, advocated expunging enemy aliens only from the areas surrounding the Boeing aircraft plant and the Bremerton Navy Yard in Washington, while Archibald MacLeish, director of the Office of Facts and Figures, emphasized the importance of maintaining civil liberties. Biddle remained adamantly opposed to mass removal. On February 17, 1942, he sent a memo to Roosevelt, noting that sixty thousand possible "evacuees" were American citizens and arguing that the military authorities and the FBI had found no evidence of an impending Pacific Coast attack.[26]

Biddle's memo did not stop momentum. By then, Roosevelt had already received a unanimous recommendation from the Pacific Coast congressional delegation, calling for "the immediate evacuation of all persons of Japanese lineage" and others who threatened the defense of the United States from California, Oregon, Washington, and Alaska. On February 18, 1942, Biddle met with Stimson and other Justice Department officials to draft Executive Order 9066. Issued the next day, it authorized the secretary of war and other military commanders to designate military areas from which civilians could be excluded. By March 2, DeWitt had issued Public Proclamation

No. 1, which established Military Area No. 1 in western Washington, Oregon, California, and southern Arizona, and Military Area No. 2, which included the remaining parts of those states. The proclamation did not exclude anyone, but it was a step toward removal.[27]

Two days after Roosevelt signed Executive Order 9066, the House Select Committee Investigating National Defense Migration, led by Representative John Tolan, a Democrat from Oakland, California, began hearings in San Francisco to discuss removal plans. Known as the Tolan Committee, it went on to hear testimony in Los Angeles, Portland, and Seattle. Many witnesses emphasized that the absence of Japanese American farmers would not be a problem. The Western Growers Protective Association in Los Angeles submitted a statement that asserted that "the flow of California vegetables to the entire county would not be affected should either or both the alien Japanese or the American citizens of Japanese parentage be removed from the vegetable industry." Similarly, H. L. Strobel, a Monterey County farmer, testified that Japanese Americans' role in agriculture "has been very much overemphasized and that the American farmer can and will take up wherever they leave off."[28] Even if some land was left unfarmed, Washington governor Arthur B. Langlie doubted that state residents would believe this to be an "adequate reason" to allow people of Japanese ancestry to remain along the coast.[29]

Other witnesses were more circumspect. Ronald E. Jones, an Oregon state senator who farmed north of Salem, explained that Japanese Americans were experts at raising celery, which required "a lot of patience and a lot of finesse and a lot of skill in the handling." Nonetheless, he believed that white farmers could become adept in a year or two.[30] Mamaro Wakasugi, a Nisei strawberry and tomato grower in Banks, Oregon, likewise noted that Japanese Americans grew "highly cultivated" crops that took "quite a bit of experience and skill to grow." Echoing Senator Jones, he concluded, "I am not saying that there is no one else that can grow these crops, but it will take time for other people to take over these operations."[31]

A handful of witnesses were adamant that Japanese American natural resource workers could not be replaced quickly and sought special arrangements to keep them employed. J. Burton Bowman of the Olympia Oyster Growers Protective Association in Shelton, Washington, argued that Japanese American removal would "practically paralyze" the oyster industry in upper Puget Sound. He explained, "We have found the Japanese very satisfactory help in years of association with them. They are good workers, dependable and thoroughly law abiding. White men will not do the work on the beds." He suggested that white superintendents could run the boats and carefully supervise them. T. M. Bunn, who owned the Salinas Valley Vegetable Exchange with Takeo Yuki, similarly requested that their Japanese American workers be housed at their labor camp, where they could be guarded.[32] And Harry P. Cain, mayor of Tacoma, Washington, called for a selective removal in which Japanese Americans in the Puyallup Valley could continue production under "due protective procedures."[33]

FIGURE 1.1 Washington State oyster growers employed workers like Mr. Okazaki, pictured here at Nemah, Washington, c. 1937. Courtesy of the Mitsuoka Family Collection, Densho Digital Repository, ddr-densho-15-96.

This debate also unfolded outside the hearing rooms of the Tolan Committee. In late February 1942, E. M. Seifert Jr., a produce shipper from Salinas, California, and president of the Salinas Vegetable Grower-Shipper Association, wrote a report to prove the "relative unimportance of truck crop production by Japanese." Contrary to assertions about the importance of the state's Japanese American tomato growers, Seifert pointed out that they only produced 11 percent of the tomatoes canned in the United States. "If this item is important enough," he continued, it could be rationed, and "we will then have an increased figure in canned tomatoes produced, instead of a decrease." He also pointed out that some growers had already begun to increase their tomato acreage and that others would take up Japanese American land. Seifert concluded that "if all vegetable acreage produced, controlled, or influenced by Japanese were completely eliminated, the loss in available fresh food supply to the United States and Canada would be entirely insignificant."[34]

Not surprisingly, growers like Seifert had ulterior economic motives. His colleague, Austin E. Anson, secretary of the Salinas Vegetable Grower-Shipper Association, traveled to Washington to urge federal authorities to remove all people of Japanese ancestry from the area, emphasizing their ability to sabotage defense installations and help invading Japanese forces. He noted, "We're charged with wanting to get rid of the Japs for selfish reasons. We might as well be honest. We do. It's a question of whether the white man lives on the Pacific Coast or the brown men." He concluded, "If all the Japs were removed tomorrow, we'd never miss them in two weeks, because the white farmers can take over and produce everything the Jap grows. And we don't want them back when the war ends, either."[35]

Lowell W. Berry of the Best Fertilizers Company made an opposing claim in a March 1942 letter to Tom C. Clark, the WDC's alien control coordinator. He noted, "It will be practically impossible to replace [Japanese] services with equally efficient management and labor. The management and planning and care of these small Japanese gardens 5 to 20 or 40 acres, requires knowledge and skill that is not properly appreciated by many not familiar with farming problems." He asked that Japanese American growers be allowed to stay on their farms long enough to harvest the current season's crops. "If this is a war of production, and surely it is," he explained, "we cannot afford to lose the productive effort of these Japanese if they can be kept at their present locations safely." He believed that confiscating their cars or guarding them, if necessary, would be "far more expedient than removal of these people to areas where their efforts will be partially or totally unproductive."[36] Berry implied that Japanese American agricultural expertise was of greatest value on the Pacific Coast.

Dave Davidson, chairman of the California Agricultural War Board, also received a rash of letters from San Joaquin Delta growers who similarly lauded the skills of their Japanese American laborers and pleaded to keep them on the job. John Zuckerman of Weyl-Zuckerman & Company and McDonald Island Farms in Stockton sent a list of his ninety-three Japanese American employees, both aliens and citizens, who comprised 15 to 25 percent of his workforce. According to Zuckerman, it took years to train these workers, who now "form[ed] the backbone of our whole organization. Most of them have been with us anywhere from 10 to 20 years continuously and they are the ones who perform the more intricate and technical phases of our farming operations." From March to July, they were "the most vital to us. It is during this period that their knowledge and experience in the irrigation and raising of crops makes them irreplaceable."[37] Fellow Stockton growers John C. Kelley, W. E. McGillvray, L. W. Moran, S. T. Moran, Gordon Lacy, and R. C. Zuckerman wrote similar letters, accompanied by lists of their Japanese American employees.[38] Together, they requested to be allowed to keep their workers on the job until the middle of July. Without these accommodations, there would be a "paralysis of our operations," which included sugar, tomatoes, and potatoes, all key wartime crops.[39]

Japanese Americans' ability to cultivate peat soil was particularly important to these growers. The delta was once a marshy swamp covered in common tule, a grasslike plant abundant in California wetlands. When the tule died every year, it decomposed into peat, a rich organic soil. Over time, the peat layer accumulated and became as deep as forty feet. This soil was extremely productive for certain crops, such as potatoes and beans, but it also posed many challenges, such as subsidence and flooding.[40] Growers insisted that these conditions were "different from almost any other farming community in the United States" and required workers trained in the "intricate phases of peat land farming," which included subsurface irrigation and the use of special machinery. In a collective letter to Davidson, they maintained that Japanese Americans had the requisite aptitude and knowledge.[41]

For all of the farming challenges generated by the delta, growers noted that its environmental features were advantageous when it came to mitigating possible security risks. They explained, "We firmly believe that the geographical nature of the Delta is ideal for a close surveillance of the Japanese working on our farms." Specifically, they toiled on islands surrounded by a wide river or artificial waterway with typically only one method of entry or exit, a bridge

FIGURE 1.2 To cultivate the San Joaquin Valley's peat soil, Japanese American workers operated specialized machinery like this Caterpillar tractor, Stockton, California, April 10, 1942. Photograph by Dorothea Lange. Courtesy of the National Archives and Records Administration.

or ferry run by the county. Moreover, given the year-round labor schedule and the many years it took Japanese Americans to hone their skills, growers asserted that they knew "by name and by sight every Japanese working on our farms."[42] Humans and nature—growers and the delta—had ensnared Japanese Americans in their web, ensuring that they were both constantly monitored and highly valued.

Even as delta growers tried to allay safety concerns, their correspondence focused, at its core, on Japanese Americans' environmental knowledge. These workers knew how to plant and harvest crops in a specific and unusual environmental context.[43] Because this kind of knowledge could not be quickly transferred to others, their absence would have a negative impact on production. These employers were not, however, promoting a wholesale rejection of removal. Rather, they simply wanted to delay Japanese Americans' departure so as to minimize economic losses. They did not question the overall necessity of removal, let alone its injustice.

Support for Japanese American farmworkers also took on a racialized edge. In a collective statement, several Stockton growers noted, "The rigors of our climate have been found to be unsuited for the most part even for the strongest of white men." By contrast, Japanese Americans were "ideally suited for all types of work in the Delta." Although farmers had employed Filipinos and Mexicans, Japanese Americans were still the "foundation of our farming."[44] These arguments were similar to earlier defenses of slavery—that nonwhites were better acclimated to certain climates and ideal for certain labor.[45] These sorts of claims were also common in the American West. Agribusiness interests deployed similar rhetoric in the 1920s when defending their use of Mexican workers.[46]

Likewise, strawberry growers wanted to keep their Japanese American laborers because they were willing to perform stoop labor, which was notoriously associated with nonwhite groups.[47] E. H. Haack, manager of the Central California Berry Growers Association, explained that American growers employed them "because this labor is skilled and strawberry culture is an eight months squatting job."[48] Similarly, Genevieve Collius of the Liberty Farm in Dixon, California, explained, "Our past experience has proved that only Japanese and Filipino labor is satisfactory for cutting asparagus or harvesting any crop that requires stoop labor."[49] Two weeks later, Liberty Farm's president R. K. Malcolm added that "there is no other than Japanese 'stoop' labor available."[50] In these cases, Japanese Americans' value was not in their environmental knowledge but their willingness to perform undesirable work.

Given their vulnerability, Japanese American growers and workers were not outspoken about removal, but Walter R. Goldschmidt Jr., a social science analyst for the US Department of Agriculture's (USDA) Bureau of Agricultural Economics (BAE), obtained a glimpse into their perspective. In March 1942, he interviewed two Japanese American farm operators in San Joaquin County, one Japanese-born and one American-born; both operated large tracts of land. They expressed their fear of reprisal "with a shrug of the shoulder." As Goldschmidt expected, they were explicit in their support of the war effort, said they would plant "whatever the Government wanted," and "in no way showed any signs of loyalty or sympathy toward the Japanese." However, one of the farmers knew of a small number of Japanese American operators who had become "panicky" and may have plowed under their crops, an action deemed an act of sabotage by the government.[51]

Goldschmidt's work for the BAE, "an all-purpose research and planning arm for the government in agriculture," was part of its larger effort to assess attitudes toward Japanese Americans on the Pacific Coast.[52] In January 1942, the BAE's Division of Program Surveys sent interviewers to San Francisco, Seattle, Los Angeles, and California's Imperial Valley to speak with residents.[53]

FIGURE 1.3 Japanese American farm laborers picking strawberries near Mission San Jose, California, April 26, 1942. Photograph by Dorothea Lange. Courtesy of the National Archives and Records Administration.

Their initial interviews found that very few people were "giving any thought to possible economic consequences in terms of disrupted food supply, rising prices, or labor shortages. In fact, very few of the people interviewed seem to think of the Japanese at all in an economic context."[54] Yet one Ventura County farmer, who rented a 325-acre farm with his father, was an outlier. Rather than supporting removal because of the possible threat to security, he advocated it because Japanese American farmers paid high rents, which raised the cost of his rent. Another county spokesperson added that they were "unfair competitors" to "American farmers" because they lived in houses "poorer than those occupied by Mexicans" and "work[ed] the entire family."[55] Economic concerns and racial antipathy intertwined, as these individuals clearly envisioned white farmers cultivating the county's soil. Japanese Americans were an impediment to their prosperity.

As debates about the status of Japanese American growers and farmworkers unfolded, Roosevelt continued to take steps toward mass removal. On March

18, 1942, he issued Executive Order 9102 to establish the War Relocation Authority (WRA) and allocated $5.5 million to this civilian agency.[56] Housed within the Office for Emergency Management of the President's Executive Office, the WRA's charge was to "formulate and effectuate a program for the removal" and to provide for the "relocation, maintenance, and supervision" of Japanese Americans.[57] DeWitt also initiated a "dress rehearsal" for mass removal with the issuance of Civilian Exclusion Order No. 1 on March 24, 1942, which removed nearly three hundred people of Japanese ancestry, both citizens and noncitizens, from Bainbridge Island, Washington, on March 30. In preparation for expunging the remaining Japanese Americans, the army divided the rest of the West Coast into 107 "evacuation districts" of one thousand people each.[58] As DeWitt issued exclusion orders for each district, Japanese Americans began packing their belongings and leaving their homes indefinitely.

"Go East, Young Japanese": Farm Cooperatives and Voluntary Evacuation

Meanwhile, some Japanese Americans came up with alternatives to forced removal. Not surprisingly, their proposals centered on their farming expertise and their ability to transfer their skills to a new environment. Hi Korematsu—older brother of Fred Korematsu, petitioner in one of the US Supreme Court cases that tested the constitutionality of removal—led the Proponent Committee for Evacuated Alien Resettlement Program.[59] The general premise was to create nonprofit farm corporations that would employ "law-abiding" Japanese aliens on large farms away from the coast. With high-paying defense jobs luring people away from agricultural work, the program would also help to alleviate the national farm labor shortage. Due to alien land laws, participants would not have any proprietary interest in the corporations and would only receive regular wages.[60] To finance the cooperatives, the group suggested the use of personal contributions and some government funds. The proposal concluded, "Japanese aliens may be productive, self-supporting and self-respecting, and without extra expense upon the Government for their detention and care."[61]

Not surprisingly, the rhetoric of loyalty and patriotism undergirded the proposal. One heading proclaimed, "ONLY LOYAL JAPANESE ALIENS CONSIDERED," then went on to explain that a "Non-Profit Farm Corporation is a *patriotic endeavor*." The writers also made a point to emphasize that the proposal was conceived by "a group of American-born college graduates of Japanese stock" and that their proposal was developed in "a spirit of coop-eration, not with the idea of assuring or interfering with any government prerogatives."[62]

Deeply entrenched racial animosity stymied Korematsu's efforts to gen-erate support for his plan. He inquired about the settlement of his group in the Columbia Basin, but H. W. Bashore, assistant commissioner of the Bureau of Reclamation, balked. He explained, "To place an undeterminate [sic] number of Japanese there, whether alien or native born, would disrupt the carefully planned pattern of settlement and jeopardize the investment of the Government." Indeed, it was especially problematic to bring in "pro-Axis saboteur suspects."[63] Bashore made it clear that he believed that there were subversive individuals within the Japanese American population, and he did not want them to settle on this reclamation project.

Hideo Hashimoto of Fresno, California, also devised a cooperative farm project that similarly focused on isolation and self-help for Japanese Americans. He proposed that one thousand families live in a "fully cooper-ative community pattern of permanent resettlement." They would move to ten to twelve thousand acres of arable land that would have three coopera-tive farms, each with 150 families, and one village for the remaining families who would find jobs in business, education, service, and industry. Farm families would live in rent-free houses with one-quarter acre of land each, while townfolk would live in apartments. Each member would be required to invest in one share at a cost of one hundred to five hundred dollars, ei-ther purchased in cash or in the conversion of tractors or trucks brought to the farm. For about two hundred hours of farm work each month, members would be paid sixty-five dollars each and receive some share of the crops. At the end of the year, they would receive rebates if any profits remained after paying loans and interest and putting aside money in a reserve fund for coop-erative education.[64]

Another group, the Nisei Writers and Artists Mobilization for Democracy (NWAMD), proposed "A Plan for Government Sponsored Farm and Craft Settlement for People of Japanese Parentage." Led by renowned artist and landscape architect Isamu Noguchi, the group recognized that it was critical for the Nisei to participate in the planning and "subsequent working out of his evacuation, temporary or otherwise." Their plan advocated a cooperative project, rather than "simple resettlement," because it brought a sense of shared responsibility and equality. They also supported the use of Japanese American skill and labor in ways that aided the war effort.[65] To that end, the NWAMD plan emphasized the shortage of farm labor that Japanese Americans could fill and, like Hi Korematsu's plan, avoided the rental or purchase of land. Instead, it asked that the government make land "suitable to agriculture or small industries" available for the duration of the war, including arable land in the public domain. Japanese Americans could even take over farms in non-military areas. The plan also acknowledged that not all Japanese Americans had farming expertise and proposed putting those Nisei skilled in other trades and crafts to work as well.[66]

None of these plans were implemented—although Noguchi traveled to Washington, DC, in April 1942 to present the NWAMD plan—but they demonstrated how Japanese Americans tried to use their agricultural skill to evade removal.[67] They accepted the fact that they would need to leave areas deemed sensitive to the nation's defense, but they wanted to do so in a way that kept some semblance of community intact and provided them with independence. Their ability to produce their own food in new environments would allow them to implement these ambitious plans. They need not drain any federal funds in the process. Away from major cities or strategic areas, they could live undisturbed and not raise the ire of suspicious Americans.

In the end, the farm cooperative proposals were unrealistic, but some families and small groups left Military Area No. 1 as part of a voluntary evacuation that *Saturday Evening Post* journalist Frank J. Taylor dubbed the "Go East, Young Japanese" movement.[68] Many participants were farmers who decided to use their skills further inland. Like the farm cooperative proposals, the idea was to move away from the coast before the WDC forced the issue. But voluntary evacuation did not enjoy widespread support, as many states were unwilling to accept Japanese Americans. Idaho governor Chase Clark, for instance, was especially vehement in his refusal to welcome any Japanese Americans. On March 18, 1942, he issued a warning in the *Idaho Daily Stateman*, imploring the existing Japanese Americans in Idaho not to encourage resettlement "because it might result in the exclusion of all."[69] Colorado governor Ralph Carr was one of the few state officials who aided Japanese American resettlement, but he faced opposition from Ed Johnson, one of his state's US senators. Johnson wrote a letter to Milton Eisenhower, first WRA director, in which he demanded that the WRA take control of these voluntary migrants. He noted, "Most certainly we ought not to be made the dumping ground for the Pacific Coast states."[70]

Even though voluntary evacuation was "a mere trickle," Eisenhower recognized that it had brought serious problems to the interior states.[71] He admitted to US Senator Elbert D. Thomas of Utah that he was "very much disillusioned" because of "the most extreme bitterness" there. He explained, "Demands arose officially in all states for the Federal Government to withdraw the evacuees, to prevent Japanese from acquiring land, to guarantee that the Japanese would be removed at the end of the War, and to give positive assurance that the whole relocation program would be on an orderly, federally protected basis." He also received warnings from governors and attorneys general that "states would not be able to maintain law and order if voluntary evacuation continued." One governor declared that "his state would not accept responsibility for the safety of a single evacuee."[72]

While government officials were aware of the volatile situation at hand, they did not always give specific examples of how prejudice manifested itself in everyday life. Junkoh Harui's experience is instructive in this regard. Along with three other families, he and his family moved from Bainbridge Island to Moses Lake, Washington, outside of Military Area No. 1, where they raised potatoes and onions during the war. Most Moses Lake residents had never seen a person of Japanese ancestry before, so the Bainbridge Island group immediately faced resistance when the men tried to find work on local farms. For Harui, his "personal trauma" came in school. One classmate "would beat the hell out of me every day in the playground, and everybody would stand around and watch." He also remembered snowball fights in which rocks were embedded in the balls that other children threw in his direction. While he eventually received some acceptance from his classmates, the antipathy that he and his family faced remained prominent memories of his time in Moses Lake.[73]

Japanese Americans from the Pacific Coast also faced hostility from existing Japanese American communities in the inland states. Tak Yamashita's parents decided to leave Southern California because of his father's ill health and settle in Greeley, Colorado. According to Yamashita, the "Colorado Japs" were less than welcoming and told them to "straighten up." He remembered thinking, "You're a Jap too. . . . You don't look like no white man. You're a Japanese boy . . . if you was in California you'd be treated the same way." While he understood that local Japanese Americans feared that the newcomers could harm their good reputation, he was still disappointed. He concluded, "Some of these Japanese guys . . . they think they were white men and it ticked us off. But that's the way it was."[74]

In the end, voluntary evacuation was not a viable option for most families. They typically needed family or friends outside of Military Area No. 1 with whom they could stay and the ability to liquidate their belongings quickly. Few families and individuals found themselves in this position.[75] Thus, only 4,889 people of Japanese ancestry left Military Area No. 1 for inland locales during the short period of voluntary evacuation. Of these "voluntary evacuees," 1,963 went to Colorado, 1,519 to Utah, 305 to Idaho, 208 to eastern Washington, 115 to eastern Oregon, and the rest to other states. Voluntary evacuation came to an end with Public Proclamation No. 4, effective on March 30, 1942, which prohibited people of Japanese ancestry from leaving Military Area No. 1 without instruction or approval from the army.[76] Thus, the vast majority of people of Japanese ancestry who lived on the Pacific Coast were removed involuntarily, under military orders.

DeWitt eventually issued exclusion orders to all of Military Area No. 1 and the California parts of Military Area No. 2 and finished forcibly removing over 110,000 Japanese Americans by early June 1942. The Wartime Civilian Control Administration (WCCA), an agency of the WDC, carried out standard procedures for removal across the evacuation districts. First, the Civilian Exclusion Order was posted throughout the area, informing Japanese Americans when to report to the Civil Control Station for registration. At registration, each family received a number and instructions to prepare for expulsion. They were told to bring their own bedding, toiletries, clothing, utensils, and "essential personal effects," with all items "securely packaged" and labeled with their name and number. When they reported for removal, WCCA officials loaded Japanese Americans on to trains, trucks, or busses that took them to one of fifteen "temporary assembly centers," which were typically located on fairgrounds or horse race tracks. These facilities were barely updated for human inhabitants, as Japanese Americans often lived in horse stalls and other nominal forms of shelter.[77] In many respects, the dismal environmental conditions at the assembly centers foreshadowed those at the ten permanent "relocation centers."

"It Is Mandatory That This Land Be Kept in Production": The FSA and Farm Transfers

In addition to removing over 110,000 individuals from their homes and placing them in the assembly centers, General DeWitt was also responsible for facilitating the sale or transfer of Japanese American property.[78] This was a significant task when it came to agricultural land that was necessary to meet wartime food demands. Out of a total of 48,926 Japanese American workers over the age of fourteen in Military Area No. 1, about 20,000 found employment in agriculture before the war. Thirteen thousand were farm laborers, while roughly 7,000 ran or managed farms.[79] With an average size of forty-two acres, these farms only amounted to about 2 percent of the Pacific Coast farming interests at the start of the war and only 0.3 percent of total farm acreage. However, because the farms were intensively cultivated, they were valued at an average of $279.98 per acre, well above the $57.94 per acre average of all West Coast farms.[80] Three out of every four acres were devoted to crops on Japanese American–operated farms, compared to only one of four acres on all farmland in the area. They often focused on specialty crops, growing 90 percent of California's strawberries, 75 percent of its celery, and 45 percent of its tomatoes. In the Northwest, they produced over 80 percent of the region's cauliflower, 70 percent of its lettuce, 60 percent of its spinach, and 50 percent of the tomatoes.[81]

Federal officials recognized that Japanese American removal had potentially serious consequences for a nation with heightened food demands. To address the agricultural component of removal, DeWitt ordered the Farm Security Administration (FSA) to participate as a member agency of the WCCA on March 15, 1942.[82] From March 15, 1942, until June 1, 1942, the FSA handled the farming interests of 6,789 Japanese American farm operators and 231,942 acres of cultivated land in Military Area No. 1. According to FSA regional director Laurence I. Hewes Jr., this was "probably one of the most dramatic events in the agricultural history of the United States. No function heretofor[e] performed in so short a period in the domestic affairs of the United States can compare in magnitude and intensity with the Japanese evacuation of Military Area No. 1."[83] The FSA's responsibilities were twofold: to insure the "proper use of agricultural lands evacuated by enemy aliens" and to ensure "fair and equitable arrangements between evacuees, their creditors, and the substitute operators of their property."[84]

To carry out its task, the FSA set up forty-eight field offices and organized three separate units. The Special Negotiations Unit helped with the transactions involving large-scale operators, while the Evacuation Control Unit went into evacuated areas to do a final checkup and assist with untransferred farms. The Wartime Farm Adjustment (WFA) unit assumed the critical tasks related to facilitating transactions between Japanese American farmers and their landlords, creditors, and prospective buyers. Initially, the WFA unit worked only with those farmers who requested assistance. Agents subsequently conducted a "systematic census" of all Japanese American farms and determined the distribution of farms and the number of farmers in the affected district. They also registered prospective operators and buyers of crops and machinery. Some individuals registered voluntarily, but FSA agents were also instructed to "go aggressively into the localities where a shortage of prospective operators appeared to exist" and to recruit through publicity or contacts with individuals or organizations.[85]

Once they identified soon-to-be-vacant farms and potential buyers, FSA agents helped with the transfer of property. Because of alien land laws, 70 percent of Japanese American farm operators in Arizona, California, Oregon, and Washington in 1940 were tenants, compared to 19.5 percent who were full owners and 6.1 percent who were part owners. Thus, most WFA transactions involved the sale or assignment of leases, the relinquishment of tenure to landlords, the employment of a substitute manager, or the division of crop proceeds. For those farms owned by Japanese Americans, FSA agents facilitated the leasing of the property or management on a share or salary basis. Most farm owners tried to negotiate arrangements that assumed that they would return.[86] For financing, the FSA asked all banks and commercial lenders to give "immediate priority" to applicants from "experienced farmers desiring to take over evacuated land." Direct WFA loans were also available for one year for production-related expenses, like seed, fertilizer, livestock, machinery, equipment, and other supplies and services.[87]

While FSA agents were familiar with farm financing and trained in "arriving at satisfactory terms and in handling special problems of negotiation," they faced a number of challenges. First, Japanese American farmers were reluctant to transfer their land until exclusion orders were issued and their removal was confirmed. In the meantime, the FSA feared that they would abandon their land, stop farming, or refuse to transfer their property. For their part, prospective operators, who were in short supply, preferred to wait until the farmers were in "an adverse bargaining position" before they began negotiating, "even at the cost of serious of agricultural production." They also hesitated to take over these farms because of a fear that a predicted labor shortage would make farming more risky. Looming over these issues was the speed with which removal was taking place. In some cases, there was simply not enough time to contact all parties involved and negotiate agreeable settlements.[88]

To overcome these challenges and encourage skilled operators to take over Japanese American farms, nurseries, and greenhouses, the FSA began a public relations campaign that invoked their obligations to help fight the war. In a press release, Hewes explained that 225,000 acres of Japanese American farmland produced "a substantial share of the nation's vegetable supply. . . . It is mandatory that this land be kept in production." He urged interested operators to report immediately to FSA agents, who would help them acquire the land and loans to keep the land in production.[89] "Often a day's delay will mean a crop loss," he added.[90] Another flyer further emphasized the urgency of the situation, proclaiming, "Production on vacated farms MUST be continued. Food is as important as guns in our national war effort. . . .You can help us win the war and at the same time make a sound farm investment."[91] Likewise, a radio broadcast script suggested that the removal of Japanese American farmers would create a "new frontier." It continued, "I'm glad to hear that word *frontier*, because frontier generally means a fight in progress. This fight is raising Food for Freedom. It makes every field harrow and garden spade a weapon, every bushel of produce a sling of ammunition. And every last man or woman who brings this produce to the markets and canneries is a soldier on active duty."[92]

FSA agents were also responsible for finding substitute operators for floriculture businesses, but patriotic rhetoric was not applicable in this arena. Instead, press releases emphasized the scarcity of operators, the economic importance of the industry, and the simple pleasure of flowers. In the San Francisco Bay Area alone, flower growers sent about $10 million worth of cut flowers, bulbs, plants, seedlings, and shrubs to urban markets every year.[93] Given that this was "almost exclusively a Japanese industry," the FSA found it especially difficult to secure suitable operators.[94] Part of the problem was that floriculture required "skilled techniques" and "relatively large investments in equipment."[95]

Indeed, Harry Bryant, a San Jose, California, landscaper, was quite troubled by the absence of Japanese American flower growers, who supplied his business. By May 1942, their expulsion had brought "an extreme shortage of flora type bedding plants." He elaborated, "Many varieties I cannot find a trace of. I am buying, and paying premium prices for scrawny, seedling-size plants (too small to plant yet). . . . By the end of this week there won't be fifty flats of decent plants in all nurseries in Santa Clara County put together." Even as the quantity and quality of plants declined, the demand was actually greater than the previous year. Bryant went on to imply that Japanese American flower growers would not be easy to replace: "Where there may be a grower, he isn't a Jap; he has no idea of demand,—no idea of marketing."[96] Without the skill and experience of Japanese Americans, many gardens would be devoid of flowers.

These emphatic pleas—whether they played on patriotic duty or the desire to maintain a marker of normalcy in the form of colorful flowers—only went to so far. FSA agents determined that they needed more authority in order to carry out their charge, specifically the power to "freeze" property and transactions. In other words, they wanted to be able "to operate, manage

FIGURE 1.4 This San Leandro, California, operation was one of many flower nurseries operated by Japanese Americans before the war, April 5, 1942. Photograph by Dorothea Lange. Courtesy of the National Archives and Records Administration.

or dispose of farm property . . . with or without the consent of the Japanese operators, their creditors or landlords" and to have the authority to act for Japanese Americans "until satisfactory substitute operators could be found and placed in control." Calvin Benham (C. B.) Baldwin, FSA administrator, granted Hewes this power in early April 1942. In addition, because Japanese Americans operated many small and specialized farms, the FSA supported the creation of corporations or other entities that consolidated and oversaw several operations. For instance, the American Fruit Growers, Inc., a fruit shipper with offices in the Newcastle, Loomis, and Auburn, California, area, created a subsidiary corporation to operate several Japanese American ranches in that area. As one report explained, this action was "absolutely necessary in order to prevent loss of crops and assure uninterrupted production."[97] The FSA later received authority to issue loans to these entities so that they could accept powers of attorney from Japanese American operators and maintain their properties until substitutes could be found.[98]

As more future detainees encountered prospective buyers intent on getting bargains, the freezing power became an important tool to promote equitable deals. While FSA agents used it only once, its very existence became a negotiating tool. In one instance, thirty Japanese American strawberry growers and the landowner were embroiled in a dispute. The very threat of the agent invoking the freezing power compelled the landowner to negotiate fairly and reach a satisfactory settlement. To further promote equitable deals, the FSA formed the California Evacuated Farms Association, a legal entity empowered to conduct negotiations if operators were subject to forced removal before their deals were finalized.[99]

After completing its work in Military Area No. 1, the FSA moved to Military Area No. 2 of California between June 1, 1942, and August 8, 1942. This area included 647 farms totaling 24,582 acres in the Sacramento Valley, the San Joaquin Valley, and the Mohave Desert. Most of these operations were focused on fruit, truck, and specialty crops, such as strawberries, tomatoes, peas, beans, and melons. As in Military Area No. 1, FSA agents registered both Japanese American farm operators and possible substitutes and encouraged "transfer transactions." However, the FSA found that work in the San Joaquin Valley was more difficult. The pool of substitute operators consisted of "financially independent farmers" who were already operating similar farm enterprises. Because of labor shortages, they were wary of expanding their holdings "except under very favorable conditions." Moreover, Japanese American operators knew that they had highly desirable farm units "for which they insisted on securing fair prices." Despite these challenges, the FSA considered its work in this valley "from the standpoint of fairness to evacuees and substitute operators, and of assured continuity of agricultural production" to be "even sounder and more enduring" than elsewhere.[100]

After nearly six months of work, the FSA concluded that it had successfully helped to ensure the "continuity of agricultural production" by putting Japanese American–operated farms "in the hands of competent management . . . without any serious interruption of farming operation."[101] Nonetheless, officials acknowledged that some changes in land use patterns were inevitable due to Japanese Americans' particular farming strategies. For instance, in the Sacramento Valley and near Puget Sound, their work was characterized by a heavy reliance on family labor and "a painstaking use of farm resources" in order to bring about the "profitable production of intensive crops on relatively poor land." They grew strawberries on "gravelly soil" and were frugal with irrigation water. Not surprisingly, FSA agents could not secure operators who used similar techniques, so reversion to pasture or extensive crops ensued. Moreover, the FSA shifted production, curtailing flowers and strawberries and focusing attention on sugar beets and vitamin-rich tomatoes, beans, peas, spinach, lettuce, and asparagus.[102]

The FSA also maintained that it had provided "maximum protection" to Japanese American farmers in the disposal of their property, but this assertion did not necessarily mirror reality.[103] Inequitable arrangements were ubiquitous. In late March 1942, the Federal Reserve Bank asked the Foreign Funds Investigative Office in San Francisco to look into alleged cases of fraud in agricultural transfers. While investigators did not find any flagrant cases, they found instances where landlords held the clear advantage. For instance, one lessor offered a Japanese American lessee a sum of money to cancel a lease on fifty acres planted with tomatoes. This amount was not commensurate with the money spent on tomato plants and to "the services to the soil," so the lessee objected. The lessee considered the second offer unfavorable too, but he felt he had no choice but to accept it. According to Rae Vader, supervising agent of the investigative office, it was "very difficult to state that the evacuee had been defrauded.... The lessee could present his claim in the proper court, but it is doubtful whether such action would be a relief to a Japanese lessee."[104]

Other stories of inadequate compensation were common. When an Oklahoma family took over the farm of Yoshihiko Tanabe's family in Fife, Washington, he remembered that five acres of lettuce were about to be harvested. The FSA made a "very low estimate" of the cost of planting the crop, "not what the crop would bring on the market, and that was what we were paid. We were in no position to negotiate with the agency and we accepted what we were given ... we were intimidated by authority!"[105] Likewise, Masaru Yamasaki remembered with great bitterness the dealings that his father, Manhichi, had with the FSA. The FSA negotiated the sale of his crop and equipment on his Florin, California, farm to George Faris, who secured a loan for an agreed-upon price. Yamasaki was sent to an assembly center before the loan came through, and Faris returned the loan to the FSA. Manhichi was due about two thousand dollars, a sum that "represented his entire life savings during his struggles to raise his family as model citizens." He tried to resolve the issue while he was confined at the Tule Lake Relocation Center, to no avail. His son concluded, "My father never received one penny from the ... transaction. The Farm Security Administration and the United States Government had a moral and legal responsibility to see that Manhichi received his rightful money."[106]

Japanese Americans also stood to lose money when their arrangements involved corporations financed by WFA loans. Most leases between Japanese Americans and corporations agreed that the former should receive 50 percent of the net proceeds from crop sales after deducting for operating expenses. However, the FSA demanded full repayment of loans before any profits went to Japanese Americans. Because corporations consolidated the holdings of several farms, it was entirely possible that "some evacuees received nothing because of poor crops on someone else's land." Even after the FSA transferred its responsibilities to the WRA Evacuee Property Division in August 1942, it retained control of its loans and insisted on a "firm collection policy."[107]

The WRA and FSA inevitably clashed over this issue of loan repayment. The case of Northern Farms, a corporation that took over twenty Japanese American–owned farms in Placer and Sacramento Counties, is instructive. When the corporation received a WFA loan, it mortgaged all growing crops on leased land. It also signed leases with individual Japanese Americans and agreed to provide each with 50 percent of annual net operating profit. At the end of the season, five of the farms turned a profit, so these owners were entitled to a total sum of $2,017.19. However, the combined operations of Northern Farms were not profitable, and the corporation could not afford to fully repay the WFA loan. According to Northern Farms secretary E. L. Schnell, the failure to turn a profit was a result of unanticipated expenses. Grapevines had not been sulfured, which resulted in stem mildew that precluded grape shipments. Winter and early spring spraying were neglected, which led to a codling moth infestation that yielded unsellable, wormy fruit. "All of these things result[ed] in increased costs to produce the crops, which with the high labor costs, prevented many of the ranches from having enough fruit to pay back the total production cost," he explained.[108]

Despite these challenges, the FSA wanted all profits applied to the WFA loan rather than distributed to individual Japanese American owners. Victor Furth of the WRA's Evacuee Property Division argued that "it seems questionable to us that it was the intent of the WFA that the evacuees' share of the net profit would not be paid to each lessor whose property showed a net income." He recommended that Northern Farms pay Japanese Americans whose farms turned a profit "even though their WFA loan cannot be paid in full."[109] The FSA refused to authorize these payments until it received such a recommendation from the attorney general.[110] This conflict and others suggested that, contrary to its rhetoric, the FSA often prioritized loan repayment over ensuring that Japanese Americans received their fair share of crop profits.[111]

Moreover, while many Japanese Americans did receive money for their crops and equipment, it was typically a fraction of what it was worth. Robert Sato's family operated a farm in Sumner, Washington. Because they were not given a firm removal date, his parents planted the spring crops. He estimated that their crops, cars, machinery, and tools were worth at least forty-five thousand dollars in 1942. His sister was able to sell everything for five thousand dollars, "although at one point my father, in utter frustration and anger, was about to abandon [it] rather than to give away his farm at such a ridiculously low price," Sato remembered.[112] Their losses proved devastating.

In addition to stories of failed or limited compensation, reduced agricultural output and uncultivated land were evident. In June 1943, the Washington State Taxpayers Association put out a report entitled "Economic Effects of Japanese Evacuation." Using data on carlot shipments of fresh produce to eastern markets, the association found a significant decline in the state's production. Between 1941 and 1942, lettuce shipments from Washington dropped from 660 to 289 tons; peas fell from 558 to 141 tons; celery declined from 386 to 56 tons; and cauliflower plummeted from 211 to 25 tons.[113] The situation on Bainbridge Island was especially discouraging. According to Edward M. Joyce, WRA evacuee property supervisor, the property there was "badly mishandled and in extremely bad shape." Neglect had led to the loss of many acres of strawberries, peas, and berry plants. Two corporations had received government loans to operate farms there, but their affairs "are in bad shape, and, as a consequence, the equities of the Japanese with whom they had dealings are endangered." [114] FSA transactions, then, failed to maintain prewar production levels.

The correspondence between Lewis Hatch and the Tanaka family corroborates this report. Through the FSA program, John Tanaka, one of the sons, sold the lease on the family's twenty-acre farm in Alderton, Washington.[115] While in Minidoka, family members corresponded with Hatch, a friend and neighbor in the Puyallup Valley who was storing their car and personal possessions. In September 1942, Hatch wrote, "Most of the people who took over the land previously farmed by Japanese have not gotten along very well, especially with vegetables." He estimated that production was half of the previous year.[116] In March 1943, he updated the family and noted, "I believe that the man who bought your lease has been more interested in working in the shipyard than in farming, at least at the road it looks like he is not doing much farming."[117]

Louis Lopez provided a more poignant story of decline and neglect. During the war, he moved to Loomis, California, next door to the Makabe orchard, which was leased to Northern Farms and occupied by Chinese laborers. When he went to the orchard to get some peaches, he saw that "the Chinamen were just laying around doing nothing. The fruit was all falling on the ground. They told me to pick what I wanted, the trees hadn't been pruned the year before and that fall the trees weren't pruned again." Aware of the deteriorating state of their farm, the Makabes contacted WRA attorney Ralph Moore in December 1942. After passing along their inquiry to WRA solicitor general Philip Glick, Moore commented, "The Japanese cannot expect to find operators as experienced as they themselves have been."[118] It is unclear if the WRA resolved the Makabes' case.

The deterioration of the Tanaka and Makabe farms probably had little impact on overall agricultural output, but their wartime transformation hints at the pockets of environmental change scattered all over the Pacific Coast. In the absence of Japanese Americans, some farms and orchards went from orderly and fecund to unkempt and unproductive. As observers drove or walked past weedy fields and unpruned trees weighed down by overripe fruit, they took notice. The physical neglect of the land was a marker of social and economic change, too. Years of hard work had been erased.

* * *

When it took over from the FSA, the WRA Evacuee Property Division adopted the conservation of property—agricultural and otherwise—as a key goal. It tried to find lessors and buyers for Japanese American property, settled claims for or against detainees, adjusted "differences arising out of inequitable, hastily made, or indefinite agreements," collected money due to detainees, and determined if property was "satisfactorily maintained."[119] It also conducted a survey of eighteen "principal Japanese populated counties," which accounted for about 80 percent of Japanese American farm ownership interests in the removal area. Here, about twenty-three hundred ownerships comprised about 71,000 acres of agricultural land valued at $21 million as of March 1, 1942. Eighty-five to 90 percent of this property was in California.[120]

The survey found a modest decline in Japanese American farm ownership and Japanese American–owned acreage. From March 2 to October 31, 1942, ownerships decreased by about 8 percent, which amounted to a 6 percent decline in Japanese American–owned acreage. By November 1, 1943, there was a net decline of about 11 percent in Japanese American farm ownerships and acreage. According to Adon Poli, an agricultural economist with the USDA, "The uncertainty of future developments in nations at war and the desire to liquidate property into ready cash for emergency use were undoubtedly strong motives for disposal of property at the beginning when evacuation measures were being formulated and publicized."[121]

These figures fail to tell the whole story, particularly since 70 percent of Japanese American farmers were tenants. In fact, almost all of their leases were transferred to non-Japanese Americans during removal. Poli noted, "Because most leases were short-term and many of the longer-term leases were canceled or reassigned during evacuation, it is likely that little, if any of the leasehold interests of former Japanese tenants will be carried over into the post-war period." The "principal remaining interest" of Japanese Americans in agricultural land was retained through ownerships, but Poli anticipated that farm owners would continue to dispose of their landholdings. He predicted that they would control no more than twenty-three percent of total prewar landholdings, including leases. This would amount to 55,000 to 60,000 acres, a huge decline from the over 250,000 acres that they cultivated at the start of the war.[122]

Meanwhile, growers still struggled with the labor void created by removal. R. K. Malcolm of Liberty Farms did not stop voicing his displeasure and even sent a wire to General DeWitt on April 23, 1942. He also continued his correspondence with Dave Davidson of the California USDA War Board. Davidson was sympathetic to Malcolm's frustration, noting, "All of us farmers are confronted with the necessity this year of using any kind of labor we can find, even though it is not immediately efficient and although it will probably necessitate considerable training before it can be used in a satisfactory fashion." Davidson was using this approach on his own farm in Tulare County. He was not happy about it, he remarked, but "I think it is what we all will have to do."[123] Malcolm, like other growers, had to resign himself to employing new workers.

For all of the people who welcomed the expulsion of people of Japanese ancestry out of economic self-interest or deep-seated racial animus, others were more circumspect about its implications for the cultivation of natural resources, especially farmland. Government officials tried to keep land in production, but they were not swayed by growers who wanted to retain their Japanese American farm laborers. Despite their well-honed skills and intimate knowledge of specific environments, their removal proceeded. As it did, patches of physical neglect and deterioration emerged on once-cultivated lands throughout the Far West.

2

Choosing Sites, Building Camps

WHEN VICTOR IKEDA got off the train in Eden, Idaho, on his way to the Minidoka Relocation Center, it seemed like "the end of the world." Situated on the high desert of the Snake River plain and dotted with sagebrush and basaltic lava flows, Minidoka was dusty, hot, and "a God-forsaken place." After growing up in Seattle, just eight blocks from the waterfront, and spending his childhood summers fishing for shrimp and rock cod or playing under the piers, his alienation and disorientation were not surprising. He had been displaced from a watery, green world and transported to a landlocked, arid one.[1] The Pacific Coast was hundreds of miles away, and his days of confinement began in earnest.

Why did the federal government choose such seemingly uninviting places? While it appeared that federal officials were arbitrarily exiling Japanese Americans to the most desolate places, the site selection process was actually quite deliberate. War Relocation Authority (WRA) and War Department officials considered over three hundred sites and reflected on their choices carefully. It was critical to locate the camps far from places of strategic importance, but discussions also included environmental criteria such as climate and soil quality. Some neighboring residents objected on the basis of environmental concerns—from pollution to finite resource supplies—but WRA officials proceeded anyway and approved ten locations. The War Department then acquired the land and began construction.

When Japanese Americans arrived at the camps, a combination of shoddy construction, wartime shortages, and harsh environmental features created unpleasant, substandard living conditions. First and foremost, detainees had minimal protection from the natural elements—dust, wind, heat, and cold. Ironically, WRA officials found themselves battling and mitigating nature at the very places that they had believed to be favorable detention sites. They had little choice but to assume a defensive posture, often dashing from one crisis to the next. As a WRA engineering section leader explained, "The construction being of a temporary nature . . . required immediate and constant maintenance and repairs."[2] Japanese Americans responded with both dismay and resolve to make the camps more livable.

The next steps in the incarceration process—site selection and construction—were thus closely connected to and shaped by the natural world. Confining thousands of people required environmental amenities and brought significant material changes to nearby lands and waters. WRA officials, local residents, and Japanese Americans simply could not shut themselves off from the nature that surrounded them. The exigencies of a nation at war, moreover, compounded the environmental limitations and unpredictability of the chosen camp sites. All parties involved learned that these human and natural forces intertwined and required frequent adaptations.

"The Inside Room in the Badlands": Choosing Sites

To understand the site selection process, one needs to understand the ideals that guided the WRA. Both Milton Eisenhower and Dillon Myer were former Department of Agriculture employees and New Deal liberals who believed in the power of the government to regulate and improve society.[3] In the case of the WRA, they maintained that they could "turn an unfortunate incidence of war into a positive social good." The camps would not be inhumane; instead, they would be planned communities that would assimilate Japanese Americans through self-government, education, and work.[4] Indeed, Eisenhower believed that working the land would allow them to prove their loyalty. They could labor on public works—soil conservation, range improvement, irrigation, flood control—or produce food and war goods. He explained, "It would give to these citizens a measure of assurance and trust should we afford them an opportunity to do their part in the war effort, with the possibility that recognition of this contribution eventually may be accorded by the American public."[5]

In some respects, Japanese American incarceration appeared as an extension of New Deal public works projects. There were, in fact, direct connections. Several Works Progress Administration staff members who had run WPA work camps went on to manage temporary assembly centers. Much like the Civilian Conservation Corps (CCC), the WRA promoted the use of labor to both improve public land and Americanize its charges.[6] But there were critical distinctions. Unlike CCC men, who enrolled and worked voluntarily, Japanese Americans labored under conditions of forcible confinement. Two-thirds of the detainees were also citizens and had no apparent need for Americanization. Eisenhower was "not at all happy" about restraints on American citizens and thus wanted good management to promote "a sound economy and a healthy democracy within each project area."[7]

WRA leaders advanced their program and sought appropriate sites to meet their objectives.[8] While some observers wanted to exile Japanese Americans to the middle of nowhere—Hearst newspaper columnist Henry McLemore suggested "a point deep in the interior . . . the inside room in the badlands"—the WRA declared that potential sites needed to provide year-round work, whether on public works, manufacturing, or food production.[9] Community and agricultural areas had to be in one block of land "to facilitate the administration and military protection of the area," and each site had to be "a safe distance from strategic works." The sites also had to be capable of supporting at least five thousand people, which meant that adequate transportation, power facilities, and water supply systems, "suitable in quality and quantity," were essential. The WRA also preferred sites on public lands "so that improvements at public expense become public, not private, assets."[10] Although the WRA privileged isolated sites with some existing infrastructure, it also considered evidence of agricultural potential, particularly climate, water, and soil.

Despite clear criteria, the WRA still received numerous unsolicited suggestions from all across the country. A handful of proposals came from Japanese Americans who hoped to establish autonomous centers. For instance, James T. Nishimura spearheaded the Happy Valley Community Project on five hundred acres of land in El Dorado County, California, owned by Helen Berry Baker. Originally proposed during the brief period of voluntary evacuation, the project was to provide work for 114 citizens who would farm and log. Nishimura also claimed that the only adjoining neighbor, May Bundy, was friendly to the project.[11] Writing to President Roosevelt, he declared, "As loyal American citizens we would like to do our part in this time of crisis, and we think we can best do this by establishing ourselves as a self-supporting community in a place where we can render our services by obtaining lumber from an isolated part of the country and thus supplying a vitally important material for the building of merchant ships."[12] However, WRA deputy director E. M. Rowalt noted that the project lacked water, power, and transportation facilities and had serious fire hazards.[13]

Whereas Nishimura and other Japanese groups were motivated by the possibility of independence, beet growers in northeastern Montana wanted to exploit a ready supply of workers. As Fred Rees of the WRA explained,

"Officials of the beet companies and a considerable part of local businessmen consider the primary purpose of the war relocation authority [*sic*] to be to provide labor for the production of beets."[14] For example, G. N. Wells, president of the Montana-Dakota Beet Growers Association, heard that the WRA was considering a site at Fort Keogh and informed Eisenhower that its timely selection would allow them to proceed with their plantings.[15] Eisenhower assured Wells that his office had "tried diligently to locate a relocation center in Montana." However, Fort Keogh's severe winters "make it very doubtful that evacuees would have any work to do for many months each year."[16] The site was rejected, although WRA leaders considered several other places in the region.[17]

Both Nishimura and Wells suggested that locating camps on their proposed sites would allow them to harness natural resources for the war effort. Wells noted, "It is our responsibility to meet the quotas of production that have been set up for us by the Department of Agriculture."[18] Yet their proposals overlooked other environmental factors that made their sites impractical. For instance, forest fires in El Dorado County could destroy the very crops and timber that Japanese Americans proposed to harvest. Moreover, they would inevitably be accused of setting any conflagration that might occur and branded saboteurs in the process.[19] The WRA's definition of environmental favorability was often in direct opposition to the views of outside parties.

A combination of infrastructure and environmental factors proved decisive in the WRA's site selection deliberations. In explaining to Senator Eugene Millikan of Colorado why the Pine River area near Durango was rejected, Eisenhower pointed to field inspections conducted by the Farm Security Administration and the Bureau of Agricultural Economics, which concluded, in part, that the cost of getting water to the land was quite high, no crops could be grown in 1942, and securing power and domestic water would be a "serious problem." A Bureau of Reclamation investigation also revealed that canal construction could not be completed until 1943, additional land could not be placed under irrigation until 1944, and the cost of extending and enlarging canals was potentially prohibitive. Pine River also faced severe winters, which blocked transportation routes. Thus, it would be "impractical" to have a camp there.[20]

As Eisenhower's letter to Millikin demonstrated, federal agencies within the Departments of Agriculture and Interior offered important input during the site selection process.[21] They also made specific site suggestions. Ira N. Gabrielson, director of the US Fish and Wildlife Service, sent Eisenhower a list of wildlife refuges where "alien work camps" could be set up. Focusing on

refuges west of the Mississippi River, he noted the size of the sites and proximity to the railroad and provided a description of the work projects. These
activities included constructing and maintaining water control structures,
fences, roads, and trails, operating tree and shrub nurseries, and conducting
soil conservation operations—all of which would "increase the value of the
refuges for wildlife."[22] None of the proposed sites made the final cut.

WRA officials proved far more interested in finding Indian reservations
"upon which the Japanese evacuees could be placed and employed in useful
work." A. C. Cooley, director of extension and industry for the Bureau of
Indian Affairs (BIA), and C. H. Southworth, acting director of irrigation,
provided a list of eight available reservation sites, three in Arizona, three in
Montana, and one each in Wyoming and Minnesota, ranging in size from
twenty-five hundred to twenty thousand acres. Drainage, canal extensions,
land clearing, and other "subjugation work" were available, but Cooley and
Southworth also suggested that the reservations were all suitable to grow
crops ranging from garden produce to forage. Despite severe winter weather,
even the Red Lake Reservation in Minnesota was "adaptable" for sugar beets,
grain, and forage crops.[23] BIA officials clearly understood the types of sites
that the WRA sought—those with agricultural potential where Japanese
American expertise and labor could be put to good use.

F. H. Daiker, an assistant to John Collier, commissioner of the BIA, was
not sanguine about placing Japanese Americans on Indian reservations. He
explained to Collier, "The logical question will be, why place them among
the Indians after all the wrongs that have been done these people? It will be
construed as just another instance of forcing something on to the Indian because he can do nothing about it." Daiker also worried about how Indians
might react to Japanese Americans: "The Indian is going to say that they are
citizens in addition to being wards of the government, and that they are giving
their young men and their dollars to help fight the very people we are putting
in their midst." They might also feel the inequity of living "under unsatisfac-
tory conditions on a sub-standard basis," while the government housed, fed,
and possibly paid Japanese Americans a monthly wage.[24] Daiker did not ac-
knowledge that two-thirds of the detainees were also US citizens. Instead, he
focused on the perception of special treatment, which might anger Indians,
given rumors of Japanese American duplicity.

While Daiker understood that Japanese Americans could improve the
reservations, he was concerned about bringing in "outside help to do the
things the Indian should do for himself." If Japanese Americans "put the land
in shape . . . the Indian may expect continued free labor to prepare and operate

his lands." It was critical that "the Indian work and . . . not have someone else do it for him," he explained.[25] Put another way, the federal government was proposing to enlist detainees to "tame the desert" for future Indian, then eventually white, use.[26]

Daiker's concerns notwithstanding, two Indian reservations in Arizona—Colorado River and Gila River—were on an April 1942 list of approved WRA relocation center sites.[27] In short order, many employees from the BIA went on to work for the WRA. Indeed, Eisenhower met with Collier and asked that the BIA operate the camp at Colorado River, also known as Poston. He agreed, but only if allowed to continue "in the spirit of the Indian New Deal and the Indian Reorganization Act." This meant, in part, making the camp "a showplace of community planning, complete with experimental farm cooperatives, schools and cultural life."[28] Wade Head, former superintendent of the Papago Indian Reservation, became the project director. Until mid-1943, Poston was the only camp administered by the BIA.[29]

After poring over the field investigations of engineers, economists, soil scientists, geologists, and agronomists, the WRA selected ten sites in rural areas west of the Mississippi River, far from major cities and strategic military works, each with a capacity to confine eight thousand to twenty thousand people. In addition to the two Indian reservation sites, the agency chose three Bureau of Reclamation sites—Heart Mountain, Minidoka, and Tule Lake—with ready access to irrigation works that were part of an extensive federal water infrastructure in the American West.[30] Manzanar, Granada, and Central Utah (Topaz) contained some private and municipal lands and thus did not fully meet the WRA's public lands criterion. Jerome and Rohwer were on Farm Security Administration land intended for subsistence homesteads.[31]

When WRA official E. M. Rowalt described five of the sites in a memorandum to the WRA staff in Washington, DC, he carefully delineated climatic, soil, and irrigation conditions for agriculture. The use of Bureau of Reclamation projects was critical, as Rowalt noted that an "adequate supply of irrigation water" was available at Tule Lake and "the full acreage can be irrigated from the present water supply" at Minidoka.[32] Water was needed so that each center could become self-sufficient in food production within one season and put any surplus toward the war.[33] Dillon Myer, who succeeded Eisenhower, even asked Secretary of Agriculture Claude Wickard which crops to grow to make "the greatest contribution to the war effort."[34]

In addition to their wartime contributions, WRA officials maintained that the camps could bring postwar benefits to nearby residents. When describing Topaz, WRA regional director E. Reeseman (E. R.) Fryer, former

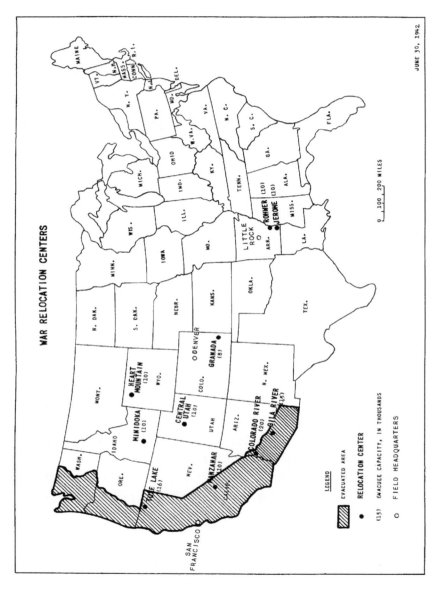

FIGURE 2.1 War Relocation Authority Centers, 1942. *Relocation Communities for Wartime Evacuees* (Washington D.C.: War Relocation Authority, 1942).

superintendent of the Navajo reservation, explained plans for Japanese Americans to develop ten thousand acres. He noted, "It would be possible and would be in line with good land use to resettle non-Japanese farmers now farming 'submarginal' land in the Delta area, on the project after the Japanese evacuees leave the project after the close of the war."[35] The *Millard County Chronicle* approved of the camp becoming a "self-liquidating project," as the land would be sold after the war, with first choice given to veterans. The government's investment would be paid back for the "betterment to us all."[36]

Japanese Americans' ability to improve the land for whites also factored into the decision to locate a camp at Minidoka. Detainees could cultivate the land during the war, after which time it would "be ready for occupation by white settlers, possibly returned service men, and a degree of cultivation will exist which should add materially to the tract and lighten the labor of reclamation usually attending the homesteading of desert land." Bureau of Reclamation Superintendent S. R. Marean was confident that "before the war is over the community will be very grateful for the farm labor that the settlement is likely to make available." He also suggested that Japanese Americans could be put to work to make improvements to the Milner-Gooding Canal.[37] Ultimately, they would give the land "long-time value."[38]

The WRA emphasized that its chosen sites had other environmental advantages, often ignoring contradictory evidence. As one report explained, "Perhaps the best evidence that environmental factors are favorable at each site lies in the fact that there are prosperous and populous communities near each project. In all cases these communities have developed under natural conditions." However, the author neglected to explain that earlier improvements—like irrigation—often made these communities possible. The report went on to dismiss the hot summers at several sites, as low humidity meant that the heat had "no serious adverse physical effects." Likewise, cold winters caused "little inconvenience or distress." In fact, most sites had fall, winter, and spring climates that were "especially mild and healthful."[39] This point was debatable. The temperature at Topaz ranged from one hundred degrees Fahrenheit to fifteen degrees below zero—not really "mild and healthful" even if the cold weather was "usually not of long duration," according to the WRA.[40] Pointing to previous crops of sugar beets, alfalfa, wheat, rye, and truck crops, WRA field investigators Fred W. Ross and Mark W. Radcliffe added that alkaline soil would create "no difficulty" in cultivating the land at Topaz and that drainage ditches would be unnecessary.[41] However, they neglected to mention low crop yields and failures due to poor drainage and that high-alkali soil inhibited plant growth.[42]

Other WRA officials were cognizant of the difficulties of growing crops at Topaz, but the ease and low cost with which they could obtain the land ultimately trumped these potential challenges. As E. J. Utz, chief of the agricultural division, explained, "Very few persons would be discommoded through the purchase of this land." More than half was in public ownership—1,400 acres belonged to the US Grazing Service and 8,840 acres to Millard County—and thirty-four people owned the remaining 9,760 acres. Only seven people actually lived on the land, and all but one of them was willing to sell. The cost was also reasonable. Millard County land was priced at one dollar per acre, whereas improved and unimproved private land cost an average of thirty dollars and ten dollars per acre, respectively. Twenty thousand shares of water stock for irrigation could be obtained for twenty dollars per share.[43]

These practical concerns were equally if not more important than environmental suitability. Still, the WRA juggled many other factors. Given security issues and anti-Japanese sentiment, the camps could not be placed in densely populated areas. Favorable conditions for agriculture were also important criteria so that Japanese Americans could minimize costs, contribute to the war effort, and even aid future land occupants. As they tilled the land, WRA officials also believed that they could prove their loyalty and become assimilated. The sites were thus integral to the promotion and affirmation of the WRA's mission and philosophy.

"The Most Illogical Place That Could Be Selected Anywhere": Protesting Site Selections

For those who lived near the chosen sites, the camps were a potential boon. Almost immediately, contractors recruited local residents to work on construction crews.[44] But in the case of Los Angeles residents and municipal officials, Idaho water officials, and Pima Indians, the WRA's selections were unwelcome. The exigencies of war ultimately overrode all of their concerns, but it was clear that the WRA lacked unanimous support for confining Japanese Americans in particular places. Opponents often associated the camps with social and environmental degradation.

Located in the Owens Valley, about 250 miles north of Los Angeles and bounded by the Sierra Nevada to the west and the Inyo Mountains to the east, Manzanar had already been the site of fierce struggles when the Los Angeles Department of Water and Power (LADWP) siphoned the valley's water and effectively destroyed the local agricultural and ranching economy.[45] The possibility of locating a Japanese American detention facility here originated with E. Manchester Boddy, editor of the *Los Angeles Daily News*. On February 9, 1942, he wrote to Attorney General Francis Biddle and suggested that Olancha in Inyo County would be an ideal place for Japanese Americans to assemble before sending them to work on Pacific Coast farming projects. It was accessible, with one weekly train and an "adequate state highway," but it was not *too* accessible, as it was separated from the Pacific Ocean "by the highest mountains in the United States." He had already mentioned the site to Alien Control Coordinator Tom C. Clark, who, in turn, discussed it with California governor Culbert Olson and General John L. DeWitt.[46]

Clark established a committee of local leaders so he could sell the project to Owens Valley residents, but his efforts fell apart when the US Army engineers contacted Harvey Arthur (H. A.) Van Norman, chief engineer and general manager of the LADWP, and demanded a lease on land in the area in early March.[47] Van Norman immediately objected, pointing to the threat of sabotage posed by Japanese Americans living at the headworks of the city's water supply. As an alternative, he suggested the use of Colorado River Indian tribes' land in Parker, Arizona, about 250 miles from Los Angeles and on the eastern side of the Colorado River. This was isolated land that Japanese Americans could clear and cultivate, resulting "in a permanent improvement that could be settled by return soldiers at the expiration of the War."[48] Los Angeles mayor Fletcher Bowron concurred. In a February 1942 radio address, he explained that the Parker site would allow Japanese Americans to be self-supporting while observing "nothing of military importance." They could also provide fresh produce to Los Angeles markets.[49]

Despite efforts to divert attention from the Owens Valley, the federal government moved forward with its plans. On March 7, 1942, the Western Defense Command issued a press release to announce the acquisition of fifty-eight hundred acres of Los Angeles land in a former apple orchard known as Manzanar. Recognizing widespread objections, the release quoted a letter from DeWitt, who explained that the project would provide "adequate provision" to protect the water from injury and pollution and would bear in mind "the needs of the City of Los Angeles for such water."[50]

These assurances did not appear to convince some Angelenos. Japanese American farmers were already facing accusations that they were poisoning food crops.[51] Now they confronted similar fears that they would poison the water supply. In a letter to Van Norman, T. Blevans explained that "it will take a great many thousand people to keep one or more of the 50,000 Japanese from crawling on their belly to get to the aqueduct and there infect the water.

If 80,000 Englishmen could not hold them back in Singapore I do not see how a few guards will be able to protect our water supply." As was common during the war, Blevans equated Japanese Americans living in the United States, the majority of whom were citizens by birth, with the Japanese enemy. He concluded, "Many of our population are very much disturbed about planting the Japanese in the most illogical place that could be selected anywhere in the State of California."[52] Although Japanese Americans on the West Coast were being expelled, in part, because of fears of another sea-based attack, Blevans believed that they posed an even greater threat in the state's interior.

H. L. Ford echoed some of these concerns and explicitly framed Japanese Americans as an environmental health hazard. He wrote, "It may be true that the Japanese could not dump enough poison in our aqueduct to kill many of us, but we do know that if they are put anywhere near the water sheds and supplies they will manage to plant Typhoid Cultures, Amebia [*sic*], Bubonic Plague, and Leprosy, and possibly other oriental diseases. We know they are capable of doing this very thing and I haven't the slightest doubt but [that] they will." A possible epidemic was "worse than machine guns," and Ford would rather the Japanese remain along the coast than "have them planted anywhere within 500 miles of our water supply, and if we permit them to be located in that vicinity we might just as well begin to look for an army of grave [diggers] and a new supply of boxes."[53] Ford assumed that all people of Japanese ancestry were inherently diseased. Like Blevans, he linked Japanese Americans' racial inferiority with their potential to bring physical harm to Los Angeles residents vis-à-vis the aqueduct.

Concerns over protecting municipal watersheds from contamination were hardly new in Los Angeles or other American cities. Beginning with the construction of Boston's and New York's water systems in the 1830s and 1840s, city and state officials erected barriers, enacted laws, and delivered sanctions to ensure the purity of municipally owned and delivered water.[54] Earlier miasmic theories, which attributed disease transmission to "bad airs" or noxious vapors, propelled such efforts, and the advent of germ theory in the late nineteenth century only gave sanitarians more powerful medical and scientific justification to protect water supplies. But just as racialized ideas of disease transmission and contagion undergirded miasmic theories, they also shaped newer ideas of germs as carriers of disease in medical and popular discourses. This "gospel of germs" carried virulent and enduring ideas of racial purity and contamination.[55]

Indeed, the rhetoric connecting public health to racial and ethnic difference was likely familiar to some Angelenos. Beginning in the late nineteenth century, Los Angeles public health officials attributed the city's health problems to the Mexican, Chinese, and Japanese populations. When the plague hit in 1924, confined mostly to neighborhoods inhabited by Mexicans, the association between filth, disease, and ethnicity was reinforced, as phalanxes of city sanitarians fumigated buildings and torched homes in these areas.[56] Such associations endured into the war years. While Japanese Americans were being forcibly removed, they still constituted a health threat—a yellow peril—that continued to define them as a racial other, unfit to be living in the city or its hinterlands.[57]

Despite this climate of racial hygiene, the *Los Angeles Times* editorial board supported the Owens Valley camp. Because the army had promised "sufficient guards" to patrol and protect the aqueduct, "Southern California residents should, as a patriotic duty, accept the Army's decision and immediately cooperate in the main objective—that of restraining the aliens from any possible acts of sabotage against our military installations, plane plants, power stations and other essential wartime key centers."[58] The *Times* editorial board asked readers to set their priorities straight. The Japanese American population was a far greater threat dispersed in the metropolitan area than it was guarded closely in a camp in the Owens Valley.

The *Inyo Independent*, an Owens Valley newspaper, also urged support among local residents. Like the *Los Angeles Times*, the editorial board emphasized residents' patriotic duty to adopt "an attitude of cooperation." The authors also emphasized tangible benefits, some environmental, for the community. Japanese Americans could provide "a large reservoir of labor for certain needed and proposed projects of present and future benefit to this region," including broad-gauging the railroad, harvesting crops, and building roads. Permanent camp buildings could also be converted into rehabilitation facilities for returning soldiers after the war.[59] Their temporary wartime presence, in other words, could bring improvements for postwar residents. This "overly promotional tone" was not unique to Manzanar and was, in fact, common among journalists who reported for newspapers in the communities surrounding the camps.[60]

LADWP officials remained firmly opposed, yet resigned, to the camp. When Van Norman replied to Ford about his fears of diseased water, he explained that LADWP would "insist upon complete guarding of our properties against any sort of sabotage, including pollution of the water" and assured him that regular water samples would be tested.[61] LADWP sanitary engineer R. F. Goudey, who also worried about exposure to "Oriental carriers of cholera, dysentery, and typhoid," tried to further ensure water purity by outlining a list of measures to keep the water clean."[62] Van Norman forwarded these recommendations to DeWitt, reminding him that all runoff from Manzanar washed into the aqueduct. Constant vigilance was imperative because the aqueduct supplied water to "over a million civilians, a large number of defense industries, and many war service units."[63] By this point in late March 1942, the first detainees from Bainbridge Island, Washington, had already arrived. Originally a reception center, Manzanar was turned over to the WRA on June 1, 1942, to be administered as a relocation center where Japanese Americans would live indefinitely.[64]

Officials at the American Falls Reservoir District No. 2 in Idaho also worried about water. They first announced their opposition to Minidoka at the end of April 1942, noting that the water supply was inadequate to irrigate nearly nineteen thousand acres of undeveloped public land that the WRA planned to use for the camp. Part of the problem was that the Milner-Gooding Canal, which was to bring water to the camp, needed repairs and this task would be "long and arduous." Even with its leaks repaired, the canal's capacity was already "taxed to the limit." They maintained that the government policy was to "first provide an adequate supply of water for the lands already under cultivation on which our people are making their home before bringing new land under cultivation."[65]

John C. Page, commissioner of the Bureau of Reclamation, responded to the board of directors of the reservoir district with both empirical and patriotic reasons to support the camp. Citing "preliminary studies," he maintained that installation of a concrete lining and the restoration of a silt blanket would reduce losses in the canal and provide enough water to support production and meet WRA needs. He also pointed out that the government was trying to reduce the costs of the camps. "In establishing camps and work areas," he explained, "preference must be given to those unentered public land areas on which Japanese can be placed on a self-supporting basis as quickly as possible." He asked for the district's cooperation, "which will be a very direct contribution to the war."[66]

When the district's attorney responded to Page, he was quick to emphasize that the board members' opposition had nothing to do with the fact that people of Japanese ancestry would be placed on the land. Instead, they were protesting "the opening and development of this tract either by the Japs or by anyone else until and after it had been demonstrated that there is sufficient additional water in the Milner-Gooding Canal to irrigate such land." The best course of action would be to repair the canal first and then determine the definite amount of water savings, although the attorney suggested that it would be "impossible" for canal repairs to save enough water to irrigate both nineteen thousand acres at the proposed camp and the remaining lands in the district.[67] The members of the reservoir district framed the problem around the imminent threat of financial losses due to water shortages and kept any racial animus toward Japanese Americans in check.

For the Pima Indians who protested the Gila River Relocation Center, the lack of consultation during the WRA's site selection process superseded any potential financial and environmental benefits to them. On April 29, 1942, the Gila River Pima-Maricopa Indian Community Council voted on a resolution to "reject the Japanese coming to our Reservation," which passed by a vote of nine to five.[68] As reservation superintendent A. E. Robinson explained, "They are an organized chartered tribe and . . . their governing body is authorized to pass upon such matters."[69] Robinson tried to gain Pima support by emphasizing the financial boon of Japanese American occupancy. To rent 6,977 acres of irrigated alfalfa land, the WRA was to pay $20 per acre annually for the land and another $3.60 per acre annually for the delivery of four acre-feet of water per acre of land. This sum would pay for the operation and management expenses for the tribe with "possibly a good margin to spare." Moreover, providing the WRA with three years of free use of another 8,850-acre tract that would be cleared and developed by Japanese Americans was "a nominal charge for the work performed."[70] Robinson also told John Collier that he believed that dissenters comprised a minority. He noted, "There seems to be comparatively little concern on the part of any except the council members who have expressed themselves."[71]

Robinson also argued that the federal government was not treating the Pima any different than many other "business concerns." Large manufacturing plants, for instance, were being called upon to produce certain war materials instead of their customary products. In this case, it was the Pima lands that were deemed an important wartime commodity. He concluded with common patriotic rhetoric: "It was not the desire on the part of the WRA nor on the part of the Department of the Interior that this should be thrust upon them without giving them an opportunity to express themselves but the emergency which this war has forced upon us has required that every American citizen heed whatever army command may be given him."[72] By early May 1942, construction on the camp had already begun. Robinson told the tribal council that he saw no possibility of "stopping the course of the project at present."[73]

When the Gila River Pima-Maricopa Indian Community signed the lease agreement with the WRA on October 7, it retained some control over its land. In the developed parcel of 6,977 acres, the WRA agreed to submit a "proposed program for the use of the lands" to the Office of Indian Affairs, which could voice objections if officials believed it "might result in substantial injury to the productiveness of the lands." In the undeveloped parcel of 8,850 acres, the WRA's irrigation work and other improvements would be left on the land as "fair and equitable compensation to the Indians for the use of their land." If the value of these improvements was inadequate, the WRA would pay the Indians "such additional sum as the parties hereto may agree upon to provide such compensation."[74]

In the end, the WRA's criteria for appropriate sites did not necessarily account for the concerns and rights of affected communities. In the case of Manzanar, Angelenos and LADWP officials viewed Japanese Americans as both contaminators and contaminants. Virulent anti-Japanese sentiment often fueled their fears. The objections of the American Falls Reservoir District No. 2, by contrast, focused on the finite supply of water and the desire to ensure that existing users had their share. For the Pima, who stood to gain improved land from their agreement with the WRA, any environmental and monetary benefits could not negate the fact that federal officials ignored their status as a sovereign nation when they decided to put a camp on their reservation. Indeed, the WRA secured the ultimate power to commandeer land and began to shape it to fit its various needs. Its visions for the land supplanted those of any other group.

"Not Fit to Be Occupied": Building the Camps

After the WRA chose the ten sites and the War Department acquired the land, private contractors began construction under the supervision of the Army Corps of Engineers.[75] Eisenhower was keen on moving Japanese Americans from the assembly centers to the relocation centers as soon as possible. He explained, "Delays result only in depressing the morale of evacuees."[76] To expedite the process, all WRA camps adopted a similar layout and design. They were arranged into several blocks, with thirty-four to thirty-six reserved for residential use. Each block housed about three hundred people and contained a mess hall, recreation hall, laundry room, and separate latrines for men and women as well as ten to fourteen barracks. The barracks were built in a modified "theater of operations" style used by the army for housing troops for no more than five years. Each barrack measured 20 by 100 or 120 feet and usually housed four to six apartments of varying sizes. Partitions between apartments did not reach the ceiling, so privacy was minimal.[77] Construction also included utilities, such as sewage disposal, electrical, and telephone

FIGURE 2.2 Camp construction required clearing extensive vegetation, like sagebrush at the Manzanar Relocation Center, June 30, 1942. Photograph by Dorothea Lange. Courtesy of the National Archives and Records Administration.

systems. By October 1942, the ten camps were up and running at a total cost of $56 million.[78]

According to WRA regional director E. R. Fryer, construction would be modified "to fully meet the climatic conditions at the project."[79] But this was rarely the case. The buildings provided little insulation, as the wood frame construction was typically covered with only tar paper.[80] According to Roscoe Bell, head of Topaz's agriculture division, the barracks were "simply a shell with the studs showing without sheet rock lining." The windows did not fit tightly, leaving space between the sashes for the "free flow of wind or dust which was all too prevalent."[81] With the exception of Granada, Jerome, and Rohwer, barrack floors were made of a single thickness of shrinking green lumber, despite the fact that War Department construction specifications mandated that flooring lumber would not have a moisture content that exceeded 10 percent.[82] Large cracks developed as the wood dried out in desert heat, letting in dust and making it difficult for detainees to keep their living quarters clean.[83] According to Toshi Takeda, a block manager at Gila River, blister beetles, scorpions, and "bugs of a thousand varieties" crawled through cracks and knotholes and "roost[ed] on beds."[84] As Topaz detainee Tom Kawaguchi explained, "We had a garden in our living room so to speak. It was awful."[85]

Shoddy construction stemmed, in part, from wartime conditions that created an "extreme demand" for all types of materials. According to one WRA report, it was "difficult, and many times impossible, to secure reasonably satisfactory material." In addition to green lumber, construction crews used secondhand water pipes that were "not well adapted to the climate and soil conditions found in a particular area." They also omitted expansion joints, which led to extensive repairs when the climate changed.[86] Windows lacked screens, so flies, mosquitoes, and other insects flew into the barracks. When residents of the Butte camp at Gila River asked for window screens, Project Director E. R. Smith demurred because screening could only be obtained "for the most important uses" due to wartime scarcity.[87] Topaz project director Charles Ernst also requested screening for barracks and latrines. In his letter to the US Army engineers, he quoted from the WRA construction standards, which stated, "All buildings will be screened unless local climatic conditions dictate otherwise."[88] Army engineers approved Ernst's request and agreed to supply the screening if camp staff installed it.[89]

The speed of evacuation and the scarcity of skilled labor also led to hasty construction. At Topaz, the barracks' terra cotta chimneys were supposed to be lined with sixteen-gauge steel. However, because of the quick arrival of Japanese Americans, builders set up pot-belly stoves before the steel liners had been received. The chimneys cracked and became serious fire hazards.[90] Inexperienced workers further undermined the quality of construction. Contractors needed twelve hundred workers, including five hundred carpenters, to build Topaz in sixty days, so it is not surprising that competent employees were hard to come by.[91] According to an article in the *Millard County Chronicle*, a foreman approached a young man and asked him, "Just how long have you been a first-class carpenter?" He looked at his watch and replied, "Exactly three hours and twenty minutes."[92] Roscoe Bell related a similar quip from a superintendent who joked, "They should name the city a 'ghost town' because there were 20 pairs of carpenters' overalls running around without any carpenters in them!"[93]

As second-rate construction crews hurried to finish the barracks, accidents seemed inevitable. In October 1942, hot roofing tar dripped through the cracks in the roof of Takako Asano's Topaz barrack, burning her right cheek, nose, back of neck, and right hand. The roofer had forgotten to lay paper over the roof before pouring the sticky black liquid. According to one report,

"The race between the arrivals of evacuees from Tanforan [Assembly Center] and the construction of living quarters continued neck and neck with the construction crew lagging slightly behind."[94] Arthur Eaton of the Housing Section later issued a warning to people living in buildings with unfinished roofs to be especially cautious of falling drops of hot tar.[95]

Several months later, Asano considered legal action against the roofing contractor because a section of her face was permanently disfigured. Topaz project attorney Ralph C. Barnhart was unsure of how to proceed because the contractor's insurance company noted that Asano was moved into the building before it was completed and so "the fault, if any, rests with the War Relocation Authority and that negligence on the part of the roofing employee is not clear." She also "had no choice but to come to the center when she did and take the quarters to which she was assigned."[96] Defending her claim, Charles Ernst noted, "The unusual circumstance of putting people into incompleted [*sic*] buildings cannot . . . excuse lack of caution on the part of the workmen."[97] By August 1944, the insurance company agreed to settle.[98]

The lack of finished roofs caused frustration for other Topaz detainees. On October 8, 1942, forty Japanese Americans who lived on blocks 33 and 34 asked to move from their apartments because their rooms "were not fit to be occupied due to the heavy rain the night before." As rain poured in, they climbed onto the roofs to tack on the tar paper, which had been left there by the carpenters who had fled indoors. Fearing that the paper might be ruined, Arthur Eaton rushed over and asked them not to fully hammer the nails down. One man became enraged and yelled, "We are trying to save our lives and property! If you don't like it, come up here and stop us!" The ten affected families were moved temporarily to another block until their barracks were completed.[99]

Construction did not keep pace with the arrival of detainees at Gila River either. This relocation center was to consist of two adjoining camps, Canal and Butte, with a total capacity of fifteen thousand. However, when Japanese Americans began moving in on July 20, 1942, there were only accommodations for three thousand people at Canal, which had a projected final capacity of five thousand. Detainees were arriving at a rate of five hundred people per day and Canal housed sixty-seven hundred detainees by August 14. As Japanese Americans arrived, construction continued, which meant that crews turned off water, electricity, and gas at random times throughout the day. By August 22, eighty-two hundred people were in residence. Japanese American Evacuation and Resettlement Study (JERS) analyst Robert F. Spencer described the crowded conditions as "rather appalling."[100]

Gila River's sanitation system created further challenges. All central pipes were supposed to meet in one large conduit, with its contents pumped into a septic tank. The water would then be pumped onto a flat space and dammed to evaporate. However, a sewer pump broke in the fall of 1942, which led to the pipe clogging and the sewage backing up along the western edge of Canal. The entire length of pipe had to be torn up, and with no pipe carrying waste from Canal, large pools of sewage formed. WRA staff worked "frantically" to address the situation, but more puddles formed on the road between Canal and Butte. To mitigate the stench, construction crews used bulldozers to turn over the sewage and mix it with sand and dirt. The detainees accepted the situation "stoically," and the younger people jokingly called the road "Sewer Lane."[101] Even by November 1942, open ditches for sewer, water, and gas pipelines remained at Butte. Planks bridged the gaps, but some detainees fell at night because they were not allowed to have flashlights or lanterns.[102]

Despite these problems, Gila River eventually became the WRA's "show-place." Crews built a roof cover with red shingles eighteen inches above every barrack. This double roof was supposed to provide a break from the heat of the sun.[103] Gila River also had white wallboard exterior sheathing, which made the camp more attractive than the other centers. This aesthetically pleasing veneer provided a perfect backdrop for First Lady Eleanor Roosevelt's visit in April 1943.[104] Of course, Spencer was quick to note that the clean, bright exterior hid the unfinished wood inside.[105]

The problems associated with delayed construction and premature occupation plagued the other camps. At Minidoka, the sewage system was not fully functional when the first detainees arrived, and it remained unfinished by December 1942 because the contractor was unable to obtain certain "scarce pieces of equipment." As a result, residents were still using outside latrines, which had become a "source of unpleasantness and inconvenience," particularly as the weather turned cold. On December 4, 1942, a sixty-year-old man got lost on his way to a latrine at 11:30 p.m. He wandered for an hour, "clad only in his underwear," before he found shelter in a dining hall.[106] Even after the system was completed, an overflow of raw sewage formed a lake near the center of camp in the spring of 1943.[107] An inspection in February 1944 found "considerable odor trouble" due to sludge remaining in the clarifier long enough to become "septic."[108]

Even Manzanar, which installed a modern sewage plant in August 1942, faced ongoing sanitation problems. After solid and liquid wastes were separated, liquids were treated with chlorine and discharged by open ditch to the Owens River, while sludge was transferred to a digestion chamber and later to drying beds.[109] However, in November and December 1942, the pumps at the plant were unable to handle accumulated sludge, so raw sewage was bypassed around the plant into the effluent channel that ran to the Owens River. While this method was used temporarily, the scum and floating solids alarmed local residents. In February 1943, John F. Baxter, sanitary inspector of Inyo County, noted that "the water was continuously discolored by sewage material all the way to the Owens River."[110] In June, he still found the river water to be turbid and discolored from one mile south of Manzanar.[111]

Aware of the explosive public relations issue, Leland Barrows, acting WRA director, identified an eighty-acre tract and asked Merritt's engineering staff to survey the property and determine its suitability for settling beds to mitigate the problem. He noted, "You and your staff should consider this proposed development in the light of its value to the authority in preventing the apparent nuisance that now exists and in providing a means of permanently disposing of the effluent in a manner that would not be criticized by the local residents or by members of the Los Angeles Water Supply Organization."[112] Given the highly charged racialized sentiments against people of Japanese ancestry, WRA officials wanted to silence any claims that Manzanar was polluting the water supply of a major metropolitan area.

Thus, despite a thorough site selection process, WRA officials did not fully anticipate the environmental problems that would ensue as the barracks and other facilities were constructed. Some problems were the result of the wartime scarcity of superior building materials and experienced workers. The speed with which Japanese Americans were pushed away from the Pacific Coast and sent to the camps only exacerbated the situation. During their initial weeks and months of confinement, then, detainees experienced the physical environment in the most direct ways: rain falling through unfinished roofs, pungent odors of raw sewage, insects and dust invading their barracks. These camps were a far cry from the idyllic planned communities that WRA leaders had envisioned and touted.

"No Life for Comfortable Human Beings": Living in a "Wasteland"

Detainees were disheartened by the rough-hewn feel of the buildings and the inadequacy of the camp facilities, but they were even more bewildered by the environmental conditions. Since most detainees came from the Pacific Coast and, in the case of many Issei, coastal prefectures in southwestern Japan, these new landscapes were wholly unfamiliar.[113] For those sent to Arkansas, the swamps, bayous, and unfamiliar weather phenomena—thunderstorms and sleet—were notable.[114] For those sent to the intermountain West, the heat and aridity made a significant impression. For example, when Kay Sakai Nakao, from Bainbridge Island, Washington, arrived at Manzanar, she could see the heat waves rising from the earth and saw men at work, tanned so brown that "I didn't even know they were Japanese." She continued, "And I said to the person sitting next to me . . . 'Oh, I'm sure glad I don't live in a place like that.' And what do you know? After a while . . . the bus turned right in there. And I'm telling you, my heart sank down to my toes. I was just devastated."[115] Washington's verdancy was replaced by the stark Owens Valley.

Likewise, Seattleite Masao Kobayashi found Minidoka to be an alien landscape with its "miles and miles" of sagebrush. In a letter to his Garfield High School teacher Elizabeth Bayley Willis, he explained, "After comparing this country with it, there's no doubt to which one I would choose to live in. . . . There aren't any beautiful mountains around like the Cascades, Olympics and Mt. Ranier [sic]. Only rolling hills with hardly any vegetation. That's the thing that struck me most. The absence of green things." Although he recognized that the region had "great possibilities," nothing compared to the "green scenery" of the Northwest for homesick Kobayashi. Living in the Idaho desert reinforced that point.[116]

Utah's Sevier Desert was just as mystifying to Californians sent to Topaz. Having read all of Zane Grey's novels in high school, Morgan Yamanaka had a romantic vision of Utah. Her hopes were quickly dashed. She recalled, "I was expecting something beautiful. No Way."[117] Yoshiko Uchida remembered, "Everywhere I looked, there was only the hard white glare of bleached sand and no sign of the renewal of life so abundant in California."[118] Daisy Uyeda Satoda added, "Topaz was one-dimensional: everything was flat, drab, dry, and colorless."[119]

Toyo Suyemoto was also struck by the aural changes. With no trees, unlike her home in Berkeley, she noticed the morning silence: "Daylight came without the twitter of city sparrows, the cooing of pigeons, or the occasional crowing of a pet rooster. This was a wasteland that overawed such remembered sounds." She and her fellow detainees from the San Francisco Bay Area spoke "wishfully" of California, experiencing "natsukashi-mi, the Japanese term for this emotional state of yearning, of longing."[120]

Rather than lament her environmental displacement, Michi Kobi found the neighboring Drum Mountains to be a source of solace and a symbol of her anger. She explained, "The fault deep underneath the Drums . . . roared with the sound of colliding boulders and thundered mightily. They expressed an emotion of fury I could not say aloud." She often took long walks along the outer rim of the camps "because I didn't want to look at the hundreds of black barracks and see the misery of the people walking around." She headed for the Drum Mountains, which became Kobi's "soul mates, my alter ego. When I heard them crashing, I wanted to really scream and release the pent-up rage of me. Nobody did. No one dared."[121]

Most detainees, however, did not find comfort in the fierce winds that characterized most of the inland West camps. While Seattleite Ishi Morishita found the sunrises and sunsets at Minidoka to be "inspirationally beautiful," the blowing wind felt "deathly cold, penetrating to the very bone." She noted, "If only the wind could be a little more kindly, life here in the wide open spaces would not be half as bad." The "climatical hardship" combined with "the strain of close living" and "all the pressure as suggested by the barbed wire fence and the watch towers" meant that camp was "no life for comfortable human beings."[122] The harsh environmental conditions only aggravated already exacting and oppressive living conditions.

The wind often set off dust storms, which became a defining feature of camp life. Bo T. Sakaguchi recalled, "Whenever the wind blew in Manzanar, we'd have these horrendous whirlwind dust storms . . . and you were just covered with dust and dirt where you'd just see the outline of your face if you wore glasses." Notably, these storms ranked alongside the deaths of three family members as his "least happy" camp memories.[123] Similarly, Henry Fukuhara remembered that the Manzanar wind "would be so bad that you could hardly walk outside. . . . the sand would come up through the cracks in the floor and would come in through the sills of the window, and it was terrible."[124] At Topaz, Maya Aikawa's mother tried to shield her family from the dust by wetting towels and sheets and putting them around the window and under the door. Her efforts had little impact, as the barrack looked "as if the whole room was filled with smoke."[125] In the aftermath of the storms, detainees were covered in dust. When he first arrived at camp, Tad Hayashi remembered seeing girls wearing what appeared to be white stockings. He thought, "Oh boy, maybe that's the style around here. . . . It just turns out that . . . the alkaline dust was so fine it just clung to their legs and looked like they had white stocking[s] on."[126]

Warren Watanabe summed up the dust situation at Topaz. He wrote, "The ever-present, all-pervading fine whitish dust that rose in clouds with each footstep and with each gust of wind had made housekeeping a nightmare and personal cleanliness an impossibility."[127] In *Trek*, Topaz's literary magazine, one writer added that dust was the "principal, the most ubiquitous, ingredient

FIGURE 2.3 Dust storm at Manzanar, July 2, 1942. Photograph by Dorothea Lange. Courtesy of the National Archives and Records Administration.

of community existence at the beginning. It pervaded and accompanied every activity from sleeping and eating and breathing on through all the multitude of other pursuits necessary to maintain and prepare the city for those yet to come."[128]

The WRA attributed the dust to the fact that the camps were built on undeveloped "desert or waste land." With no roads or water to stabilize the soil, "They proved to be miniature dust bowls."[129] Moreover, the construction of the camps necessitated the removal of natural ground cover, which exacerbated the dust problem.[130] According to a Community Analysis Section report from Minidoka, strong winds had created dust storms nearly every day since the first Japanese Americans moved in on August 10, 1942. The dust was so thick that "traffic was forced to a standstill." One could not see from one barrack to the next one, a distance of forty feet, and the "fine, powdery dust" seeped through the window cracks. Some detainees devised masks and filters or plugged their ears and noses with cotton to keep the dust out.[131] The winds even created a "dust pall" that extended as high as four hundred feet, and the buildings would often fill with a "dusty haze" so that "one end would be practically invisible from the other."[132]

FIGURE 2.4 The dust created by camp construction was evident at the Minidoka Relocation Center, August 18, 1942. Photograph by Francis Stewart. Courtesy of the National Archives and Records Administration.

For the editorial board at the *Gila News-Courier*, dust storms were signs of more pleasurable natural phenomena to come. On the one hand, the dust "ferreted out every corner and crevice in the apartments" and left a "dusty twilight" that "brought gloom to the brightness of an Arizona afternoon." On the other hand, dust storms sometimes preceded rain. "And rain is an anodyne. It brings a past of rain on the green hills of California. It erases the reality of dust and heat. That rain that came drumming on the roofs of the barracks early one morning in strong gusts was followed by two days when sleep came without effort at night, and the air was dust-free," the editorial explained. Dust storms also brought lightning displays in which "jagged bolts split the night's darkness." Thus, for the "rain-conscious and beauty-conscious people" of Gila River, "the dust storms are viewed with a commingling of despair and hope."[133]

WRA officials soon embarked on a variety of projects to protect detainees from the dust. The first step was watering and oiling the roads. In early June 1942, Manzanar looked "substantially as it was when the land first was cleared of the native sagebrush growth. . . . With the destruction of the natural ground cover, the dust problem was acute on windy days."[134] By the end of the month, WRA crews had sprayed eleven of Manzanar's fifteen east-west thoroughfares with oil-asphalt to provide quicker transportation and eliminate "clouds of dust in pedestrian faces when vehicles pass."[135] These efforts may have mitigated dust loosened from construction, but they did not get rid of the dust from the dry bed of Owens Lake, a fine, alkaline dust that embedded heavy metals in people's lungs.[136]

Ultimately, landscaping was the primary strategy to mitigate the dust, heat, and mud. Mandated by Administrative Instruction No. 89, the WRA allowed for the purchase of ground cover to control erosion and landscaping materials for the agricultural program and the areas around the schools, hospital, and administrative offices. At Gila River, the task initially seemed "almost impossible." But after recruiting experienced gardeners who began to plant around the community buildings, lawns seemed to spring up "as if by magic." This vegetation managed dust and reduced indoor temperatures.[137] As Gila River administrator David Rogers explained, "In these hot, inland valleys of Arizona it is important that shade and grass be provided as quickly as possible so that living conditions will at least be bearable during the summer

FIGURE 2.5 To keep down the dust, Manzanar crews hosed the streets with fire equipment, July 2, 1942. Photograph by Dorothea Lange. Courtesy of the National Archives and Records Administration.

months." He recommended planting summer and winter grasses, flowers, and hardy, fast-growing trees, at least four to eight feet in height, the latter being of utmost importance because animals and people were "susceptible to heat prostration unless provided with shade."[138]

E. W. Nichols, who headed the Grounds Section at Gila River, was especially intent on obtaining trees that would provide shade. He recommended species known for their "rapid and hardy growth" in the area, including Chinese elm, black locust, cottonwood, green ash, Russian olive, silverleaf poplar, and china berry.[139] He explained, "Trees are one of the best and most permanent improvements that we can add to the project. Shade and ornamental trees will be of great help during the hot summer months." In December 1942, he requested trees that were eight to ten feet in height in order to have "immediate shade this next summer."[140]

Projects intended to mitigate heat were sometimes at odds with other inadequacies in the camps' infrastructure, namely a short supply of water. Gila River detainees installed evaporative coolers in their barracks, but water shortages made it difficult to use their equipment to full effect. Administrators urged residents to use the minimum amount of water and to keep coolers off before noon unless the outdoor temperature was over one hundred degrees Fahrenheit.[141] Thus, even as they tried to address one environmental challenge, they confronted another.

Moreover, problems that emerged during one time of the year turned into different problems within a matter of months. At Minidoka, dust from the sun-parched earth turned into sticky mud when the rain and snow fell in the winter. This impeded walking around the camps in any efficient manner. One sixth-grade student at Minidoka even wrote a poem about the mud: "I start to school in the morning / And my shoes are spic-and-span / When I come home at noon-time / They're like a muddy van."[142] WRA administrators, then, had to address environmental conditions that changed seasonally, trying to mitigate both problems without worsening either. In this case, the solutions were straightforward: shade trees and gravel and rock sidewalks.[143] In other instances, they were more elusive. To seal up cracks and make barracks "liveable during the winter period," Manzanar crews installed 2.5 million square feet of plasterboard on the walls and ceilings and Mastipave, a durable covering, on the floors. However, these materials also trapped desert heat inside during the summer and made the barracks unbearable.[144] Nature was a moving target that often eluded WRA officials' best efforts.

Detainees also devised their own solutions to the heat. At Gila River, residents asked the WRA for awning materials or air conditioners, but then took matters into their own hands.[145] Kazumi Yoneyama's father dug a four-foot-square basement beneath their Gila River barrack, accessible through a trap door in the floor, in order to stay cool.[146] Yasu Kayamatsu Momii's brother fashioned a cooler by moistening excelsior wood shavings with a drip system and blowing a fan through them. The efficacy was questionable—Momii remembered that "if you sat in front of it you'd . . . just get so sticky"—but the contraption spoke to Japanese Americans' willingness to try anything to make living conditions more bearable.[147]

These personal strategies to mitigate nature, however, came with risks. At Manzanar, four boys were caught driving off with a load of special gravel, which they planned to use as flooring for one of the boys' barrack basement. In addition, carpenter foreman Kaneshige Kato was caught ordering a driver to deliver twenty-one leftover pieces of floorboard to his home. While project attorney Robert Throckmorton did not explain their motivations, both thefts may have stemmed from environmental conditions. The basement was probably intended to provide some respite from the heat, while Kato likely wanted the floorboards to provide extra protection from dust storms.[148] As punishment, Kato was demoted and not permitted to be a foreman for six months. In addition, he and the boys, from 6:00 p.m. to 8:00 p.m., had to help excavate a drainage ditch, the boys working five nights and Kato ten. Throckmorton observed them "wielding their picks and shovels and not in the least regarding the undertaking as a frolic."[149] Indeed, this outdoor labor punishment only served to remind them of the harsh environmental and social conditions in which they lived and worked.

* * *

At the end of March 1942, *Los Angeles Times* journalist Tom Cameron declared that Japanese Americans sent to Manzanar "couldn't wish for better scenery or a cleaner, more healthful atmosphere."[150] The reality was far more complex. While each site met specific criteria, WRA officials encountered countless complications once the barracks were built and the detainees moved in. They could not even begin to think about trying to assimilate Japanese Americans until they provided basic protection from the natural elements. Hasty construction and second-rate materials only exacerbated the inconveniences created by extreme temperatures and unpredictable weather. When one problem appeared solved, another one often emerged, and the next dust storm or snowfall was always imminent. There was no easy way to address the inherent problems of detaining thousands of people in desolate, volatile environments. Maintaining the infrastructure of the camps was a struggle from the arrival of the first detainees to the departure of the last.

Japanese Americans, of course, endured this struggle too. They understood the unforgiving environment as they swept their barracks after a dust storm or walked under the blistering sun. They also experienced these challenges through their labor on the land. Intent on making the camps self-supporting, WRA officials put Japanese Americans to work. In theory, this labor was supposed to keep them occupied and aid assimilation. In practice, the federal government was placing detainees' own basic needs squarely on their shoulders.

3

Maintaining the Camps

AFTER ENDURING THE heat and dust of the summer, Japanese Americans began to feel the temperature drop in the fall of 1942. In the Arizona desert, Gila River detainees were "anxious to get the chill out of their bones." As they awaited the installation of oil-burning stoves, they resorted to building bonfires outside their barracks.[1] Dr. Jack Sleathe, chief medical officer, urged camp officials to secure heat as soon as possible and warned of a "serious medical problem" with the advent of cold and pneumonia season.[2] The plunging mercury also consumed Topaz, where crews worked frantically to finish the barracks and winterize them with wallboard.[3] This extra layer, however, could only do so much. As Grace Oshita explained, winterizing "didn't mean extra insulation. It just meant hammering on the plaster boards."[4] According to fellow Topaz detainee Jean Kariya, it got so cold that "I could hardly open my eyes because the moisture from the eye formed ice crystals."[5]

Heating the barracks was one of several maintenance tasks that required Japanese American labor. Most detainees complied with WRA demands to work, but a small group believed that "as long as the government had placed them in these camps, the government should take care of their needs." According to Russell Bankson of the WRA Project Reports Division, these individuals asserted that "Self Help is Forced Labor."[6] With this forthright stand, they implied that working at the behest of the WRA—even if they were making their own living conditions more tolerable—was akin to slavery, or, perhaps, convict labor.[7] They lived in a country that had long since outlawed human bondage. They had not been tried for or convicted of a crime. Why should they toil for a pittance so that they could perpetuate their own unjust confinement? This was a minority stance, but it spoke to a larger issue: maintaining the camps would be next to impossible without Japanese Americans.

As the frigid barracks suggested, harsh environmental conditions further shaped the labor situation. Japanese Americans often balked at working in such severe conditions. To exact concessions from WRA officials, they pointed to the ways in which natural fluctuations added to and aggravated their job duties. However, some environmental conditions compelled them to work. Their resistance had limits, particularly when the environment could be so unforgiving and their basic comforts were at stake. Like the workscapes of western extractive industries or southern slave plantations, the camp workscapes reflected the intersection of dynamic natural forces and Japanese Americans' circumscribed power.[8]

The question of whether to work for the WRA sometimes drove a wedge between different groups of detainees or exposed latent divisions. This wartime discord often reflected the prewar diversity of the Japanese American population. In any given camp, detainees came from rural and urban areas and represented a range of occupations, from farmers and foresters to skilled professionals and business proprietors.[9] For instance, nearly 73 percent of Topaz's population in 1942 came from prewar communities of over 25,000 people. As urbanites mixed with country dwellers, conflicts sometimes emerged.[10] Incarceration also triggered new sources of tension. Specifically, labor disputes created and exacerbated conflicts between those who cooperated with federal authorities and those who pushed back.

Several war-related issues—chronic shortages and the use of second-rate materials—continued to provide the backdrop for some of these struggles. At times, erratic or inadequate supplies were even more vexing than the inhospitable environment or recalcitrant workers. On other occasions, they simply augmented the existing difficulties of maintaining the camps. These were the challenges that were part and parcel of the incarceration process. WRA officials could not predict which human or natural factor would hold the most influence at any given moment. Meanwhile Japanese Americans were constantly negotiating and renegotiating shifting WRA demands and environmental conditions. Given these complexities, many detainees were sometimes left, quite literally, drenched and in the cold.

"The Worries of a Fuel-Less Winter": Heating the Camps

After forcibly removing Japanese Americans and confining them in camps, the WRA was "to provide for their needs in such manner as may be appropriate."[11] Adequate heat during the winter was one of those needs. In fact, the WRA construction standards—established in a June 1942 agreement between General John L. Dewitt and Colonel L. R. Groves from the Office of the Chief of Engineers—mandated "space heating in suitable form depending on climate and fuel most easily and economically obtained."[12] At Minidoka and Topaz, coal was the fuel of choice, but WRA officials faced chronic difficulties securing an adequate supply. In this instance, labor was not the key problem. Instead, national wartime demands thwarted efforts to mitigate nature and keep the barracks warm.

At the end of October 1942, the temperature dipped to twelve degrees at Topaz and lower at Minidoka. WRA Regional Attorney Edwin E. Ferguson explained that the "coal situation has overshadowed every other activity at the Projects. The evacuees have been physically cold and if the cold weather increases, it will become more and more difficult to interest them in any other activity other than keeping warm." He estimated that Minidoka and Topaz each needed forty thousand tons of coal for the 1942 winter. Without sufficient coal and an adequate reserve, moreover, a sudden drop in temperature would "paralyze both Projects as it would be necessary to shut off and drain the water from the water systems in order to keep the pipes from bursting."[13] Coal was thus central to both Japanese American morale and basic camp infrastructure.

Coal was also essential to fighting the war. According to a Department of Interior publication, coal was the "greatest single source of energy for the Nation," key to building Liberty ships, tanks, and bombers. To prosecute a successful war, the authors argued, mine output had to be increased and "available where and when needed."[14] To this end, United States production of bituminous and lignite coal reached its wartime high of 620,000,000 net tons in 1944.[15] The western coal fields were not a significant percentage of this figure, but Utah, Wyoming, and Montana provided a greater share than before the war. This expansion met local demands, such as Utah's iron and steel industry and West Coast markets.[16]

With the nation's coal output funneled to wartime industries, it is not entirely surprising that the camps' supplies were unreliable. Gordon Creek Mine in Helper, Utah, was supposed to provide thirteen thousand tons to Minidoka, but no coal was received. Independent Coal and Coke Company of Salt Lake City, Utah was supposed to deliver another seven thousand tons at the rate of two cars (ninety tons) each day, but it stopped deliveries due to "differences" with the Quartermaster's Division. Project director Harry Stafford cobbled together a supply, making purchases in amounts as little as five tons and bringing them to Minidoka by truck or "any other means of conveyance available." By October 15, 1942, however, there was insufficient coal to heat the barracks. The hospital, kitchens, and administration buildings were maintained, but guards watched the coal bins to prevent residents from stealing for personal use. Soon, it was "a common sight to see a group of evacuees gathered around a bonfire made of sage brush on the edges of the relocation center."[17]

Indeed, T. Matsumura, who lived at Minidoka, recommended that everyone stockpile sagebrush for emergencies. He wrote, "If we have the good luck to get our normal coal supply, we can always use this wood mixed with coal and get more efficiency out of the coal. Or we can take the chill out of our rooms in the mornings in the early spring with a light wood fire." According to his calculations, thirty-two hundred pounds of sagebrush was equivalent to one ton of "good grade" coal. "In this time of emergency, if we can produce any fuel in this project and save coal, we will help the industry and will be of benefit to our country," he concluded.[18] For Matsumura, using local fuel sources instead of scarce coal could be a patriotic gesture. Whether or not they were motivated by Matsumara's ideological arguments, men and women still "made it a daily business to carry sage brush home on their backs." This practice continued despite warnings that the high tar content of sagebrush would ruin coal-burning stoves.[19] It is unclear how much sagebrush Minidoka detainees actually harvested and whether it had a substantive environmental impact. Nonetheless, detainees clearly adapted to their natural surroundings to keep warm.

The shortage was so critical that staff had to resort to stopgap measures. In early November 1942, a group of men drove a fleet of twenty-two 1.5-ton trucks to an abandoned Civilian Conservation Corps camp north of Rupert, Idaho, where three hundred tons of coal were scattered down a hillside. The men gathered fifty tons of coal, enough to meet Minidoka's heating needs for one day. With the temperature dropping to around twenty degrees, Stafford estimated that the center would soon need 125 tons of coal each day.[20] Residents of block 21 also devised a method to distribute the limited coal supply on a "fair basis," issuing each apartment a ticket that could be redeemed for a set amount of coal when submitted to the "coal pile watchman."[21]

Minidoka's coal shortage prompted A. E. O'Brien, acting project attorney, and Stafford to travel to Utah to investigate the situation. They discovered that the Gordon Creek Mine had not operated since 1939, and the foreman estimated that it would take thirty days to produce coal "at the scale called for by the Minidoka contract." They also found that Independent Coal and Coke had failed to make deliveries because the Quartermaster required a coal sample analysis. Once this provision was waived, it resumed deliveries. The Quartermaster then secured another contract with a Denver mine to deliver ten thousand tons at a rate of four or five cars per day. If this contract was "promptly carried out," Minidoka was in a position to build up a stockpile of coal "to maintain this Project for some time to come."[22] Soon, ten to twelve carloads of coal arrived each day, which meant that "the worries of a fuel-less winter are over."[23]

While the coal supply was addressed, the labor supply was not. With only a few dump trucks available, the Coal Division delivered only one or two car loads each day, with high school students supplying much of the labor. As more coal arrived in Minidoka, WRA officials had to mobilize "compulsory volunteers." They devised a plan in which each block was part of a rotation and furnished men to haul and deliver coal. If they did not cooperate, they would not receive coal. Such threats did not seem necessary, as Edward Osawa, supervisor of the coal division, noted that he was receiving "splendid cooperation . . . and I'm sure the colonists appreciate the volunteer services of those who are contributing their time and labor to the welfare of the community." However, C. T. Takahashi remembered that it took cajoling to motivate disgruntled "older folks" to help. He told them, "We're going to unload that damn coal off the cars before they grab the coal and take it back somewhere else."[24]

FIGURE 3.1 Workers unloading a coal delivery at Minidoka, c. 1943–1945. Courtesy of the Bigelow Family Collection, Densho Digital Repository, ddr-densho-156-26.

By the end of January 1943, thirty thousand tons of coal had arrived at Minidoka, with an additional twenty thousand tons scheduled to be delivered by the end of the March. With ample coal for the year, Minidoka officials asked that each block recruit volunteers to dig two pits, each twenty-five feet square and one foot deep, for their coal supply. At this point, the coal situation seemed stable, and the coal crew, which consisted of 162 workers as of March 1943, enjoyed considerable respect. According to a Community Analysis Section report, most Japanese Americans appreciated the coal crew. Their soot-marked faces made it hard to imagine that they were not working hard. Moreover, because detainees felt their work "biologically"— they had warm barracks and warm bodies—they "cheered them as saviors and heroes."[25]

Obtaining adequate coal was also an urgent matter at Topaz. On October 1, 1942, the Willow Spring Coal Company was supposed to begin delivering 150 tons of coal daily to fulfill a 25,000-ton contract. By October 23, it had only delivered 40 tons, so Topaz officials had to contract with other companies.[26] In early November 1942, senior engineer Henry Watson called for a 15,000-ton stockpile "at the earliest date." He estimated that this amount was required to maintain round-the-clock fires during the winter. He explained, "The situation is acute as we can anticipate extreme temperatures any time coupled with wet and almost impossible roads."[27] At this point, coal was being trucked in from a mine at Castle Gate, Utah, about 150 miles and across two mountain ranges from Delta. From there, the WRA had to use its own trucks to bring the coal another seventeen miles to the camp. Two snowstorms at the end of October made this arrangement untenable. Because this coal was consumed "as fast as it arrived," Japanese Americans were also burning brush and "scraping up the coal dust from the floor of the coal bins with whisk brooms."[28]

By the late fall, Topaz's coal supply began to grow. Starting November 9, 1942, Consolidated Coal and Coke Company of Denver was contracted to ship 6,000 tons, a two-month supply. Another 75 tons per day were delivered from Castle Dale. William W. Hunter, head of the Procurement Section, noted that his goal was to ensure a "constant and adequate supply" and to allow for the accumulation of a stockpile "to guard against future emergency."[29] All told, Topaz officials purchased 28,279 tons of coal between September 1942 and June 1943. As of June 30, 1943, they had a 6000-ton stockpile, in part, because of a relatively mild winter. For the fiscal year 1943, the center received 10,500 tons from the Deer Creek Mine and 14,500 tons from American Fuel.[30]

The other challenge was finding workers to transport the coal by truck from the Delta railroad yards to Topaz. In December 1942, the Employment Division issued a plea to Topazeans. If several men volunteered to work for two weeks, "Your rooms will be warm. Your children and old folks can have a real Christmas and New Year. Let us have no shortage of coal."[31] WRA officials essentially evoked feelings of guilt and obligation to recruit workers. They emphasized the physical and emotional warmth associated with coal.

Although coal supplies were secure, detainees still behaved as if another shortage was imminent. Don Nakahata remembered the intense struggle for coal whenever dump trucks made deliveries at Topaz. With the coal heaped into a pile, everyone would clutch a coal scuttle—a metal pail—and "run out there to get coal." Being a shy kid, "I wouldn't get in there and elbow people out of the way which is really what you had to do . . . we'd have to fight it out." Nakahata remembered this experience as "dehumanizing."[32]

The "arbitrariness" of life in camps likely contributed to this behavior. When coal deliveries came, Harry Kitano's father, who was a block manager at Topaz, told the residents of his block, " 'This is all the coal we have, so ration it.' " But then "two minutes later," another truck would dump even more coal. "So now you start thinking the whole thing is gone, and then we find out later that maybe that was the coal supply for three months. All of these kinds of things that just throw you off in terms of any kind of regularity," he explained. They could not plan "much more than day-by-day because you never knew when another disaster would come."[33] Detainees could not know with any certainty when or if another coal delivery would arrive, so most were willing to push aside their neighbors to take care of their own needs.

For their part, WRA officials were cautious about the coal supply and encouraged conservation. In November 1943, Charles Ernst sent out a letter to all residents and employees, asking that they redouble their efforts to conserve resources, including coal. He explained that disputes within the coal industry had resulted in a decline in supply. Topaz had an "ample supply on hand to meet unforeseen emergencies," but Ernst warned that deliveries might be reduced or stopped if an acute shortage developed. He asked everyone to burn only the coal that they needed to be "comfortable" and to regulate their fires throughout the day. He warned them that lumps of coal should not be used as "boundary markers or in decorative designs," as this "creates the impression of waste regardless of the fact that the coal may be burned later." Coal piles were to be "neat and orderly" and away from buildings, kindling, or any "combustible" that might start a fire, resulting in "a most serious loss."[34]

Similar calls for coal conservation went out to Minidoka residents, including detailed instructions for using their coal-burning stoves.[35]

WRA officials were trying to anticipate the unexpected. They knew that the winters were cold at Minidoka and Topaz, but they had no way of knowing exactly when heat would be necessary. To compensate for an unpredictable nature, they needed ample supplies of coal and labor. While they eventually secured the latter, the former proved elusive. Mitigating the cold required a natural resource that, due to the war, had an erratic supply. All parties involved learned that transcending adverse environmental conditions demanded flexibility and vigilance.

"A Howl of Protest": The Minidoka Boilermen and Janitor Dispute

While detainees burned their much-coveted coal in their individual pot-bellied stoves, other workers were hired to tend the stoves in public spaces, including the laundry rooms and lavatories, and to fire the boilers that provided hot water. These workers—mostly middle-aged or older Issei—became the center of a Minidoka labor dispute beginning in July 1943. The precipitating event was a WRA-wide personnel cutback that was supposed to remove about twelve hundred people from the camp payroll and reduce the number of Japanese American employees to twenty-nine hundred.[36] The Maintenance Division of the Engineering Section experienced a "sizeable cut" as a result. Before, each block had a staff of eleven people: four janitors, two janitresses, two stove tenders, and three boilermen. One relief worker for four blocks was also on the payroll. After the cuts, each block had to make do with just four workers: one janitor, one janitress, and two boilermen. The four-person crew was manageable during the summer but not in the autumn and winter, which required regular tending of stoves and boilers. Seasonal changes in the environment and increased duties led janitors and boilermen to "immediately set up a howl of protest."[37]

Because of their recalcitrance, Glenn (G. R.) Green, superintendent of construction and maintenance, issued a memo to all maintenance workers on November 8, 1943, and detailed a specific schedule. In the morning, the boilermen were to build all fires in the laundry room, lavatories, and the boilers to heat the water. From noon until dinner, one janitor would keep the fires going. After the evening meal, the second janitor would stay on duty until 10:00 p.m., at which time he made sure that the fires were "properly banked so that as much heat as possible will be retained in the building to keep the plumbing from freezing." Green struck a stern tone at the end of the memo, threatening dismissal if they did not follow these orders. At the same time, he tried to appeal to some sense of obligation among the workers. He noted that frozen or broken pipes would shut down water, "making it very inconvenient to the people in the respective blocks." Thus, "We feel that it is the duty of each and every janitor and boilerman to accept this responsibility for the people they are serving."[38]

Maintenance workers believed that the memo was "undiplomatically written," but it also annoyed them because Green rejected the "status hierarchy of jobs" that had developed within their division. As a Community Analysis Report explained, "Men who have been classed as boilermen have acquired a certain status and are resolved only to perform the tasks which they feel are boilermen's jobs. Lighting laundry room and lavatory fires are not considered in their category. The janitors, on the other hand, do not feel they should tend the boiler room fires since this is boilerman's job."[39] In short, these workers rejected the merging of job duties and caring for the laundry and lavatory fires, which was the purview of the recently dismissed stove tenders. They responded by writing to project director Harry Stafford on November 18, noting that Green's orders and his threat of dismissal were not "in accord with our democratic principals [sic] as it gives no consideration for the rights of the workers to bargain with their employers."[40]

The workers went on to explain how various environmental factors and safety considerations made the labor cuts untenable. Cleaning up winter mud typically kept janitors busy for a full eight-hour shift. The use of an inferior grade of coal with a mixture of rock, gravel, sand, and dirt created additional work for boilermen, who had to screen out the extraneous material. Indeed, the boilermen were already stretched thin because the camp was filled to capacity and the hot water system was "pressed to its full load." They also objected to leaving the boilers and stoves unattended after 10:00 p.m., as "late hour stragglers" might open the damper or tamper with the fire and "invite danger of a fire." This tinkering might also cause the fire to burn out sooner than expected and result in frozen pipes. Fuel would be wasted because additional coal would have to be burned to bring the thirteen-hundred-gallon hot water tanks back to the proper temperature. In light of these issues, the maintenance workers requested two additional stove tenders for each block.[41]

Two days later, Stafford met with the maintenance workers and rejected their request to continue the separation of job duties. He reasoned that conceding to their demands might lead to a full employment situation. If

FIGURE 3.2 Winter rain and snow at Minidoka created mud that augmented the cleaning duties of the janitors, December 10, 1942. Photograph by Francis Stewart. Courtesy of University of Washington Libraries, Special Collections, UW21143z.

all detainees were working, they would be less inclined to participate in the WRA's relocation program.[42] This program began in May 1942, when the WRA allowed detainees to attend college or work as seasonal farm field hands outside the exclusion zone.[43] By July 1942, WRA officials began to develop a more comprehensive program to allow "loyal" American citizens to leave the camps indefinitely so that they could accept full-time work and "establish residence in normal communities." By the end of September, the policy expanded to include non-US citizens.[44] The rationale was that relocation would disperse people of Japanese ancestry throughout the nation, breaking up the insular ethnic enclaves of the prewar years.[45] WRA director Dillon Myer added that the camps were established "primarily as an expedient—to provide communities where the evacuated people could live while long-range relocation plans were being developed." As it became clear that "valuable skills were obviously not being put to full productive use" behind barbed wire, it made sense to roll out the program.[46]

In addition to supporting relocation, Stafford also rebuffed the contention that the winter would bring a dramatic increase in janitors' cleaning responsibilities. He granted that "there will be a lot of dirt in the winter time," but he also believed that "we won't be quite as bad off this year." The sidewalks, which had not been installed the previous winter, would miti-gate some of the mud. R. S. Davidson, assistant project director in charge of operations, asked Harry Hatate, supervisor of the boilermen, if parents, block managers, or residents could take measures to make sure that the children used the sidewalks. Hatate was doubtful that such behavior could be mandated, while Joseph Beeson, relocation program officer, spoke out against such mandates. "We want our children to live as nearly like normal people as possible. You expect children to walk in the mud," he explained.[47] Nonetheless, most Minidoka officials maintained that the quantity of winter mud was diminishing, making more workers unnecessary.

While administrative officials did not accept the seasonal increase in cleaning responsibilities, they did concede to the seasonal increase in fire sur-veillance. During the summer, workers did not need to maintain the boilers between 10:30 p.m. and 6:30 a.m. because pipes would not freeze. But in the winter, G. R. Green explained, "There is no question that twenty-four hour service will be maintained." Stafford agreed, but once again he did not want to hire additional workers. Instead, he and Davidson recommended that the two boilermen and one janitor each work an eight-hour shift, leaving the janitresses to clean the women's part of the building during the day.[48]

According to the workers, maintaining round-the-clock fires required the burning of what amounted to coal scraps. As Hatate explained, the residents took the lump coal and left them with dust and slack to fuel the boilers. Part of the problem was that the camp was using low-quality lignite coal, which broke apart easily. Stafford suggested that the boilermen secure voluntary co-operation of the residents and "tell them to get three parts dust or slack coal and one part lump." Hatate countered that this sort of request was not real-istic. "Naturally, it is human that they should pick the big [lumps] first," he explained.[49] Despite Hatate's thorough explanation, it was clear that the ad-ministration was not going to assist the boilermen as they tackled additional winter job duties.

Indeed, Stafford's dismissive attitude morphed into disdain. He suggested that the boilermen were often idle on the job, only busy when loading coal into the stoves and removing the cinders. Stafford went on to reveal that he had heard many stories about boiler room poker games.[50] Short of calling them lazy, Stafford implied that each boilerman needed to put in a full eight-hour day and simply deal with the coal slack and dust if necessary. Hatate retorted, "You talk about the boilerman just sitting and giving little coal, but as far as

I am concerned they are busy every day. . . . I don't know how each janitor or boilerman can take care of janitorial work and attend five or six stoves on each block." He reiterated his request for two additional stove tenders who would prevent fires and freezing pipes during the winter. Stafford firmly told Hatate, "You don't need more people."[51]

Following the meeting, the boilermen and janitors adhered to their customary schedule and job duties for much of December. As temperatures continued to plummet, however, Green recognized he needed to take action to prevent freezing pipes.[52] On December 28, he informed Hatate that the twenty-four-hour schedule would go into effect on January 1, 1944, and that all maintenance workers would assume the job title of "janitor." While three janitresses agreed to the new schedule, the rest of the maintenance workers submitted their resignations effective December 31. Hatate was adamant that "the changing of the name of the boilermen to janitor and forcing them to do extra work was unjustifiable." Some detainees believed that the WRA was trying to make living conditions intolerable to compel them to leave Minidoka and participate in the relocation program.[53]

The boilermen and janitors gave the administration a brief reprieve and agreed to work until January 4. When that deadline passed, they insisted that they could not do both boilermen and janitorial jobs, emphasizing that Idaho's harsh environmental conditions made this merging of job duties impractical. One janitor noted, "We should have more [workers]. Project located in a warm climate [does] not need as much as a Project located in a cold climate."[54] After walking off the job, workers in other divisions—especially those who performed "hard and dirty labor"—joined them. The garbage crews stopped delivering kitchen refuse to the hog farm; the coal crew only hauled fuel to the hospital and dining hall kitchens; and truck convoy services were irregular. A group of thirty motor pool workers even engaged in an act of sabotage, pouring water and snow on fires in the laundry rooms and lavatories. Since they controlled truck deliveries, they threatened to curtail food supplies to any block that relit them.[55]

Acting project director R. S. Davidson immediately called a meeting of administrative staff on the morning of January 5 to strategize their next steps. Frustrated, he concluded, "There is no basis for their argument at all. They don't want to work and I think that the only thing they want to do is to raise cane [*sic*] with the administration." Dean Miller, assistant project director in charge of administration, was more pragmatic and suggested that they turn off the water and drain the pipes in order to protect government property. He also recommended asking the block managers to help find volunteers to maintain the fires. Green, however, warned of violence. "We might do that but could we get volunteers who are willing to get their heads knocked off? What protection can you give them if they do build fires? What are you going to do if the worker is molested? We will have to be prepared for any emergency," he cautioned.[56]

To maintain at least the semblance of control, six administrative officials later met with the block managers and tried to reason with them. They began by warning them that the lack of twenty-four-hour coverage for the boilers could lead to a fire or frozen pipes. Either way, the block would be left without water. Superintendent of education R. A. Pomeroy then expanded the discussion and spoke of detainees' larger obligations to the nation. He noted, "Our Country is at war and the cut in the budget has come about in order to save some money. Patriotic citizens will understand that situation and will attempt to meet it by working a little bit harder." He bristled at hearing a comment that suggested that a country spending so much money fighting the war surely "could spend a little more money to hire a few more boilermen." In his mind, loyalty to the nation was supposed to supersede loyalty to fellow detainees.[57]

As the walkout continued, most detainees directed their anger at the WRA administration. A group of women was so outraged about the lack of hot water that they wrote WRA director Dillon Myer to remind him that they "were guaranteed to lead a normal life, but as it is now, we cannot live normally without hot water for bathing babies, washing and general cleaning, which is absolutely necessary for our daily living." They had to endure these hardships even though "a little effort on your part may straighten out this uncomfortable situation in which we are only victims of circumstances."[58] While bathing in cold water, particularly during the dead of winter, probably seemed cruel to these women, Myer was not sympathetic. He insisted that the WRA was fulfilling its responsibilities by maintaining facilities, supplying fuel, and paying workers.[59] It was up to Japanese Americans to provide the necessary labor to generate the coveted hot water.

Some detainees decided to offer their labor rather than endure the frigid water. On block 8, the manager encouraged his residents to keep the fires going. Not surprisingly, other Japanese Americans frowned upon this strategy. Some dumped the block's food on the ground and delivered its meat allotment—"all fat and bone"—in a "filthy paper carton." According to one report, others described block 8 as *eta mura*, a village or community inhabited by *eta*, a Japanese outcaste group. During the Tokugawa period, *eta* performed police and jail duties, like guarding prisoners, and were associated with "polluting" occupations, such as working with leather or disposing of animal carcasses.

While these categories were abolished in the Meiji period, the stigma carried over with emigrants.[60] In this case, detainees used the *eta* designation to criticize those Japanese Americans who seemed to be cooperating with or aiding the white administration.

Other supposed administrative sympathizers or collaborators were labeled *inu*, or dog. During the war, Japanese Americans used this term to refer to spies or informers who, like dogs, "sniffed" around for incriminating information that was leaked to the federal government.[61] Mr. Urakawa, a placement officer, received a threatening *inu* note after he began trying to find replacements for boilermen and janitors. Written in Japanese and posted on his door, it read, " 'Dog.' You go away as far as possible. Otherwise your life is in danger." While Urakawa insisted that he was not afraid, he tendered his resignation because he did not want to be "misunderstood by my people."[62] The Community Analysis Section reported two other individuals who received *inu* notes, but Urakawa was the only person who had any direct role in the dispute. It was possible that these notes "were the work of a crank who capitalized on the incident to vent his spleen on individuals he disliked."[63]

The *eta* and *inu* designations may have also been indicative of larger tensions within the camps. During the war, the leaders of the Japanese American Citizens League (JACL), an organization founded in 1929 to facilitate Nisei integration into American life, adopted an ultrapatriotic position and emphasized Nisei loyalty to the United States. They also collaborated and cooperated with the federal government and discouraged dissent. Many critics charged that the organization "had sold Japanese Americans down the river in an effort to gain political acceptance and national influence." Thus, in the midst of the boilermen's dispute, Urakawa and others may have been viewed as individuals who perpetuated rather than protested confinement, similar to JACL leaders.[64]

By the fifth day, some detainees grew weary of the strike. According to a report from the WRA Community Analysis Section, they began to feel that "they were the ones who were suffering not the administration and the issues should be settled as soon as possible."[65] On the afternoon of January 10, the mediation committee and Stafford agreed to a settlement that restored the status quo. The twenty-four-hour schedule was retracted, and boilermen and janitors had separate schedules and job duties. While not explicitly delineated in the agreement, it was also assumed that the responsibilities for tending the stoves in the laundry rooms or lavatories were left to each block to address.[66]

Although hot water and janitorial services were restored, Minidoka detainees had to fire the stoves on a voluntary basis, a development that angered some Japanese Americans who believed that this "should be the responsibility of the administration and that the administration staff is shirking its duty by laying the work upon the shoulders of the evacuee residents." One Issei even argued that the walkout had saved 282 tons of coal, which amounted to enough money to hire one stove tender for each block for one month. Nonetheless, six days without hot water may have "dampened" Japanese Americans' enthusiasm to further agitate the WRA administration.[67]

WRA personnel attributed this dispute to detainees' pent-up resentment and accumulating grievances against the administration, but that account marginalizes the importance of environmental conditions.[68] The changing seasons shaped patterns and practices of Japanese Americans' labor and affected when and why they pushed for concessions. In the end, however, their power was limited. Hot water may have been, in the words of mediation committee leader, Yoshito Fujii, "a necessity of camp life, as vital as food, shelter and clothing."[69] Nonetheless, the WRA made it clear that they were only obligated to provide a regular supply of coal. It was up to detainees to unleash the energy stored in these lumps of carbon and provide for their own warmth and material comfort.

"The Willpower of the Workers": Pipeline Labor at Topaz

Similar to the Minidoka boilermen and janitors, Topaz workers also withheld their labor to resist the WRA administration. In this case, they did not go on strike but rather rejected a specific job. The job in question—fixing and replacing the water pipelines—emerged, in part, because of Utah's environmental conditions, which corroded the pipes. Detainees denied any responsibility for the repairs, but, much like their Minidoka counterparts, found that their power to resist was circumscribed. The Topaz dispute likewise heightened tensions between detainees, some of whom rejected pipeline work and associated it with lower social status.

The source of the problem was the Sevier Desert's alkaline soil. According to Roscoe Bell, who served as chief of agriculture and later assistant project director, the army engineers believed that Topaz would be a short-term project. Thus, during the installation of the domestic water system, it used lightweight twelve- and fourteen-gauge welded steel pipe, some of which had been reclaimed and reconditioned. The pipe was unwrapped and installed without expansion joints, and due to a shortage, seventy valves were eliminated from the system. These pipes corroded in the soil, and leaks developed around

February 1943. The administration began to keep records of the location and size of pipe damage, using this data to apply to the War Production Board (WPB) to replace the service line, which consisted of 2.5-inch twelve-gauge pipe. The WPB approved the project on July 28, 1943, and authorized the expenditure of $11,400.[70]

Meanwhile, leaks popped up everywhere. By early September 1943, the situation was so serious that Henry Watson, senior engineer, wanted to enlist volunteers from all blocks to cooperate with Frank Iga, the plumbing crew foreman, to repair leaks for two weeks.[71] Iga concurred that the leak situation was serious—he and his crew had already repaired approximately 447 leaks and still had another 100 to fix—but he wanted to expedite the repairs. He approached George Ochikubo, chairman of the Community Council, which functioned as "the sole channel through which the residents can voice their collective desires to the Project Director." He asked him to urge the

FIGURE 3.3 After Japanese American workers installed these water mains at Topaz in October 1942, they began to deteriorate in the alkaline soil. Photograph by Tom Parker. Courtesy of the National Archives and Records Administration.

administration to hire outside contractors to complete the pipeline replacement before the winter and prevent future leaks.[72]

Topaz administrators, however, did not seek other workers and continued to recruit detainees. This proved to be a frustrating task. By October 22, 1943, Watson had been requesting workers from the Community Council and the block managers for three weeks. While they had enough cast-iron pipe to lay service lines in seven blocks, only seven plumbers were on hand to carry out the work. Watson wanted to secure at least twenty more permanent plumbers' helpers and twenty to thirty men to repair leaks. He emphasized that permanent crews were needed because volunteers "cannot be controlled" and could not complete the work efficiently. In fact, the situation was so dire that he proposed that "all construction and other operations of the Operating Division which is [sic] not vital to protection of Government property and life . . . be stopped and these [laborers] assigned to the pipe line work."[73] He then increased his estimate for the number of needed workers to eighty-five: ten men to lay pipe on the main lines, ten men to lay pipe for the service lines, twenty-five men to repair leaks, and forty men to finish the hand work behind the trencher and dig out bell holes and valves.[74]

At the suggestion of James Hirano, chairman of the block managers, Watson tried to entice workers with larger meals and a special dining hall or table. Pipeline workers suggested a sample menu, including breakfasts of cooked cereal with cream, fried potatoes or hotcakes, toast, two eggs, and bacon, ham, or some meat, along with coffee and fruit juice. Lunch would consist of "plenty of rice, at least two big mush bowl[s] per person," cooked meat with vegetables at least three times per week, "chop suey or hash or some substantial food with vegetables" or some meat dish at least two days per week, fish one day per week, dessert at least three times per week, and bread, butter, milk, coffee, and fruit.[75] Such large meals likely exceeded wartime ration points and daily meal budgets, but Watson did not question their request. The bodily exertion required for digging up the wet, muddy soil gave pipeline workers some leverage.

Even with bigger and heartier meals, labor recruitment was difficult, given the negative connotations of pipeline work among detainees. These associations were affirmed in an article in the October 26, 1943, edition of the *Topaz Times*. Published in the Japanese language section of the newspaper, the author, supposedly a sixty-four-year-old man who had volunteered on the pipeline crew for a couple of days, wrote, "A group of old folks with one foot in the grave are digging holes for the pipes with pick and shovel. Sooner or later they will die and we will have to dig graves, but those are holes we should dig for them." The writer then concluded with the expression "Consider it practice and keep digging." Digging ditches for the pipeline was, in other words, akin to digging their own graves.[76] Deeply offended, the pipeline crew of eight to ten men quit.[77]

According to Watson, the article was written in response to the employment of workers who had recently arrived from the Tule Lake camp. These "Tuleans" moved to Utah following loyalty registration, which started in early 1943. A collaborative effort of the WRA and the War Department, registration was supposed to provide "a comprehensive examination of the loyalties of all the inmates" in order to recruit Nisei men for the armed forces and to expedite the clearance process for the relocation program. All detainees over the age of seventeen were required to register and fill out a loyalty questionnaire. Question 27 asked respondents if they were willing to serve in the armed forces. Question 28 asked them if they would swear "unqualified allegiance" to the United States, defend the nation from attack, and "forswear any form of allegiance to the Japanese Emperor or any other foreign government, power, or organization." Those who answered yes were eligible to serve in the armed forces. Those who answered no or offered qualified responses—about 10 to 15 percent of the population—were known as "no-no boys" and sent to Tule Lake, the designated "segregation center" for so-called disloyal detainees.[78]

Tule Lake's "loyal" detainees were, in turn, transferred to the other camps. The Tuleans sent to Topaz, mostly prewar farmers, were, according to project director Charles Ernst, "virtually forced" to work on the pipelines or face unemployment. Taking this job compounded their feelings of inferiority, as most Topaz residents were urbanites from the San Francisco Bay Area and appeared to be "more cultured and sophisticated than they." While the Tuleans expected "an appreciative attitude" since they were completing "a disagreeable task," Ernst added that the *Topaz Times* article instead "assigned them to an inferior social status or inferred that their services were of inferior quality."[79]

The assignment of "inferior social status" came with the author's association of digging ditches for the pipeline with digging graves. This dirty work had long-standing connections to immigrant and nonwhite workers in the United States.[80] Moreover, it is possible that *eta* continued to be relevant to some Japanese Americans, as those who worked in death-related jobs—undertakers, executioners, grave watchers—were *eta* throughout Japan. In some parts of the nation, well diggers—similar to pipeline work—were also *eta*.[81] Unlike the Minidoka detainees who shunned the residents of block 8, this author did not explicitly use the *eta* label. Nonetheless, his implication that Tuleans were engaged in an impure, polluting form of labor associated with an outcaste group could be perceived as a huge affront. He insisted that he was referring to his own experiences and that his article "was definitely not intended as a slur to any particular group." The crew accepted his explanation and returned to work.[82]

For Watson, any flip comments were unwarranted because the failure to repair the pipeline system had grave consequences. Harmful microbes might enter the water system, or the fire protection system would not have ample water. Moreover, the camp could be forced to draw too heavily on the wells, depleting groundwater reserves and limiting or potentially exhausting the water supply. Once again, he recommended that "all operations in the Operations Division cease until this work is adequately taken care of." He also asked Bell to submit an article to the *Topaz Times* to highlight "how important it is that we get men to work on these pipe lines and get the job done."[83] The next issue of the newspaper in late October 1943 had a front-page article about the pipelines, quoting Watson's repeated warnings about potential health problems and depletion of the camp's water supply should detainees fail to work on the project.[84]

Still, pipeline work proceeded with limited labor into the fall of 1943. Harry Yamasaki oversaw a crew of seven men who repaired leaks and then set up temporary lines to dry up wet areas. Emergency crews from the blocks then dug these lines up. Under the leadership of Harry Tsugawa, a plumbing crew of six men followed and laid the auxiliary and permanent service lines. According to the *Topaz Times*, these crews were doing the work of fifty men in repairing and replacing twelve miles of pipeline. The plumbing crew in particular, given its responsibility to maintain all plumbing in the camp, was so overtaxed that the administration asked appointed personnel to work on the crews.[85] The replacement of the service pipelines in the blocks was eventually completed by November 19.[86]

Watson turned his attention to the replacement of the main lines, but he also explored other options to stop further pipe corrosion.[87] Specifically, he was interested in cathodic protection. According to Eldon McEntire of Salt Lake City, corrosion occurred as a result of the pipes passing through two or three types of soil, some very wet and some dry. This created cathodic and anodic places in the system, the former attracting positive charge and the latter attracting negative. Using an electrical power source, the pipeline could be made cathodic, preventing further corrosion.[88] Watson forwarded McEntire's report to Bell and noted that they already found two direct-current generators, which he planned to install to see if they reduced corrosion and leaks.[89] Rather than actually changing the pH of the soil—which was impractical—the cathodic protection system might allow camp officials to transcend the corrosive effects of alkalinity. However, the system was ultimately not very effective because Topaz's grid system had several cross currents that were impossible to neutralize. This tactic was abandoned in the summer of 1944.[90]

Meanwhile, Watson continued to look for workers even as detainees continued to leave the camp under the auspices of the relocation program.[91] Ernst provided monetary incentive by approving the employment of pipeline workers at the wage rate of nineteen dollars per month, a significant concession. The WRA's wage scale ranged from twelve dollars per month for apprentice workers to nineteen dollars per month for professional or highly skilled workers and "those carrying supervisory responsibilities or engaged in unusually difficult and essential jobs." Most workers received the middle wage of sixteen dollars per month.[92] Even in offering the highest wage, Watson reported in April 1944 that he had not been able fill the crew. The situation was serious because ten fire hydrants were not working, and other pipeline jobs, including half of Jasper Avenue, needed to be completed.[93] The larger issue was the deteriorating state of the main line between the water tanks and the camp. If it failed, the entire camp would be left without water.[94]

Once again, new workers were not forthcoming, and the pipeline replacement project had to rely on volunteer construction crews from the Engineering Section to work on a rotating basis. Perhaps in an effort to instill guilt among the detainees, the Engineering Section issued a press release, published in the May 31, 1944, edition of the *Topaz Times*, that singled out plumbing foreman Harry Tsugawa for praise. The article noted, "There should be gratitude and thankfulness realized by every person in the center for his services; and crews should be organized immediately from the center to assist him in this work in order to maintain his present spirit and civic pride." The article concluded, "The Project Director has declared that the pipeline replacement is the most important task and rates the highest priority of any work on the project."[95]

The work became even more critical in early June 1944 when heavy rains fell and created mosquito-infested puddles. By June 14, 66 out of 116 fire hydrants were out of service. The Community Analysis Section explained, "In terms of health, comfort, sanitation and water conservation, the pipe line is a major problem. Yet in spite of this critical situation sufficient workers cannot be recruited to repair the breaks." Moreover, because the workers spent so much time repairing leaks, progress on pipeline replacement stalled. Thirty high school boys were on the job, but they were inexperienced and could not be depended upon to work throughout the summer. Although Watson preferred to have men accept regular assignment to the pipeline crew, he conceded that the "only solution" was to form block crews that worked on lines and leaks in their respective areas.[96]

On June 19, 1944, Luther (L. T.) Hoffman, who succeeded Charles Ernst as project director, added an official stamp to Watson's recommendations. He issued a directive to "the residents of Topaz," reiterating that the pipeline replacement project was "the most important of current tasks to be done on the project." To expedite the repairs, he announced that each block was to recruit five workers for temporary assignment to the pipeline crew when repairs reached their vicinity. Hoffman concluded, "Residents of Topaz are urged to accept regular assignments on the water line in lieu of their present work. . . . The cooperation of every resident in camp is hereby solicited, because it will be only through unified effort of all that this problem can be solved and grave danger to our water supply averted."[97]

While workers made some progress during the summer of 1944, a crippling camp-wide labor shortage emerged in September. The pipeline crew found itself in need of seventy-five full-time workers and twenty-five part-time workers.[98] This huge shortage developed when forty-five high school boys quit after their first day on the job. Since work on the pipelines had "practically ceased," Topaz leaders had no choice but to terminate a contract on a trencher, a crucial piece of equipment for the pipeline work. Watson also requested that WRA community analyst Oscar Hoffman investigate "what is behind the whole matter of refusing to work on the pipeline."[99]

Hoffman was attuned to the reasons that pipeline workers were hard to find, including an overwhelming feeling of indifference among Topaz residents. They often felt no need to help, "so long as pipeline leaks merely make unsightly ponds in scattered areas in the Center, so long as seepage does not visibly undermine the health of the resident population, and finally . . . so long as an adequate water supply comes through the faucets in the kitchen, latrines, and laundries."[100] Because leaky pipes had been a problem for so long, detainees "merely shrugged their shoulders" unless affected directly. Moreover, the WRA had helped to create the labor shortage by sending Japanese Americans out on seasonal agricultural leaves. When they returned, they often settled in for "a good, long rest or a vacation" and had no interest in taking on other jobs.[101]

Japanese Americans also rejected pipeline work because they did not see it as their responsibility. The WRA was supposed to provide them with "health, food, hospital facilities and lodging," so many detainees believed "that the Army Engineer should have provided an adequate domestic water system which would have lasted for the duration of the project."[102] Hoffman elaborated, "After all, so ran the argument, the residents should not be required to maintain basic camp equipment."[103] Mrs. Minoru Iyaki, coordinator of the Maintenance and Operations Office, bluntly wrote, "Having such poor quality pipes installed meant that WRA was making fools of the Japanese people in camp."[104] They were not going to look even more foolish by fixing a problem that was not of their making. The federal government, then, had to be held accountable for the pipeline repairs.

Another issue was inadequate pay. As one leader explained, "We are saving WRA a lot of money, working as we do on the pipelines for 50 cents a day. If an outside contractor were to do the pipeline job, it would cost WRA possibly $150,000. We will get it done for about $15,000."[105] Others argued that "there is no place in these United States where people are being employed at 'slave' wages outside the Centers, except perhaps in the prisoners-of-war and prison camps."[106] For some workers, their labor situation approached the most repressive conditions of human servitude.

The wages were especially offensive because they were not commensurate with the dirty and arduous nature of pipeline work. When repairing lines, workers dug four-foot-deep holes, pumped out water, and climbed to the bottom of the hole to clamp and plug it shut. When installing new pipe, they worked in four-foot deep trenches, caulked, handled both rusty old pipe and tar-covered new pipe, and poured "molten" leadite onto the joints. They got wet, sticky, and muddy and risked getting burned.[107] Indeed, Roscoe Bell described the pipeline as "one of the most miserable jobs" at Topaz.[108] George Shimamoto, who worked on many construction and maintenance projects, added that the job was especially taxing during the winter. Digging up the pipes and plugging holes in the "cold chill days" was hardly enticing.[109] Just as at Minidoka, seasonal changes degraded labor conditions.

Watson recognized the filthiness of pipeline work. While he could not radically change the actual work involved or the physical conditions of this labor, he wanted to mitigate the effects of the mud and grime by issuing coveralls. Keeping the workers' clothing and bodies clean, Watson believed, would "increase the moral[e] and the availability of workers to handle this job." He even recommended that this clothing be washed in the hospital laundry. However, he was naive to think that coveralls would dramatically change detainees' attitudes. After all, they only provided superficial protection from the physical discomforts and inherent dirtiness of the job. The coveralls, moreover, did not protect the workers from the stigma associated with such grimy—even polluting—work. And they did not hide the fact that their labor was the direct result of the government's short-sightedness.

Ultimately, the WRA had to resort to more coercive measures to secure enough workers to replace the pipelines. In October 1944, a labor adjustment policy transferred construction crews and men working on other nonessential work to the pipeline project.[110] Topaz officials also recruited men returning from seasonal leave, some of whom found that more desirable jobs were scarce due to the labor transfers. Those shifted from other sections had to accept their new positions or be fired. A Japanese American supervisor explained, "So what else could the fellows do when they were faced with a financial curtailment; their pay checks and family clothing allowances would be stopped. To many it is forced labor, therefore the pipeline unit may have the manpower but they do not have the willpower of the workers." Nonetheless, Hoffman claimed that most Japanese Americans were appreciative and even "inclined to give credit to the Administration for taking rather strong steps in recruiting workers."[111] Hoffman's report undoubtedly did not represent the sentiment of most Japanese Americans at Topaz.

Work on the pipeline was completed on May 10, 1945. All told, the improvements to the service lines and the installation of the main water lines cost $63,727.99. The final report of the Engineering Section noted, "The pipe line replacement program has been the most difficult construction program which the Engineering Section has endeavored to undertake." They attributed this challenge to the problem of securing labor, even though pipeline work "was no more difficult than a number of construction jobs on the Center."[112] While it may not have been harder, it carried negative connotations that compelled Japanese Americans to reject it.

Ultimately, the pipeline dispute further suggests how nature shaped labor relations at the camps. Topaz's alkaline soil necessitated the pipeline repairs and shaped Japanese American resistance. Because they deemed the work undesirable, they withheld their labor to protest low wages and to demand that the WRA fulfill its mandate to provide adequate facilities. They had not moved voluntarily to a camp with disintegrating pipes, so they should not have to fix them. But in the end, administrators compelled the detainees to work by threatening one of their only sources of income. The fact that the WRA had to force them to work testified to the efficacy of Japanese American tactics, but it also underscored their limited power.

* * *

In October 1944, the WRA Community Analysis Section released a report entitled "Labor Relations in Relocation Centers." To explain the source of labor strife, the author called attention to numerous factors, including the insolence that characterized the "Self Help Is Forced Labor" philosophy. As one detainee informed the author, "We did not ask to come here. We were forced to leave our legitimate type of work for the Caucasians to take over and make money on during the war. Therefore, if we choose not to work the government still has the obligation to see to it that we are treated right."[113] Since the federal government bore complete responsibility for his losses—economic and otherwise—he felt absolutely no duty to work.

The author also made a point to distinguish between the "normal communities" on the outside and the "abnormal" communities at the camps. In the former, labor disputes usually involved only a business and its workers, but in the latter, "Employment exists chiefly to provide residents with necessary services." As a result, the "entire center" often became embroiled in labor disputes, with community sentiment sometimes "determin[ing] the strength of many strikes." In the former, wages were a bargaining point, but in the latter, "their uniformity and seeming unchangeability" provided "a weak basis for special negotiations" and served to remind detainees of "their reduced economic status and subordinate role in the employment hierarchy of the centers." Moreover, because very little money separated unskilled and professional positions, "Men often do not want to do strenuous or unpopular work for the same wage paid to office workers and others in what are regarded as 'soft' jobs."[114]

For all of the report's insightful observations, the author neglected to address the influence of the environment. The "necessary services" that workers provided often reflected the harsh environments in which the camps were located. WRA officials had to scramble to secure coal deliveries and maintenance workers because the winters were so cold and heat and hot water so essential. They had to fix the Topaz pipelines because the soil corroded the secondhand pipes. The labor required to address these problems led to the creation of the "strenuous or unpopular jobs" that detainees often avoided. Part of what made these jobs undesirable was the fact that they were dirty and unpleasant tasks or they forced Japanese Americans to toil in an unmediated nature. In other words, labor relations were thoroughly enmeshed in the natural world.

As workers and WRA administrators quarreled, the relationships between Japanese Americans also shifted. The author called attention to detainees' appreciation for laborers who worked jobs with no "prestige" and their role in bringing about timely resolutions to strikes.[115] However, he did not delve into the animosity that developed among detainees. Labor disputes shaped the social dynamics within the camps and highlighted that Japanese Americans were not a united group, despite their near unanimous frustration with their confinement.

In the end, human and environmental factors shaped the labor associated with maintaining the camps. Not only did WRA administrators encounter shortages and substandard materials, they also had to contend with unforgiving, unpredictable environmental conditions that increased labor requirements, deterred detainees from working, and strained their authority. These issues were also central to the WRA's agricultural program, which proved to be just as challenging as keeping detainees warm and their water pipes flowing.

4

Desert Agriculture

IN JANUARY 1943, Commissioner of Indian Affairs John Collier issued a memorandum entitled "Unrealized Food Production Capacities at Japanese Relocation Centers." In it, he lamented that the WRA was not producing "foodstuffs beyond the immediate needs" of detainees. Considerable acreage—including large tracts on two Arizona Indian reservations—was being "withheld from full production capacity, while the Japanese who reside in the areas make only partial use of their abilities." Collier went on to criticize the WRA's wage scale as a "commanding reason for the failure to advance more rapidly with the program and to secure more active cooperation from the Japanese." As an alternative, he advocated the formation of cooperative groups so that detainees could "share in the benefits of increased production." "The evacuees are not kept at the relocation centers for punitive reasons," he reasoned. "There is no rationale in asking them to work hard in the absence of any kind of normal economic motivation."[1] Since Collier did not see the camps as prisons nor the detainees as convicts, he believed that agricultural productivity should be tied to monetary incentives. With higher wages or profits, they would clear more acres, plant more crops, and work more efficiently.

Collier's memo may have reflected his power struggle with WRA director Dillon Myer. On November 17, 1942, just days after Collier had emphasized the creation of a stable, vibrant Japanese American community at Poston, Myer visited the camp and announced the WRA relocation program. Encouraging detainees to leave camp was at cross-purposes with Collier's vision. He was also upset because Myer disregarded Milton Eisenhower's previous agreement to allow the Bureau of Indian Affairs to administer this camp. Notably, President Roosevelt had actually considered Collier for the position of WRA director after Eisenhower's resignation in June 1942 but chose Myer instead.[2] As this memo suggests, Collier would have taken the WRA in a much different direction had he received the position.

Still, his statement overlooks many other factors that may have led to "unrealized food production." In many cases, workers were trying to grow food on submarginal land that was unsuitable for farming. Unpredictable natural phenomena made their task all the more difficult. Wartime conditions—from equipment shortages to rationing—also limited productivity, as did the objections of nearby landowners. Looming over all of these issues were chronic labor shortages. According to Collier, this was partially a problem "of [the WRA's] own making," because the agency encouraged Japanese Americans to take seasonal leaves or participate in relocation.[3] As these environmental and social factors intersected, farm leaders saw yields compromised and months of work potentially erased.

While these challenges paralleled other maintenance issues, the agricultural program was distinct. The objective was not to simply keep the camps up and running. As Eisenhower explained in April 1942, "It is highly desirable that at each of these [center] locations there be opportunities for the evacuees to produce their own food and also for sale if possible . . . it will reduce the cost of this whole undertaking and it will help produce food for the Army."[4] Cultivating the land was seen as a way for Japanese Americans to assert their loyalty to the nation and contribute to the war effort.[5] Some detainees were not swayed by this rhetoric and scoffed at farm labor. Ultimately, a program intended to bring self-sufficiency, instill patriotism, and save federal funds often teetered on the edge of waste and inefficiency.

Making Them "Pay Their Own Way": Agricultural Operations at the Camps

While growing food was a critical task, it was an especially complex issue, given wartime rationing at the behest of the Office of Price Administration (OPA). Detainees were not exempt from this program. The central OPA office allocated ration points to the Washington WRA office, which then distributed them to the camps.[6] Because WRA policy mandated that "at no time shall evacuee's food have higher specifications than or exceed in quantity what the civil population may obtain in the open market," point allowances for detainees and staff were the same as regular civilians: forty-eight processed food points, sixty-four meat points, and two pounds of sugar per month. When vegetables could not be grown, processed food points were used up to the limit. The consumption of camp livestock and low-point or no-point foods helped slow down point depletion. Given public criticism that detainees were "pampered," WRA staff members were quick to emphasize that they received no "special" treatment when it came to their food allotments.[7]

Each camp's Mess Operations Section had to work with these points and "provide good, wholesome, nutritious, palatable food at a daily cost of not more than 45 cents per day per resident." The camp farms helped the WRA meet these goals. For instance, by 1943, Manzanar was asked to spend no more than thirty-one cents per day for food purchased outside the camp and to produce at least fourteen cents' worth of food per day per person. When the camp closed, it had never exceeded the thirty-one-cent maximum. In fact, during the summer, it only spent twenty-two to twenty-four cents per day per person on outside goods. From March 1943 to August 1945, it used 68.4 percent of its processed food ration points, 83.5 percent of its points for meats, fat, and cheese, and 98.4 percent of its sugar points.[8]

WRA director Dillon Myer also envisioned an agricultural program that would substantively contribute to the war effort. WRA Administrative Instruction No. 14, issued June 23, 1942, noted that, after providing food for detainees, the "second objective" of the crop production program was to "grow such products as are most urgently needed for supplying the armed forces and for sale to or through the Office of Lend Lease Administration to provision the United Nations." This included both food and fiber crops, like cotton, as well as seeds and oil crops, like soy and castor beans. To determine which crops were "needed particularly in the war effort" and to avoid competition with "established farmers," he consulted with Secretary of Agriculture Claude Wickard. Because Myer anticipated that production for subsistence would take up a relatively small proportion of the land, he proposed the dehydration of vegetables to be sold directly to the Lend-Lease program or the armed forces.[9]

Myer's desire to embark on such an ambitious agricultural program was not surprising, given his previous positions in the Agricultural Adjustment Administration and the Soil Conservation Service.[10] He and other New Dealers believed that an increase in rural purchasing power would allow farmers to buy manufactured goods, thereby supporting industrial recovery. To augment rural incomes, they adopted a variety of conservation policies, such as land retirement, soil restoration, and flood control. After 1937, they also focused on "rehabilitation in place": keeping farmers on their existing land by implementing measures to increase productivity.[11] This ethos of enhancing submarginal lands may have influenced Myer as the WRA's agricultural program unfolded.

Ultimately, numerous obstacles prevented Myer's original vision from coming to fruition. Food dehydration was not viable, as the War Production Board gave priority to canneries for the necessary equipment. The WRA also found it difficult to obtain machinery to prepare the land for farming. Before machinery could be ordered, the War Food Administration had to issue a certificate of necessity. The WRA received only a small number of requested certificates and sometimes found it difficult to find manufacturers to supply its needs.[12] Most importantly, the WRA grossly overestimated the available labor supply. Myer assumed that 50 percent of the workforce at each camp would be employed in agriculture, which amounted to 25,000 to 30,000 people. When it was clear that such a large labor force would not be available, the WRA in 1943 shifted its plan for agricultural production, which was to "be limited primarily to the production of commodities needed for subsistence."[13] In February 1943, WRA Administrative Instruction No. 14 was revised to reflect this scaled-back approach. It stated, "If land and labor in addition to that needed in the production of subsistence crops and livestock products are available, they should be used in the production of commodities needed in the war effort."[14] This effectively de-emphasized production for the war effort.

With a shortage of equipment and labor, the WRA's Agricultural Division had to make "more careful preparation" for the 1943 production program. In addition to deprioritizing production for outside use, staff members consulted with nutrition specialists at the Department of Agriculture to discern detainees' dietary needs. They identified a fondness for leafy green vegetables and food "not normally consumed by the average American," such as daikon, gobo (burdock) root, and soybean products, as well as a preference for rice, instead of potatoes, for their primary starch. They also explored the production capacities of the camps based on soil and climate and met with Japanese American and white agricultural staff to devise production schedules. They stressed crops that yielded "a large amount of digestible nutrients" per acre with "a minimum amount of labor."[15]

WRA staff members were also mindful of developing a production program that promoted interdependence between the camps. If one camp was well suited for growing a certain crop, the surplus could be sent to camps with less favorable conditions. For instance, Gila River had ideal growing conditions for leafy green vegetables from October to May, and shipments of these crops to other camps became commonplace during the winter and early spring. The WRA also favored storage crops, such as potatoes, carrots, cabbage, onion, and squash. They were stored at Tule Lake, Minidoka, Heart Mountain, Granada, Topaz, and Manzanar, then shipped to other camps as needed. "Less essential" or "luxury" crops, like cantaloupe, cucumbers, and watermelon, were discouraged for intracamp shipments. Gila River and Tule Lake, the biggest suppliers, shipped just over 7 and 5.3 million pounds, respectively, to other camps in fiscal year 1944. Distributing crops between camps meant that purchases on the open market "in competition with the armed forces and the civil population generally" were minimized.[16]

This system of intracamp shipments tried to unify diverse landscapes into a coherent whole. The growing conditions in Arizona and Idaho, for instance, were dissimilar, yet the agricultural strengths of one place offset the agricultural weaknesses of another. Likewise, bumper crops at one camp could compensate for disastrous ones elsewhere. While the actual climate or soil could not be transferred, the crops could. The objective was to reduce costs, but the impact was to create a similar diet for all detainees, despite the deserts and mountains that often separated them.

In many respects, the agricultural program achieved its chief objective of limiting the inshipments of food. When WRA representatives from each camp met at Gila River in February 1944 for an agricultural conference, they celebrated the fact that the camps' farms accounted for about 20 percent of the total food cost for all ten centers in 1943, thereby making "a substantial contribution toward a reduced cost of project operation." The conference report continued, "This production represented a material reduction in the volume of critical and perishable commodities withdrawn from quartermaster supplies or diverted from the consuming public."[17] However, even with intracamp shipments, most camps experienced difficulties obtaining "a uniform seasonal distribution of vegetables." The WRA hoped to tap into the expertise of state agricultural extension specialists to address this issue.[18]

In addition to providing food for detainees, Ernest H. (E. H.) Reed, who worked as WRA head of agricultural marketing and later head of the agriculture section, believed that the agricultural program could improve public relations. When the camps were established, critics called attention to the costs of feeding and caring for the detainees. As these detractors learned that Japanese Americans were helping to produce food, a "typical" response was, "Well, that puts a little different light on it. I am certainly glad to learn that the War Relocation Authority is trying to make them pay their own way." Reed noted that "public relations would have been much more difficult had it not been for the agricultural program."[19] In producing their own food, he implied, detainees helped to support the camps' very existence. This point was galling for Topaz detainee Maya Aikawa, who recalled, "Whatever the government was subsidizing to the real Japanese-American centers, it sure wasn't used for the food, because we were actually doing the farming. Things like that were very degrading."[20] Indeed, as detainees cultivated the land, they perpetuated their own confinement.

"They Are Used to Farming ... under Much Different Conditions": Agricultural Labor

Some Japanese Americans, at least initially, framed farming as an admirable task. According to an editorial in the *Minidoka Irrigator*'s inaugural issue of September 10, 1942, detainees from "climatically temperate cities and the lush, verdant valleys of coastal Washington and Oregon" were confronted with "a vast stretch of sagebrush stubble and shifting, swirling sand—a dreary, forbidding, flat expanse of arid wilderness." Nonetheless, they were determined to convert "a wasteland into an inhabitable community" and create "an oasis." The editorial concluded, "Our great adventure is a 'repetition of the frontier struggle of pioneers against the land and the elements.' Our future will be what we make it, and there is no reason to despair."[21]

This pioneering rhetoric could be interpreted in vastly different ways. Because many Americans understood the frontier as a place that had created loyal, self-sufficient citizens, it reinforced the assimilation goals of the WRA program. This probably pleased the WRA officials who controlled the content of the camp newspapers. At the same time, the frontier could also be seen as a potentially subversive place where detainees could claim a distinctly American identity at a time when they were widely shunned. If they could turn desolate land into productive fields, like the white pioneers before them, their confinement might appear all the more undemocratic. The foreboding landscapes of the camps, in short, could become a source of power in their wartime struggles for inclusion.[22]

In practice, claims that the camp farms would engage detainees in "a worthwhile undertaking" did not always find a captive audience.[23] To be sure, some Japanese Americans found meaningful and fulfilling work on the farms. However, the size of the labor pool was often unpredictable, and its quality and efficiency were spotty for several reasons. The WRA began to encourage detainees to participate in the relocation program or take seasonal agricultural leaves, effectively undermining its efforts to operate productive farms. Moreover, some Japanese Americans shunned farm work due to the harsh environmental conditions, while others found that their farming knowledge had limited applicability to their new locales.

The agricultural crew at each camp consisted of both white appointees and Japanese Americans. White personnel included a chief of agriculture and a farm superintendent who oversaw the programs, but the WRA tried to hire detainees in the positions of assistant farm superintendent and farm foreman to boost worker morale. This point was made clear in the fall of 1942 when one hundred Manzanar farmworkers walked off the job to protest the employment of five white foremen, who served "mainly as escorts and overseers."[24] As qualified individuals began to leave camp for seasonal leaves and the relocation program, agricultural officials anticipated that much of the farm work would be done by older men and women and high school students.[25]

The depopulation of the camps led to concern about whether or not the WRA could maintain agricultural production. The total camp population dipped from 110,353 to 95,576 between February 1, 1943, and February 1, 1944. Gila River lost 3,611 people during that same time period, dropping to 9,800 people.[26] At the February 1944 agricultural conference, attendees noted that all of the camps needed to bring about "a drastic tightening-up of the requirement of work efficiency of the evacuee." In order develop independent farm operations, the centers needed to reduce "excess employment" on all activities and cut back on employment in "less essential activities." They also recommended that the WRA director distribute a statement that delineated the objectives of the agricultural program and its importance to overall WRA operations.[27] The implication was that agriculture took priority, with the labor supply allotted accordingly.

While detainees were not fleeing in droves at any given moment, the camp labor pool sometimes became drained at inopportune times in the planting and harvesting cycle. For instance, at Manzanar, the agricultural section was short 30 percent of its labor quota for spring farm work in May 1944. Twenty-five men left on seasonal leave, while another three participated in the WRA's relocation program. Fifteen others resigned. Farm supervisors secured an additional forty-one workers, but they were mostly older men and women who could "hardly be expected to produce as much work as the younger more able bodied men who left the Center." To address the labor shortfall, agricultural chief H. R. McConnell received approval to discontinue the beef cattle and meat chicken programs, the nursery, and the construction of winter storage facilities.[28] By June, the labor situation improved, as several boys on summer vacation began to work on the farm.[29] But in September, the agriculture section had to enlist 132 students to temporarily help with the harvest on Saturdays.[30] Minidoka actually gave high school students a "harvest vacation" for three weeks in October so that they could work during this crucial time.[31]

Even detainees with agricultural backgrounds were far from ideal workers because their skills did not always transfer to new environments. Japanese Americans soon learned that their previous experience on small- or medium-sized specialized farms was very different from the extensive and diverse operations at the camps. As E. H. Reed, explained, "The evacuees['] technical knowledge of the cultural practices, irrigation methods, etc., which were applicable on the West Coast was not wholly applicable at the relocation centers." Despite their lack of knowledge, Reed claimed, they held firm to their own methods or were unwilling to accept advice from other personnel.[32] Indeed, Louis E. Rice and Rhuel D. Beebout of Minidoka's agriculture section noted that irrigators, despite "numerous warnings," overirrigated a potato and a celery field, leading to stunted growth.[33]

Learning these methods proved especially difficult at Minidoka. Since this camp drew its population from the Pacific Northwest, the farmers were used to regular precipitation and were unfamiliar with open-ditch irrigation. With sagebrush-dotted land, irregular topography, and dry soil, irrigation at Minidoka was challenging even for experienced people. Rice and Beebout

FIGURE 4.1 Japanese American workers planting celery at Minidoka, c. 1943. Courtesy of the National Archives and Records Administration, Densho Digital Repository, ddr-densho-37-47.

noted that low yields often resulted from too little or too much irrigation, which ultimately reflected "the inability of the evacuee to cope with farming conditions new to them." Nonetheless, Japanese American irrigators discovered that the placement of medium-weight waxed paper or old burlap sacks helped to prevent erosion and aided water control. But once they attained some experience, they often relocated or left for seasonal leave. The agricultural staff was at square one again.[34] To address this issue, Reed recommended the organization of "several irrigation 'schools' or 'demonstrations' at which your evacuee irrigation foreman would demonstrate proper methods of irrigation."[35]

Reed also pointed to the Japanese Americans' lack of financial incentive as another source of labor inefficiency. Similar to John Collier, he argued that detainees "could not become enthusiastic" about the WRA's pay scale of $12, $16, or $19 per month when wages for farm labor outside the camps ranged from $132 to $164 per month. In some cases, they had been led to believe that a cooperative profit-sharing plan might be developed on the farms. Since this arrangement would have undermined the relocation program, it was never implemented. Detainees were subsequently disappointed because "there was little or no hope of individual reward for exceptionally meritorious work." Some Japanese Americans with agricultural experience thus took less physically taxing jobs. Others embraced new vocations.[36]

Many of these labor issues—shortages, resistance, lack of efficiency—played out at Gila River. Because the camp was populated with many farmers from California's Tulare County, Charles Kikuchi, Japanese American Evacuation and Resettlement Study (JERS) fieldworker, initially predicted that it "will not lack for experienced hands."[37] Yet some detainees quickly rejected farm work. One JERS report pointed to the desert heat as a deterrent, as "few saw fit to endure the Arizona sun for eight hours when they could get off with fewer hours in a mess hall that had ice in drinking water and was generally much cooler."[38] Kikuchi affirmed this sentiment and added that one leader from Tulare County was "sabotaging the farm labor effort" by telling workers "that it is not much use to work because everything will be provided for them anyway."[39] According to JERS fieldworker Shotaro Hikida, Nisei in particular were taking a greater interest in other jobs. Hikida, an Issei, found this tendency to be unfortunate, since many of their fathers were gifted farmers who had contributed "much toward agricultural developement [*sic*] of this country."[40]

Gila River farm superintendent David Rogers was more sanguine about the labor situation. In September 1942, he reported that ten Japanese

Americans had been trained in using farm equipment and eighty-one workers were in the field. He explained, "I am not discouraged with the progress we have made so far in land preparations or the attitude of the Japanese people in general." Because they were quick learners, he was confident that "when we get the fields planted they will be able to carry along in excellent shape."[41] But one month later, the age and physical strength of the farmworkers were problems. Acting project director E. R. Fryer asked for the transfer of young workers (under the age of thirty) from kitchen and mess hall jobs to agricultural production. He justified this request by noting that older detainees should not be denied the kitchen and mess hall jobs and that younger detainees should be employed in "work in which there is an opportunity for job training and production both for the Community and the Nation."[42] By the following summer, the labor situation appeared to be sorted out. When Reed and fellow WRA agricultural staff member William (W. M.) Case visited the camp in June 1943, they praised the "high quality" of the staff and "the fine spirit of teamwork" among its 150 to 800 workers.[43]

Final WRA reports from Gila River expanded upon these sentiments, praising Japanese American expertise and emphasizing the positive impact of farm labor on them. Despite their unfamiliarity with the climate and the "experimental" nature of their farming, one report explained, they applied their "hard-won skills" and made vegetables grow on desert land only recently reclaimed. Most workers took "great pride in their work," as evidenced by "the fine crops grown under their care." Another report concluded that their labor was "inspired by the spirit of cooperation only." Because they were not motivated by "a large pay envelope," the success of the farming program deserved "more credit than normally would be extended to those who had the profit motive as an incentive for their participation."[44] According to this report, then, Gila River met the material and social goals of the WRA's agricultural program, simultaneously producing food and compliant Americans.

These glowing reports were tempered by suggestions that Japanese Americans were neither consistently content with their work nor the most productive workers. While the quality of their work was generally "very good," the "quantity of work was nearly always less than could have been accomplished by hired labor at the going wages for that type of work." According to WRA community analyst G. Gordon Brown, detainees were conscientious about farming, but they also did not want to work "too hard" or cooperate "too closely" with the administration. As a result, they were "very careful to do no more than their quota."[45]

Working on the farm did give Japanese Americans some measure of control by helping them maintain their foodways. With the expertise of Shinjiro Hamasaki, who had thirty years of experience in growing commercial vegetable seed in San Jose and Gilroy, California, Gila River's seed farm produced large quantities of seeds for carrots, onions, peas, lettuce, and garlic as well as Japanese vegetables.[46] The seed stock of daikon, napa cabbage, mizuna greens, and other crops from Gila River was distributed to other camps. According to one WRA report, "Without this seed farm there would have been no supply of these vegetables especially desired by the Japanese people." Even as the camps' populations began to decline, the WRA still asked Gila River to focus its seed production on "Japanese type of vegetable seeds which are not available generally on the market."[47]

WRA leaders found Japanese American expertise less desirable when it came to planning the types of crops to grow. At Topaz, W. M. Case noted that the agricultural program "should be developed in cooperation with

FIGURE 4.2 Japanese American workers harvesting daikon at Gila River, November 25, 1942. Photograph by Francis Stewart. Courtesy of the National Archives and Records Administration.

the evacuees, but final determination should be made by the Agricultural staff so that the production of the center meets the most important food requirements locally as well as fitting into the total food production program of all centers." He reminded project director Charles Ernst that Japanese Americans' judgment "on what is best at Topaz is not apt to be as good as the staff who understand local conditions regarding soil, climate and irrigation problems." Thus, Ernst's staff needed to assert more control over "what shall be planted and where and when." Frost-sensitive watermelon and cantaloupe had to be abandoned, and more root crops, cabbage, beans, spinach, chard, and grain crops grown.[48]

Case's advice ultimately produced results. As George Sugihara, who worked for the WRA's Project Reports Division, noted, "All crops handled in accordance with recommendations and plans prepared by the agronomist or in accordance with well-recognized practices in the community [have] shown excellent results."[49] It was reasonable to privilege the knowledge of local agronomists, given the unique growing conditions in the Sevier Desert, but this facilitated increasing white control over Topaz's agricultural program.

In his unpublished memoir, Topaz's agricultural head Roscoe Bell painted a more generous image of his work, emphasizing the farm's efforts to train and educate detainees. He knew that "economic operation could not be a prime objective," particularly as the WRA's relocation program drained the labor supply, but he believed that the program was worthwhile because it provided "constructive employment." In fact, he explained that the "first objective" of the agricultural program was to train people. Bell noted, "Obviously you can't just hire people for $16.00 a month and expect them, if money is the only objective, to work with diligence, whereas, if they are anxious to learn, they will do a better job and the production will take care of itself." The farm was a "training ground" for detainees who wanted to learn a trade or further develop their agricultural expertise.[50]

Topaz developed several educational programs, ranging from food crops and swine production to machine operation and farm construction. For instance, the twenty-week vegetable-gardening program covered plant propagation, seeding and transplanting, land preparation and cultivation, machinery operation and maintenance, insect and disease control, harvesting and packing vegetables, and storage.[51] Taught by George McColm, Topaz's farm crop supervisor and a former Soil Conservation Service employee, the program also delved into soil care and the particular growing requirements of a variety of crops, from greens to root vegetables.[52] McColm's expertise proved to be instrumental to the success of the Topaz farm. He noted, "Everybody assumed that we were bringing in people that knew all about how to grow crops. Well, when we brought them in we found that we had only 200 out of the 8,000 that had ever lived on a farm." Even men with greenhouse experience did not know how to work with the alkaline conditions. McColm taught them furrowing methods to move the alkaline content up and away from the root zone of the crops, thereby changing the pH of the soil.[53]

During his two years at Topaz, McColm grew especially fond of Bob Sakata, whom he described as "my very best young man that showed the greatest ability with vegetable crops." He soon became McColm's "right-hand man."[54] Sakata was just a teenager at the time, but his father had a ten-acre farm in Alameda, California, before the war. He walked the fields with McColm to collect soil samples, then conducted soil tests in the lab in the evening. Sakata recalled, "Once we discovered that we could grow the crop, and allocated the amount of water that was available . . . I was assigned to create the budget of what we can grow there and how many . . . acres and what kind of equipment we need and so forth." Sakata enjoyed working with McColm, whom he described as an "outstanding fella," but soon decided to leave for Brighton, Colorado, where he built a long career in agriculture.[55]

The experiences of Bell and McColm corroborated other WRA assessments of the agricultural program. In his final report, E. H. Reed confirmed that novices gained marketable skills for outside employment. If they could grow crops in the camps, they could "again be successful in growing crops under conditions differing from those on the West Coast or in the Relocation Centers."[56] Indeed, former Pacific Coast growers were exposed to "whole new fields of agricultural endeavor, greatly widening their opportunities for relocation." Some learned to raise livestock, while others simply became accustomed to larger operations. Even former city dwellers gained vocational experience that could open employment opportunities in many agricultural areas in the nation.[57] WRA leaders thus emphasized how cultivating the land facilitated the agency's efforts to aid Japanese Americans' "gradual reabsorption into private employment and normal American life."[58]

However, some detainees did have preexisting agricultural knowledge to apply to the camps. When Bell started the agricultural program at Topaz, the WRA staff "knew that there was talent if we could just locate it." Several key individuals soon volunteered their services. According to Bell, they were "well qualified, experienced, and dedicated to serve and to train people who might not be experienced in various aspects of agriculture." He eventually singled out George Nakano and Vernon Ichisaka as instrumental to the success of the vegetable and farm crops.[59] Nakano was a flower grower in San Mateo

County before the war, and he began conducting soil surveys for the agricultural department shortly after his arrival at Topaz in September 1942. While he recognized the poor soil quality, he noted that "we will try our best" to grow crops and contribute to "making this a livable camp."[60]

For all the WRA staff members and Japanese American farmworkers who viewed the agricultural program in a positive light, others expressed frustration. In August 1944, Topaz's Wendell Palmer noted that Japanese American foremen "have continuously stated that there is a general feeling in the center that the Agricultural program is superficial since the government has guaranteed that evacuees would be fed while in centers." They believed that they received very little support in building the program, with one foreman noting, "The feeling that the Agricultural program is unimportant is so rampant in the center that it is not only destroying center support but also the morale of many of our workers."[61] At this point, the Topaz farm did not have enough workers, and the people who did tend the fields were either "high school boys" or people over fifty or sixty years of age.[62]

Nonetheless, urgent moments brought detainees to the farm involuntarily. At the end of June 1943, Ernst pleaded with "every able-bodied resident" at Topaz to help the farm crews to plant the crops. He noted, "We must plant NOW or never! The Agricultural Division, therefore, is calling upon each activity in the Center for its contribution of workers and supervision."[63] At the time, the farm crew only had 35 regular workers, well short of the estimated 120 workers needed to maintain the food crop program from April 1 to November 1.[64] This small group of workers, augmented by some volunteers, was able to plant all of the vegetables for the season. However, because many of the crops were planted late, they required "excellent care" to bring them to maturity before the first frost. In particular, the onion and tomato fields were so weedy "that it will be necessary to abandon certain fields unless they can be hoed immediately."[65] The urgency of the situation prompted Ernst to institute a special food crop assignment program, which transferred fifteen workers from seven blocks to the farm each day.[66] The program concluded in September, saving six thousand bags of onions and between fifty and seventy-five tons of cabbage.[67]

When faced with the threat of a wasted harvest, WRA administrators did not just transfer workers within camps but also between camps. This was necessary because of the interdependence of the camps' agricultural programs. A labor problem in one camp might create food shortages at all the camps. This was especially a possibility at Tule Lake, which, along with Gila River, shipped the most produce. It was also an incredibly volatile place in the wake of the loyalty questionnaire. When twelve thousand "disloyal" detainees descended on the camp after it was designated the "segregation center," the population swelled to over eighteen thousand, far exceeding its original capacity. Internal conflicts developed between newcomers and "old Tuleans" who refused to move to other camps, so the WRA added soldiers, fences, and guard towers.[68]

The new Tule Lake arrivals recognized substandard living and working conditions and, already highly disaffected with the WRA, started to organize. In the wake of a farm truck accident that injured five people and killed one, farmworkers went on strike in October 1943 to protest unsafe working conditions. With valuable crops awaiting harvest, WRA administrators recruited workers from the other camps. As Charles Ernst explained, Topaz detainees initially resisted, preferring to be "satisfied with less food this winter . . . than to be accused of unfriendliness by their fellow evacuees at Tule Lake," about fourteen hundred of whom had previously lived at Topaz. He continued, "Surely WRA could not expect Topazeans to stab old evacuee friends in the back and make themselves the most despicable of creatures!"[69]

However, when Ernst learned that the Tuleans did not feel that they should harvest crops for other centers, "The residents of Topaz began to feel that their helping with the harvest could no longer be construed as an attempt to break a strike."[70] Thirty-two Topazeans—all but two had previously lived at Tule Lake—along with several dozen other workers from Poston and Heart Mountain soon arrived in far northern California. They worked sixteen- to eighteen-hour days until the end of November and earned $1.00 per hour, which meant that they could earn as much in one day as they could in one month at Topaz. In the end they saved a harvest that provided sixty-one carloads of produce to other camps and was worth $250,000. According to Topaz detainee Mike Maruyama, who served as foreman, most of the Topazeans decided to participate in order to show their loyalty to the United States.[71]

The presence of these workers, of course, created a potentially explosive situation. Dillon Myer visited Tule Lake on November 1, met with a negotiating committee, and promised to investigate workers' complaints. Three days later, a group of Tuleans spotted a truck convoy leaving the camp and suspected that it was carrying their crops to other camps or to the workers, whom they regarded as strikebreakers. When they tried to block the trucks, a "brawl" ensued, with several detainees beaten. On November 14, the army declared martial law, which lasted for two months, and built a stockade to confine about 350 protesters.[72]

The interdependency of the camps' farms added a layer of complexity to the situation at Tule Lake, whereby the environmental strengths of certain camps compensated for the deficiencies of others. Because Tule Lake was vital to the system, the labor transfer was necessary. While Tule Lake workers chose an opportune moment in the agricultural cycle to go on strike—at the peak of the harvest—the importation of workers ultimately undercut the efficacy of their labor protest.

Of course, most farm labor protests did not result in violence, but they still involved environmental conditions. In August 1943, Minidoka agricultural staff met to discuss discontent among the farmworkers. One issue was Dillon Myer's enforcement of the eight-hour workday. According to farm foreman George Kamaya, "Some of the workers work longer than 8 hours a day and others don't work but 6 ½ hours but they get the same pay. It isn't fair. I want to treat the boys fairly." His workers also complained "that the sun is too hot and that the dust makes it terrible to work. There is a lot of difference in working inside and out in the hot sun." Stafford suggested providing part-time work with part-time pay for people "who can't stand the heat," a proposal ultimately deemed impractical.[73]

Farm supervisor W. E. Rawlings suggested that they compute workers' hours on a weekly rather than a daily basis. He explained, "You cannot work on the farm by the clock entirely. If there is a job to be done the workers should stay on the job until it is finished rather than working 8 hours and then quit whether or not the job is finished." Stafford liked the idea, as "a fellow would get the benefit of a long day against a short day." Assistant project director R. S. Davidson concurred, adding that irrigators might need to work ten or twelve hours a day, but then "they could lie around for a few days."[74] Once again, the environmental complexities of agricultural labor caused unrest and necessitated compromise.

"Unfit for Agricultural Use": Environmental Obstacles to Cultivation

The desire to make the camps self-supporting also ran up against unforgiving landscapes. While most of the camps were on land that had been previously farmed or ranched, the WRA's program was larger and more ambitious.[75] This enlarged scope often amplified the environmental problems. Even Gila River, which had more favorable growing conditions than the other camps, faced a variety of complications. For instance, the Pimas' horses routinely wandered onto the farm, trampling the fields and eating the crops. Gophers dug around the irrigation ditches. During the summer, floodwater from the San Pedro River flowed to the San Carlos Irrigation System, drenching the fields with muddy water just as the staff was trying to plant fall vegetables. A grasshopper infestation in the fall of 1944 and spring of 1945 required insecticide and the burning of two pastures.[76]

The environmental challenges were arguably more pronounced at the other camps. Minidoka consisted of "raw land" covered in sagebrush and lava rock outcroppings. Farmworkers cleared the first eighty acres by hand, then developed their own machinery to complete the task.[77] Topaz was hampered by poor soil conditions and the short growing season. As Roscoe Bell drove to Utah, he noticed greasewood and other vegetation that was a "prime indicator of alkali soil. It was, indeed a discouraging start, to think of trying to develop an agricultural program to feed 10,000 people—trying to produce crops on soil that was so obviously alkali and very difficult . . . to manage productively and successfully."[78]

Utah scientists, state officials, and residents had been dealing with many of these problems for decades. In 1917, they established Millard County Drainage District Number 3, which used bond sales, drainage taxes, and federal funding for "the improvement of agricultural and health conditions through effective land drainage." In the late 1930s, the district built 20 miles of new open drains and rebuilt 5.3 miles of tile lines—a plumbing system installed below the agricultural fields to remove excess subsurface water. Drainage reduced alkaline content in order to bring "satisfactory crop production." However, because the Sevier River watershed was experiencing a wet cycle during the war, water tables were high, resulting in the upward flow of water into the soil and higher alkali concentration due to evaporation. With about 65 percent of the camp located within the district, the need for "immediate and effective drainage activity" was pronounced.[79]

WRA officials knew that this would not be an easy task. The tile drains were filled with roots, soil, and debris, and the system lacked an outlet, with the water emptying into an open slough located one mile west of the camp. "As the depression fills up," Wendell Palmer, Topaz's final chief of agriculture, explained, "the water backs up some distance into the main drains."[80] Moreover, the Sevier River meandered through and received drainage water from low-lying valleys with alkaline soil. By the time its runoff was conveyed from the Sevier Bridge Reservoir to Topaz, it contained "a very appreciable quantity" of soluble salts—1,700 parts per million. Soil damage was "a very distinct possibility" when this water was used, unless there was good drainage and the application of "sufficient water" that could "percolate through the soil profile and into the drains so that at least some of the salts may be carried away rather than being continuously built up in the root zone of the soil."[81]

Topaz's problems were so pronounced that the WRA requested that the Soil Conservation Service and the Utah Agricultural Experiment Station conduct a soil survey of 18,840 acres from 1942 to 1943. In addition to assessing drainage, alkali conditions, erosion, and climate, surveyors identified five different soil groups, ranging from light-textured surface soils to miscellaneous nonarable land. Within each group, surveyors assigned a land use capability rating that assessed its suitability for agriculture. No areas were rated Class I, V, or VI, which were "lands suitable for cultivation without special practices," lands "not more than slightly susceptible to deterioration and not requiring special practices of measures," and lands "moderately susceptible to deterioration," respectively. Over 51 percent was considered Class IV—"not suitable for continuous or regular cultivation"—and over 17 percent was in Class VII, "highly susceptible to deterioration requiring severe restrictions in use with or without special practices." Just under 8 percent was class II—suitable for cultivation with "simple practices"—and over 23 percent was class III, which required "complex or intensive practices." Roughly 83 percent of the soil was moderately to very heavy and hard to till, while nearly 50 percent of the soil had an undulating surface that would require "considerable leveling" for irrigation.[82]

Topaz moved forward with the planting of 472 acres of vegetables in 1943, but even this modest program encountered environmental limitations.[83] In July 1943, W. M. Case visited Topaz and reported back to E. J. Utz, chief of the WRA's Agricultural Division, "Neither the soil nor the climate are well adapted to production of vegetables." Because of the 117-day growing season, planting needed to proceed on schedule. The poor soil—heavy in texture and lacking organic matter—had to be handled with "extreme care." In fact, the majority of the land was "unfit for agricultural use." He concluded, "The scattered small patches of cultivated land cannot be handled efficiently, except to be pastured by livestock"; these programs needed to be "pushed as rapidly as possible."[84]

Just a few months after Case visited Topaz, the farm crew faced the first killing frost of the season. The weather bureau warned of its arrival, which prompted "feverish activity" to save the crops left in the fields. Two hundred volunteers from Topaz High School joined the regular farm crew and "swept into the fields" on October 12 to harvest two hundred lugs (about thirty pounds each) of tomatoes and seventeen tons of cantaloupes. Working well into the night, they also harvested entire crops of eggplants, peppers,

FIGURE 4.3 To prepare Topaz's soil for planting, Japanese American workers applied barnyard fertilizers to a bank of soil, October 17, 1942. Photograph by Tom Parker. Courtesy of the National Archives and Records Administration.

cucumbers, and green beans. Because the farm crew had planted the crops late, they were fortunate that this killing frost came three weeks later than usual for this area.[85] George Sugihara of the WRA's Project Reports Division concluded that Topaz could grow much of its own food, but the staff had to "work diligently or give more attention to details than ordinarily would be required to produce an equal amount of food in almost any other location."[86]

Weather-related challenges persisted in 1944. In March, the farm crew only enjoyed ten days of good weather and did not get any substantial seeding done until April. As an agricultural report explained, "After a storm occurs here it is usually several days before we can work the land because of the clay sticky nature of the soil." In May, a hard, drying wind "sealed over the topsoil" and prevented carrot seedlings from getting out of the ground. Cool weather in June stunted growth, and a killing frost on September 15—twenty-eight days earlier than in 1943—destroyed eggplants, peppers, cucumbers, and squash.[87] In an undated chart, agricultural staff delineated crop losses due to "unpreventable causes." The list included many human-related factors—lack of equipment, labor shortages, late plantings—but it also pointed to environmental problems: hot weather, alkali soil, frost, insect damage, and "unadapted" plants.[88]

Topaz production was also limited by the constant experimentation required to grow diverse crops on marginal soil. In 1944, the staff tried some "questionable" crops in terms of their suitability to the environmental conditions. Their failed attempts to diversify the harvest "took time away from some of the other crops that would do best." The staff also tried to gauge the alkaline content on different tracts of land and planted accordingly. For instance, they surmised that heavier soils had more natural fertility and lower alkaline content. However, they did not realize that these soils also remained colder during the late spring, and when they became alkaline, the concentration was high. As a result, some crops planted in this soil, such as tomatoes and onion, grew poorly, despite the "quite good care" that the crew gave them. But the farm crew did reap the rewards of the decision to plant hardier vegetables on the sandier soils.[89]

Even as agricultural staff members repeatedly called attention to the difficulties of farming at Topaz, they promulgated an upbeat public image of the farm's productivity. In an August 1943 edition of the *Topaz Times*, a headline declared, "Plenty of Home Grown Vegetables for September–October Assured; Topaz Soil Proven to Be Fertile." The author explained that the soil was "almost unbelievably fertile" and that good crops yields resulted with "little or no application of fertilizer." In fact, they might match "California standards."[90] Given the importance of maintaining detainee morale, this positive spin is not surprising, even if it contradicted the constant troubleshooting in which farm supervisors engaged.

Topaz's farmworkers were so proud of their accomplishments that they decided to show off their vegetables and animals "in the manner of the old fashioned country fair." In October 1943, the event was staged at a recreation hall, with livestock corrals set up outside. Russell Bankson of the WRA Project Reports Division estimated that "every person within the center who was able" visited the recreation hall—roughly six to seven thousand people. Topaz staff also invited businessmen, professionals, and "leading agriculturalists" from the community.[91] Charles Ernst addressed the attendees and noted, "When I think back of the dusty barren days of a year ago, I am pleased and proud of what the residents of Topaz have been able to do to assist in supplying the food which is being consumed within the center."[92] During the 1944 festival, a representative from the Utah State Agricultural College "expressed amusement at the food produced on this submarginal land." He asked for additional information so that he could publicize the camp's activities.[93]

While the farm only operated for two full years, its yields were not insignificant. The farm crew only harvested about 187 of 472 acres planted in 1943, but they brought in over 660,000 pounds of produce. In 1944, they pared back the program to 329 acres, planted many seedlings grown in the camp's greenhouses, and divided the acreage into five units, each with a separate foreman and work crew. With these changes, they harvested 237 acres, which yielded over 776,000 pounds, in spite of a late spring planting and a mid-September frost. Some crops—including onions, chard, napa cabbage, spinach, mustard, daikon, summer squash, and green onions—had excellent results in one or both years.[94] The beef program produced enough meat for the camp and also sent 263 head to Minidoka, while the hog program met the full needs of the camp by the fall of 1943.[95] However, Topaz grain production only met one-third of the camp's livestock needs, and the meat chicken program was "mainly a failure."[96]

Manzanar's agricultural program also reflected unpredictable environmental conditions and spotty production. From the beginning, WRA leaders were pessimistic about its agricultural prospects. R. B. Cozzens, WRA assistant regional director, did not think that the camp should accommodate more than ten thousand people because of the limited agricultural potential of the site. He noted, "We are of the opinion that this area will not produce the type of agriculture which the Japanese have been used to cultivating and that any type of leafy vegetable produced in this area would probably not be suitable for market."[97] Two months later, Cozzens added, "It is evident that this project will not, from an agricultural standpoint, be a self-sustaining economic unit for 10,000 evacuees, nor will it have long-time economic value after the war is over." As a result, other industrial development would be necessary to employ detainees.[98]

Despite this relatively gloomy outlook, Manzanar's farm program began in earnest in the spring of 1942. Led by Horace (H. R.) McConnell, who was farm superintendent from May 1942 until April 1945, and Henry Hill, who worked as his assistant and later his successor, it encountered immediate environmental challenges. Annual precipitation averaged 4.5 inches of rain and snow; the temperature ranged from 10 degrees below zero to 108 degrees Fahrenheit; and the growing season was 120 to 180 days per year. Moreover, as McConnell and Hill explained, "Desert winds of high velocity blow much of the time from early March until late June. These winds were detrimental to the successful production of vegetable crops." The soil lacked nitrogen,

potash, and phosphoric acid, so fertilizers were necessary, as was regular irrigation given arid conditions and sandy soil.[99]

The farm was also established on long-neglected "wastelands" that were
"covered with brush and badly hummocked with dunes caused by hard
winds." This desolate state was a legacy of the City of Los Angeles's acquisition of the land in the 1920s. Before the city bought up property in the Owens
Valley, Manzanar was a small farming community that raised apples, pears,
vegetables, and alfalfa. Because the Los Angeles Department of Water and
Power (LADWP) was not interested in agriculture, most of the farms and
ranches were abandoned and overrun with weeds and brush.[100] Thus, the
first task was to clear the land. In April 1942, workers began digging up sagebrush, rabbit bush, and willow trees using only shovels, rakes, and hoes. They
eventually cleared about 120 acres and reconditioned about eight miles of
ditches. Plantings began in May, and the farm produced eight hundred tons
of vegetables by the fall.[101]

Manzanar officials immediately began to plan the next season, applying
their recently acquired knowledge of both the land and Japanese Americans.
This precipitated disagreement with the WRA regional office, which sent a
recommended seed schedule for the camp. Ned Campbell, Manzanar's assistant project director, insisted that modifications were necessary because of
local tastes. For instance, the WRA recommended twenty acres of beets, but
he wanted to reduce the acreage to five because "the Japanese do not eat many
beets." He wanted to abandon Swiss chard altogether, as "the Japanese prefer
both nappa [cabbage] and spinach." Other recommendations were based on
environmental considerations. While the WRA wanted ten acres of corn, he
called for twenty-five acres, in part because it could provide a windbreak to
protect other crops. He also wanted to increase the acreage of Hubbard and
banana squash because both varieties grew well at Manzanar and lasted many
weeks after harvest.[102]

Nonetheless, the variability of Manzanar's environmental conditions
made any schedule, whether developed on the ground or from a distant
office, difficult to implement. As the 1943 season got underway, Manzanar's
farm crew faced a potential disaster. On May 6, a wind storm began at 10:00
a.m. and blew continuously from the northwest until 5:00 a.m. on May 7.
The cold, dry wind caused "an excessive loss of plant moisture resulting in
stunting plants and a bad condition of wind burn." In other words, plants
could not absorb water as fast it was lost. Corn was "completely flattened to
the ground," pea vines, only eight inches high, were "blasted," and all of the
young alfalfa was destroyed. Because of the heat, the alfalfa fields could not be

replanted until the fall. Adding to the farm crew's woes, the unusually warm May temperatures melted the snow pack faster than desirable, so McConnell anticipated a shortage of irrigation water during August and September if the weather did not cool down.[103]

Just as Manzanar's agricultural staff was recovering from this calamity, a ten-hour sand- and wind-storm hit on June 1. It completely destroyed another ten acres of peas and 90 percent of the bell pepper and chili pepper crops. Tomatoes, potatoes, sweet potatoes, and cucumbers were also hit hard. In the storm's aftermath, the crew inspected the fields and decided which crops could be saved and which had to be replanted. However, they could not re-plant pepper and eggplants due to insufficient seedlings, and no potato seed was available. New tomato and sweet potato plants were put in the ground right away.[104] Ultimately, "ideal weather" and "heavy irrigations" helped these replantings. While irrigation water was in short supply in August and September, McConnell organized three shifts of irrigators who worked around the clock to minimize crop losses.[105]

Environmental fluctuations were chronic and required constant attention. On March 13, 1944, a strong wind that blew up to thirty-five miles per hour lasted ten days, and the temperature dropped to twenty-two degrees. Six acres of early carrots were "cut off at the ground by wind and sand," and about half of the cabbage plants incurred severe damage.[106] Growing conditions improved in June. Although the harvest of tomatoes, peppers, and eggplants extended into November, warm weather led to the rot and shrinkage of potatoes stored in root cellars. Agricultural staff began to sort the potatoes, emptying bins and removing the spoiled tubers.[107]

The long summer also led to water shortages due to evaporation, pointing to yet another variable that agricultural staff had to monitor: irrigation.[108] Manzanar's irrigation system consisted of twelve miles of ditches and pipelines that diverted water from George's, Bair's, and Shepherd Creeks, all of which were fed by Sierra Nevada snowmelt. Because of fluctuations in flow and the late summer drying up of Bair's Creek, the system was supplemented by City of Los Angeles wells. In addition, the engineering section built concrete dams on Shepherd Creek and George's Creek, which were then connected by a concrete pipeline to Bair's Creek. The outlet emptied into open ditches that brought water to the south field.[109]

This intricately engineered system did not guarantee a continuous flow of water. Shortages threatened vegetable crops and livestock alike. Crops of al-falfa and corn to feed cattle were limited because of a lack of irrigation water. As a result, the staff was doubtful that Manzanar's beef herd would reach "slaughtering condition" without outside feed. Because stock feed costs were high in 1944, "It was deemed advisable to close out the beef herd and resume buying beef through the Quartermasters Corps of the Army." The agriculture section liquidated its beef herd in December 1944.[110]

Despite these numerous challenges, the Manzanar farm produced about 80 percent of the vegetables consumed at the camp in 1943 and 1944. McConnell and Hill reported, "Costs of producing vegetables were less than the costs of purchasing on the outside. Vegetables were fresher and more desirable." The program also had the advantage of growing food "usually eaten by the Japanese people but unobtainable on the open market due to war time conditions."[111] In effect, the farm reduced operating costs and provided food that aligned with Japanese American tastes. Given severe environmental constraints, this was no small feat.

"Hampering the Activities of the Agriculture Section": Shortages and Protests

While labor and environmental conditions persistently challenged WRA agricultural leaders, they also faced shortages of materials, equipment, and storage facilities. Some of these problems reflected the hasty construction and inadequate infrastructure of the camps, while others stemmed from an atmosphere in which certain goods and services were scarce. In the case of Manzanar, farm leaders faced the additional challenge of addressing the complaints of the local landowner, the LADWP. WRA leaders and farm laborers often grew frustrated with these additional limitations on their operations.

At Gila River, workers worried that a shortage of crating supplies would result in squandered crops. According to a December 2, 1942, article in the *Gila News-Courier*, farm crews allegedly plowed under lettuce and spinach as a result.[112] Gila River project director L. H. Bennett later explained that "some of the boys" spread this story to discourage fellow detainees from stealing the shipping crates. He concluded, "The evacuees realize their patriotic duty and are making every effort to support themselves and thus save the Government cash which would otherwise be necessary in the purchase of this material on the outside market, and also save outside vegetables for the use of the civilian population."[113] Bennett knew that plowing under crops was a serious allegation, and he tried to allay concerns about the loyalty of his workers.

This publicity stunt notwithstanding, the real issue of crop shipments and efficient distribution remained. Crops that languished too long in desert heat could be rendered inedible without ice, packing materials, and reliable transportation. Months of planning and labor, in turn, could be wasted in just a matter of days. As Paul Robertson, head of WRA agricultural marketing, explained, it took six or seven days by rail to deliver lettuce to the nearest camp at Poston, a distance of about two hundred miles. Because this was an unthinkable proposition without ice, he suggested that the food be trucked or sold to local buyers instead.[114] A few months later, these issues still worried Gila River farm superintendent David Rogers. He explained to Bennett, "We have produced tons of high quality produce on the project but due to natural dehydration in the field caused by warm weather and unreliable railroad service the product has reached its destination in poor shape."[115] Arizona's warmth made year-round production possible, but it also threatened to destroy the crops that fed detainees at other camps. Favorable environmental conditions alone could not ensure the success of the WRA's agricultural program.

Bountiful harvests and inshipments from other camps could also go to waste if storage facilities were inadequate. In the fall of 1943, a Manzanar warehouse collapsed with ninety tons of produce inside. Banana squash and sweet potatoes were also lost due to the lack of storage space.[116] To store carrots, agricultural crews resorted to digging pits.[117] H. R. McConnell later complained that many crops were stored in warehouses "which are neither strong enough nor warm enough to be used for winter storage while in their present condition." He recommended the refurbishment of four buildings and the construction of an additional root cellar and a packing and sorting shed. "Until such facilities are provided, no satisfactory preservation of fresh vegetables can even be hoped for," McConnell warned. The project director approved his request and construction was promised for the spring of 1944.[118]

The lack of processing equipment and materials at Manzanar also created food waste. In 1943, one hundred tons of surplus tomatoes were sold to a Southern California cannery due to inadequate canning machinery at the camp.[119] Food preservation was also stymied by sugar rationing. OPA regulations allowed certain institutions to use additional sugar for canning fruit, but it did not have similar provisions for the canning or pickling of vegetables. As Manzanar project director Ralph Merritt explained, "If we do not pickle them and lose the vegetables, we will have to buy processed vegetables on the market. It seems to me then that it naturally follows that the government and the taxpayers will save money if OPA allows us the sugar necessary to pickle these vegetables."[120] He asked Dillon Myer to take up this matter with the OPA, but he was unsuccessful.[121]

This outcome was not surprising, since sugar had been a source of great controversy at Manzanar. In late 1942, Harry Ueno, head of the Mess Hall Workers' Union, accused administrators of selling the camp's sugar rations on the black market. He was also embroiled in a larger conflict with the Japanese American Citizens League (JACL), which often cooperated with the WRA administration and marginalized the Issei and his fellow Kibei, those born in the United States and educated in Japan. He was later arrested for allegedly beating Fred Tayama, a JACL leader favored by WRA officials. Believing that Ueno was being unjustly targeted because of his sugar accusations, many detainees protested on December 6, 1942, culminating in a riot that left two detainees dead and at least nine wounded.[122] For Manzanar to receive additional sugar in the wake of the riot could have raised eyebrows, even if used for food preservation.

Manzanar's efforts to produce its own food also faced challenges from neighboring municipalities. According to H. R. McConnell and Henry Hill, the LADWP's opposition to Manzanar "had a definite bearing in hampering the activities of the Agriculture Section."[123] One major source of conflict was the hog farm. In November 1943, the Board of Water and Power Commissioners of the City of Los Angeles wrote to Ralph Merritt, alleging that the hog farm would threaten "the purity of our water supply" because of its location about one and one-half miles west and above the aqueduct. While the board was "heartily in favor of enabling the inhabitants of Manzanar to supply food for themselves," it asked that the farm be moved below the aqueduct.[124] Dillon Myer immediately wired Merritt and asked him to "come to an agreement" with the LADWP so that the hog farm could continue.[125]

The situation deteriorated by January 1944, when H. A. Van Norman, chief engineer and general manager of the LADWP, requested "immediate measures" to remove the "menace" to the city's water supply: "The Department desires to avoid unnecessary friction with the local Manzanar authorities, but, unless the hog nuisance above the City aqueduct is removed forthwith, it is our intention to seek civil and criminal remedies against the individuals in charge of the Manzanar Relocation Area."[126] Merritt responded that he was committed to protecting Los Angeles's water supply, but he also noted that several other hog farms were within the city's watershed. Manzanar was not the only threat.[127]

Van Norman and Merritt continued to spar, both arguing that they were discharging their patriotic duties. For Van Norman, the LADWP was responsible for providing clean water to army and navy installations and L.A. residents, who "should not be secondary to the Manzanar Japanese

FIGURE 4.4 Hog farm at Manzanar, 1943. Photograph by Ansel Adams. Courtesy of the Library of Congress, Prints and Photographs Division, LC-A351-3-M-31.

Relocation Project."[128] Merritt quickly repudiated Van Norman's assertions, accusing the board of "waving a red herring across the trail of the real issue. The red herring in this case is a little pig."[129] He implied that the uproar about the hog farm obscured the necessity of confining ten thousand people behind barbed wire—and protecting the nation from potential subversives.[130]

Unmoved, the Los Angeles City Council adopted a resolution requesting that the City Health Department, the State Health Department, and the US Public Health Service investigate and work with the LADWP to "correct any condition deemed to be against the health and safety of the people of Los Angeles and our armed forces."[131] Charles Senn, director of the Sanitation Section of the Los Angeles City Health Department, and Councilman Carl Rasmussen, chairman of the Health and Welfare Committee, then traveled to Manzanar to inspect the hog farm. They looked over the gutters and feeding platforms and pens and examined the various measures to prevent hog excrement from flowing into the aqueduct. Merritt and his assistants also explained why moving the hog farm below the aqueduct was impractical. Relocation would require transporting hogs and garbage over a narrow bridge that crossed the aqueduct, both of which could contaminate the water. Because the area below the aqueduct was outside center boundaries, guards would have to be hired to escort Japanese American workers at a cost of at least six hundred dollars per month.[132] Thus, keeping the water clean would create a costly policing problem. Wartime frugality and wartime security were at odds.

Ultimately, Senn concluded that the hog farm was not a public health threat to the city of Los Angeles.[133] Although Van Norman recommended that no further action be taken, he insisted that his employees would "keep constant watch to see that nothing objectionable develops."[134] The Los Angeles City Council and Health Department also asked that the number of hogs not be increased and that the farm "be kept as clean and sanitary at all times as it was on the day of the inspection." Manzanar officials agreed.[135] By the time the camp closed in 1945, Japanese Americans had slaughtered over two thousand hogs, which yielded over 395,000 pounds of pork worth over sixty-seven thousand dollars.[136]

* * *

With continued camp depopulation and the impending reopening of the Pacific Coast and closure of the camps in 1945, WRA leaders scaled back the agricultural production schedule after the 1944 season. Labor was scarce, and there were simply fewer mouths to feed. At Manzanar, for instance, H. R. McConnell called for all planting to cease in 1945. By the time the crops would reach maturity, he explained, sufficient labor would not be available for harvest.[137] Thus, the labor problem solved itself at all of the camps except Gila River, Poston, and Tule Lake, which continued growing food in 1945.[138]

Of the ten camps, Gila River had the most successful agricultural program. During its first season, farmworkers planted a mixed vegetable crop on 1,289 acres, producing 1,464 tons of food for Gila River detainees and an additional 1,341 tons for other camps. The second year of operation, fiscal year 1944, saw the peak of Gila River production. The camp produced 4,804 tons of food crops, with 3,027 tons shipped to other centers and 1,777 tons consumed at Gila River.[139] By the time the camp closed in 1945, it had produced over 16,000 tons of produce, 176,000 dozen eggs, and 159,000 gallons of milk. In cultivating forty-eight crops on 4,434 acres, Gila River surpassed all of the camps in the number of acres harvested and crops grown.[140]

These statistics affirmed the WRA's belief that submarginal lands could be made productive, but they obscure the difficulties of cultivating desert lands. While geographer Karl Lillquist contends that infrastructure and labor issues "arguably played the greatest roles in limiting the success of the agricultural programs," these problems had deep environmental roots. Farm crews could never completely control or overcome aridity, poor soil, fierce winds, and killing frosts.[141] Inhospitable growing conditions necessitated more equipment, more expertise, and more labor.

These challenges undoubtedly limited the farms' productivity. All told, detainees consumed about $50 million worth of food but produced only about 14 percent of this total. Despite this subpar figure, a WRA report from 1946 concluded that the agricultural program was "a sound investment for the government and a valuable means of preserving the initiative and self-respect of the evacuated people during their enforced exile from their homes and their normal occupations."[142] Although the latter point was certainly debatable—not all Japanese Americans viewed the farms as uplifting—WRA leaders clearly believed that detainees' work on the land could serve bigger purposes. Indeed, they enlisted their participation in a variety of other projects intended to show their support for the war effort and prove their loyalty to a nation that had spurned them. Nature and patriotism intertwined in ironic ways, but once again, Japanese Americans did not always embrace the rhetoric that surrounded these activities.

5

Environmental Patriotism

WHEN THOMAS L. CAVETT of the Dies Committee interviewed James F. Hughes, Topaz's assistant project director, he inquired about the fierce winds and dust storms that obliterated visibility and infiltrated the barracks. Hughes responded that irrigation and cultivation had mitigated these "objectionable features of the weather." Cavett fired back: "Do you believe that these people when eventually turned loose after having undergone the beating that they are taking from the elements in some of these desert areas, particularly this one, would tend toward instilling patriotism into them?" Hughes replied, "I can say that none of them are particularly happy about their present residence."[1]

Cavett insinuated that the harsh environmental conditions at Topaz and the other camps would undermine Japanese American patriotism. Given the charge of the Dies Committee—to investigate potentially subversive activities among individuals and organizations with communist ties—his line of questioning was not surprising. He seemed to fear that such horrendous living conditions would do nothing to inspire a love of country and would instead breed communists. Yet some detainees did not see the unforgiving environment as a foil to their patriotism. On the contrary, they discovered that improving and engaging with these desolate landscapes was a way—at least superficially—to demonstrate their loyalty and their commitment to the war effort.

Indeed, all across the nation, natural resources figured prominently in mobilization efforts.[2] A savvy propaganda campaign of posters, films, and advertisements encouraged Americans to save materials—metal, rubber, paper, kitchen fats—and to safeguard precious natural resources to ensure Allied victory[3] If they were not vigilant, they would be providing direct aid to the enemy. At the same time, the federal government facilitated the rapid exploitation of resources deemed necessary to fight the war—Sitka spruce trees, oil, fish stocks—often at the expense of previous environmental regulations.[4] Natural resources were thus militarized and turned into weapons for victory.[5]

This ideological transformation of natural resources was part of President Franklin Delano Roosevelt's larger effort to create one front that "extends from the hearts of the people at home to the men of our attacking forces in our farthest outposts."[6] Forging this connection between home front and war front helped to legitimize the expansion of federal authority and the creation of a "warfare state" in which government officials compelled civilians and soldiers alike to "reorient their productive energies toward reworking the nation."[7] While enthusiasm for wartime sacrifice varied, many citizens accepted the expanded scope and power of the federal government and eagerly made their homes and workplaces "war-minded."[8] In this context, compliance with mandates on natural resource use became a way for citizens to express a broad commitment to the war effort.

Environmental activities deemed crucial to winning the war, in turn, became couched in the rhetoric of environmental patriotism, the idea that one's devotion to nation could be expressed through engagement with the natural world.[9] This rhetoric pervaded the camps, where numerous environmental pursuits—from growing vegetable gardens to cultivating certain plants—became connected to the war effort. Transforming the environment in particular ways was supposed to contribute to the defense of democracy and the destruction of fascism, reinforcing detainees' American identities in the process.

In practice, the rhetoric of environmental patriotism served different ends. For federal officials, it was used to encourage Japanese American participation in specific labor projects. For a small number of detainees and their white sympathizers, it was deployed to improve Japanese Americans' social status and expose the hypocrisy of incarceration. If they participated in environmental activities and proved themselves to be loyal Americans, how could they continue to be confined behind barbed wire? Environmental patriotism ultimately proved to be more of a rhetorical tool than a shared ideal. Nonetheless, its extensive deployment suggests that the camps were not isolated from a larger wartime process in which certain interactions with the natural world became steeped with cultural and political meaning.

"Food Production Is War Production": Working the Land Behind Barbed Wire

During World War II, victory gardens became a common sight in urban, suburban, and rural environments across the nation. In the cities, for instance, vacant lots, once dotted with litter and weeds, were soon full of bean bushes, tomato vines, and strawberry patches. Victory gardens also altered the environments of the incarceration camps. Tucked in between the barracks or in the firebreaks, their harvests supplemented those of the farm projects. As detainees tended these plots, they joined the ranks of nearly twenty million Americans who relieved pressure on national food supplies and freed up food for Allied troops by growing their own produce.[10] Even as victory gardening embodied environmental patriotism, Japanese Americans worked the land behind barbed wire for reasons that did not necessarily reflect a steadfast devotion to the war effort.

The victory garden campaign of World War II stemmed, in part, from Roosevelt's commitment to the "freedom from want," one of the "Four Freedoms" articulated in his famous January 1941 speech. The Atlantic Charter of August 1941 further confirmed that this freedom was "essential to framing a stable postwar society." As food became an important freedom for which the nation was fighting, food production became a crucial activity on the home front, both for practical and for symbolic reasons.[11]

The War Food Administration, a program within the US Department of Agriculture (USDA), revived the victory garden campaign first initiated during World War I.[12] According to a 1943 USDA publication, one-fourth of food production in 1943 was needed for the armed forces, allies, "fighting men, and the workers who made their weapons." Moreover, because the Axis powers had established a strategy "to use starvation to beat conquered peoples into submission," it was crucial that the military accumulate food stores. By growing their own food, victory gardeners could reduce demand on commercial food supplies, make more food available for military and Lend-Lease needs, reduce demand on scarce metal supplies used for canned goods, and free up trucks and trains to transport war supplies instead of civilian produce.[13]

The central slogan of the campaign was "FOOD PRODUCTION IS WAR PRODUCTION." To this end, propaganda encouraged all Americans to participate. In rural areas, the USDA called on farm families to expand their gardens so that they could produce a year's supply of food. Suburbanites were told to use "open sunny garden space and fertile ground" to grow vegetables and fruits, while urbanites were encouraged to tend community gardens on vacant industrial property or on the outskirts of town. School gardens were also deemed important to provide vegetables for school lunches.[14] In short, no pocket of bare land was to be left uncultivated.

To motivate these diverse Americans, the USDA invoked their personal connections to the war effort. It explained, "By growing a Victory Garden you can make it easier for your boy or your neighbor's boy or your big brother somewhere in our armed forces, or soldiers in the Russian Army, the British Army, or any of the other United Nations' armies to get the food they need to fight for you."[15] Because all Americans could directly help their own family members serving in the armed forces, there was simply no excuse not to participate.

To the USDA, it was critical that the land be transformed in an intelligent, planned manner. Victory gardeners were to choose well-situated plots, prepare the soil, and "plant carefully so as not to waste seed." Whatever was not eaten fresh had to be stored and preserved for the winter. Those without knowledge of gardening or food preservation had to get the advice of "a good gardener in your neighborhood" or a county agricultural agent.[16] The USDA also enlisted victory garden "leaders" who were told to be on the lookout for wasteful practices. For instance, victory gardeners had to stay on top of weeding: "Don't let a single gardener abandon his army of vegetables to the enemy weeds at a time when every bit of food is needed to help win the war." The use of pesticides was also deemed necessary to facilitate strong production. The *Victory Garden Leader's Handbook* stated, "Don't let your Victory Gardener be dismayed at the onslaught of greedy bugs, any more than at the fifth column of weeds. Local experienced gardeners will tell you how to blast the miniature Japanazis in a hurry." In the end, "Every successful Victory Garden is a blow to the enemy."[17]

The militaristic metaphors equating insects to "Japanazis" and gardens to bullets tried to make a clear connection between home front and war front. Victory gardeners were on the front lines of battle even if their weapons were shovels and hoes, not rifles and grenades. By cultivating the land in a specific manner, they could feed their families nutritious meals and help support the troops in all theaters of battle. The simple act of gardening allowed them to contribute to an important campaign to produce food for victory.

In the camps, Japanese Americans answered the call to garden. At Manzanar, victory gardens fulfilled the basic mandate of the campaign by providing food for the mess halls and hospitals.[18] In August 1942, one kitchen had already received sixty crates of vegetables from victory gardens, which helped to supplement the food provided by Manzanar's farm.[19] Between

July and September 1942, over 120 families worked individual victory garden plots, while other detainees tended to six larger tracts.[20] By March 1944, two hundred Japanese Americans had joined the Victory Garden Association, sponsored by the Community Activities Cooperative Association, with each family working plots as large as thirty by fifty feet.[21] During the summer of 1944, they cultivated a total of fourteen acres.[22] All told, Manzanar officials estimated that one thousand detainees participated in the victory garden campaign.[23]

WRA administrators were often supportive of victory garden efforts. At Topaz, the Engineering Section agreed to level the land after plowing, make irrigation ditches and headgates, and provide water for a ten-acre victory garden plot east and south of the center. In addition, the Agricultural Section committed to plow land, provide advice on planting, insect control, and irrigation, supply and apply two hundred pounds per acre of commercial fertilizer, and contribute small tools, insect control dusts, and certain seed varieties

FIGURE 5.1 Japanese American woman tending to her Manzanar victory garden, July 2, 1942. Photograph by Dorothea Lange. Courtesy of the National Archives and Records Administration.

totaling over 280 pounds.[24] With this level of support, Japanese Americans only needed to provide their labor and expertise to plant and maintain the gardens.

Curiously, neither Japanese Americans nor WRA officials emphasized the patriotic nature of their environmental transformations. Indeed, they acknowledged that Japanese Americans raised victory gardens for their own pleasure and purposes, not necessarily to show their support for the war effort. In one WRA report, Aksel G. Nielsen, head of the Community Activities Section at Manzanar, emphasized that the gardens proved particularly beneficial for the Issei who did not often participate in other social activities. He concluded that they "would derive tremendous pleasure out of being able to raise what they pleased in their little plots," perhaps dining on their harvest on occasion.[25] An article in the *Manzanar Free Press* further noted that the victory gardens provided food, boosted morale, helped to beautify the landscape, and offered "an experimental station for the community."[26] The Japanese American writer did not make connections to the "food for victory" campaign. The emphasis was instead on the benefits for the Japanese American community.

Nonetheless, WRA officials also acknowledged that Japanese Americans explicitly called their plots victory gardens, even if they did not highlight the ways in which their gardens directly contributed to the war effort. This suggested some awareness of the rhetorical and symbolic power of participating—at least in name—in this campaign. When one administrator expressed concerns that the Manzanar victory gardens were competing with and duplicating the farm project, Lucy Adams of the Community Management Division explained that it was important that Japanese Americans continue to grow produce "in view of the general national propaganda of more vegetables through Victory Gardens." She also believed it would be a "great mistake" to ask them to focus solely on growing flowers, which were used for weddings, funerals, and other events.[27] Adams wanted to create the appearance that they were conforming to national mandates on food production. A victory garden still had to be a victory garden.

At Minidoka, educators incorporated victory gardens into the summer school curriculum, but explicit patriotic cues were similarly absent. During the summers of 1943 and 1944, each elementary school class had a victory garden plot. Students were responsible for preparing the soil, planting seeds, tending the crops, and harvesting. According to a WRA report, "Much incidental learning took place in the field of mathematics, English, agriculture, and geography." Yet the report did not suggest how victory gardening also tied into social studies lessons, despite an American educational tradition of using nature study to cultivate civic values.[28] Nonetheless, Minidoka educators embraced the opportunity to develop curriculum that was integrated with community life.[29] Victory gardens clearly contributed to this larger goal. As at Manzanar, this program was important for reasons that did not necessarily coincide with government propaganda. There is no doubt that Japanese Americans produced food, but they did not necessarily produce food for victory.

"The Beet Knife Is Your Sword": Farm Work Beyond Barbed Wire

While some incarcerees tended to the soil of the camps, others moved beyond the barbed wire fences to harvest crops. This work took to them to farms throughout the intermountain West and as far away as Seabrook Farms in southern New Jersey. With sixty square miles of farmland, modern processing facilities, and advanced equipment, Seabrook was the major military supplier of canned, frozen, and dehydrated vegetables and produced one-fifth of the nation's frozen vegetables during the war. Facing an acute labor shortage, the company began to recruit Japanese Americans in the camps in early 1944. By the end of 1945, nearly seventeen hundred Japanese Americans were working for Seabrook, both in the fields and in the processing plants, and living in company-owned barracks.[30]

Japanese American labor in the western sugar beet industry also proved to be vital. Wartime circumstances created a sugar shortage, as Japan occupied the Philippines and Java, both major sugar producers. At the same time, the Allies needed more sugar to convert into industrial alcohol for the production of synthetic rubber. To keep up with wartime needs, federal officials rationed sugar, but they also allowed farmers to expand sugar beet acreage by over 25 percent. As these fields grew in the interior West, the labor supply contracted due to the military draft and the lure of lucrative production jobs in urban areas.[31] Japanese Americans soon filled the void, thinning and topping beets and ensuring that they did not rot in the soil. For many farmers and sugar processors, their active engagement with these cultivated environments became vital to the war effort.

The idea of enlisting Japanese Americans to work in the sugar beet fields emerged just weeks after Roosevelt issued Executive Order 9066. In March 1942, Montana growers, who had an earlier planting season than other areas where sugar beets were grown, began to put pressure on state politicians and WRA officials to provide Japanese American labor. Because farmers had planted over one million acres of sugar, half of which were in the intermountain West, they "nervously hoped that their labor problem would soon be resolved." Sugar refineries also worried about the labor shortage and "foresaw eroding profits if their plants could not operate at full capacity."[32]

In response to both increasing pressure for Japanese American workers and public resistance to Japanese American settlement in the western interior, WRA director Milton Eisenhower and Colonel Karl Bendetsen, General John DeWitt's assistant chief of staff in charge of civil affairs, convened a day-long conference of the governors and state and federal officials from the ten western states, excluding California, on April 7, 1942, in Salt Lake City. One of the goals was to provide a volunteer workforce in the region. At the conference, Eisenhower explained that Japanese Americans could be released from the camps, provided that their physical safety, housing, and round-trip transportation were secured. But governors and state representatives were not keen on his proposal, as they feared that Japanese Americans would settle permanently in their states at the end of the war. Certain that Japanese Americans would face hostile and potentially dangerous conditions, Eisenhower reported to Secretary of Agriculture Claude Wickard that they could not be transferred, even temporarily, to private farm employment.[33]

As the labor situation grew serious, attitudes began to change. With nearly thirty thousand acres of sugar beets planted, growers in eastern Oregon pressured Governor Charles A. Sprague to sign a private employment agreement in May 1942. DeWitt then authorized the release of four hundred Japanese Americans from the Portland Assembly Center to thin and top beets in Malheur County, Oregon. Idaho governor Chase A. Clark agreed to a similar arrangement, but he still spewed anti-Japanese rhetoric at every opportunity. In response to his critics, he finally stated that Japanese American workers who helped to thin the beets had "a fine opportunity to demonstrate their loyalty. Any that are doing this I am ready to give my praise."[34]

As Japanese Americans moved from assembly centers to the relocation centers, the WRA and the USDA formalized arrangements for "seasonal work leaves." According to the *WRA Handbook*, the purpose of this type of leave was to "assist in alleviating the serious manpower shortage which exists in seasonal agriculture," with the primary objective of helping "all eligible evacuees to return to normal life outside the centers."[35] Before detainees left camp, they had to meet certain conditions detailed by the WRA and the US Employment Service (USES) of the War Manpower Commission. First, they could not be gone for more than seven months. The relocation supervisor—a

WRA employee who sought out job opportunities in designated areas—had to determine that local sentiment was such that workers "can successfully maintain employment and residence there." For their part, employers had to pay "prevailing wages" approved by the USES or another federal agency and cover the cost of workers' round-trip transportation to and from camp and the job site.[36]

Once employment offers were approved, sugar companies often sent representatives to the camps to recruit workers. In September 1942, officials from four sugar companies went to Topaz. In announcing their visit, WRA official Vernon W. Baker made a patriotic appeal in the camp newspaper: "In view of the great need for peak agricultural production, residents on the project may consider their cooperation at this time as a patriotic gesture [on] behalf of the defense effort."[37] In March 1943, Jack Maynard of the Great Western Sugar Company, which operated in Colorado and Nebraska, traveled to Gila River and told detainees about "steady employment" and free transportation, housing, water, and a garden plot provided to all workers.[38] In addition to recruiting field hands, sugar companies also began to seek farmers who could put their agricultural knowledge to use and grow crops. In February 1943, three representatives from the Utah-Idaho Sugar Company traveled to Manzanar to meet and interview prospective sugar beet farmers who would cultivate land in Montana and Idaho on a share crop basis.[39]

Sugar companies also placed advertisements in the camp newspapers and tried to entice detainees to sign contracts by emphasizing the myriad benefits they would derive from this work. The Utah-Idaho Sugar Company's full-page ad in a March 1943 edition of the *Minidoka Irrigator* proclaimed, "YOU DON'T NEED TO WAIT ANY LONGER TO GET OUT." It went on to list the "rewards" of working for this company, from the personal—freedom, high wages, a chance to make new friends—to the collective—helping "America win the war and the peace to follow." The Amalgamated Sugar Company's ad likewise explained that there were "practical and patriotic reasons" why Japanese Americans should work in the sugar beet fields. The company expressed its long-standing commitment to enabling "thousands of trustworthy and loyal persons of Japanese ancestry . . . to contribute to the war effort by helping to produce this essential food . . . beet sugar." The ad concluded, "The beet-growing areas of the West need your help, and you have an opportunity to improve your circumstances by volunteering for farm work at once."[40] Japanese Americans' ability to contribute to the process by which beets were harvested from the fields to be converted into sugar would help to improve their social status and allow them to escape the confines of camp.

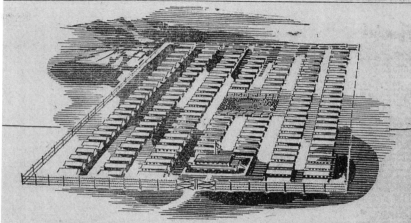

YOU DON'T NEED TO WAIT ANY LONGER TO GET OUT

Every evacuee has been looking forward to the day when he could permanently leave the relocation center that has been his temporary residence, but not a real home, these long and tiresome months.

"Some day," he has said, "I'll leave here . . . to return to my former home, or to start over in a new and friendly community. Some day I'll be a part of America again . . . to produce or fight for it."

Well, that day has come to those who will take it. . . Here's how: Get yourself a job on a farm . . . to begin with. Sign up for thinning and blocking beets; that's one of the first jobs of the season.

Pick yourself a friendly community, where a variety of crops are grown. Then work through the spring and summer, taking the crops as they come along . . . returning to sugar beets in the fall.

HERE ARE THE REWARDS:

1 Freedom to work for yourself and your family at prevailing high wages (rates of minimum pay for beet workers are guaranteed by Federal order);

2 Adequate housing (the Federal government requires every farmer to supply this before his offer of employment can be officially approved);

3 A new chance to make friends for yourself and for all other persons of Japanese birth or ancestry;

4 A stepping stone to permanent year-round employment in agriculture, or industry;

5 Healthful employment . . . for yourself and for other members of your family, if you have one, even down to fourteen-year-old boys and girls;

6 An opportunity to produce more food for freedom, thereby helping America win the war and the peace to follow;

7 A means of earning money for an education or for profitable investment, now or in the future.

SUGAR BEETS are the best way out for the greatest number of evacuees. When you accept a beet contract, take one with the organization that pioneered the way for evacuee job seekers nearly a year ago; take one with an organization that can give you a wide choice of locations and climates.

Utah-Idaho Sugar Company has factories in five states from the Dakotas to the Pacific Coast. Thousands of growers in hundreds of western communities are looking for evacuee help. We can put you in touch with the right place for you. For complete information see your project employment director or write to this pioneer sugar company.

UTAH-IDAHO SUGAR COMPANY

Home office: Salt Lake City, Utah. Factories in Utah, Idaho, Montana, South Dakota, Washington

FIGURE 5.2 Utah-Idaho Sugar Company advertisement, *Minidoka Irrigator*, March 6, 1943.

This message was reinforced through illustrations. The Utah-Idaho Sugar Company advertisement was accompanied by a line-art drawing of the barracks surrounded by a barbed wire fence. Sugar beet work offered the opportunity to escape such confinement, the ad implied. The Amalgamated Sugar Company advertisement featured a photograph of white Idaho high school students and Japanese American workers from the camps. Standing or kneeling shoulder to shoulder, they all smiled broadly with no lines, real or imagined, segregating Japanese American from white. They were working together for a common cause. In harvesting the sugar beets fields, the ad suggested, one could possibly gain acceptance from white America.[41]

These patriotic appeals were also evident in the *Rupert Laborer*, the newspaper for the Rupert farm labor camp, located about thirty miles east of Minidoka. The editor, Arita Ikegama, wrote, "The beet knife is your sword and the potato basket is your knapsack . . . at last 'they' know you want to help; 'they' know you want to see the harvest through. . . . For no one compelled you to do this work. You asked; you even begged for the privilege that is now yours. THIS IS YOUR CHANCE TO DO FOR AMERICA!"[42] In this case, it was not WRA and sugar company officials who were trying to play on Japanese American patriotism, but another person of Japanese ancestry. Ikegama suggested that sugar beet work offered the opportunity to bridge the divide between "us" and "them" for a larger cause. They were not fighting on the front lines of battle, but their labor in the sugar beet fields was no less important.

The extent to which Japanese Americans heeded patriotic appeals varied. In many cases, they were purely self-motivated. When a Topaz man left camp to pursue farm work, he noted, "It was such a good sensation to be moving along on those dirt roads away from camp. As we traveled along further, I filled my eyes with the sight of green lawns, individual homes, paved streets, and actually water fountains. I never realized how much I missed those things that I had seen so often in San Francisco."[43] Likewise, a Manzanar man noted, "The feeling of seeing life in a normal city is wonderful. . . . I'm not going to go back to Manzanar if I can help it."[44] Some detainees, however, became disillusioned about the promises of better living conditions outside the camps. One Topaz detainee went to the sugar beet fields to get away from "the damn dust storms," but the difficult work took its toll. He explained, "I felt like a goddam fool for ever leaving the camp where I could loaf around."[45] A Manzanar man concurred, "The freedom we enjoy in a country town . . . isn't worth the backaches."[46]

Nonetheless, it is possible that some sugar beet workers were driven to prove their loyalty. At Topaz, Roscoe Bell, head of the agricultural division, noted that some of his men volunteered because "they feel they are contributing to the good relations between the people of Millard County and our city of Topaz by their efforts."[47] Of course, Bell's perception probably did not match their actual motives. As a WRA official, he was more inclined to couch their work in a principled way. In other instances, some combination of factors probably influenced decisions to accept sugar beet work. For instance, Harley Ito from Los Angeles volunteered to harvest sugar beets as a "patriotic gesture" and as a way to "get on the opposite side of barbed wire."[48] For him and others, the two motivations were not mutually exclusive.

Yet some Japanese Americans grew weary of patriotic platitudes. After receiving letters of complaint from many workers, G. J. Inagaki and Scotty H. Tsuchiya from the national office of the Japanese American Citizens League (JACL) conducted a survey in the beet-growing areas of Idaho and Montana in an effort to protect seasonal laborers "against possible exploitations, hostilities, and other difficulties." During their fifteen-day investigation, Inagaki and Tsuchiya spoke with many workers who disliked the sugar company officials' continual use of patriotic rhetoric to coerce them into working. They would often state, "You have an obligation as patriotic American citizens to save the sugar beet crop." According to Inagaki and Tsuchiya, "The boys feel that exploitation of patriotism on the part of the Sugar Companies is not patriotic in itself, that the sugar companies should cooperate with the laborers by providing reasonably acceptable conditions and thus working together in the patriotic duty of harvesting the maximum amount of sugar beets possible to meet our country's need."[49] In other words, workers believed that their employers should also act in the interest of the nation. An obligation to contribute to the war should provoke all parties, not just Japanese Americans.

Regardless of their motives, Japanese Americans found that toiling in the sugar beet fields was backbreaking work with limited remuneration. The season typically started in the spring with thinning and concluded in the late fall with topping and loading the beets. Lily Hioki remembered her first year of sugar beet thinning as "torture." To thin the beets, workers stooped over using a short-handled hoe to remove everything but one plant every eight inches. As she described it, "with . . . the right hand you're using the hoe to remove and with the left hand . . . you hold the one you want to save and you remove this, and then you take another step and move and then save this, and it's just a continuous step over step and removing and saving."[50] To harvest the beets, workers used knives to hook them out of the ground and cut off the tops.[51] Earnings were meager because field workers were paid by the piece or by the pound. For Tosh Yasutake, this was a serious disadvantage because he worked on a farm with small beets. He had "to work twice as hard to get our money out of it."[52] One worker lamented that after all his hard work, he returned to camp with only a new jacket to show for it.[53]

Low wages sometimes stemmed from environmental conditions. In their beet survey, Inagaki and Tsuchiya reported that climate along with a labor shortage during the growing season yielded a poor crop, which meant that beet toppers were receiving unsatisfying returns. As a result, "Those on the poor fields are working as hard as the others on good fields and yet, barely making expenses." Inagaki and Tsuchiya recommended that those working low-yield fields receive higher pay, or pay should be set on an hourly rate.[54]

After toiling in the fields, Japanese Americans returned to housing facilities that provided nominal protection from the natural elements. Many workers in Idaho and elsewhere lived in Farm Security Administration or similar camps, where their shelter consisted of tents. During the harvest months of October and November, they provided little protection from the cold temperatures in the interior West. In Conrad, Montana, Inagaki and Tsuchiya even found workers living "in a very dilapidated box car-like shack next to the pig-pen, huddled around a stove." Before the war, many Japanese Americans who worked in the sugar beet fields "had attained a much higher standard of living than that which is offered them now and . . . they will struggle with greater fervor against any forced retrogression in the standards."[55] Given their often urban backgrounds and higher class status, they expected better accommodations.

While they experienced little financial security or physical comfort, Japanese American detainees did contribute to the wartime harvest. In 1942, eight thousand Japanese Americans left their confinement to harvest approximately 80,000 acres in Idaho, Montana, Wyoming, Utah, Colorado, and Oregon, 17 percent of the crop in those six states. But given the ongoing labor crisis, beet farmers could not keep pace the following year and only planted 619,000 acres, well short of the USDA's goal of 1,050,000 acres for that season. Nonetheless, between 1942 and 1944, sugar beet growers executed over thirty-three thousand labor contracts with Japanese Americans living in the assembly centers and relocation centers.[56] They clearly helped to transform the environment in these states, toiling in the fields to ensure that thousands of acres of sugar beets were tended, harvested, and sent to the refineries.

Some anecdotes suggest that residents of the intermountain West recognized Japanese American contributions.[57] For instance, a Twin Falls, Idaho, farmer explained that his Japanese American workers had no experience but quickly adapted "so that they could be called 'excellent farm hands' of this territory."[58] The Preston Chamber of Commerce praised workers from Topaz who "conducted themselves in a true American manner" and "saved our beet crop" in Franklin County, Idaho."[59] Herbert Tiegs of Nampa, Idaho, added that the fifteen Japanese American women from Portland who came to his farm "did good conscientious work" topping beets. He concluded, "I'm glad that I had the opportunity to meet these young women. Not only because they helped save a large part of my crop, but because the friendship that has been formed will help to strengthen our country to unity again."[60] Tiegs's positive experience affirmed the sentiment behind environmental patriotism. Japanese Americans could prove their loyalty and their worth to American society by working the earth and keeping the land in production.

Of course, Japanese American beet workers often received mixed receptions, even from Japanese Americans who were longtime residents of beet-growing regions. A Japanese American farmer in Idaho noted, "The workers recruited for the beet fields should be men who really want to work and not those who want to go out and have a good time. . . . If we are going to show the American people that we really are going to help out in the labor shortage, we must go out with the idea of helping the war effort as patriotic Americans. We should think of other things than just earning money. We should think in terms of helping this country win this war."[61] While this farmer was not forcibly removed from the Pacific Coast, he found some common bond with the laborers, as indicated by his use of the pronoun "we." Nonetheless, he also believed that some workers were not taking advantage of the improved public image that could be forged for all Japanese Americans. Their failure could hurt him too.

A USDA Bureau of Economics survey conducted in November and December 1942 further confirmed farmers' diverse responses to Japanese American seasonal farmworkers. Researchers conducted interviews with 109 farmers from sugar beet farms in Colorado, Wyoming, and Montana and long-staple cotton farms in Arizona, New Mexico, and Texas, concluding that growers who had previous experience with "a *variety* of types of so-called foreign labor," including Russians, Germans, Filipinos, Mexicans, and earlier Japanese migrants, were more likely to view Japanese American workers in "pragmatic terms." They had "grown accustomed to the utilization of what-ever labor is at hand during the busy harvest time" and were satisfied "as long as the work is done."[62]

USDA researchers also found that farmers were more likely to accept Japanese American workers if they came from farming backgrounds. Their evidence came from Yellowstone County, Montana, and Big Horn County, Wyoming, both near the Heart Mountain Relocation Center. While only 6 percent of Yellowstone County farmers stated that they would reject the use of Japanese American labor for the 1943 season, 68 percent of the Big Horn County farmers would. Researchers attributed this discrepancy to the fact that Yellowstone County farmers probably secured workers who had more farm experience and were willing to accept long work hours and "primitive living conditions." Because the workers who went to Big Horn were mostly urbanites accustomed to an eight-hour day and modern housing with sanitation and heat, they found rural life unpleasant and failed to meet farmers' expectations. Researchers concluded, "When both farming skills and rural cultural background are lacking it is especially difficult for newcomers to become satisfactory farm labor." To address these problems, they recommended that inexperienced workers work under seasoned leaders and that training programs be instituted in the camps.[63]

Inagaki and Tsuchiya diverged from the USDA study and believed that the treatment of Japanese American laborers should not be dependent on their skill. Regardless of their experience and productivity, employers should recognize the "loyal citizen status" of these workers and that "these people are intelligent, well-educated, and Americanized well above the type of labor which had been employed heretofore." Indeed, Inagaki and Tsuchiya made it clear that Japanese American workers were, put simply, a class above prewar sugar beet laborers. While many were from cities and lacked agricultural experience, their willingness to work in the beet fields was all the more evidence of their patriotism and commitment to the war effort.[64]

Harry Stafford, Minidoka project director, recognized the contingent nature of farmers' attitudes toward Japanese American sugar beet workers. In an October 1942 report, he noted that there was "general tolerance and little open discrimination" toward the twenty-three hundred detainees engaged in outside farm labor because they relieved an acute labor shortage and were spending money in local stores.[65] However, a few months later, he noted that some farmers in the Caldwell and Boise areas ostracized their neighbors if they used Japanese American labor, which he attributed to their ignorance of the leave process by which workers were "determined eligible and trustworthy."[66] As the fall 1943 harvest approached, Stafford recognized that "if farmers get the labor they need there will be a good feeling toward the evacuees, and if crops suffer from insufficient workers the evacuees will be criticized."[67]

This was the scenario that unfolded when a "very serious labor disturbance" erupted in Hazelton, Idaho, in November 1943. Farmers reported that several Japanese Americans from Minidoka refused to work. Because of poor weather, farmers were "jittery" that they would lose their crops. As a result, they were particularly competitive when it came to securing labor. Taking advantage of the situation, work crews asked for higher pay. The situation became so volatile that a group of employers told WRA investigators that if they did not take the striking crew back to Minidoka, they would be lynched at night. Fearing for their safety, Stafford sent a truck to Hazelton to bring this group back to Minidoka.[68] For Hazelton farmers, the beet workers' audacity in demanding higher wages compromised the war effort and made them possible targets for racial violence.

In the end, invoking environmental patriotism only went so far when it came to Japanese Americans' work in the sugar beet fields. In leaving the camps, they sometimes raised the suspicions and animus of nearby residents who simply could not see their work as patriotic. To be sure, Herbert Tiegs and others extolled Japanese Americans' virtues, but some only saw grave deficiencies in their work. Even the farmers who valued their contributions did not necessarily see their labor as an expression of patriotism. As the USDA survey noted, many farmers viewed Japanese American workers as yet another group of nonwhites who could get the sugar beets out of the ground and to the refineries. Farmers appreciated their skill and efficiency above all else, while Japanese Americans often relished the chance to leave the camps. Not unlike the victory garden program, patriotism often took a back seat to more compelling and pressing motives for participation.

"Further Proof of Their Loyalty": Growing Rubber at Manzanar

Growing rubber offered a potentially more fertile expression of environmental patriotism than victory gardens or sugar beet work. Because the Axis powers had gained control of areas in the Pacific and Southeast Asia that supplied rubber from *Hevea braziliensis*, the rubber tree, scientists increasingly turned their attention to guayule, *Parthenium argentatum*—a small, woody drought-resistant shrub that resembled sagebrush and was native to the southwestern United States and northern Mexico—as a possible domestic source of rubber.[69] As they determined the viability of guayule, Japanese Americans worked to solve a major wartime problem and reinforced their commitment to the nation.

Although the federal government organized national scrap rubber drives and encouraged rubber conservation, it also moved toward a major commitment to this possible "agricultural solution" to the rubber crisis. On February 28, 1942, Congress passed a bill that created the Emergency Rubber Project (ERP) and authorized the planting of seventy-five thousand acres of guayule and the purchase of all US assets of the Intercontinental Rubber Company, which had conducted extensive prewar guayule experiments in Salinas, California. With the creation of ERP, previous contracts between the Intercontinental Rubber Company and scientists at the California Institute of Technology (Caltech) became "null and void."[70]

Caltech scientists, led by Robert Emerson, decided to launch their own project. A Quaker and pacifist who was against incarceration, Emerson recognized the talents of many Japanese American detainees—some of whom were formerly employed as chemists, botanists, and nursery men—and believed that they could help to determine the potential of guayule. One of Emerson's colleagues, Robert Millikan, president of Caltech and 1923 Nobel Prize winner in Physics, added that he did not want to see these talented scientists "locked up" at Manzanar with "nothing to do but wash dishes." Emerson also believed that their work on the guayule project could prove that they were "more than willing" to serve their country.[71]

After securing ERP assistance and receiving permission and limited financial support from the WRA, Emerson had to convince Japanese Americans to participate.[72] This was not an easy sell for all potential workers. Homer Kimura was reluctant because rubber was a military material, and he did not want to help producing something that would prolong the war. Two other Japanese American scientists eventually convinced Kimura to join the project. As Emerson noted, "They explained to Mr. Kimura that my principal purpose in developing the guayule program was to help some Japanese families to re-establish themselves in American society, and to contribute something toward the re-building of good-will in Americans toward other Americans of Japanese ancestry."[73]

Guayule work at Manzanar began in earnest in the April 1942 when Emerson hauled fourteen gunnysacks of guayule cuttings to the camp. Immediately, the Japanese American scientists faced challenges. Strong winds destroyed one lath house, a structure with narrow wooden slats on the roof that allowed air and light in. Jackrabbits ate the plants. Tending to thousands of guayule seedlings was challenging in the extreme climate of the Owens Valley. Nonetheless, Japanese American participants persevered. By June 1942, they had planted 169,000 guayule plants grown from cuttings, and the first yellow flowers began to bloom on the plants in the lath house. By the end of June, four plots with different types of soil, drainage, and location were set aside for guayule experiments, and three chemists, one statistician, two plant propagators, and sixteen nurserymen worked on the project.[74]

The *Manzanar Free Press* soon embraced this project, espousing the rhetoric of environmental patriotism. One article noted, "If the experiment at Manzanar proves successful, it would mean that the Japanese will have contributed a substantial share toward national defense and the Japanese residents are happy to receive their opportunity to give further proof of their loyalty."[75] Another article explained that Japanese American contributions to meet the rubber shortage would produce "something more valuable than a product for cash sale. They will have contributed toward the building of good will between the Japanese in America and their Caucasian friends and fellow

FIGURE 5.3 Robert Emerson inspecting guayule plantings with Japanese Americans at Manzanar, June 28, 1942. Photograph by Dorothea Lange. Courtesy of the National Archives and Records Administration.

citizens." Because this goodwill would benefit the entire Japanese American community, the writer concluded, "Their efforts merit your interest and appreciation, and, whenever possible, your cooperation."[76] This language of wartime unity is not surprising, given the WRA's editorial control over the newspaper.[77] Nonetheless, it demonstrates that Japanese American journalists understood how to deploy ideas of loyalty and patriotism to frame the guayule project and potentially garner the support of all incarcerees.

Grace Nichols, a journalist and Quaker activist, also lauded the environmental patriotism of Japanese American guayule scientists. In an unpublished manuscript, she wrote, "Superior skill in growing plants whose requirements are exacting has long been recognized as one of the native gifts of the Japanese." She went on to explain that those who worked on the guayule project "welcomed it as an opportunity to demonstrate in humble ways that a man's loyalty and patriotism, his love and devotion to his country and its ideals and principles, are elements which can never be measured by the narrow bounds of race or lineage or ancestral origin,—nor can the privilege of striving and sacrificing for those things in which one believes most deeply be limited to any one race or group." Although they had been "deprived of" their homes and businesses, "Their first thought is still to be of service to the country which has denied them the rights of free men." To corroborate this point, she quoted a "statement of policy" that hung on a Manzanar bulletin board: "Day after day, through wind and dust storms, we work with willingness and without complaint—not for individual profit, but for the success of the project as a whole. . . . we are hoping that the day may come when we are able proudly to place our accomplishments before the people." Nichols clearly wanted to expose government hypocrisy as Japanese Americans participated in a crucial war project from behind barbed wire.[78]

The success of the Manzanar team soon attracted media attention. In September 1942, journalist Neil Naiden wrote about Walter Watanabe and Morganlander Shimpe Nishimura, both experts in plant propagation, for the *Washington Post*. They intended to cross-pollinate different strains of guayule in order to increase the rubber content of the plant. Suggesting innate if positive racial traits, Naiden explained, "The inborn horticultural talent of the Japanese may be what all the previous experiments lacked." He also singled out Nishimura for his "unbelievable patience. He will stand rooted by an experiment for hours at a stretch in order to place a drop of water or seemingly magic compound on a plant at the proper moment." While these men had "extra incentive" to work hard and prove their loyalty, Naiden believed that the guayule project would be "encouraging" to the average American citizen.

Even as it responded to military necessity, the government had "given the evacuated Japanese an experimental task which will keep them active and curious."[79] Thus, the camps were not oppressive places; they enabled Japanese Americans to prove their devotion to the United States.

The Manzanar guayule project was not just a front for patriotic rhetoric. Japanese Americans conducted numerous experiments that yielded important findings. In February 1943, Emerson submitted a report to the US Forest Service and the Bureau of Plant Industry to explain the three areas of Manzanar research: propagation of guayule from cuttings, suitability of different guayule strains to the Manzanar climate, and extraction of rubber. Between August and November 1942, researchers made over ninety thousand guayule cuttings that were cut from different parts of the stem, treated with different chemicals, and put in different grades of sand and gravel to root. They tried different methods for quick rubber extraction, with the hope that these techniques might have potential value for commercial applications.[80] All of these experiments yielded tangible results. Japanese Americans succeeded in getting cuttings to grow by applying plant-rooting hormones;

FIGURE 5.4 Walter T. Watanabe and George J. Yokomizo examining guayule plants at Manzanar, June 29, 1942. Photograph by Dorothea Lange. Courtesy of the National Archives and Records Administration.

developed hybrids that could survive in the harsh Owens Valley environment; and devised "an innovative, effective, and energy-efficient method of milling the guayule that yielded a low-fiber rubber extract" that had the potential to "revolutionize and modernize" this process.[81]

While the guayule project clearly involved indoor laboratory work, it also required detainees to actively engage with Manzanar's natural surroundings. First and foremost, they had to grow their own shrubs upon which to experiment—no small undertaking given the sometimes unforgiving environmental conditions. It was only when they successfully grew guayule that they could determine its viability as an alternative source of rubber and hybridize more resilient varieties. They simply could not solve the rubber problem and aid the war effort without planting and tending hundreds of guayule shrubs, altering the Manzanar environment in the process.

According to WRA community analyst John Embree, Emerson's leadership ensured the guayule project's success. His enthusiasm for guayule and his commitment to Japanese American "cultivators" helped to stimulate interest among "old Japanese nurserymen and young Japanese American soil chemists and plant cytologists." He took the time to explain the project to these skilled men, "who in turn could and did recruit helpers on their own." Ultimately, their discoveries had "very important implications for the development of rubber for the whole United States."[82]

Nonetheless, Japanese Americans' work sparked controversy. The fact that Japanese American researchers were able to accomplish so much with such limited resources proved embarrassing for the ERP scientists, who received large federal appropriations. After the *Washington Post* article was published in September 1942, Fred McCarger, secretary of the Salinas Chamber of Commerce, wrote a letter to Federal Bureau of Investigation director J. Edgar Hoover, expressing doubts that the Manzanar researchers could have accomplished as much as the hundreds of individuals working in Salinas. This sort of pressure led to declining support for guayule research at Manzanar. WRA officials shut off the water that irrigated the guayule plants and told Grace Nichols not to publish her article about the guayule research. But given Japanese Americans' important contributions to guayule research, this moment of contraction was brief. By spring 1943, Millikan secured grant money and other funding, while ERP director Paul Roberts promoted government monies. The pace of research at Manzanar accelerated.[83]

Merritt affirmed the contributions of Japanese Americans when he wrote to WRA director Dillon Myer in August 1943. He explained that Japanese American horticulturists, chemists, and engineers at Manzanar had confirmed that rubber could be produced from guayule. "Who are these men who are pioneering the way toward heavy duty rubber production in the United States," Merritt asked. "Their leaders are highly skilled and educated in our schools and universities. They give the answer to the question, 'what do the Japanese bring to our culture that is important?' It denies the assertion that the Japanese are purely imitative. It proves that the Japanese trained in our schools are of the most creative type. . . . I could preach a sermon from the text: 'The stone that the builders rejected has become the head of the corner.' "[84] Merritt singled out those American-educated Japanese Americans for praise because they had distanced themselves from Japanese culture and proven their assimilation and devotion to the nation. Their exile had not precluded them using their expertise to make essential contributions to the US war effort.

Merritt's praise was aimed at saving guayule researchers from banishment. During the loyalty questionnaire process, Masuo Kodani answered no to Question 28, while Shimpe Nishimura and Takashi Furuya applied for repatriation and expatriation, respectively, to Japan.[85] As a result, all three men were to be transferred to Tule Lake. Merritt pleaded with Myer to make exceptions "where men are engaged in work necessary to the war effort." He argued that their actions were not "in any way a reflection of an anti-American view or a pro-Japanese political view." Kodani's wife, Fumi, was a Japanese immigrant whom he met while they were students at the University of California, Berkeley. Fearing that she would be sent back to Japan, he answered no so that they would not be separated. Merritt thus insisted that his response should not detract from his "thoroughly American" point of view. He concluded, "If the United States is to produce heavy duty rubber from the only known source and the only known method, the men I have mentioned must be kept together and allowed to continue their work undisturbed by the regulations that are applied to others."[86] Ultimately, these pleas went unanswered. Kodani and Furuya were transferred to Tule Lake, although it does not appear that Nishimura joined them.[87] Nonetheless, Merritt suggested that Japanese Americans may have been unpatriotic in one context, but their efforts to produce guayule proved otherwise.

Toward the end of the war, Merritt wrote an essay—his intended audience is unclear—once again extolling the environmental patriotism of Manzanar's guayule researchers. He began by noting that scientific research had flourished in an unexpected place: "behind barbed-wire fences in a soldier-guarded, wartime barrack settlement located on the desert in the shadow of our highest mountains." He thanked the various agencies and universities that had supported the research, then concluded that "the highest tribute goes to the large group of loyal men of Japanese ancestry who, after an evacuation that took them from their homes and former fields of productive activity, worked without hope of reward or regard to long hours, under many hardships and despite an antagonistic public press that they might make their wartime contribution to the economic up-building of America." Merritt concluded that their research served "as evidence that science has no limitations of racial intolerance and that those of Japanese blood may offer cultural and creative values to American life."[88]

Merritt's essay was a rousing defense of Japanese Americans, but not an explicit refutation of incarceration. According to WRA staff member, Solon T. Kimball, Merritt viewed himself as the "father of Manzanar," committed to helping his charges learn "American ways."[89] Given its contribution to the war effort, the guayule project supported this goal, allowing Japanese Americans to express their patriotism and loyalty to the United States. The government's betrayal of the ideals of freedom and equality were not part of Merritt's rhetoric surrounding the guayule project. Instead, he chose to emphasize how the camps facilitated the creation of devoted Americans.[90]

Photographer Ansel Adams reinforced Merritt's point of view. Friends through the Sierra Club, Merritt invited Adams to Manzanar in 1943 to document life in the camp "in a way that stressed [Japanese Americans'] loyalty to the U.S. government." To this end, Adams depicted detainees as proud, resilient Americans. He also took landscape shots that featured their "fine crops"—including the guayule fields—and picturesque ornamental gardens. Through these photographs, Adams showed how Japanese Americans had "responded to the resonances of their environment" while also establishing "a democratic internal society."[91] When he published his photographs and essays in *Born Free and Equal* in 1944, his main objective "was to celebrate Nisei Americanness defined by loyalty, energy, ingenuity, and pride."[92] The image of guayule fields, bursting with full-grown shrubs, was evidence of these laudable qualities.

While Merritt, Emerson, and others clearly invoked environmental patriotism to describe the guayule project and to either defend or challenge the incarceration of Japanese Americans, it is not clear to what extent men like Kodani and Nishimura pursued this work in an effort to prove their loyalty. Perhaps they were driven by a simple desire to advance scientific knowledge. Perhaps their work gave them some purpose and autonomy, filling what would have otherwise been somewhat monotonous, regimented days.

FIGURE 5.5 Japanese Americans' success with growing guayule was evident in this 1943 photograph, one year after the project began. Photograph by Ansel Adams. Courtesy of the Library of Congress, Prints and Photographs Division, LC-A351-3-M-15-B.

Whether their discoveries improved their position in American society may not have been a paramount consideration when they chose to participate in the guayule project. Indeed, they actually had no need to prove their loyalty because they saw themselves as Americans who were doing their part to contribute to the war effort.[93]

But the fact that Merritt and Emerson believed that Japanese Americans had valuable environmental knowledge to impart and that this knowledge could both undermine anti-Japanese sentiment and affirm their American identities is noteworthy. Japanese Americans could plant and tend guayule seedlings in the desert, conduct experiments, and make scientific discoveries that might be crucial for the wartime state. For Merritt, this work proved their assimilation and the success of the WRA's mission. For Emerson, Nichols, and others, this work challenged any questions about their loyalty, weakened arguments for their incarceration, and reinforced the dissonance between the wartime rhetoric of democracy and freedom and the oppressive nature of the camps. Both Merritt and Emerson worked from within the accepted patriotic framework of wartime America to advance their distinct claims.

* * *

In the end, the various parties involved in the Japanese American incarceration used the rhetoric of environmental patriotism selectively. In some cases, as with victory gardens, it proved somewhat inconsequential or ambiguous. Given the popularity of victory gardens and the emphasis on democratic participation—federal propaganda implied that anyone could and should grow a victory garden—it is not entirely surprising that Japanese Americans tended these plots of land for their own personal purposes. Their engagement did not really stand out amid the millions of other Americans who also had gardens.

As for sugar beet work, sugar companies and WRA officials appealed to Japanese American patriotism to get them to sign labor contracts, but their toil in the fields was unlikely to improve their status among wary white onlookers. Moreover, many farmers viewed Japanese American workers as just another group of marginalized people of whom they could take advantage. For their part, many Japanese Americans did not really fall for the patriotic rhetoric and simply used it to leave camps. Performing undesirable, racialized stoop labor for the war effort expanded the permissible physical spaces that Japanese Americans could occupy.

In the case of guayule, environmental patriotism proved central to the narrative that surrounded the project. Only a small group of Japanese Americans possessed the requisite expertise to work on this project, making their wartime contributions arguably more exceptional than those of other home front Americans. Indeed, Robert Millikan and Robert Emerson did not want Japanese Americans to be reduced to unskilled laborers and believed that they could make meaningful scientific contributions and aid the war effort. However, their moment of distinction was short-lived, their success a liability amid other rubber research programs. ERP ended in 1945, and scientists pursued synthetic rubber derived from petroleum to solve the rubber crisis.[94]

In invoking environmental patriotism, government officials, Japanese Americans, and others demonstrated the intimate connections between nature and nation. They tried to promote certain environmental activities by tapping into people's abiding devotion to a nation fighting a principled global war. In the process, natural resources gained civic meaning and influenced who was included and excluded from the American polity. Yet these invocations of loyalty were haphazard and inconsistent. Throughout their incarceration, detainees engaged with nature—both inside and outside the barbed wire fences—for reasons that had nothing to do with their devotion to nation and instead spoke to their personal needs and desires.

6

Outdoor Recreation

THE BARBED WIRE fence was a volatile issue for Japanese Americans who lived at the Minidoka Relocation Center in Idaho. During its installation, they were "so incensed" that they tried to tear it down and disrupt construction. The contractor responded by hooking up the fence to an electrical generator, a practice that was discontinued once War Relocation Authority (WRA) officials found out. According to project director Harry Stafford and reports officer John Bigelow, the residents were bitter because they did not feel it was fair "after they cooperated to the fullest extent with the administration in keeping within bounds for the three months before the fence was built. The fence seems to symbolize their confinement more than anything else."[1] Adding to their frustration was the fact that the fence ran through the middle of the camp's ice skating rink. Several skaters had slid into the wire and gotten cuts, prompting them to slash the fence and roll it back.[2]

The barbed wire fence running through the skating rink serves as a powerful metaphor for the pursuit of outdoor recreation in the camps. Both Japanese Americans and WRA officials were constantly negotiating the fence, weighing the costs and benefits of their participation. On the one hand, WRA officials came to recognize the benefits of providing outdoor recreational opportunities. They provided detainees with a sense of purpose, staved off boredom, and even facilitated assimilation in certain instances. With the advent of ornamental gardening, the appearance of the camps also improved immeasurably. On the other hand, as WRA officials increasingly relaxed regulations and surveillance and allowed Japanese Americans to pursue recreational activities, they had to address criticism from those who did not approve of these outings and bristled at detainees' increased mobility.

For their part, many Japanese Americans began to embrace opportunities to venture outdoors. Despite their initial bewilderment with the camp environments, they came to genuinely enjoy swimming and hiking, fishing and gardening. While their outings typically lacked spontaneity—WRA Internal Security officials required detainees to obtain passes to leave camp— Japanese Americans could escape the rows-upon-rows of barracks to achieve some semblance of freedom.[3] These interludes of independence were particularly important given the overwhelming lack of privacy in the camps, from the cramped barracks to communal latrines. As they trekked beyond camp boundaries, the environment also became a source of spiritual renewal and cultural expression. With these myriad benefits, some detainees asserted their autonomy and engaged in outdoor recreation on their own terms. They pushed at the boundaries, cutting away at the real and symbolic fences that marked their confinement.

"One of the Few Things to Look Forward To": Hiking, Fishing, and Swimming

While most of the camps were dry, dusty, and desolate, they also afforded, in some cases, spectacular scenery and ample recreational opportunities. Manzanar was bounded by the snow-capped peaks of the Inyo Mountains and the Sierra Nevada, one of the most majestic ranges in the American West.[4] The landscapes around Arizona, Idaho, and Utah provided their own scenic qualities. Gila River was set in the Gila River Valley, with the Sacaton Mountains three miles to the south. Minidoka was located on the high desert in the Snake River plain, surrounded by sagebrush and basaltic lava flows, while Topaz lay in the Sevier Desert edged by mountains on all sides, with Mt. Topaz to the west, the Drum Mountains to the north and east, and Mt. Hinckley to the south.[5] These environments were distinct from the places from which detainees came—the tree-lined waterways of Puget Sound, the rolling hills of the San Francisco Bay Area, the fertile agricultural lands of the San Joaquin Valley, the sandy beaches and chaparral-covered mountains of Los Angeles—but they quickly recognized that they held opportunities for escape, pleasure, and even resistance.

For many Japanese Americans, a simple picnic or short stroll was a welcome break from camp life. In the Utah desert, Yoshiko Uchida remembered fondly her early evening walks along the edge of camp. After the blistering heat of the day, she enjoyed "watching sunsets made spectacular by the dusty haze and waiting for the moon to rise in the darkening sky. It was one of the few things to look forward to in our life at Topaz."[6] Some Topaz detainees ventured even further. Along with an experienced Issei hiker, one man remembered hiking "as far as we could go and still see Topaz," at which point they dug a hole to store extra water and planted a flag attached to a long pole. They would then hike until they could barely see the flag before returning to camp.[7] At Manzanar, Sanezumi Nagano trekked south of camp, where a fire had destroyed two square miles of tall weeds. There, he stretched his body on the new, soft grass and looked at the blue sky before walking along the creek with his companions.[8]

These jaunts helped to change some detainees' previous bewilderment with and hostility toward the camp environments. For instance, Harumi Iwakiri Serata, from Fife, Washington, initially found the Minidoka desert to be "forbidding," particularly in contrast to the Pacific Northwest, "a land full of greenery with tall trees and rolling hills." But she and her fellow detainees discovered an array of rocks and flora, including "little bluebells that smelled like onions," "twisted gnarled branches of the bitterbrush," and "tumbleweed that rolled across the landscape with the wind." As Serata remembered, "We began to see the beauty of the desert; it was not so desolate after all."[9]

Fishing was another popular form of recreation. With his homemade white pine pole and scavenged wire, "Mr. M" fished along the Gila River canals, often giving away his catch to his friends or frying it up to eat. He took particular pride in a nineteen-inch-long fish he caught.[10] At Minidoka, Issei men enjoyed fishing along the nearby irrigation canal, part of the federal government's prewar efforts to irrigate the arid West.[11] According to Superintendent of Education Arthur Kleinkopf, they would sit for hours, "mostly to pass away the time but hoping that if an occasional fish goes by he will at least stop to nibble and thus relieve the monotony and divert the fisherman's thoughts from his own sad plight to the joy of outwitting some unsuspecting and wandering fish." Some men even built shacks out of rock and sagebrush on the banks of the canal.[12] That these men were fishing along an artificial river seemed inconsequential. Kleinkopf suggested that it was the very act of fishing, of having something to do, that made it worthwhile.

For Japanese Americans at Gila River and Topaz, hiking was especially enjoyable because it coincided with efforts to create art. At Gila River, Issei men organized walks to collect manzanita wood, which resembled ebony found in Japan. Polishing and carving the wood into flower stands and other decorations had given them "a new lease on life."[13] After learning that Topaz was built on the former bed of Sevier Lake, a vanished inland sea of the late Pleistocene, many artists began to dig for unbroken fossilized shells and trilobites in a drainage ditch and old slough a few miles beyond the camp. They then washed and bleached these items and glued them together to make pins in the shape of flowers and "other beautiful things."[14] Collecting shells provided much-needed exercise and "a feeling of freedom, a realization that they are out of the reach, at least for the moment, of WRA and other restrictions," explained a WRA Community Analysis newsletter.[15] They also made sketches and paintings and pursued wood carving, basketry, and lapidary work. According to agricultural chief Roscoe Bell, these individuals—previously too busy to "express themselves"—"blossomed in the desert."[16] Rather than viewing the desert as a cause of distress, some Japanese Americans began to see that it could also be a source of personal liberation and beauty.

WRA officials endorsed these activities in a variety of ways, from building new facilities to making others available for recreation. At Manzanar, they allowed children to wade in an irrigation dam leading from Shepherd Creek during the scorching summer months.[17] They also established picnic areas, both within and just outside camp boundaries, as part of a larger effort to provide recreational facilities that would encourage the Japanese Americans to develop "a sense of permanence in regard to their new home."[18] Even as Japanese Americans began to leave the camps to work or attend school in the Midwest or East, officials anticipated that the camps might be open for the length of the war.[19] Thus, encouraging connections to the surrounding environment through recreation appeared to be a strategy to limit discontent and diminish feelings of boredom and confinement.

But tensions emerged between providing Japanese Americans with recreational opportunities and adequately policing their movements and activities. At Gila River, many Issei began pursuing the Japanese custom of "moon walking," or "moon viewing," strolling into the desert during the full moon to recite haiku and tanka poems about the beauty of nature and the "serenity of the moonlight." According to JERS fieldworker Robert Spencer, the Issei did not pursue this custom prior to evacuation because they simply did not have time. He elaborated, "Now, however, that there is leisure time, and that the moonlight nights are reminiscent of those of Japan, the desire to do this has returned on the part of some." Nonetheless, they could not leave camp limits and "thus do not dare indulge in this custom to the extent that they would desire."[20] As they revived a cultural tradition, their movements were carefully circumscribed by WRA rules and regulations.

Keeping track of Japanese Americans was especially vital at Manzanar, where WRA officials needed to protect the adjacent Los Angeles Aqueduct. When project director Roy Nash discovered that water from a small dam used for wading near the Bairs Creek picnic grounds flowed into the aqueduct, he

FIGURE 6.1 Japanese American children cooling off in a creek that bordered the Manzanar camp, July 2, 1942. Photograph by Dorothea Lange. Courtesy of the National Archives and Records Administration.

promptly prohibited swimming in these streams.[21] The dam was later removed so that it no longer impounded water.[22] Yet four days later on July 7, 1942, assistant project director Ned Campbell announced that the boundaries of Manzanar were to be extended into the foothills. He explained, "Picnics and outings can now be held at any time although the residents are cautioned to use their own discretion in keeping the grounds clean and observing reasonable hours." He also reiterated that swimming in the creeks was prohibited, and fishing was only allowed with a permit. If these rules were not followed, "The extended boundaries may be revoked."[23]

After one group purportedly went swimming in the settling basin for Manzanar's water system, about one-half mile northwest of the center, the new boundaries were rescinded.[24] The July 9, 1942, edition of the *Manzanar Free Press*, published a notice that proclaimed, "Watch That Line!" Administrators stated that Japanese Americans could no longer venture beyond the west boundary because of complaints of swimming in the reservoir and the aqueduct streams.[25] Nash insisted that there was to be no swimming except within camp boundaries, where a small board had been placed in a creek channel on Georgia Street to provide wading pools.[26]

The creeks that proved so tempting for swimming were also ideal fishing spots. For Japanese Americans at Manzanar, fishing provided a bit of subversive adventure to otherwise regimented lives. Three creeks tempted young boys to sneak away from their barracks to fish for rainbow trout. As Sets Tomita recalled, "It kind of reminded me of Huck Finn."[27] For Archie Miyatake, it was deeply satisfying to leave camp and fish without getting caught.[28] Government reports corroborated these memories of clandestine fishing expeditions. In August 1942, employees of Los Angeles Light and Power reported seeing Japanese Americans leaving from the west side of the camp after dark, staying out overnight to fish in local streams, and returning in the morning. In response, Roy Nash established additional military patrols in this area and installed four additional watch towers.[29]

Numerous reports of "WRA laxity" when it came to maintaining boundaries and allowing Japanese Americans to leave Manzanar without white supervision led to an investigation conducted by P. J. Webster, chief of the WRA Lands Division. Local residents and officials were suspicious when they saw Japanese Americans outside of camp, because facilities run by the Sierra Talc Company and the Southern California Minerals Company, which included explosive magazines and storage, were close by.[30] Thus, in early September 1942, Webster spent three days in the area to look into these claims and inspect the military police guard system. He concluded, "There is little doubt that Japanese have done considerable fishing and some swimming outside of the Relocation Area and, in all probability, some fishing is being done at the present time."[31]

Webster's findings were based partly on an investigation conducted by Aksel Nielsen, supervisor of community activities, and partly on conjecture. Nielsen followed Shepherd Creek from the water reservoir toward the mountains and cut across to Bairs Creek in order to find out if any of the creeks had been dammed for swimming holes. Along Bairs Creek, he found three dams that appeared to have been built before Japanese Americans were confined in the area. Between the picnic grounds south of the lath house and the road that led to the garbage dump, he also came across six dams that may have been constructed since the previous spring. Two dams in particular appeared to be large enough to be used as swimming holes.[32] In addition to on-the-ground investigations, Webster also interviewed twenty-four people. While "no one had personally seen any Japanese swimming," he speculated where Japanese Americans could have swum. Given the constant patrols by the City of Los Angeles, Webster was doubtful that they had ventured into the aqueduct.[33]

When it came to fishing, Webster had more definitive evidence. E. B. Austin of the Los Angeles Department of Water and Power saw a Japanese American man fishing with a homemade willow pole and carrying a bag with thirty-five to fifty fish on August 22, 1942, two miles west of Manzanar on Shepherd Creek. Austin was angry because he assumed he had no fishing license and no right to fish there. When the two men began to talk, the Japanese American fisherman told him that he fished there "often" along with other detainees. Austin reported the incident to the military police at Manzanar, but the on-duty guard was not especially concerned, as "he frequently heard that the Japanese got out of the center with a permit on detail and then sneaked away and went fishing." He also informed the game warden, who explained that he had not been able to catch Japanese Americans in the act of fishing outside of camp.[34]

Maul Miller of the Sierra Talc Company also claimed to have witnessed four Japanese Americans fishing on Georges Creek, about five miles from Manzanar boundaries, on August 30, 1942. Upon further questioning, he admitted that he did not actually see them fishing, but rather saw them scurry into the bushes by the creek bed. When Webster prodded further, Miller noted that he was about one-half mile away from the group. Webster thus questioned his story, explaining, "One might raise the question whether a Japanese could be distinguished from anyone else at this distance." Perhaps recognizing the speculative nature of his account, Miller went on to tell Webster that he had a friend who had seen eight Japanese Americans "actually in the act of fishing" along Shepherd Creek.[35]

Austin's and Miller's stories were accompanied by a handful of other accounts. Mrs. George Johnson, for instance, claimed that her husband saw two Japanese Americans fishing west of Manzanar boundaries earlier in the summer. K. Horton, chief of Internal Police, explained that "he had no doubt that Japanese working on the garbage crew had been fishing in the Owens River in connection with their trips east of camp to dump garbage." In fact, Japanese Americans had found other ways to get out of camp on official business in order to fish. Horton reported that nine or ten detainees were found fishing three or four miles west of Manzanar on Georges Creek after receiving permission to collect native plants for landscaping. Webster saw this as "simply a case of their taking advantage of the situation."[36]

Concerned about the policing of the Manzanar boundaries, Webster met with Captain Archer and Lieutenant Buckner of the Military Police. With

120 soldiers and eleven guard posts to oversee, they insisted that they could not post an adequate number of guards on the west side of the camp round the clock. Indeed, when Webster inspected the western line of Manzanar, which was about seven-tenths of a mile long, he found that it was patrolled lightly, so "a person could go over the line without being noticed." Moreover, there was a trash-burning dump a short distance from the western boundary, for which a long trench had been dug. The dirt formed a five-foot-high barrier. Webster explained, "If a person gets over this barrier he can proceed a considerable distance to the west, out of sight of anyone patrolling the west boundary. Furthermore, at night there are no search lights along the west boundary."[37]

Japanese Americans could slip away from Manzanar with apparent ease, but Webster also noted that the guards had been instructed to shoot "anyone who attempts to leave the center without a permit, and who refuses to halt when ordered to do so." Buckner expressed doubt that the guards would bother to ask someone to stop, as they "were finding guard service very monotonous and that nothing would suit them better than to have a little excitement, such as shooting a Jap." Thus, Webster concluded that if Japanese Americans were leaving the west side to fish or swim "they are doing so at great peril to themselves; and that, if they continue this practice, in all probability one of them will get shot." The dangers were mounting, as Archer's request for eight additional watch towers and twelve search lights had been approved. "When this is completed," Webster explained, "it appears very unlikely that any Japanese will leave the Center without permits during hours of darkness."[38]

But the memories of Manzanar detainees call into question the supposed quick triggers of the guards. According to Fred Nagai, the military police did not stop him from leaving camp. He recalled, "They didn't care if you wanted to sneak away from there, you have to climb the big Sierra mountains. Heck, nobody'll make it."[39] Mas Okui related an even more poignant story in which he went fishing on Bairs Creek with friends. He knew they were in a forbidden area and understood the risk of being shot, but a guard actually tossed them a bag of frames, fishing line, and hooks over the fence. He explained, "He saw what we were doing and went out of his way, it was an act of kindness."[40] Thus, the actual dangers of sneaking away from camp may have been exaggerated.

It is unclear how WRA regional director E. R. Fryer responded to Webster's report or if he took any definitive action. What is clear is that some Manzanar detainees were not deterred from sneaking away from camp to pursue recreational activities. In February 1943, the *Manzanar Free Press* published a warning to residents with the headline, "No More Hikes up to Mountains." The short article reminded them that they could hike within the park but were prohibited from "going to the foot of the mountains for snow parties and hikes."[41] The fact that such reminders were necessary suggested that Japanese Americans were making these jaunts in violation of WRA regulations and that they felt that the freedom to move without constraint was worth the risk, whether real or overstated.

For instance, Hank Umemoto, a high school student, snuck away from Manzanar to climb the nearby Alabama Hills with a friend. With "rather lenient" security, they had no problem crossing the barbed wire fence and fording George's Creek to continue to their destination. Nonetheless, they were acutely aware of their unfree status and hiked along a ravine instead of the crest to escape detection. When the boys reached the top of the ridge, they resisted the urge to explore the area and instead briefly took in the view, "gazing down on Manzanar with its checkerboard of tarpapered barracks." In retrospect, the excursion gave Umemoto hope that he would someday be able to see the "beauty and grandeur" on the other side of the Alabama Hills and even climb California's tallest peak, Mount Whitney.[42]

In the case of Manzanar's Kenji Itamura, the desire to fish led to the violation of state law. In June 1943, the California State Legislature amended Section 427 of the California Fish and Game Code to prohibit the issuance of sport and commercial fishing and hunting licenses to "alien Japanese."[43] Itamura, an Issei, was ineligible to receive a license, but he falsified his application and claimed that he was born in Los Angeles County. According to Manzanar project attorney J. Benson Saks, a representative of the California Fish and Game Commission "was quite disturbed by the evacuee's actions" and insisted that the WRA handle the situation.[44] Itamura was tried at Manzanar, convicted, and fined ten dollars.[45] While his punishment was minor, his move was bold. Itamura could have gone fishing and risked being caught without a license. The fact that he actually applied for a license and blatantly lied about his citizenship reveals some level of defiance and discontent with the discriminatory state laws and federal policies that controlled his recreational activities and mandated his incarceration.

Hiking, picnicking, swimming, and fishing were just as popular at other camps and came with varying restrictions. At Topaz, detainees had more opportunities for spontaneous hikes without advance permission, as project director Charles Ernst declared in November 1942 that he was "extending the freedom of the entire Project to all the residents in this City." This meant that they could pass from the "Center" into the "outer Project" by simply presenting their personal identification card at the gates. The entire project encompassed eighteen thousand acres, which they could access between sunrise and sunset without a pass. Ernst warned that they should never leave or enter by "crawling through the fence," and he noted that the boundaries of the project were clearly marked with red warning signs placed one hundred yards apart. Not unlike Manzanar's officials, he emphasized, "There is little possibility that these boundaries can be overlooked and you are asked to cooperate by observing all of the regulations in this respect."[46]

To monitor detainees' movements, Ernst advocated a simple system of checking in and out of the gates "so that there would be some means of ascertaining that no one had been lost or injured somewhere outside." This was especially necessary in the spring, as more residents were taking advantage of the warm weather to "wander out across the desert."[47] Ernst was not being paranoid when he made this statement; accidents did occur when Japanese Americans ventured beyond the barbed wire fences. At Minidoka, Takaji Edward Abe died of exposure when he left camp on the morning of December 1, 1942, to search for greasewood to make into "artistic articles." He became separated from his friend, and when he did not return by nightfall, a search party began to comb the area. Abe's body was found on December 3, about four miles northeast of camp. In his confusion during a snowstorm, he had walked parallel to the camp for over ten miles instead of toward it.[48] Project director Harry Stafford noted that this death taught everyone about "the treacherous nature of sagebrush-covered plains and gullies in the project area."[49]

Drowning was another ever-present danger associated with outdoor recreation. At Minidoka, swimming often took place in the North Side Canal to the south of the barracks. Recognizing the potential dangers, Stafford announced in March 1943 that the North Side Canal Company had granted permission to develop two protected and controlled areas off the canal for swimming pools, in order to control swimming and reduce drowning accidents.[50] Before ground could be broken, however, Noboru Roy Tada, age eleven, drowned in the canal. He was playing along the banks, slipped, and fell into the irrigation stream, which was about fifty feet wide. His body was found about forty-five minutes later a mile downstream.[51]

In early September 1943, Japanese American volunteers completed construction on a fifty- by twenty-five-foot swimming pool south of the warehouse area and a few feet away from the North Side Canal. It was a simple pit about six feet deep with a short ditch that connected it with the canal. Volunteer life guards received training to patrol the new facility.[52] But the

FIGURE 6.2 Japanese Americans enjoying the swimming pool at Minidoka, August 28, 1943. The North Side Canal is at the upper right. Courtesy of the National Archives and Records Administration.

pool still did not keep detainees away from the canals. Tragedy struck again when Yoshio Tamura drowned there, within a week of the pool's opening. One WRA report noted, "Occasionally talk was heard to the effect 'WRA must think the Japanese certainly are causing a lot of trouble. After all the warnings people still can't stay out of trouble.'"[53]

When Minidoka detainees wrote a report to the Spanish Consul—the diplomatic intermediary that communicated Japanese nationals' grievances with the US government to the Japanese government—their interpretation of the swimming situation specifically and the recreation issue more broadly was different.[54] They called attention to government publications that vowed to provide recreational facilities "inasmuch as this is one of the necessities for a normal pursuit of social life. It is even more so in a conjested [sic] community where thousands have to live in a limited space. . . . There are no outdoor facilities for play provided, which all account for a lack of stimulus to uphold the morale of the residents in general."[55] The Spanish Consul claimed that the Minidoka administration had failed to keep its promise to build swimming pools, which led to the two drowning accidents in the canal.[56]

Though not wholly accurate, the report's more salient point was that these Japanese Americans saw recreational activities—both indoors and outdoors—as critical to their overall well-being and their ability to endure their incarceration. Without places where they could play games or go swimming, the camp seemed less like a normal American community than a place of oppression and discontent. A swimming pool thus held a great deal of symbolic meaning in the context of incarceration.

Even after the pool was operational for nearly a year, the irrigation canals still proved to be troublesome places. On May 15, 1944, officials from the Twin Falls–North Side Canal Company reported that eighteen hundred feet of rip-rap—sagebrush set into the canal bank in order to prevent washing—had been burned by four detainees. The WRA had had a "tacit arrangement" with the company that allowed Japanese Americans to use this area for fishing and bathing. This was the first incident of damage, but the destruction was serious because canal waters were rising with the beginning of the irrigation season. Two weeks later on June 1, 1944, a group of young boys were digging off the banks of an irrigation canal and running water over it when they were caught by the foreman. Because the canal supplied water to 130 acres of crops at the camp's farm, Minidoka official William Maxey explained, a break "could very easily have caused complete loss of a major portion of the crop. . . . the section would have been completely washed out in a short time, if our forman [sic] had not repaired the bank."[57]

One can only speculate as to why Minidoka detainees were continually drawn to the canals and why they engaged in activities that could be easily construed as sabotage. Perhaps they were attracted to the canals' recreational flexibility. Perhaps they were attracted to the fact that their activities along the canals were only tacitly approved of by the administration and the canal companies. The very act of breaking the rules may have provided a sense of empowerment and control to some detainees. Regardless, the canals became sites where both Japanese Americans and WRA officials tried to assert their power and dictate acceptable activities.

The ongoing problems with the canals also demonstrate how the WRA had to juggle competing interests in detainees' pursuit of outdoor recreation. Benefits notwithstanding, they had the potential to anger suspicious neighbors. In addition to their run-ins with the North Side Canal officials, Minidoka detainees were the source of gossip in the summer of 1943, when a group of 270 picnicked at Shoshone Falls, a park in Twin Falls, about twenty miles from camp.[58] Claude Detweiler, president of the Twin Falls Chamber of Commerce, had "no objection to the proposal," but local residents were critical when five trucks transported the picnickers and made several trips back and forth.[59] A similar problem emerged at Topaz. Project director Charles Ernst announced in December 1942 that the Rationing Board had asked him to discontinue the use of trucks "for the purposes of outings or picnics."[60] Almost two years later, residents engaged the services of a Delta, Utah, resident, Mr. Hunsaker, who transported them to Oak City Canyon and provided a meal of chicken, corn, salad, and French bread. Grace Oshita remembered these picnics fondly, especially the beauty of the canyon and the feeling "that we were in heaven for a day." But in October 1944, the Delta Ration Board denied Hunsaker gasoline for private "hauling."[61] During a time of gasoline and rubber rationing, it probably appeared frivolous to use scarce resources for Japanese Americans' picnics.

Fishing at Topaz also raised the eyebrows of Utah conservationists. In May 1943, project attorney Ralph C. Barnhart received a letter from a Delta conservation group that expressed "great alarm at the depletion of the fish in the local area if large numbers of our Topaz residents are permitted to fish."[62] Along with two other Topaz officials, he later met with a group of representatives from Millard County conservation organizations. According to Barnhart, their concern stemmed from "their lack of information about the project in general, including our attitude on the subject and whether or not large numbers of evacuees would have the opportunity of fishing." Once the Topaz administrators told them that they did not issue passes explicitly for fishing and that hiking parties did not go "in the direction of any of the streams or reservoirs where fish may be taken," the conservationists' fears were allayed. They "merely want assurance that their work of a number of years in stocking certain streams and reservoirs would not be obliterated in a short time by a multitude of evacuee fishermen."[63]

Once again, WRA officials found themselves torn between allowing detainees to pursue recreational activities and policing their charges in a way that maintained boundaries between Japanese American and non-Japanese American, camp and the outside world. Sometimes, they allowed them to cross the real and metaphorical barbed wire fences, but at other times they actively enforced the demarcated lines. For their part, Japanese Americans often defied these decrees, sometimes at terrible costs. Nonetheless, as they engaged in outdoor recreation, their perceptions of the camp environments shifted. Once deemed categorically oppressive and forbidding, the natural world became a place of pleasure and even inspiration.

"Most of the Barriers Had Been Broken Down": Scouting in the Camps

Japanese American youth who went on camping excursions under the auspices of the Boy Scouts and Girl Scouts of America enjoyed little administrative opposition to their recreational activities. WRA officials pledged "full cooperation" with the establishment of "a vigorous Boy Scout program," as it was consistent with the "WRA policy of encouraging evacuee identification with groups typically American in concept" and helped to reinforce Japanese American patriotism.[64] In providing youth with the opportunity to escape the camps, it may have also eased the anxieties of their confinement.[65] But in the end, scouting, much like other forms of outdoor recreation, was still limited by the barbed wire fences, as children could not participate in the same ways as non-Japanese American youth.

Scouting in the context of the incarceration built on decades of discussions surrounding the benefits of outdoor life for young people. Beginning in the nineteenth century, advocates of camping and nature study argued that outdoor play revitalized youth exposed to urban-industrial ills and made them better citizens. During World War II, they added that summer camps served as refuges from the anxieties engendered by war.[66] The civic benefits of scouting seemed to be paramount for the WRA. The "Statement of Joint Policy" for the WRA and the Boy Scouts of America, signed in June 1943, noted that Scouting had the potential to make Japanese American youth "acceptable" to their communities when they returned home. WRA officials suggested that participation in an organization that supposedly battled moral degeneracy, built character, and "advocated conformity through citizenship training and insistent Americanism" had the potential to alleviate anti-Japanese sentiment.[67]

Scouting seemed to have had this desired effect at Minidoka, where Japanese American troops joined white troops from southern Idaho on a weeklong camping trip in August 1943. One hundred thirty Japanese American Boy Scouts, most between the ages of twelve and fourteen, camped in the Minidoka National Forest in two groups of sixty-five, accompanied by five Japanese American scout leaders and a member of the WRA staff. The first group camped in an area on Porcupine Creek, while the second group camped at Penstemon, a developed site about two miles from Porcupine and forty-eight miles from Minidoka. White troops from Twin Falls, Hansen, Kimberly, and Murtagh, Idaho joined them.[68]

An initial period of apprehension between the white and Japanese American scouts was followed by camaraderie. Because of some antagonism from the "Caucasian scouts," the two groups camped separately at first. But by the end of the week, "Most of the barriers had been broken down. . . . Several of the [Japanese American] boys became very popular and were invited to other camps for meals."[69] Japanese American scouts were included on hikes "with no discrimination whatever," and "it certainly did not take the boys long to get over this feeling" of hesitancy. One white Eagle Scout spent considerable time with the Minidoka scouts, who all participated in hiking and playing ball with the other group. At the end of their time, they exchanged addresses and agreed to keep in touch.[70] Their shared affiliation with the Boy Scouts and their shared experience in the Idaho wilderness seemed to have broken down social barriers in a way that would not have been possible in another context.

Topaz scouts also had camping facilities that provided personal pleasure and the opportunity to achieve loftier civic goals. Initially, the unforgiving landscape surrounding Topaz was discouraging to would-be campers. As one report explained, "For miles and miles in every direction lay the barren, level desert with widespread alkali 'slicks' glistening in the sun's rays." Nonetheless, beyond these expanses of flat, apparent nothingness, there were mountain ranges toward which "planners turned their eyes. Somewhere up there perhaps a place could be found that would suit the purpose." The Community Activities section sought an appropriate camp site for Topaz youth and came upon an abandoned Civilian Conservation Corps work camp at Antelope Springs, thirty-eight miles west of the center. At the foot of Mount Swasey and "walled in on three sides by the abrupt mountain slopes," the site was "a beautiful and majestic amphitheater" with running mountain water and grounds for sleeping, cooking, and recreation. The US Department of the Interior's Grazing Service allowed the WRA to occupy the land during the summer of 1943 and use all of its facilities. During that time, 198 boys and 140 girls attended camp, including four different Boy Scout troops, a YMCA group, and two Girl Reserves groups. They all enjoyed a program of swimming, hiking, fossil-hunting, nature study, scavenger hunts, sports, and astronomy. In addition, eighty-seven Cub Scouts and ninety-three Brownies made day trips.[71]

While the Topaz summer camp program was part of a larger summer activities program for school-age children, its goals aligned with the larger philosophy behind the Boy Scouts: "improvement of physical and mental health" and "stimulation of nature interest," as well as "civic betterment" and "opportunity for self-expression." In camping in the shadow of Utah's scenic mountains, children escaped the confines of camp. At the same time, they were expected to follow camp rules, clean the facilities, participate in group activities, and cooperate with the running of the camp.[72] In the process, campers would become happier, healthier children and better citizens who cared about their community and their fellow campers.

But these benefits were not open to all Japanese American youth. At Manzanar, scouts could only camp within center boundaries at Reynold's

Ranch, which ultimately curbed the success of the scouting program there. As one Nisei leader explained, "The trouble is that you are limited in what you can do in a place like this. The kids want to take overnight hikes like the other scout troops do. They want to take trips up into the hills for nature study. We haven't got the inducements for them."[73] This leader suggested that scouting was synonymous with camping, and without camping, Boy Scout membership would languish. Likewise, Gila River scouts had few opportunities to camp outside of boundaries. When the WRA arranged to use a YMCA and an Episcopal church camp near Prescott to accommodate about four hundred Boy Scouts, Girl Scouts, and Girl Reserves, Arizona governor Sidney Osborn "objected very strenuously 'for the safety of the children.'" The WRA canceled its plans, which brought "great sorrow and distress to the youngsters."[74]

Even at Topaz, where the scouting program was strong, scouts had to abide by strict regulations for overnight outings. They had to secure a permit at least one week in advance, with names and addresses of each member of the group, the location of the camp site, and the time of departure and return.[75] Scouting opened up opportunities for Japanese American youth and allowed them to participate in a quintessentially American activity, but their movements remained restricted and monitored.

"A More Livable Habitat": Creating Gardens, Planting Greenery

Hiking, swimming, fishing, and scouting allowed Japanese Americans to engage with their local surroundings, but they did little to actually change them. Ornamental gardening, on the other hand, gave detainees considerable power to transform the environment. Mostly Issei gardeners helped to landscape wide swaths of the camps, designing parks and planting greenery around public buildings and personal barracks in an effort to beautify the camps and mitigate dust and heat.[76] In the process, ornamental gardening became a meaningful outdoor activity. As an article in the *Minidoka Irrigator* explained, "We hadn't learned to appreciate the good that comes with Nature—until Minidoka. . . . A struggling green shoot became a dear thing to be coddled and petted."[77] As they made the desert bloom, the camps came to reflect their expanded environmental knowledge of the arid surroundings and their visions of beauty. Detainees still had to navigate WRA regulations, but they asserted more control over the conditions of their confinement and changed oppressive landscapes into more "survivable places."[78]

It is not surprising that many Japanese Americans chose to grow things when they arrived at the camps. Dating back to the early twentieth century, many Issei worked as gardeners on the West Coast, gaining the reputation as "the finest in garden maintenance." In the two decades preceding World War II, Japanese Americans made up 70 to 80 percent of all gardeners in the Southern California region. This was an appealing occupation because it did not require large capital investment or special skills, provided steady income, and brought minimal competition from whites.[79] Topaz, Manzanar, and Gila River confined the largest number of individuals involved in a prewar "gardener occupation," with 928, 902, and 761, respectively. This category included gardeners, groundskeepers, nursery owners, flower growers, nursery and landscaping laborers, dayworkers, housemen, and yardmen.[80] Only a small percentage of these individuals constructed camp gardens, but they brought important skills to the task.

Gardens quickly dotted several areas of the camps. Some detainees worked as volunteers or paid WRA employees to landscape public areas, such as the camp entrances, administrative buildings, and hospitals. When they received remuneration, gardening could not be considered a purely recreational activity. Nonetheless, it provided welcome opportunities for detainees to embrace nature and improve their surroundings. They also worked together to construct mess hall gardens, which were "something pleasant to look at" while they waited in line before each meal.[81] The most common gardens were the smaller plots that adorned individual barrack entries and "front yards," the open areas between facing barracks. Together, they showcased "the craft and skill of the resident and embellish[ed] both the barracks and the community space."[82]

The WRA maintained that these material improvements would help the camps lose "much of their pioneer appearance and character." In fact, they would resemble "an ordinary American city of 10,000 or 15,000 inhabitants."[83] To reinforce this transformation, Topaz officials even named the north-south streets after trees (Cottonwood, Willow, Poplar) and the east-west roads after gemstones (Tourmaline, Jasper, Agate).[84] Such misleading place names, of course, were not nearly as important as real changes on the ground. At Gila River, E. R. Fryer, who served as acting project director before becoming a regional WRA director, emphasized that the camp should reflect "the personal pride of those who have their homes here and who want this community to blend with the natural beauty of its surroundings."[85] Japanese Americans' environmental enhancements would hopefully mitigate their discontent and make their incarceration seem more benign.[86]

Landscaping efforts often began with Japanese American initiative and volunteer labor. At Gila River, a group of eleven gardeners started planting at Butte's administrative office on October 3, 1942, which was followed by volunteers in block 58 planting around their mess hall. According to Superintendent of Grounds E. W. Nichols, "Other blocks in rapid succession began the planned development of their mess halls. Upon completion of these buildings, other units within the block were landscaped." Soon, the Gila River administration hired additional gardeners to supervise the block work and "consolidate their plans toward a uniform design." These basic plans were also adopted at Canal camp. By the end of December 1942, the Grounds Section employed ninety-nine detainees and two white supervisors, and they had planted over 47,000 flower plants and 14,000 pounds of grass seed.[87] During the first quarter of 1943, they planted 960 trees and 8,650 pounds of grass seed and built twelve basketball courts, three tennis courts, eight baseball diamonds, and five playgrounds.[88]

Two nurseries at Gila River, operated by the Farm Division, supplied flowers, trees, and shrubs, with many species propagated from stocks of seed and plants brought by detainees who had operated nurseries in California. According to one WRA report, they were initially wary of the extreme Arizona heat. But once lath houses were made from scrap lumber to provide shade, "to their joy they found that the nursery plants thrived very well here." Trees, shrubs, and bedding plants from the nurseries were distributed to the Public Works Division for "center beautification." Detainees took "great pride" in this growth, which did "much to nullify the otherwise drab appearance of the camp." In fact, those who had visited other camps commented that Gila had a "better general appearance" because it had more "green plant life."[89]

Landscaping plans were just as ambitious at Topaz. Roscoe Bell, head of the agricultural division, announced a program for "community beautification" that called for trees, shrubs, lawns, and athletic fields. In September 1942, he explained that each block would have its own "miniature park" in the area opposite the recreation hall. The trees, shrubs, and lawns would be "laid out in accordance with the desires of the residents on the block. Considerable leeway is being provided for the expression of individual initiative and taste, and the final appearance of the City will depend largely upon the amount of effort the residents are willing to expend for beautification." The greenery and improved roads would also help to eliminate the dust clouds that "plague the City."[90] By the following month, crews were building a nursery on a ten-acre site next to the southwestern edge of the recreation field to propagate vegetables and plants.[91]

FIGURE 6.3 Paul S. Goya, a nurseryman from Sierra Madre, California, tending to summer sweet peas, April 24, 1943. He was in charge of the flowers grown at the Gila River nursery. Photograph by Francis Stewart. Courtesy of the National Archives and Records Administration.

Given the arid conditions at most camps, water was crucial to gardening and landscaping projects. At Minidoka, water came from the North Side Canal, designated for fire protection, dust abatement, and gardens and landscaping.[92] The camp was later divided into four sections, with two men overseeing each section to deliver water to the blocks according to a fixed schedule. These efforts soon paid off. In April 1944, camp official William Maxey noted, "Grass which has been planted in the boulevard areas around each block now has attained a good stand almost everywhere. Irrigation of those areas once each week will greatly improve the appearance of the center and will aid materially in controlling dust and mud."[93]

Minidoka benefited from the fact that it was located on Bureau of Reclamation land and was thus served by irrigation canals, but this was not the case at Topaz. Officials there had to provide landscaping water in other ways. In August 1943, Henry Watson, senior engineer, announced "immediate steps" to build irrigation ditches and road crosses for landscaping

FIGURE 6.4 To beautify Topaz, Japanese American workers prepared to move this tree to an area near the hospital, October 16, 1942. Photograph by Tom Parker. Courtesy of the National Archives and Records Administration.

areas north of the project and in between the barracks and administrative offices. He noted that it was "important that we have irrigation water for the resident blocks by next spring for gardens and lawns."[94] Roscoe Bell then pronounced that workers would dig ditches in the fall and winter to bring water to the resident area "so that gardens and lawns may be green next summer."[95]

Landscaping projects also benefited from the expertise of detainee gardeners who adapted their skills to new environmental conditions. Akira Nishi, who worked for thirty years cross-breeding roses from his San Fernando, California, nursery, continued his trade at Manzanar. He started with about four thousand wild Sierra roses, known as Maneta rose bushes, and grafted buds from domestic varieties onto them. His hope was that using the "rugged local plants" as the base would help the roses to "weather withering hot summers and cold winters."[96]

In addition, WRA officials tapped into the expertise of locals who were familiar with growing conditions. In October 1942, Roscoe Bell wrote to

J. Whitney Ford, extension forester at the Utah State Agricultural College, to obtain trees and shrubs that would be adapted to the soil and climactic conditions of the area so that "the residents of the city will be enabled to improve their surroundings during the course of their stay in the Relocation Center." According to Bell, many skilled gardeners at Topaz were "greatly interested in landscaping and improving the ground. I am sure that any plant materials which could be furnished from the college nursery will serve as a demonstration of what can be done through careful and skillful handling."[97] It is unclear if Topaz received plants and shrubs from the college, but it did obtain 365 trees valued at almost four hundred dollars from D. Stevens and Company at no cost other than labor required to move the trees to the center. Bell thanked William J. Starley of D. Stevens, noting, "You can well appreciate how welcome these trees are when they are planted throughout the city. A little touch of green makes a lot of difference in the way people feel."[98]

Donations from nearby residents gave gardeners a good idea of what grew in these particular locales, but Topaz detainees also visited private gardens and the high school in nearby Delta. At the high school, they saw Japanese creepers, red cedar, lilacs, junipers, and various perennials and annuals "growing vigorously." They also visited the garden of Mrs. Ward Moody. According to Topaz landscape architect Tom Takaki, Moody's garden "probably surpasses the ordinary California gardens of equal designs in planning and attractiveness."[99] While the conditions were not as temperate as their homes in the San Francisco Bay Area, the gardeners saw that they could still beautify and improve the appearance of the camp.

Soon after these visits, landscaping began to occur at a brisk pace at Topaz. By mid-November 1942, Japanese Americans had planted four large junipers, found on government land west of camp, around the hospital and thirteen smaller ones outside of two administration buildings. On other field trips, they returned with more than one thousand tamarisk shrubs from Clear Lake, about forty miles away. The landscape department ordered an additional fifty-five hundred trees and two thousand shrubs, including five black locusts and twenty-nine hundred Russian olives.[100] A month later, they found Liberian elms, varying in height from thirteen to forty feet, which they dug up and planted around the public buildings. They also found tamarisks, willow, Carolina poplar, and green ash trees.[101] As Bell explained, "It is the aim and hope of the landscape group that we might have some 'green' all the year around. If we can, even to a slight degree tame this wild, barren desert . . . , [our] efforts shall not have been in vain."[102]

Some gardeners wanted to encourage more widespread participation in landscaping efforts. In November 1942, Tom Takaki and the Topaz Community Activities section sponsored "Arbor Week" to teach residents how to garden and plant shrubs in the area surrounding each block.[103] Gardeners also obtained 4,000 willow saplings, with each block receiving 150. According to one WRA report, Arbor Week was a testament to detainees' initiative and perseverance in confronting "unfavorable climatical and soil conditions." Indeed, the environmental challenges they encountered were significant: poor drainage, alkaline soil, a constant threat of freezing, and the need to irrigate with open ditches.[104] But they were still able to implement their visions. Acting Project Reports chief Frank S. Twohey concluded that the new greenery did "much toward banishing the 'bare' look of the project and the flat monotony of the land."[105]

Camp administrators eagerly publicized Japanese American efforts to green the desert, from planting patches of grass to creating ornamental gardens. Manzanar project reports, typically sent weekly to the WRA's Washington, DC office, documented this transformation. In June 1942, while chatting from their stoops in the evenings, residents of barracks 12 and 13 on block 6 decided to plant lawns. After receiving permission from the administration, they prepared the soil and sprinkled grass seed ordered from Sears and Roebuck. By the end of July, residents had planted over one hundred lawns between barracks, and administrators expected "that nearly half of the Center will be landscaped with lawns before winter." Visitors even "ohed and ahed with sincere admiration" of the greenery.[106] One month later, the number of lawns doubled to over two hundred, made possible by the distribution of sixty tons of lawn seed.[107]

Likewise, a Minidoka project report praised gardening efforts and emphasized the satisfaction Japanese Americans derived from their transformations to the land. Before they arrived from "the green hillsides and valleys of the coast," Minidoka was "dessicated [sic], drab and dusty." Because "life is not worth living for these people unless they have some green to cultivate," they began collecting mosses, cattails, reeds, willow, cactus, bunchgrass, and rocks. Singling out Tomo Akiyama, the report detailed how he built a steep mound to represent a hill, which leveled into a pond surrounded by willow, swamp grass, and other plants. He even made a "little natural pagoda" out of flat rocks. Until Akiyama could return to his home in Seattle, the report explained, "He will spend many happy hours with his garden."[108]

Yasusuke Kogita's rock garden at Minidoka also helped him endure his confinement. A willow tree from Seattle shaded his garden, but he collected

FIGURE 6.5 Japanese Americans raking the soil for a barrack garden at Minidoka, c. 1943–1945. Courtesy of the Bigelow Family Collection, Densho Digital Repository, ddr-densho-156-38.

many materials nearby. He wandered the area for two months to gather volcanic rocks, fashioning a hand cart with scrap wood and water pipes to haul them back to camp. Native flora, perennials and annuals grown from seed, and two ponds populated with fish from a nearby stream also adorned his garden. His sons, Ted and Paul Kogita, later explained that the garden was profoundly important to their father because it allowed him to tune everything out and provided him with something he could control.[109] For Issei men like Kogita, having something to control was important, as their social power weakened when the Nisei assumed leadership positions in the camps.[110] Ironically, this garden—created in oppressive circumstances—also prompted Kogita to forge a deep connection to his place of incarceration.

While Akiyama and Kogita made do with mostly local materials, Francis Miosaku Uyematsu transplanted pieces of the Pacific Coast to the desert. A successful nurseryman in Montebello and Sierra Madre, California, he donated about five hundred flowering cherry trees, twenty wisterias, camellias, and various other plants to Manzanar and shipped them at his own expense. Project director Ralph Merritt allowed Uyematsu to travel back to his business, Star Nursery, to collect his prized flora and to care for the trees and plants for the duration. He described the wisteria as "one of the most beautiful among flowering plants" and maintained that the Manzanar soil was "very suitable" for this plant. According to his granddaughter Amy Uyematsu, "He really wanted to share his magical touch with plants with his community."[111]

The camp communities often cherished the beautiful gardens that detainees cultivated. As an article in the *Topaz Times* explained, "We, who have lived near the rolling green hills of California with its lush poppies and wild plants, the scented gardens, immaculate lawns and thriving flower beds of the bay area, yearn for Nature's expression of greenery."[112] Given this longing, Topaz detainee Toyo Suyemoto explained, "The non-gardeners did appreciate the efforts of the others. They would saunter around the block, occasionally to other blocks, to see the gardens and comment encouragingly about the plantings. The evacuees favored making Topaz a more livable habitat."[113]

Perhaps the most famous and elaborate garden was Manzanar's Merritt Park. With WRA sponsorship, Kuichiro Nishi, older brother of fellow gardener Akira Nishi, led a group of landscape architects, nursery owners, and gardeners to design and build the Japanese-style garden. In addition to ponds, bridges, and a teahouse, they installed a rock that resembled a turtle, which symbolized "endurance, long life, and reflection" in Japanese tradition. Upon its completion, Merritt Park became "the most photographed place within the barbed wire fence," as one could be pictured "in a beautiful setting without a backdrop of tarpapered barracks."[114] In his dedication, inscribed on a wooden sign in the teahouse, Nishi wrote, "Although we were ushered in this place

FIGURE 6.6 Yasusuke Kogita's garden, no date. Courtesy of the National Archives and Records Administration, Densho Digital Repository, ddr-densho-37-737.

with the breaking of friendly relations between the two countries, we have come to enjoy this qui[et], peaceful place."[115] As Hank Umemoto recalled, it was at Merritt Park where detainees "patiently dreamt of better days to come amid the serenity and beauty of gardens and ponds with cascading waterfalls and carp whirling in the waters under black locust trees."[116]

Merritt Garden—like many other barrack gardens—was a Japanese-style garden that included the use of rocks, water, and plants, arranged asymmetrically, to "depict nature in miniature." Barrack gardens of all sizes fit these basic criteria and incorporated other traditional elements, from stepping stones and lanterns to ponds and islands.[117] For instance, at Gila River, JERS fieldworker Yataro Okuno observed carp ponds surrounded by shrubs and cactus planted between rocks and stone lanterns fashioned from "fancy shaped stones which must be gathered through many tiresome trips to the neighboring mountains."[118] However, gardens in the administrative areas did not typically have these characteristics and adopted more of a military style, with expansive lawns and rocks arranged in straight lines. The Japanese style was reserved for residential areas where it boldly asserted gardeners' Japanese heritage.[119]

FIGURE 6.7 Merritt Park, 1943. Photograph by Ansel Adams. Courtesy of the Library of Congress, Prints & Photographs Division, LC-A351-3-M-11.

The WRA sometimes faced criticism for the camp gardens, but mainly for their perceived expense. A June 1942 editorial in the *Inyo Independent* asked why Manzanar detainees were allowed to travel "almost a hundred miles round trip" to procure a Joshua tree when nearby residents were participating in a national scrap rubber drive. "Maybe it's more worthwhile to get Joshua Trees by driving many miles on valuable rubber than it is to conserve rubber," the editorial concluded sarcastically.[120] The Joshua tree in question was likely for one of the administrative area gardens, as the WRA provided financial support only for landscaping in public areas. For gardens in residential blocks, WRA Administrative Instruction No. 89 mandated that they "be carried out with materials and labor provided by the residents and without cost to the Authority; except that surplus materials may be made available by the Project Director for such purposes."[121] Nonetheless, the tenor of the editorial suggested that Japanese Americans were being profligate with scarce wartime resources in order to beautify the camps. In response to similar complaints, R. S. Davidson, Minidoka's Agricultural Division chief, made a point to emphasize that the camp's landscaping would use considerable nursery stock, seeds, cuttings, and bulbs donated from nearby towns. He explained, "The impression we are attempting to make upon the general public is that expenses for non-essential items will be held to the minimum."[122]

Much as with the hikers and swimmers, the WRA also had to make sure that gardeners adhered to regulations and heeded camp boundaries. These issues came to head when seven gardeners involved with Manzanar's Merritt Park were caught "out of bounds" on their way to get a pine tree. Ironically, project director Ralph Merritt, the park's namesake, presided over a hearing and emphasized that their infraction was a serious offense. All seven men were ineligible for passes for three months, and Kuichiro Nishi had to report to the Internal Police Station weekly. While there was confusion as to where the crew had been allowed to go, Nishi's greatest concern was the pine tree, which he had to abandon when the military police found him. Merritt responded that he would send someone else to pick it up. Photographs indicate that the coveted tree was later transplanted to Merritt Park.[123]

WRA officials found themselves in a quandary. The beautification of the camps made them appear less austere. Green lawns, billowing trees, and flowering shrubs also provided evidence that detainees were engaged and productive. But these activities could also be perceived as rather trivial and unnecessary when men were fighting overseas. In a sense, then, the camps could not be too attractive. Given suspicions surrounding Japanese Americans, WRA officials also had to reinforce regulations at the expense of garden collecting activities. For their part, Japanese American gardeners proceeded with their plans on shoestring budgets and did not seem concerned about outside perceptions. Refusing to see the land solely as an oppressive force, they tried to make the camps beautiful or at least comforting and more familiar.

Some scholars have argued that the gardens were expressions of defiance, "a subversive response to internment, where individual and collective gestures were a way of denying the camp administration and environment," in the words of Kenneth Helphand.[124] However, most gardeners did not so much deny the WRA and their natural surroundings as negotiate with or try to assert control over them for their own purposes. In the process, the gardens became "restorative agents" that provided Japanese Americans with pockets of beauty and serenity amid the most oppressive circumstances.[125]

* * *

While outdoor recreation was often limited in scope, WRA officials often viewed these environmental activities as tools to reinforce the incarceration of Japanese Americans. If detainees enjoyed themselves in the outdoors, they would have fewer reasons to object to their confinement. If Japanese American youth became perceived as more "American" through scouting, their incarceration might actually aid in their assimilation. And if the camps really did come to look like an "ordinary American city" with landscaped streets and flower gardens, this wartime policy might not appear abnormal or inconsistent with wartime rhetoric. But arguably of greater significance were the benefits Japanese Americans derived from their outdoor activities. Some came to recognize the beauty of the environment and were rejuvenated by their brief escapes from the barracks. Isolating landscapes became therapeutic, emboldening, and even pleasurable.

Yet outdoor recreation sometimes reinforced the presence of the barbed wire fence and reaffirmed Japanese Americans' confined status. WRA officials told them when and where they could go hiking or swimming or collecting flora—whether they could go beyond the barbed wire or had to remain confined within. As Minidoka's ice-skating ring demonstrated, the barbed wire fences were human impositions on the landscape, ropes of twisted, sharp metal that had little bearing on natural forces. But Japanese Americans could not completely ignore them, lest they incur harm and censure. Over time, WRA officials gave detainees more autonomy. Still, Japanese Americans were taking risks—albeit decreasing—when they left camp without permission. True freedom remained elusive.

In the end, outdoor recreation attained an empowering influence. When Yataro Okuno wrote about fishing at Gila River, he explained that the carp was associated with many important stories and traditions in Japan. It was understood to be a strong fish that was able to swim against the current. He elaborated, "It is an emblem of an undaunted spirit to get over any hardship which may come in front of you." As he perused the barrack gardens and saw fanciful ponds stocked with carp, Okuno noted, "I like to stop very often to watch them—the emblem of undaunted spirit."[126] He seemed to liken the detainees to the carp and suggested that perhaps they drew inspiration from the very fish that they had caught and then placed in their ornamental gardens. Ultimately, this "undaunted spirit" remained indispensable when Japanese Americans were displaced yet again at the end of the war.

7

Dispersal, Resettlement, Return

AFTER LIVING IN the Granada Relocation Center for less than one year, the Sato family, originally from Stockton, California, resettled in Keenesburg, Colorado, to farm. While several California neighbors had already returned to the coast by the fall of 1946, Mr. Sato was unsure if his family would join them because of the unfavorable living and farming conditions. Still, he felt a close connection to the Golden State. He explained, "Regardless of the obstacles one likes to return to familiar places. For instance, the native farmers don't mind the severe winter here in Colorado, but a native farmer who visited Central California returned here and told me he couldn't stand the heat and the summer there." Sato was accustomed to the Stockton weather as well as "the mountains, the rivers, and the place in general. Somehow all these familiar experiences and places make us feel that 'this is home.'" Keenesburg had rich soil, but "with the market and the weather against us I don't see how we can continue for very long."[1]

Sato's story paralleled that of Kazutoshi Mayeda, whose family cultivated a celery farm in Southern California before spending the war years in Manzanar. In 1945, they resettled in Brigham City, Utah, where they first worked at the Brigham City Laundry and Dry Cleaning Company. His uncle, however, wanted to farm again, so they moved to American Fork, Utah, in 1946. They planted onions, cabbage, and celery, but the experience was "a fiasco." A frost hit during the harvest and destroyed the cabbage crop. The price was too low on celery to make money. Mayeda noted, "If it were not for the onions, we would have been poverty stricken. The summer's hard labor was all for naught." Forced to return to the Brigham City laundry, he lived in a one-bedroom apartment with his mother. "I can not help but wonder what might have been, if only, we were allowed to live in Venice, California," he lamented.[2]

Like many other former detainees, Sato and Mayeda tried to start anew in the inland West after the war. In the process, they discovered that their Pacific Coast roots distinguished them from Japanese Americans who already lived in these areas. Divergent perceptions of the environment fed these differences, as "native" Japanese Americans bristled at former detainees' antipathy for and unfamiliarity with the new natural surroundings. The social and environmental conditions in the interior thus stood as a final barrier to freedom in the wake of American victory. Many Pacific Coast Japanese simply bided their time and made plans to return home.

Those who headed west directly from the camps also encountered numerous challenges. As one WRA report explained, the Issei in particular were uncertain "how they could reestablish the broken economic systems on which their old communities rested."[3] For many former detainees, these economic systems were firmly embedded in natural resource industries. In their absence, production costs had skyrocketed, and business practices had changed. Land had often been neglected. In some cases, hostile neighbors tried to prevent detainees' return with intimidation and violence. The postwar years revealed many stories of loss, anger, and rejection and of dreams deferred or abandoned.

It would be easy to conclude the environmental history of incarceration with the end of the war, the closing of the camps, and the departure of the last detainees. But that would imply that there was no environmental component to their dispersal from the camps, their resettlement in the interior, or their return to the Pacific Coast. On the contrary, the environment continued to play an important, if overlooked, role during the postwar years, particularly for Japanese Americans involved with agriculture. Their confinement was officially over, but they confronted yet another environmental displacement. Once again, their experiences were structured by social inequalities and environmental limits.

"Your Transition Back to Private Life": Relocation and the Opening of the Pacific Coast

The WRA's relocation program, which allowed detainees to leave the camps and take jobs outside of the Pacific Coast, initiated the process of dispersal. It became a major undertaking, with field offices extending from the Rocky Mountains to the eastern seaboard. Agents at these offices helped Japanese Americans find housing and jobs while preparing the receiving communities for their arrival. They encouraged Japanese Americans to establish them-selves, make friends, and develop a "normal, satisfying life for yourself and your family," in order to "create a public attitude favorable to yourself and to other Americans of Japanese ancestry." One WRA pamphlet explained, "In a sense, you are an 'ambassador' for the entire group of evacuated people. If you keep this thought in mind, your own relocation is pretty likely to be a success from every point of view."[4] The WRA also encouraged resettlement in small groups, widely dispersed so as to ensure integration and acceptance into American society and preclude the creation of insular "Little Tokyos." Of nearly 30,000 people who resettled before January 1, 1945, Illinois recorded the highest number of 7,652, with 6,599 going to Chicago alone. Colorado, Ohio, Utah, Idaho, and Michigan also had sizable numbers of resettlers, with 3,185, 2,854, 2,427, 2,084, and 1,990, respectively.[5]

The WRA was eager to publicize stories of successful resettlement. One press release told the story of Mickey and Amy Furuta, newlyweds and vege-table farmers from California who made their way to Milford Center, Ohio. It noted, "Like many others, they awaited the opportunity to prove their loyalty to the United States by removing to parts of the country where the Japanese population was less concentrated and the chance for fruitful work would be greater." There, they worked on Cone Howard's one-thousand-acre farm. According to the press release, Howard "readily agreed" to use Japanese American labor, while the Furutas "felt no resentment against their govern-ment for their condition into which they had been thrust by the war." The two families enjoyed "an atmosphere of friendly cooperation" that proved "that Americans, of whatever race or color, determined to work together can achieve wonders."[6]

But this feel-good story obscured significant anti-Japanese sentiment. New York City mayor Fiorello H. LaGuardia, for instance, maintained that "it is manifestly unfair to turn these people loose, and because the Western states do not want them back, to force them upon New York City."[7] Similarly, near Hamburg, Iowa, Norman Kishi, Sam Mayeda, and T. F. Konno tried to purchase 612 acres of farmland, only to be rebuffed by local residents who passed a resolution, sent to Dillon Myer, protesting the settlement of any person of Japanese ancestry in their community. While WRA officials met with community leaders, the would-be farmers eventually abandoned their transaction and never settled in Iowa.[8] Even in Chicago, Japanese Americans escaped the worst of the city's racism because they were not black, but they still faced limited housing and job opportunities.[9]

The WRA's relocation program accelerated with the reopening of the Pacific Coast to people of Japanese ancestry. On December 17, 1944, General Henry C. Pratt, new head of the Western Defense Command, announced the end of the exclusion of Japanese Americans beginning January 2, 1945. He did, however, retain the right to exclude certain individuals from the coast.[10] According to Secretary of the Interior Harold Ickes's press release— the Department of the Interior had assumed control over the WRA in 1944—this announcement meant that the relocation program expanded to "cover the entire country including the West Coast. It most definitely does *not* mean that there will be a hasty mass movement of all evacuees back to the coastal area." While he expressed the WRA's continued commitment to relocating Japanese Americans to other parts of the United States, he offered aid to those "who prefer to exercise their legal and moral right to return to the West Coast." He called the detainees "casualties of war" and urged every American "to do everything he can to make easier the return to normal life of these people who have been cleared by the Army authorities. By our conduct towards them we will be judged by all of the people of the world."[11]

Despite Ickes's public support for Japanese Americans' efforts to settle anywhere in the nation, he preferred that they avoid the Pacific Coast. In a letter to the remaining detainees, he recognized their sacrifices and praised "the patience and understanding which the great majority of you have displayed as cooperative and law-abiding residents of relocation centers." He then noted that the people who had already left the camps had proven that "opportunity, acceptance and personal satisfaction may be yours in states other than those which were your former homes." In fact, he believed that "a wider opportunity, for most of you, lies in states east of the Sierra Nevadas [*sic*], where your friends, and in many instances members of your families, are establishing new and successful homes." Of course, he also assured the detainees that "regardless of where you finally decide to relocate," the WRA would "make every reasonable effort to facilitate your transition back to private life."[12] Still, Ickes reiterated his preference behind the scenes. In a memorandum to WRA staff, he asked them to remember the importance of "carrying out the desire of the President to continue and intensify the effort to relocate as many of these people as possible in places other than the West Coast area."[13]

Dillon Myer, however, was less concerned about a mass return than with the state of mind of the remaining Japanese Americans. In a confidential letter to the project directors, he explained that individuals and families would be on their own and would be uncertain of what awaited them. As a result, "We cannot expect therefore that the opening of the Coast will be greeted with joy and determination by more than a small minority. For the great majority it will mean an upset of the relative security they have adjusted themselves to during the past two and a half years. The definite knowledge that the centers will be closed in the near future will mean the necessity for concrete planning, for decision—but still in a context of some uncertainty." He warned the directors that they might be dealing with "a disturbed and upset community," made up of some individuals who had hoped to stay in the centers until the war ended. Thus, he encouraged them to provide "vigilant" and "persistent" leadership, establish good communication, and clarify WRA services.[14]

The next day, Myers provided the project directors with more specific instructions. He was adamant that they quickly empty the camps, as he wanted to get the Japanese Americans resettled while there was still demand for their labor. He explained, "As we approach the end of the war, these opportunities will not be so plentiful. . . . It will be almost impossible if evacuees have to compete with returning soldiers and with other people who may be seeking adjustment during the reconversion period." Myers also told the directors to discourage detainees who wanted to regain possession of their land on the coast from breaking leases or instituting legal proceedings to eject tenants. "It will certainly result in adverse publicity and make the job of orderly resettlement more difficult, not only for the individual concerned but for other evacuees," he concluded.[15]

Japanese Americans' precarious status was evident when Harumi Iwakiri Serata's father began to consider a return to his hometown of Fife, Washington, an agricultural area south of Seattle. Upon the announcement that the Pacific Coast had been reopened, he traveled from Minidoka to Tacoma, Washington, with a group of other men in order to assess the housing and labor situation. After he received a threatening phone call, he decided to return to Minidoka the next day. That unpleasant encounter convinced Serata's father that they could not return directly to Fife. He instead moved his family to Eden, Idaho, where they all worked on local farms to save money for their eventual return to Washington.[16]

Lewis Hatch in the Puyallup Valley described a similar situation to the Tanaka family. In February 1945, Ed Tanaka wrote to Hatch and inquired, "How is the people's opinion towards the Japanese people out that way."[17] Hatch replied that anti-Japanese sentiment was strong in the farming areas of Puget Sound, especially where Japanese owned land. He went on to relate an incident of arson and "white people trying to make life miserable" for returning Japanese. If Tanaka's sons wanted to visit, he did not expect them to be physically harmed, but they would have to endure insults and name

calling. In addition to social hostility, Hatch also informed Tanaka that land
to purchase was expensive, and land for rent was scarce and "not of very good
quality."[18] The family may have taken Hatch's assessment to heart. In January
1946, they were living in Pocatello, Idaho.[19]

WRA officials also tried to investigate the situation on the Pacific Coast,
particularly with regard to agricultural opportunities. At the beginning of
August 1945, they sent a query to the camps, asking how many detainees
wanted to return to the Los Angeles area to engage in agriculture; 263 families
and 154 single people responded affirmatively. Meanwhile, E. H. Reed of the
WRA's agricultural section traveled around Southern California, inquiring
about supplies, credit, and marketing for returning farmers and gathering
leads on job opportunities. While some growers were amenable to employing
Japanese Americans, others, like Rae Koenig of Chula Vista, noted "that a
white man could not compete with them and that if they returned and went
into the vegetable business again, he would quit farming." In the Imperial
Valley, many people wanted to hire former detainees, but were waiting for the

FIGURE 7.1 The graffiti on this Seattle home were indicative of the larger anti-Japanese
climate encountered by many Japanese Americans who returned to the Pacific Coast, May
29, 1945. Courtesy of the Seattle Post-Intelligencer Collection, Museum of History and
Industry, Seattle.

approval of the Imperial Valley Farmers Association, which had voiced firm opposition to their return.[20]

With dubious options for resettlement, Japanese Americans left the camps slowly at first, then more swiftly as the closing dates neared. Not surprisingly, some detainees did not want to leave. When Myer met a group of elderly men who worked on the Minidoka farm crew, they told him that they liked it there and were going to stay.[21] George Nakagawa's family was among the last to leave Heart Mountain because neither of his parents "had any inkling of what to do." His father had been a tenant farmer in Washington before the war and had "nowhere to go and nothing to go back to."[22] By late February 1945, only 539 people had left the camps and returned to the Pacific Coast. An additional 1,200 had decided to head to the interior West, the Midwest, and the eastern seaboard.[23] The pace of departure picked up considerably in the following months. By July 1945, 45,000 Japanese Americans had left the relocation centers.[24] The WRA gave twenty-five dollars to each individual—families received fifty dollars—paid for train fare, and shipped personal effects to their destination. Of the 75,000 individuals who left the camps after January 1, 1945, over two-thirds returned to California, Oregon, and Washington. Tule Lake remained open until March 1946, but the other camps were closed by the end of 1945.[25]

"One Can Get Along": Resettlement in the Interior West

Although Japanese Americans were free to return to the coast in 1945, many remained in the nation's interior. Colorado was a popular destination for those with agricultural backgrounds. In 1946, an estimated thirty-two hundred people of Japanese ancestry lived in Colorado's rural regions, half of them former detainees.[26] From August to November 1946, Toshio Yatsushiro, a sociologist who conducted wartime research for the Bureau of Sociological Research at the Poston camp, traveled all over the state to interview some of these individuals, both former California farmers as well as "natives"—Japanese American residents of Colorado who had not been subject to removal and confinement.[27] He was part of a team of fieldworkers gathering information for the War Agency Liquidation Unit, a federal agency that was finishing the work of the WRA following its termination in June 1946. The product of their work was *People in Motion: The Postwar Adjustment of the Evacuated Japanese Americans*, published in 1947.[28]

People in Motion detailed regional variations in the resettlement process, but the authors also made important generalizations. "The most notable characteristic of the evacuated Japanese Americans is a feeling of unsettledness, of having unanswered questions concerning location, economic activity and social adjustment," the authors asserted.[29] Indeed, former detainees felt some trepidation and anxiety wherever they went. Yatsushiro's conversations also revealed that environmental factors—from the challenges of farming under new conditions to a powerful longing for the Pacific Coast—added to their resettlement difficulties in the Rocky Mountain state. In other words, that "feeling of unsettledness" had a significant environmental dimension for some Japanese Americans.

Whether they came to the interior West during or immediately after the war, former Far Westerners immediately noticed the different farming strategies. Sam Sameshima, originally from Salinas, California, noted, "You know, Colorado farming is very different from California farming. In California the farmers use big machinery and equipment and farm on a big scale, but here the farmers use smaller machinery and equipment." He also explained that California farmers would often gamble on one crop, "while here in Colorado a farmer just can't take that gamble, as you can easily lose everything for the year. Since I have been farming in Colorado I have learned to farm according to the farm methods here. There are good reasons why farmers farm the way they do here. Farming in Colorado, in general, isn't too bad."[30]

For Sameshima and others, taking gambles was unadvisable because of the weather. Roy Uyesaka, originally from Torrance, California, farmed in Greeley, Colorado, and explained: "The weather here is the greatest problem. Boy, if the hail hits your farm you're wiped out for the year. I've had three years of bad luck with weather, and this is too much for me. I'm definitely pulling out of here. . . . I'm fed up with this Colorado weather. . . . The first chance I have I'm going to hit for California."[31] Reverend K. Sasaki, pastor of Denver's Community Methodist Church, added that the weather bred vulnerability, citing a recent hailstorm that destroyed crops in Brighton, Greeley, and Ft. Lupton. Sasaki concluded, "In California the weather is not a problem. They can farm practically year round and the risk is not as great."[32] Roy Nakano, a Nisei journalist at the *Denver Post*, believed that Californians had to adjust their methods and "learn to play along with the weather instead of trying to fight it."[33]

In addition, overproduction plagued agricultural markets after the war.[34] George Ohashi's parents-in-law—who once farmed 300 acres in Guadalupe,

California—tilled about 160 acres of vegetables in Ft. Lupton. They were doing "satisfactorily," but could not make very much money when prices for onions were only twenty-five cents per sack.[35] Hitoshige Okabe, who worked at a produce packing shed, added, "Farming here is a waste [of] time. . . . The farmer here hasn't got [a] chance. He farms and harvest[s] his crops, but he can't sell anything until the shipper calls him up on the phone and requests certain farm products. . . . Now out in California . . . [t]he farmer is sure to sell his products. There's a bigger market demand there."[36]

To address these challenges, former California farmers had varied advice. Mr. S. Kobayashi, an Issei sugar beet farmer from Stockton who began farming in Keenesburg during the war, recommended farming on a small scale using family labor. As Yatsushiro explained, "This is to insure the farmer from incurring any big loss, especially here in Colorado where farming is comparatively risky with weather so unpredictable and the market not always good. If one engaged in big scale farming and hired many paid laborers, his loss will be proportionately bigger if the hail hits his farm or if the market is so poor that it is unprofitable to sell his crops." With small family farms, the only loss was "the labor put into the farm by the family."[37] But Mr. Hori, also from Stockton, advised, "If you are going to farm here you have to farm big. You see, you can't make too much farming here, so if you farm small your earnings are very small. The way I see it, one has to farm big here to make any sizable income. "Not surprisingly, Hori had no intention of staying on his Swink, Colorado, farm and was biding time until he could return to California.[38]

Despite environmental and economic adversity in Colorado, many Californians remained because of the uncertainties that faced them on the Pacific Coast. Fred Mikuni, from Salinas, farmed on a sharecrop basis in Pierce, twenty-five miles northwest of Greeley. He did not want to return to California because he believed that it would throw them into the "old Japanese community" where they would face "worse discrimination than elsewhere." Much like WRA officials, he believed it was necessary to disperse, rather than congregate in ethnic enclaves.[39] For Sam Sameshima, his enormous wartime losses precluded his return west. He explained, "I can't go back to California now. There's nothing there [if] I could go back to. Any way I don't think it's a good time to go back."[40]

Many former detainees' ties to California simply ran too deep to want to stay in the interior West longer than necessary. F. I. Kaihara, editor of the *Colorado Times*, explained, "I've contended all along that you can't keep the Californians out of California, regardless of what legal restrictions there are. Sooner or later they will all trek back to California."[41] John Horie, executive secretary of the Colorado Japanese Vegetable Growers Cooperative Association, expressed similar sentiments: "I guess it's human nature to prefer living in a place where one lived most of his life. One gets used to the surroundings and environment. The Californians are used to California and are strangers to Colorado, and it's natural for them to want to go back." While he knew of a few California farmers who intended to stay, most were "very anxious" to return. The only reason that they had not left already was a severe housing shortage in California.[42]

Other former detainees were more sanguine about staying in Colorado. The Nishimura family exchanged four hundred acres in California for sixty acres in Colorado. George Nishimura noted, "Oh, we're just gardening out here, compared to the farm we operated out in Guadalupe, California. . . . But it hasn't been bad farming out here. . . . you can [not] expect to make a huge profit farming in Colorado, but one can get along."[43] Mr. Kobayashi concurred. He saw numerous farmers and farm hands in Keenesburg return to California in early 1946, but they did so "purely for sentimental reasons." Given the scarcity of good land and high labor costs, "So many of them are having a hard time now." He elaborated, "I've always contended that native Japanese farmers have been able to farm in Colorado . . . over a period of many years, and that if they can do it, so can the evacuee farmers. . . . I haven't heard very many evacuee farmers who have returned to California making [a] big success out there. I've heard a number of cases where the evacuee farmer has regretted returning and wished he had remained in Colorado."[44]

However, former detainees who remained in Colorado did not necessarily find a welcoming community among the "native" Japanese Americans because they were new economic competition. Mrs. John Numoto of Greeley noted, "Around here they all raise onions and cabbage. I don't see why some of them don't go into some other type of farming. . . . That's one of the reason[s] the market is flooded with onions and the price is so low this year."[45] They also contributed to elevated land rents. As John Horie explained, detainee farmers paid forty-five to fifty dollars per acre, whereas native farmers never paid more than twenty-five dollars. "Naturally, the Caucasian landowners raised the rent on native Japanese farmers. . . . This infuriated the native Japanese farmers," he concluded.[46]

The presence of former detainees also seemed to undermine previous Japanese American efforts to gain acceptance from the larger community. A Nisei woman in Greeley claimed that Japanese Americans were in the process of being integrated before the war. However, with the arrival of Californians, whom she described as "clannish," the Japanese presence became more prominent and "undermined the good will that the native Japanese residents had established in the community." Thereafter, the Japanese community became a target of suspicion, and she began to lose some of her Caucasian friends.[47] Yatsushiro clarified, "Naturally with a large group of evacuees coming into a small community at about the same time, the native Japanese were identified with the evacuees and prominently focussed in the eyes of the community. It made the native Japanese a little more self-conscious about being of Japanese ancestry in their dealings with the larger community."[48]

In addition, former detainees also created tension with non-Japanese farmers, which further undermined native Japanese Americans' efforts to blend into the community. As John Horie explained, Italian farmers in the Brighton area grew lettuce, celery, carrots, turnips, beets, green onions, broccoli, and radishes, while native Japanese grew cabbage, dry onions, beans, peas, and tomatoes. In other words, "There was an informal unwritten agreement between the Italian farmers and the native Japanese as to what farm crops they were to specialize in." However, detainee farmers began to raise the same crops as Italians farmers. "This antagonized the native Japanese too, as it caused the heretofore pleasant relationship between the Italian and native Japanese farmers to become strained somewhat," he concluded.[49]

Tension also stemmed from divergent approaches to farming. Reverend Eizo Sakamoto, who worked at the Baptist church at Rocky Ford, explained that former detainees had a "philosophy of 'getting-rich-quick,'" so they gambled on risky crops like tomatoes. He also described the California farmers as "big operators" who bought "big machinery and equipment, rode around in big nice automobiles, and many of them antagonized the native farmers." [50] According to T. Doisaki, he and his fellow Colorado farmers, on the other hand, were aware of the capricious climate and farmed more conservatively, growing sugar beets and hay, "which cannot easily be destroyed by hail."[51] Indeed, Horie described former detainees as arrogant and criticized them for showing off and acting superior to native farmers.[52]

Native farmers saw themselves as far more cautious and humble. John Numoto, who sharecropped twenty-five acres of onions and cabbage in Greeley, perhaps personified a native farmer. He did not expect to make a big killing in a single year and was instead "satisfied if he is able to provide food and other necessities for his family from year to year."[53] Fred Hisamoto, an Issei farmer who had been tilling land in the Greeley area since 1922, added: "The California farmer is very much like the Jew. He is extremely money-conscious. All he thinks about is money, money, money. . . . If he doesn't make a huge killing in one year he is disappointed. He is terribly upset if his crops are destroyed one year by hail or bad weather. He figures he must be making money every year." Curiously, Hisamoto deployed a derogatory ethnic stereotype to describe fellow Japanese. In his mind, former detainees constituted a distinct cultural group that had nothing in common with Colorado farmers, who were more "easy-going," content to maintain a steady income with no expectation of making a fortune overnight. They did not quit if they had one bad year; they simply hoped that the next year would be better.[54]

Native farmers also came to resent former detainees' constant refrain about the unfavorable growing conditions in Colorado. According to Yatsushiro, Colorado farmers did not deny that the farming conditions in California were better, but they grew annoyed at constant reminders. Bright Hoshiko noted, "You hear the Californians talk, you'd think that California is the only place there is to live."[55] Fred Hisamoto added, "You know, what really got me was what the evacuee farmers told us Colorado farmers. They said we were crazy to continue farming in Colorado. . . . I resent very much they saying we're 'crazy' here in Colorado." Hisamoto went on to suggest that the short growing season in Colorado was actually advantageous. He explained, "Yes, it's true that in California one can farm year around[,] while here, one can farm only during the summer season. But I've heard that most of the Japanese farmers in [California] were just able to provide their livelihood while they worked right throughout the year." By contrast, Colorado farmers did not work during the winter months and essentially enjoyed a three-month vacation. He concluded, "I don't see why Californians think they're better off just because they can farm year round."[56]

Different relationships with the natural world contributed to a sense of mutual distrust, but the native and detainee farmers also influenced each other in more positive ways. Upon hearing about farming in California, Reverend Kaihara noted, some Colorado farmers decided to pick up and move west to seek out "golden opportunities." "Maybe the California farmers did the local people some good by stimulating them to greater activity," he concluded.[57] In other communities, former detainees became integrated with the native farmers. For instance, in Littleton, Colorado, two families from Washington and California got along with the other Japanese farmers and had no intention of returning to the Pacific Coast.[58] In fact, the two groups of farmers eventually came "to understand each other much better and there is a good deal of visiting between evacuee and native families."[59]

The tensions and challenges in Colorado were replicated in other interior farming communities. In Brigham City, Utah, local Japanese Americans resented that the former detainees had more financial means to buy equipment. Moreover, ill feelings emerged when newcomers refused to "take the advice of the old residents as to what to farm, how to farm and what to do in order to get along in the Caucasian community." An older Nisei from the area remarked, "We had become well established in our community ... people knew us and respected us. The Californians moved in and they soon outnumbered us 2 to 1. They did not know how to act. They thought they were better than we were. We didn't like that." However, he acknowledged that they eventually were able to make "the right kinds of adjustments."[60]

Former detainees who pursued farm labor in Caldwell, Idaho, found a more promising economic situation. Many had worked in the sugar beet fields during the war, so they were familiar with the labor involved, as well as the Caldwell Farm Labor Camp, where they had done wartime stints. Built in 1938 to house migrant workers, it consisted of temporary, uninsulated barracks called "shelters" and permanent family cottages of "rather good construction." Each cottage had two bedrooms, a bathroom, a living room, and a small kitchen, with a lawn and garden plot. In the fall of 1946, 260 Japanese Americans lived at Caldwell out of a total population of 550, most of them in the cottages as family units. According to John deYoung, former WRA community analyst at Minidoka and fieldworker for the War Agency Liquidation Unit study, Caldwell resembled a WRA camp, but it had better living quarters and the freedom to work at prevailing wages.[61]

Since cottages rented for only ten dollars per month, Japanese American families at Caldwell often made a good living. During the summer and fall harvests, a worker could earn twelve to fifteen dollars per day. Those who did piecework with lettuce and potatoes could make up to twenty-five dollars per day. If employed throughout the year, one worker could average between three thousand and thirty-five hundred dollars per year. Farmers respected Japanese Americans and demanded their labor. As a result, few families were planning to return to the Northwest. Most of them had no property, and many believed that they were better off than they were before the war. Those who did return often came back, or they gave discouraging reports on housing and job prospects. As a result, deYoung predicted that these Japanese Americans might develop into a "unique labor unit that will last for many years to come."[62] Their fortunes appeared much brighter inland than back on the coast.

Some detainees continued to move to Seabrook Farms in New Jersey. By December 1945, 1,688 former detainees were living and working there. By January 1947, that population had climbed to between 2,300 and 2,700. Many stayed indefinitely by force of circumstance. As Mamoru Ogata explained, "I didn't want to go there since my home and farm was in California. But we had nothing, so we decided to go to Seabrook." He ended up working there for twenty-one years, retiring in 1969 and finally returning to California in 1976. Some individuals put down permanent roots; in 1970, 530 people of Japanese ancestry still lived in the Seabrook area.[63] Setseku Fuyuume's father was one of them. He saved up his earnings and eventually bought his own New Jersey farm, raising strawberries and vegetables until his death at age eighty-five.[64]

Still, most former detainees saw New Jersey and the interior as way stations between incarceration and freedom.[65] As they set their sights on the Pacific Coast, they dispersed from other locales. Seabrook's Japanese American population dropped to twelve hundred by 1949.[66] In Garland, Utah—near the Utah-Idaho border—all but three families, or eighteen people, had left by February 1947, a significant drop from its peak of eleven families, or fifty-seven people. The families returned to San Jose, California, because they did not like the climate and farming methods in Utah, had farms to which to return, and were unhappy with their profits given the amount of work involved.[67] Their environmental displacement was short-lived, but the conditions further west were far from ideal.

"I Am Taking a Gamble": Returning to the Coast

The coast was the ultimate destination for many former detainees who once worked in agriculture and also in the fishing industry, but re-establishing their livelihoods was an uphill battle. Many farmers came back to land and equipment that had deteriorated in their absence, due to tenant "neglect and destruction" that, according to the WRA, "far transcends the ordinary carelessness of tenants."[68] Moreover, discriminatory laws and anti-Japanese sentiment restricted their access to certain lands and waters. Although they returned to familiar natural surroundings, their successful postwar adjustment was far from guaranteed. In fact, economist Adon Poli doubted that they would "regain any prominence in the agriculture of the West Coast." Nonetheless, many former detainees had "a deep devotion to the land" and believed that their ability to harvest nature on the Pacific Coast was the key to their future.[69]

Japanese Americans who once fished out of Terminal Island, California, faced an especially challenging postwar situation. During their wartime absence, the navy had razed their homes and businesses.[70] Moreover, the state legislature had amended the Fish and Game Code in 1943 to prohibit Japanese aliens from obtaining fishing licenses, a measure that ruled out a return to their previous occupation. Because singling out "Japanese aliens" could be deemed unconstitutional, legislators revised the measure in 1945 to bar "aliens ineligible to citizenship" from fishing licenses.[71] The change in language, however, did not alter the law's impact.

This statute affected all but 10 of the 107 fishermen who were confined at Manzanar. While the men and their families could be split up, relocation program officer Walter Heath argued that it would "be easier . . . if fishing could be reopened to them. This group is loath to change their occupation." Indeed, sixty-one had no secondary occupation, and sixty-two were over the age of fifty. Heath hoped that the New Jersey coast could be opened to them to fish; otherwise, he warned, "I know of no other mass relocation opportunity that would interest them."[72] Nonetheless, it does not appear that these fishermen plied Atlantic waters in the postwar years. Of thirty-seven prewar Terminal Island Issei interviewed in California in 1946, only one was fishing. Seventeen were working in canneries, three were gardening, and two were farming. Seven had retired.[73]

Japanese Americans farmers likewise encountered constrained options. Asael T. Hansen, a former WRA community analyst at Heart Mountain, worked in California's Santa Clara Valley for the War Agency Liquidation Unit study and recounted many stories of loss.[74] For instance, Ted's family had to sell their Cupertino farm because of forced removal. He returned to nearby San Jose in 1945 and eventually leased six acres in South Palo Alto. He continued to look for property to buy, but the prices were very high and the produce and flower markets unstable. Ted concluded, "I've sure regretted we sold our place in Cupertino. If we had had that to come back to, it would have been easy."[75] Similarly, Mr. Oshiro, an Issei bachelor, had farmed twenty acres by Berryessa and had two houses before the war. While in camp, "everybody" told him to sell his land. He relented, receiving $650 per acre. The same land was worth $1,500 per acre in 1946. When Hansen spoke with him, he was living in a hostel, working as a farm laborer, and spending his evenings drinking with a friend. Oshiro was resigned and said that there was "no use" looking back. He had to start over again and work even faster.[76]

Other Japanese Americans were more circumspect and realized that they would need to be patient in order to re-establish themselves in farming. Hansen interviewed a family that had farmed twelve acres of berries in the Santa Clara Valley for more than twenty years before the war. Ham, one of the children, returned to San Jose in July 1945 and got a job as a caretaker on a Los Altos estate, which provided housing for his entire family. He did not think they would be able to get back into farming for at least two more years.

He noted, "We can't take a chance right now even if we could get a piece of land. Everything costs so much. This would be all right if the price of berries would stay the way it is now. But if the price should slip a little, with production costs the way they are, we could lose $3000 or $4000 easily. Then our capital would be gone. So we are going to wait until things are more settled before we risk what we have."[77]

The Yokota family was rare in that they were able to return to the same farm they had leased before the war. They left voluntarily for Colorado before forced removal began and farmed there during the war. In January 1945, one of the sons visited their former landlord in the Santa Clara Valley and "he was really glad to see me. He had been having an awful time trying to run the place himself with the kind of labor he could get during the war." With an invitation to take over the farm, Yokota brought his family back in February and planted ten acres of strawberries and two acres of tomatoes. Hansen believed that they would "come out all right."[78]

In the midst of his investigations, Hansen made some preliminary conclusions. He believed that resettlement had three phases. The first phase took place from August to October 1945, during which time Japanese Americans sought any available housing and steady winter employment. By the summer, they began to seek better jobs, housing, and wages. The idea was to save money until they could enter the third phase—to get back to farming through the purchase or leasing of land.[79] In general, he believed that Japanese Americans in the Santa Clara Valley had a brighter future because they faced "less articulate" prejudice. This stemmed, in part, from their focus on berries and vegetables, which allowed them to avoid direct competition with white orchardists, who long associated fruit-growing with whiteness.[80] The fact that 84.4 percent of Santa Clara County's prewar Japanese American population had returned by 1946 was an indicator of their positive assessment of the region's prospects.[81]

War Agency Liquidation Unit fieldworker Tom Sasaki found a more complicated situation in the Los Angeles area.[82] Given the numerous agriculture-related businesses in the region—gardens, truck farms, wholesale markets, nurseries, and flower markets—the relative success of Japanese Americans' resettlement often varied widely. Gardening jobs proved relatively easy to obtain. According to Fred Ota, "All they have to do is to know someone who is a gardener and he can get a job anytime."[83] Japanese American gardeners' favorable reputation opened up gardening contracts regardless of their previous experience. For many former detainees, gardening was not their first-choice occupation. Prewar flower farmer Sakujiro Kawaguchi became a gardener only when he could not get his Dominguez Hills farm back.[84] For others, it was a temporary line of work. According to Bob Kodama, they wanted "to get out of it as soon as the boom is over. It is too hard work for those people who are not gardeners. . . . They are making good money, anywhere from $250 to the top limits of $600.00 a month. But it is hard work."[85] Ultimately, gardening proved to be a permanent postwar occupation for many Japanese Americans, evidence of their labor segregation and, in the case of former farmers, their downward mobility.[86]

Truck farming was far more difficult for Japanese Americans to re-enter. Although they had once dominated numerous crops, they faced poor postwar markets and high land prices in Southern California. Mits Aiso, who once ran a boardinghouse for gardeners, related the story of a group of farmers who grew cabbages at a cost of twenty-five cents per crate. The market was only paying twenty cents. Rather than sell at such a loss, they plowed them up.[87] Given market uncertainties, Kodama added, "The Japanese are holding out to see what the situation is. The leases are high, and it will pay to hold back until they see which way the wind blows."[88]

The fate of the truck farmers affected the wholesale and retail markets. Before the war, a vertical organization developed, with ethnic continuity between production and distribution. Japanese American wholesalers often specialized in crops controlled by Japanese American truck farmers and then sold this produce to Japanese American retailers. They also provided financing to farmers.[89] This business model was not reconstructed after war. In addition to having less produce to sell, wholesalers felt the impact of supermarket chains, which competed with Japanese American retailers and bought fewer crates of vegetables.[90] As a result, Japanese Americans wholesalers only accounted for about 14 percent of the commission merchants (individuals who received crops from producers for sale on commission) and stall operators at three Los Angeles markets in 1948, compared to nearly 41 percent in 1941.[91]

Japanese American floriculture in Los Angeles also had a vertical organization, but it rebounded faster. This can be partly attributed to the Southern California Flower Market, a Japanese American organization that supported and managed business in this industry. Members opened the Southern California Flower Market in 1913, which controlled competition by limiting participation to members. The organization went on to provide many services, including advertising, financial advice, and mutual aid.[92] It also provided indispensable support after the war. Before Japanese American flower growers even left camp, it helped them to secure leases on land and obtain equipment. As their numbers grew, the Southern California Flower Market reopened in

September 1946. In 1947, more than 110 flower growers were back in business, although they farmed in different areas than before the war. Leadership also passed to the Nisei with the reorganization of the Southern California Flower Market as the Southern California Flower Growers in 1950.[93]

Those who returned could be subjected to hostility. Howard Itamura, the first Japanese American to return to the flower market on February 17, 1945, encountered signs that read, "No Japs allowed between 7th and 8th Street on Wall." Fearing for his safety, "I stayed inside the building, not daring to stick my head out." A couple of months later, vandals broke the store windows. Fortunately, Itamura and other Japanese American flower growers had allies. William Carr, Friends of the American Way activist, secured a police presence at the market, while the Norman Seed Company extended credit and sold insecticides to Japanese Americans at no profit. This assistance was particularly important because the flower growers lacked capital, and other seed companies had boycotted their business.[94]

Japanese American nursery operators also had to overcome boycotts. Shig Higashi, a nursery worker-turned-broker before the war, noted that white nurserymen refused to buy from or sell to Japanese Americans when he first returned to Los Angeles in March 1946. They also boycotted anyone who bought goods from them. According to Higashi, they were afraid that Japanese Americans would take away their business. He expressed a desire to "get back at these selfish Caucasians who are trying to prevent the Japanese from coming back into business." In one spiteful gesture, he charged a nursery an extra three dollars for a plant, as "I had him eating out of my hand because I knew that he couldn't get them anyplace else."[95]

Because of their exceptional ability to grow beautiful plants and flowers in Southern California, Japanese Americans were optimistic about their future in agriculture-based industries. They monopolized gardening again, Higashi explained, because "their quality of work is far superior to anything that any other group of people can do. Take a look at the Beverly Hills section, when you compare it to what it looked like during the war, the place is a paradise." Likewise, Japanese American nurserymen grew better plants than their competitors. He concluded, "No matter what one says, the Japanese know how to grow. And over the past year, the Japanese have grown their stuff with such speed that it is amazing." They might be viewed with suspicion at first, but they would soon be "judged according to [their] merits."[96]

Mr. Yagi of the Southern California Flower Market concurred. He asserted that Japanese Americans could compete with the best growers in the country. He explained, "During the war the white growers got away with large scale flower growing, but I don't think the public will stand for second grade goods. Already many of the people who used to buy from the Japanese have come back because they know that they can get the best flowers from the Japanese." Despite several challenges—the loss of good-quality seed and favorable land for growing—Yagi had faith that Japanese Americans would adopt new growing methods, produce better flowers, and expand into eastern markets, securing their future through their transformation of the land.[97]

This optimism, however, ran up against many practical economic problems in the postwar flower and nursery businesses. For instance, Ed Yonai had a counter at the flower market and grew flowers on land that he owned. In October 1946, he remarked that business was slow because the high cost of living deterred people from buying flowers. The market was also flooded, so the prices of flowers had declined. The high cost of labor, the difficulties securing materials, and the deterioration of his equipment during his war-time absence made the situation even more difficult. Nonetheless, Yonai saw his investment as long term. "I am taking a gamble just like the rest of these growers," he noted.[98]

Yonai's experiences indicate that access to land did not ensure success. Even as Japanese Americans engaged in their prewar environmental activities, their postwar resettlement was hampered by larger social and economic factors. Like Yonai, Frank Matsuoka, an Issei farmer from Venice, had his own land and leased it to one of his workers during the war. Upon his return, he found his plants dying and greenhouses deteriorating. To rebuild his business, Matsuoka was planning to mortgage the property for a loan. According to Tom Sasaki, "He still will have tough sledding for the next couple of years to get his place back into shape. Much money and time will be spent."[99]

For many Japanese Americans, wartime losses were not simply economic. In 1938, Mitsuo Usui's family started the Cren-Club Nursery in Los Angeles. They bought the property for $10,000 and had $4,500 in equity at the time of removal. Forced to leave the coast quickly, they sold everything for $1,000. After the war, Usui's father tried to get the nursery back, but the owner wanted $13,000 for the land and the $13,000 for the inventory. Outraged, Usui kicked over a five-gallon plant and showed him the writing on the bottom. He explained, "It says this plant was planted from seed on this date and was transplanted into a gallon can on this date and finally in this 5-gallon can on this date. My mother planted these plants in these 5-gallon cans and all those big trees in the back, and now you want to sell it back to us at these outrageous prices?" The owner replied, "Well, that's the way the ball bounces." Usui's father wept when he heard this story.[100]

Agricultural communities outside of Los Angeles told similar tales of loss and uncertainty. In Orange County, Japanese American returnees tilled between one thousand and twelve hundred acres of land in November 1946, a sharp decline from the twelve thousand acres in prewar years. Those who did farm saw their profits decline because of high operating costs and taxes.[101] According to Sasaki, many Japanese Americans in Orange County felt that they had been reduced to the status of menial laborers, as they had been when they arrived from Japan. In a sense, they had been set back one generation.[102] In the Imperial Valley, less than 10 percent of the prewar population had returned by October 1946. The major explanation was the low rate of land-ownership before the war. Of the 212 Japanese-run farms in 1940, 177 were operated by tenants. Only 18 were fully owned and 2 partly owned. Given that the price of leasing land had doubled since before the war, non-landowners had little incentive to return. In addition, rumors of hostility permeated the valley.[103] However, many white residents maintained "that actually only a few in the valley were against the return of the Japanese."[104]

Oregon's Hood River Valley, which had a vibrant Japanese American farming community before the war, became a fierce locus of anti-Japanese sentiment. When Min Asai, Sat Noji, and Ray Sato returned to the valley shortly after the lifting of the Pacific Coast exclusion order in January 1945, members of the Hood River American Legion threatened violence. The situation soon escalated under the leadership of Legionnaire Kent Shoemaker. In February 1945, he took out a full-page ad in a local newspaper that proclaimed "JAPS ARE NOT WANTED IN HOOD RIVER" and listed eighty-seven Japanese-owned properties. He also published a list of nearly five hundred residents who had signed a petition in opposition to their return. Two weeks later, he took out another ad, reiterating, "SO SORRY PLEASE, JAPS ARE NOT WANTED IN HOOD RIVER."[105]

For Japanese American farmers and orchardists, this hostility only added to their difficulties in re-establishing their operations. Their first challenge was to reverse years of environmental deterioration and neglect. Weeds abounded, and trees had been unpruned. After cleaning up their fields and squeezing out a harvest, they were "pushed out of line" when they brought their first crop to the Apple Growers Association. Packers also threatened to strike, but they backed down when former detainees agreed to deliver their goods after white growers.[106]

With this backdrop, Chop Yasui, son of Hood River Valley leader Masuo Yasui, returned to his family's farm in April 1945. Like many others, he found the orchards in near ruin and his farm equipment in disrepair. Since local merchants would not take his business, he traveled as far as Boise, Idaho. Fortunately, Chop received constant encouragement from his father, who was still interned at the Santa Fe Detention Center, and benefited from the kindness of a few white friends in the valley. Anti-Japanese sentiment eventually subsided, partly due to Japan's surrender on September 2, 1945, and partly because many Japanese Americans chose not to return. The postwar population was about the half the size of the prewar population, so it was not an economic threat. However, it took years for orchards to recover, if at all.[107]

Given the hostility encountered by returning Japanese Americans up and down the Pacific Coast, WRA officials developed a protocol intended to combat racial intolerance. The first strategy was to maintain a "reasonably constant flow of evacuees" into the former exclusion zone. Their presence would provide a "focal point" for their allies, who would otherwise be fighting prejudice "in a vacuum." Another strategy was to set up field offices that encouraged the formation of "local committees of fair-minded citizens" who assisted Japanese Americans and distributed information that "counter[ed] the lies and the misinformation which were being disseminated

FIGURE 7.2 Like other Hood River, Oregon farmers, Gene Asai and his parents had to tend to neglected orchards upon their return to the Pacific Coast. Here, they are thinning apple trees, May 21, 1945. Photograph by Hiraku Iwasaki. War Relocation Authority photographs [graphic]: Japanese-American evacuation and resettlement, BANC PIC 1967.014—PIC Volume 54 Section F WRA no. I-921. Courtesy of the Bancroft Library, University of California, Berkeley.

by the hostile groups." Still, some Japanese Americans continued to face acts of "terrorism"—a term that Dillon Myer used to describe an attempt to dynamite and burn a fruit-packing shed in Placer County, California, and dozens of shooting incidents directed at Japanese Americans' homes.[108]

Anti-Japanese sentiment eventually subsided, but the challenges of finding agricultural land persisted. In January 1946, Lewis Hatch informed Ed Tanaka that there were "a number" of Japanese in the Puyallup Valley. They were "not popular with some people but I have not heard of anyone attempting to do violence. I think that the opposition is dying down all the time." However, even if hostility had cooled, little land was available for Japanese farmers. "Without a doubt somewhere in the Puyallup Valley there is some land that can be rented but I do not know where it is," Hatch concluded. Nonetheless, he invited Tanaka and the rest of the family to make a "personal investigation of the situation" and invited them to stay at his home.[109]

Other Washington communities affirmed the scarcity of land available to returning Japanese American farmers. Of the roughly sixty families who were forcibly removed from Bellevue, Washington, only eleven returned. Most were landowners. Those who had leased farmland before the war found that white property owners were selling their land to suburban housing and commercial developers. This trend pushed them into urban areas. As David Neiwert has detailed, Bellevue became a thriving postwar suburb on land that had been cleared and cultivated by prewar Japanese American strawberry growers.[110] In the White River Valley, George Nakagawa likewise remembered few farmers returning. Recognizing their limited economic prospects, the most industrious farmers from the area left camp earlier and went to eastern Oregon, Idaho, or California. His family was eventually able to return to farming, but not until 1950. His older brother, Giro, bought a farm in Kent for their father, who was then sixty-two years old and "too old to farm by himself." He worked for five or six more years with the help of his children.[111]

Nakagawa's story alludes to the enduring power of alien land laws. His father remained barred from buying land, which undermined his and other Issei farmers' efforts to re-establish themselves in Washington. This legislation had a similar effect elsewhere on the Pacific Coast. In Oregon, the legislature strengthened its existing alien land law in March 1945, making it illegal for an alien ineligible for citizenship to acquire leases or agreements for agricultural land in the name of a spouse, child, or "any other person" and then live, cultivate, and enjoy "beneficial use" of the land.[112] This amendment helped to reinforce a House Joint Memorial, passed one month earlier, in which Oregon legislators requested that Roosevelt "issue such orders and directives as will

FIGURE 7.3 Emon Ikuta was another Japanese American who was able to return to farming in the White River Valley, Kent, Washington, May 13, 1945. Photograph by Hiraku Iwasaki. War Relocation Authority photographs [graphic]: Japanese-American evacuation and resettlement, BANC PIC 1967.014—PIC Volume 53 Section F WRA no. I-879. Courtesy of the Bancroft Library, University of California, Berkeley.

prevent the return of said Japanese aliens and said citizens of Japanese extraction to the west coast states for the duration of the present war with Japan."[113]

California's alien land legislation also received renewed attention. The law mandated that any property acquired or transferred "with intent to prevent, evade, or avoid" the statute would "escheat"—transfer—to the state. Intent was presumed when an alien ineligible for citizenship paid for land that was transferred to a citizen or an alien eligible for citizenship. While many Issei had technically shown intent when they bought land in the name of their American-born children, enforcement was lax before the war. This changed after Pearl Harbor. In February 1942, state attorney general Earl Warren convened a meeting of district attorneys and sheriffs where he explicitly linked alien land law violations to national security. After Warren became governor in November, Robert Kenny assumed the position of attorney general and began to initiate escheat proceedings.[114] In October 1944, Dillon Myer urged Kenny to defer these cases because defendants found it difficult to retain California attorneys and prepare cases while detained out of state, but he proceeded anyway.[115] For defendants who settled their cases, the costs were high. For instance, Fumiko Mitsuuchi paid seventy-five thousand dollars to the state to quiet, or establish, title for her seventy-one-acre truck farm in the Sawtelle area of Los Angeles.[116]

The most famous escheat case involved Fred and Kajiro Oyama. In the 1930s, Kajiro gave his son Fred, a Nisei, two parcels of land in the San Clemente area. While the Oyamas were in Utah during the war, Kenny began escheat proceedings, claiming that the transfer of land from Kajiro to Fred was an evasion of the Alien Land Act. The Oyamas decided to try a test case and received legal representation from Japanese American Citizens League counsel Abraham Lincoln (A. L.) Wirin, who was also head of the Southern California branch of the American Civil Liberties Union, and Hugh Macbeth, executive secretary of the California Race Relations Commission and stalwart defender of Japanese Americans.[117]

In San Diego Superior Court in February 1945, Wirin and Macbeth argued that the Alien Land Act "was conceived in race prejudice and penalized the defendants solely because of race, and was thereby unconstitutional." After the superior court and the California State Supreme Court ruled against the Oyamas, they appealed to the US Supreme Court. Wirin argued that the Alien Land Act violated the Fourteenth Amendment "by imposing solely on [Japanese Americans], and not on citizens of any other ancestry, that the burden of proof that any land they received from a parent ineligible to citizenship was intended as a gift and was not made in order to avoid escheat." In a six-to-three decision, the court ruled in favor of the Oyamas on January 19, 1948. While the majority opinion agreed that the Alien Land Act violated the constitutional rights of citizens, it did not broach the issue of whether aliens had the same right to equal protection.[118]

As the Oyama case wound its way through the legal system, California embarked on several other escheat actions. All told, the state's attorney general office brought fifty-nine escheat actions against Japanese aliens between 1942 and 1947. The proceedings created a "sense of insecurity" for all Japanese American farmers that likely compounded the other challenges they faced as they tried to re-establish themselves on the coast.[119] Even for the Oyama family, their victorious day in court did not create a clear path to agricultural prosperity. The escheat proceedings led Kohide Oyama, Kajiro's wife, to view the old farm as bad luck and insist on selling it. They turned their attention to a sixty-acre farm in Palm City. Fred left farming altogether and became a middle school math teacher.[120]

Japanese alien fishermen likewise challenged the California legislation that barred them from holding commercial fishing licenses. Represented by Wirin, Saburo Kido, and John Maeno of the Japanese American Citizens

League, Terminal Island tuna fisherman Torao Takahashi agreed to serve as the test case. In *Takahashi v. California Fish and Game Commission*, the Los Angeles Superior Court ruled in his favor. However, the California Supreme Court reversed the lower-court decision on appeal, arguing that the state could restrict fishing licenses as a conservation measure. Takahashi's legal team appealed to the US Supreme Court. In a seven-to-two decision issued on June 7, 1948, the majority argued that the right to equal protection in the Fourteenth Amendment extended to both citizens and aliens. A concurring opinion by Justice Frank Murphy also called attention to the discriminatory intent of the law.[121] Even with this favorable ruling, the prewar Japanese American fishing communities never recovered. Takahashi fished for a few more years until his death in 1953, and Terminal Island became home to shipping terminals, shipyards, a Coast Guard facility, and a federal penitentiary.[122]

Ultimately, the odds were stacked against Japanese American farmers and fishermen who returned to the Pacific Coast. Even Hideo Mori, who bought his land before the passage of California's Alien Land Act in 1913, faced numerous challenges. During the war, he rented his ranch to "local Spaniards." He explained in a letter to Dillon Myer, "They milked it for all it was worth, never bothering to keep up nor improve it, knowing that during the term of their lease no one would come to inspect their work. . . . The result is that the productivity of the ranch is now but a fraction of its full potential, thereby making it a poor prospect for sale or lease." WRA officials told him that if he chose to file a lawsuit against his tenants, his chances of success were "very poor though the evidence be substantial." Incensed, Mori asked, "Is it not only fair that restitution for such losses incurred as a result of this evacuation—proper restitution to put us back on the economic status from which we were forced—be treated by a measure as forceful as our evacuation?" Not surprisingly, Myer's response was unsatisfying. While he was "deeply disturbed" by Mori's losses, neither the WRA nor any other federal agency had the authority to make restitution.[123] Mori—and many other Japanese Americans—had to eat the losses that were no fault of his own.

Japanese American farmers and fishermen who returned to the Pacific Coast still had the skill and knowledge to till and ply coastal lands and waters, but they struggled to practice their trades. They found it difficult to secure access to land or water and also encountered discriminatory legislation, anti-Japanese sentiment, and a variety of economic difficulties. Even when farmers had land, weedy fields, unpruned trees, and withering flower beds were material evidence of Japanese Americans' wartime absence. Given these obstacles, they were sometimes pushed into completely new lines of work. It was evident that their engagement with Pacific Coast fields and waters would not match the prewar years.

* * *

The WRA was well aware of Japanese Americans' postwar struggles. According to one report, the number of Japanese-owned and Japanese-leased farms dropped from nearly seven thousand before the war to a little over two thousand after the end of exclusion. Another report concluded, "The loss of hundreds of property leases and the disappearance of a number of equities in land and buildings which had been built up over the major portion of a lifetime were among the most regrettable and least justifiable of all the many costs of the wartime evacuation."[124] The agency blamed anti-Japanese sentiment along with local and state law enforcement officials and the federal government for not adequately protecting property.[125]

Property losses were economic, but they also had a devastating impact on Japanese Americans' sense of emotional security and overall well-being. Particularly for the Issei, starting over was a daunting, if not impossible, undertaking, as countless personal stories confirm. Noriko Bridges's family ran a small truck farm in Santa Ana before the war. They left their farm equipment and tools to a man who paid them five dollars. After the war, they "struggled and failed to reach economic independence approaching what we had had before we were wrenched from our farm, our source of livelihood." Her parents looked at resettlement "with foreboding, for they lacked the resources to resume farming."[126] Thomas T. Shigio's family incurred a loss of about ten thousand dollars before the war because they had to leave their Sumner, Washington, truck farm before they had a chance to harvest the crop. When they returned, the farm had deteriorated and financing from local banks was not forthcoming. He believed that the incarceration set back his family's finances by ten years.[127]

By mid-1947, the West Coast was once again the center of the mainland Japanese American population.[128] One can speculate that many Japanese Americans may have found it more desirable to face the challenges and uncertainties of postwar life in familiar surroundings. The environment of the Pacific Coast was tangible, even if they had lost everything there. For example, when Japanese American farmers returned to Florin, California, in the spring of 1945, they found neglected Tokay grapevines and strawberry fields. Nonetheless, one WRA report claimed that the men were "resourceful farmers" who could rotate crops, experiment, and work a little harder. They were happy to be home again, "even if they had to start out once again as they had years ago."[129]

Whether in California or Colorado, Washington or Utah, Japanese Americans confronted another environmental displacement when their confinement ended. Wherever they resettled, they found unfamiliar social and material circumstances, not unlike when they first arrived at the camps in 1942. Once again, they had to adjust to discriminatory attitudes and environmental constraints. Rather than picking up where they left off, they had to rebuild their lives and navigate a new set of challenges in postwar America.

Epilogue

EMANATING FROM THE SOIL

"MANZANAR, WAR-BORN JAP Town, Dismantled," declared a headline in the
Los Angeles Times on December 2, 1946. Written by journalist Frank Finch,
the article reported on a two-week sale that disposed of many of the former
camp buildings. Each twenty- by one-hundred-foot barrack was available to
veterans for $333.13. Once disassembled, the buyer was left with eight thou-
sand square feet of lumber, one thousand square feet of wallboard, twenty-two
slide doors, four interior doors, two hundred feet of wiring, and six electrical
outlets. Glendale architect Erwood P. Eiden, previously an army major, even
drew up four different house floor plans that specifically used the salvaged
barrack materials. Former Manzanar director Ralph Merritt noted, "One of
the finest ways government money can be spent is in giving these veterans a
home at a bargain. And please say that Manzanar is not being demolished—
it's merely being redistributed." By the end of the sale, nearby Bishop veterans
had purchased fifty-two barracks. Lone Pine and Independence veterans
accounted for another thirty-two and twenty-eight, respectively. All told,
750,000 board feet of lumber were sold.[1]

Finch's article also featured the story of Joseph and June Guzman of
Keeler, California, twenty-five miles south of Manzanar. Joseph had served as
an infantryman in the army and worked in the local talc mill to support his
wife and two children. While they had wanted a bigger home, June Guzman
explained, "We felt that we couldn't afford to build until we heard of this
deal." Thanks to the sale of the Manzanar barracks, the couple hoped to move
into their new home in Lone Pine "just as soon as Guzman finds time to
build it."[2] The article was accompanied by a photograph of the couple, June

beaming as she sat atop the salvaged lumber with Joseph by her side, both gazing intently at a blueprint for their future home.[3]

Finch juxtaposed this rosy portrait of postwar home ownership with explicit allusions to mass destruction. In the wake of the barrack sale, he noted that Manzanar looked "like it had been the target of an atomic bomb." Taking this comparison even further, the caption, "Like Hiroshima," accompanied a photograph of the dusty remains of the camp, lumber strewn about the ground with the majestic mountains towering in the distance. Finch also observed that Merritt Garden, a horticultural delight that had captured photographer Ansel Adams' attention in 1943, was now "overrun with weeds"; the "once-verdant nursery" was "being returned to the desert."[4] Whether through simple neglect or intentional human actions, the material evidence of Japanese Americans' wartime incarceration was vanishing.

Finch's article highlights a postwar paradox. On the one hand, he implicitly rejected Merritt's use of the term "redistribution" and implied that the demolition of the camps was part of a larger, violent story in which the federal government destroyed places inhabited by people of Japanese ancestry, whether in the United States or Japan. At the same time, he suggested that this site of Japanese American confinement had become a wellspring of postwar optimism and possibility for returning veterans. The Guzmans could own a single-family home, thanks to the materials from Manzanar. Of course, the ultimate irony was that former servicemen, who had fought an overseas war to defend freedom, benefited directly from a massive violation of civil liberties on American soil. This process extended beyond Manzanar, as veterans also received priority to purchase land and barracks at Topaz, Minidoka, and Tule Lake.[5]

With the dismantling of the camps, the physical remnants of the incarceration were at least partially erased from the landscape. Some fragments were left behind, but they were largely forgotten or ignored by Japanese Americans and nearby residents alike. In many ways, this process mirrored the near-erasure of the incarceration experience from the memories of former detainees. Many Japanese Americans marched into the postwar years determined to put their wartime trauma behind them, rarely speaking of it in any detail.[6] Starting in the 1960s, however, a growing number of activists, scholars, former detainees, and their descendants began to call for the reclamation of these memories. These efforts highlighted the overwhelming importance of the natural world to Japanese Americans' wartime experiences.

"It Just Floods the Memories": Returning to the Camps

Until the early 1960s, government officials, social scientists, and Japanese American Citizens League leaders promulgated a story of patriotism and cooperation when it came to representing Japanese Americans' wartime experiences. As historian Alice Yang Murray has demonstrated, this narrative coincided with media depictions of Japanese Americans as the successful "model minority" who achieved upward mobility through education and hard work rather than vocal protests. However, many third-generation Sansei and some Nisei began to reject these depictions, instead noting that the incarceration "left a legacy of internee suffering and communal trauma." Silence, Murray notes, "was a sign not of recovery but of psychological damage, repression, feelings of shame, and continued victimization. The real lesson of internment, according to these activists, was that Japanese Americans needed to confront memories of the wartime experience."[7]

This confrontation occurred in many public and private venues, but it was of particular importance in 1981 when the Commission on Wartime Relocation and Internment of Civilians, a bipartisan congressional body set up to investigate the wartime incarceration of Japanese Americans, held eleven hearings across the nation.[8] Some were standing-room-only events, and over five hundred Japanese Americans testified. Despite their divisions, the hearings offered them an opportunity to display "a sense of pride in asserting control over the history of internment" and rally around the idea that "the incarceration was unjust and internees deserved monetary compensation." Inspired by forthright testimonies, many other Japanese Americans subsequently began to share their wartime memories with friends and family.[9]

At the hearings, several Japanese Americans spoke of the environmental dimensions of their economic losses and wartime confinement. Because financial redress was one of their central goals, former farmers, nursery owners, and fishermen discussed valuable land, crops, boats, and equipment sold for a pittance or left behind. They spoke of their lost earnings because they could not return to these occupations after the war. They also described experiences that could not be monetized, namely the indignities of their living conditions. For instance, Haru Isaki, who was confined at Topaz, remembered how dust became a "second skin" in the summer months and concluded, "Our physical surroundings in camp—the climate and living accommodations—were as harsh as the Topaz desert, itself."[10] These conditions sometimes had dire health impacts. Dr. Mary S. Oda recounted that her older sister developed bronchial

asthma due to Manzanar's dust storms and died at the age of twenty-six. Her
father, also sensitive to the elements, had "constant nasal irrigation" and ultimately died of nose and throat cancer.[11]

While sharing memories was important, revisiting the physical sites of
confinement became another crucial element of confronting the war years.
Beginning immediately after Manzanar closed, Reverend Sentoku Mayeda,
a Buddhist priest, and Reverend Shoichi Wakahiro, a Christian minister,
returned to Manzanar every year to pray for the dead buried there. Over two
decades later, plans emerged for a larger pilgrimage. Southern California an-
tiwar activists Warren Furutani and Victor Shibata, both children of camp
survivors, began to brainstorm ideas for "organizing people to bring about social change and a better society for all." Inspired by the March on Washington
for Jobs and Freedom in 1963 and the United Farm Workers' march from
Delano to Sacramento in 1966, they considered a march to Manzanar. They
made an initial scouting visit at which time they came across the white obelisk
cemetery monument, erected in 1943, the camp dump site, still strewn with
wartime artifacts, and the apple orchard that ringed the camp's perimeter.
Furutani noted, "Just as the camp experience bears fruit for those individuals
who want to pick and harvest the lessons and knowledge to be learned, these
trees blossom every spring."[12]

Instead of a march, Furutani and Shibata scheduled a bus pilgrimage in
late December 1969. Furutani admitted that the winter timing of the event
reflected their lack of "deep knowledge of the camp experience." After a long
bus ride from Los Angeles, they encountered the wind "scream[ing] down the
[Owens] valley, armed with a million grains of sand." The frigid temperature
also provided a lesson in "how life must have been in camp."[13] Activist Edison
Uno added, "The bitter cold reflected the strange feelings and emotions that
overcame all of the weary travelers as they viewed the desolate scene." The 140
participants soon got to work, clearing vegetation, repainting the monument,
and laying wreaths and flowers at the base. They then held a short Buddhist
dedication service in which Reverend Lloyd Wake, a former detainee, called
on those gathered to "dedicate ourselves to the causes of freedom so that no
other people shall go through what we had to go through." At the conclusion
of the program, Jim Matsuoka, who had been incarcerated at the age of seven,
proclaimed, "When people ask me, 'How many people are buried in this cemetery?' I say a whole generation is buried here. The Nisei Americans lie buried
in the sands of Manzanar."[14]

Matsuoka's comment sparked controversy for his brazen critique of the
Nisei and their postwar silence, but what is striking is that he and the other

FIGURE E.1 Participants gathered in front of the cemetery monument at the first Manzanar pilgrimage, December 1969. Photograph by Evan Johnson. Courtesy of the Manzanar National Historic Site and the Evan Johnson Collection, Densho Digital Repository, ddr-manz-3-29.

pilgrimage organizers and participants derived meaning from the desolate nature that surrounded them. For Furutani, the harsh weather highlighted his naiveté and ignorance of the wartime incarceration. For Uno, it served as a metaphor for his abrupt awakening to the trauma and suffering of the camp survivors. In traveling to Manzanar on a cold December day, they gained a visceral appreciation of what it meant to be incarcerated. For Matsuoka, the physical site of Manzanar symbolized the suppression and erasure of the war years from the Japanese American experience. As participants unearthed the camp remnants, he implied that survivors should likewise excavate their wartime memories.

Emulated by Minidoka, Tule Lake, Amache, and Heart Mountain, the Manzanar pilgrimage has remained an annual event. Organized by the private nonprofit Manzanar Committee, over one thousand former detainees, family members, students, teachers, and other interested people, including many non-Japanese Americans, gather every April to remember and commemorate the incarceration.[15] According to religious studies scholar Jane Naomi Iwamura, the pilgrimage "is at once festival, political forum, and religious ceremony." Important activities—from the offering of flowers at the cemetery obelisk to participation in the *tanko bushi* (coal miner's) dance to honor the dead—tied Japanese Americans to their ancestors and allowed other participants to be "drawn into the history of internment." In the process, they considered "the consequences of injustice and betrayal" and the persistence of "perseverance" and "hope."[16]

Manzanar's environment—the temperature, the wind, the view of Mount Williamson—intensifies the symbolic power of the gathering. Kiyo Tanaka, who was fourteen when Japan bombed Pearl Harbor, noted that when she returned to Manzanar in 1991, she "just wanted to look at the mountains." She explained, "It just floods the memories."[17] For Tanaka and others, remembering the incarceration went hand in hand with being at the site of confinement. Encountering the built and natural environment seemed to facilitate or at least support the process of remembrance.

In the years since the first Manzanar pilgrimage, the federal government has begun to formally protect the former camp sites. Manzanar and Minidoka became national historic sites, administered by the National Park Service (NPS), in 1992 and 2001, respectively, and in 2008 Tule Lake became a unit of the World War II Valor in the Pacific National Monument, a conglomeration of sites in Hawaii, Alaska, and California.[18] These sites are joined by the Rohwer, Heart Mountain, Topaz, and Granada camps and the Rohwer Memorial Cemetery on the National Register of Historic Places, also managed by the NPS. In addition, the Rohwer cemetery, Heart Mountain, Topaz, Granada, Tule Lake, and Manzanar are National Historic Landmarks, a special category of properties within the register. National Register designation provides formal recognition and access to federal grants and tax incentives, but does not offer the protection of national historic sites or national monuments.[19]

Of the ten former camps, Manzanar is the most developed for visitors. Housed in the restored Manzanar High School auditorium, the Manzanar Interpretive Center opened in April 2004. In September 2005, the NPS erected a reconstructed guard tower, and the following year, archaeologists began to excavate the ornamental gardens that once dotted the camp. In January 2011, an exhibit opened in a restored mess hall, which had been moved from the Bishop County Airport to the Manzanar site in 2002. Four years later, two reconstructed barracks were opened to the public, featuring audio and video stations with forty-two oral history clips. Visitors can also take a self-guided auto tour to see the remaining orchards, sentry posts, rock gardens and ponds, building foundations, and cemetery.[20] In the future, visitors' experiences may be enhanced by the rehabilitation of more gardens. In December 2015, archaeologist Jeffery F. Burton developed the *Garden Management Plan*. While five specific gardens are slated for restoration, the majority of the gardens are to be left in "their state of abandonment" in order to "evoke the dry, harsh condition of Manzanar when internees arrived, and the inexorable way the desert has reclaimed the site."[21]

Other confinement sites have been preserved by nonprofit organizations. The Heart Mountain, Wyoming Foundation was founded in 1996 to preserve and memorialize the camp site, educate the public about the war years, and support research and outreach. In August 2011, it opened the Heart Mountain Interpretive Center, a museum "dedicated to passing on the Heart Mountain story to future generations."[22] Similarly, the Topaz Museum Board, initially an ad hoc committee, was formed in 1991 after a Delta, Utah, family donated half of a Topaz recreation hall. The building was restored and dedicated in July 1995, and the Topaz Museum Board was incorporated in 1996 to preserve the Topaz site and build a permanent museum.[23] It began buying the land encompassing the former camp site, surveying the property, and raising money for the new museum, which opened in July 2017.[24]

The Japanese American Confinement Sites (JACS) grant program has supported these public and private efforts. Created with the passage of the Preservation of Japanese American Confinement Sites Act in 2006, this program authorized the NPS to award $38 million in grants to "identify, research, evaluate, interpret, protect, restore, repair, and acquire historic confinement sites."[25] Shortly after the bill passed, the NPS held a series of "public listening sessions" in Nevada, Washington, Oregon, California, Colorado, Arizona, Utah, Arkansas, Hawaii, Illinois, Minnesota, and Washington, DC, to discuss criteria for the program. A subsequent NPS newsletter quoted one attendee who stated, "The heart of internment is the camps themselves, the hallowed places, remote as they are. When people visit the site, they feel the onus of the incarceration. It emanates from the soil, the temperature whether hot or cold, the desolation, and they know the injustice of internment. Protecting and interpreting those places is paramount."[26] For this interested citizen and others, the history of the incarceration is embedded in the nature of the confinement sites.

As of fiscal year 2017, the NPS has awarded 186 JACS grants totaling almost $24 million. Projects related to the WRA camps, assembly centers, isolation centers, and facilities administered by the Department of Justice, US Army, and Federal Bureau of Prisons are all eligible for funding. Many grants have focused on educational projects, such as curriculum development, documentary films, digitization of original documents, and construction of the Topaz Museum. Other grants have preserved the sites of confinement, from the reconstruction of a guard tower at the Minidoka National Historic Site to the restoration of the Heart Mountain hospital chimney.[27]

Visitors can now descend on many camp sites and view where Japanese Americans endured the war years. They can imagine an earlier era by gazing at historic photographs and artifacts or walking through a restored barrack and the remnants of an ornamental garden. In the process, they might sense the presence of the past. As photographer Todd Stewart explained with regard to his visit to Manzanar, "What surprised me most . . . was the immediacy of the experience. Although the landscape had been abandoned for fifty years, the presence of ten thousand internees was unmistakable."[28]

Visitors might also detect, to some very small degree, what detainees experienced during the war. Depending on the time of year, they might encounter the blistering sun or a swirling dust storm. Regardless of the season, it would be difficult to escape the isolation and barrenness of the landscape, as most sites have not experienced significant economic development since the end of the war. This unchoreographed sensory element to a camp visit suggests how the remembrance and commemoration of the incarceration have entwined with the land.

"A Sense of Coming Home": Restoring the Nature Left Behind

These larger efforts to preserve the confinement sites exist alongside individual endeavors. In some cases, survivors and their descendants protected and restored the nature left behind—both on the Pacific Coast at the start of the war and in the camps at the end of the war. These environments inspired contemplation and helped them to remember and honor their families' wartime experiences. Although some of these efforts began as personal initiatives, they gained attention in the local and national media. As a result, they came to serve as public examples of the importance of nature to Japanese Americans' wartime memories.

Junkoh Harui's drive to restore his family's Bainbridge Island nursery stands out as an especially poignant story of environmental renewal. His father, Zenhichi Harui, had emigrated from Japan to Washington State in the early twentieth century and worked at the Port Blakely lumber mill with his brother. They saved their earnings to buy twenty acres on Bainbridge Island, where they started Bainbridge Gardens, an operation that included a grocery store, gas station, greenhouse, nursery, and Japanese gardens adorned with

willow trees and carp ponds. Before the federal government ordered Harui
to leave the island in March 1942, he leased the grocery store and the other
facets of his operation, then planted several Japanese red pine saplings, grown
from seeds brought from Japan, in the shade near the nursery. According to
Junkoh Harui, he cherished those saplings and did not want them to die in
his absence.[29]

Instead of spending the war years in camp, the Harui family participated
in the short period of voluntary evacuation, making their way to Moses Lake,
Washington, east of the Cascade Mountains and outside of the exclusion
zone. They returned to Bainbridge Island in 1946. While the tenants at the
grocery store were responsible—the rent allowed the Harui family to pay
the taxes on the property and retain ownership—the tenants at the nursery,
gardens, and greenhouses were negligent, and the property had been looted.
According to Junkoh Harui, "The greenhouses had collapsed and the nice,
beautiful gardens my father had made were gone. We had left everything
to some individuals who didn't take care of it. Everything was destroyed or
taken by thieves." When the family drove around the island, Zenhichi Harui
pointed out some of his nursery's "finest specimens" adorning the yards of
"opportunistic islanders." At this point, he was too old and had too little
capital to completely rebuild the prewar operation, and the family struggled
to get by with a nursery, produce garden, and greenhouses. Zenhichi Harui
passed away in 1974, four years after his wife's death.[30]

FIGURE E.2 Panoramic view of Bainbridge Gardens, 1930s. Courtesy of the Bainbridge
Island Japanese American Community Collection, Densho Digital Repository,
ddr-densho-34-18.

After working for more than thirty years as a florist on another part of the island, Junkoh Harui decided to rebuild and restore Bainbridge Gardens in 1988. Initially, he resisted this prospect because it was "a ghostly place with sagging and rusted reminders of all that his father built and lost." But Harui also discovered evidence of his father's horticultural prowess. For one thing, many of the Japanese red pines that Zenhichi Harui had planted in the frenzy of removal survived and thrived. Moreover, the old nursery stock of poplars, holly trees, birch, ash, and cedar had grown into miniature forests, and a pear tree, which his father had turned into a pear-shaped topiary, remained. He decided to carve a nature trail through the trees with the pear topiary at the center of the Harui Memorial Gardens, a plot that honored his parents and the Japanese American community's horticultural heritage. As Junkoh Harui began this project, community members saw photographs of the prewar gardens and returned two cast-iron lion statues that had been stolen during the war.[31]

The restored Bainbridge Gardens only occupies seven of the original twenty acres, but it has become a local institution. According to island resident Cassie Picha, "There's something poetic about the closed circle of Junkoh picking up where his parents left off."[32] Donna Harui, Junkoh Harui's daughter, elaborated, "Dad, I think, really felt at peace, as he started to explore the property, tear away the weeds, and find some of the treasures, and find some of his memories, too. I saw him really feel a sense of coming home, of peace. It's something I can't quite describe, but I could see the change in him as he felt that this was the right thing to do, the right way to honor his parents."[33] Junkoh Harui passed away in 2008 at the age of seventy-five, but Bainbridge Gardens remains open to customers and visitors.

The story of the Harui family demonstrates how wartime removal disrupted human relationships with the environment. While Zenhichi Harui did not lose his property, its wartime neglect and his inability to regain his prewar productivity were common. Yet some of his changes to the land endured the war years: the towering Japanese red pines and the pear-shaped topiary. Junkoh Harui's restoration of Bainbridge Gardens ensured that his father's prewar environmental legacy was not erased. Bainbridge Gardens continues to honor the Harui family, but the business also reflects Japanese Americans' deep ties to the Pacific Coast, ties that transcend the war and continue to be remembered by subsequent generations.

Rather than preserving the nature left behind in Washington, Yasusuke Kogita brought several pieces of the Idaho desert back with him to Seattle when Minidoka closed. Unwilling to completely abandon his beautiful camp garden, he hired a trucking company to transport his prized rocks and several plants back to Seattle. His sons, Ted and Paul Kogita, remembered loading those rocks, some of them weighing over one ton, for their journey back home. Initially, their father recreated the garden in front of his International District hotel. Later, Paul Kogita brought the rocks to his Seattle garden, where they line a small pond and walkways.[34]

The story of Yasusuke Kogita's rocks may have remained private and hidden had it not been for Anna Tamura, who completed a master's thesis about the incarceration camp gardens in 2002. During her research, Tamura corresponded with the Kogita brothers and visited and photographed the rocks. Their story was then featured in Kenneth Helphand's book *Defiant Gardens: Making Gardens in Wartime*. In his discussion of the Japanese American camp gardens, Helphand pondered Kogita's decision to move parts of his Minidoka garden back to Seattle. He explained, "Only Kogita knew whether this reconstructed garden was a reminder of the camp and its indignities or a source of pride of what he had accomplished under those dire circumstances; perhaps it was both things to him."[35] Regardless, the rocks serve as tangible evidence of Kogita's connection to the incarceration camp environment and enduring reminders of his efforts to beautify the Idaho desert.

The chain of remembrance continued when Ketzel Levine of National Public Radio interviewed the Kogita brothers for a story on Helphand's book in 2006. Paul Kogita noted, "Oh that garden meant so much to him, probably more than life. If he lost that garden, he would've lost his hope."[36] Moving back to the Pacific Coast likely filled Yasusuke Kogita—along with thousands of other Japanese Americans—with uncertainty. The presence of those rocks may have mitigated some of those fears. They had become an integral part of his personal story of survival, from confinement to freedom.

While the Haruis focused on preserving the Bainbridge Island land that had languished during the war, the Kogitas gathered nature from Minidoka and incorporated it into postwar Seattle. These families focused their efforts on nature that originated in opposing places, but their stories are part of the same narrative. In both cases, the war years brought environmental changes, whether in coastal Washington or southern Idaho. In both cases, the families did not want those changes to be buried under weeds or dust. In both cases, the families decided to excavate these environmental reminders of the war and put them on display, either for the general public or for themselves. In both cases, nature was not forgotten or lost in the turmoil of their wartime removal and postwar return.

The importance of nature to the incarceration experience was further made public with the release of the 2012 documentary *The Manzanar Fishing Club*. Cory Shiozaki, a television cameraman and fisherman whose mother and father had been detained at Topaz and Minidoka, respectively, decided to make the film after reading a 2004 *Los Angeles Times* article about a Toyo Miyatake photography exhibit at the Eastern California Museum in Independence. Miyatake had been a successful Los Angeles photographer before the war and smuggled a camera lens and film plate holder to Manzanar, where he secretly took photographs of his fellow detainees. He later received permission from Ralph Merritt to set up a photo studio and eventually took hundreds of photographs of camp life.[37]

The article featured his photograph of a man known as "Ishikawa" holding a string of golden trout. As journalist Darrell Kunitomi wrote, "No one knows

FIGURE E.3 Heihachi "Joe" Ishikawa with a string of golden trout, Manzanar, no date. Photograph by Toyo Miyatake. Courtesy of Toyo Miyatake Studio.

exactly how Ishikawa slipped away to go fishing. He holds the only evidence of his travels, freedom in a string of trout. His portrait embodies the vibe of Cole Porter's 1944 song 'Don't Fence Me In.'" Kunitomi speculated about Ishikawa's movements, noting that when he hiked into the mountains, he "must have felt he was on the roof of the world, compared to his government quarters below at Manzanar." He imagined him sitting by the fire, feasting on his catch, and gazing at the Milky Way. Finally, Kunitomi surmises, Ishikawa "looks up in perfect silence, free."[38]

After Shiozaki read the article, he was immediately intrigued by Ishikawa's story. He knew that golden trout were a much-prized fish, only found in lakes above eight thousand feet. Since Manzanar was at an elevation of thirty-seven hundred feet, he wondered how Ishikawa got his catch. He remembered, "It triggered my imagination. It became a very big mystery—how did he get the fish? I wanted to find out more about this guy." Shiozaki's investigation quickly broadened to include all Manzanar detainees who ventured beyond the barbed wire fences and went fishing while in camp. He began scouring museums and libraries near the camp and eventually becoming a docent at the Manzanar National Historic Site interpretive center. As word of his fascination with the fishermen spread, filmmakers Lester Chung and John Gengl contacted Shiozaki and asked him about making a film. Shiozaki's friend and journalist Richard Imamura joined the crew as the film's writer.[39]

As Shiozaki began to interview fishermen, they put him into contact with other fishermen. The team eventually interviewed twenty-six individuals, either Manzanar fishermen or their family members. Many of them spoke of the "illicit pleasure" of fishing. As Archie Miyatake, Toyo Miyatake's son, explained, fishing under the cover of darkness provided "a satisfying feeling because you feel like you can put one over on the government." The filmmakers also identified the mysterious "Ishikawa" as Heihachi "Joe" Ishikawa, fifty-three years old when he arrived at Manzanar. He was known for hiking into the high country and fishing the streams and alpine lakes by Mount Williamson.[40] Reflecting on his motivations, his grandson, Dale Ishikawa, speculated, "You know, he probably wanted the challenge and he met the challenge, and he came back with evidence of the challenge. And he has the attitude, you can see it in his face. He was proud of what he did. That was the satisfaction in it all. But it was his own private challenge."[41] By travelling alone into what appeared to be the impenetrable mountains surrounding Manzanar, Ishikawa seemed to transcend the physical and psychological confines of incarceration.

Indeed, the film suggests that fishing in the creeks and lakes surrounding Manzanar had profoundly personal meaning for detainees. At the close of the film, Ray Chomori is shown fishing in the present-day eastern Sierra. He notes, "Each of us had our own reason for going fishing. I've been coming back to the Sierras every year. I taught all my kids to fish. I think the reason why is the freedom I feel when I'm out here. That comes from my time at Manzanar."[42] Paradoxically, Chomori felt freedom most keenly when he was fishing in the shadows of the former camp. In some ways, his experience parallels that of Yasusuke Kogita's. Neither man could completely abandon or forget the environments of his wartime incarceration.

The "Unchanged Presence of the Past": Protecting the Manzanar Viewshed

With a heightened desire to protect and remember the camps—both their human and natural features—potential threats to the former sites could become a source of controversy. This was the case at Manzanar. In 2009, the Los Angeles Department of Water and Power's (LADWP) Board of Commissioners approved a renewable energy project, the Southern Owens Valley Solar Ranch (SOVSR), that included the installation of solar panels on 616 acres of the now-desiccated Owens Lake. The panels would generate power for Los Angeles and potentially reduce the dust storms that rose from the dry, alkaline lakebed.[43] As interim LADWP chief S. David Freeman explained, this area was an ideal place to build this facility, as it was "blessed with the 'best sun in the country.'" Given the agency's long history of exploiting the region and its "near feudal reign over the valley," some Owens Valley residents were skeptical of the proposal. Others were intrigued by promises of local jobs and a plan to restore a large portion of Owens Lake with mudflats and ponds for wildlife habitat.[44]

Over the next few years, the SOVSR expanded to encompass twelve hundred acres for a two-hundred-megawatt photovoltaic plant with one million solar panels. The project would be located three and a half miles east of the Manzanar National Historic Site (MNHS), appearing as "a thin, dark strip at the base of the Inyo Mountains."[45] Soon, MNHS administrators and members of the Manzanar Committee voiced concerns. As Les Inafuku, then MNHS superintendent, explained, the plant would have "an irreversible, negative impact on the culturally significant views from Manzanar."[46] *Los Angeles Times* reporter Louis Sahagun elaborated, "Views of a solar complex in the distance would destroy an important element in understanding what internees here experienced 70 years ago: To be in Manzanar felt like being in the middle of nowhere."[47]

The idea of preserving a "viewshed" was not unprecedented. At Gettysburg National Military Park, National Park Service officials cut shrubs and trees to preserve views of the battlefield as it appeared in 1863. Such modifications were part of creating an "authentic landscape."[48] At Manzanar, the viewshed idea also gained traction. Inafuku elaborated:

> I think it's really important for the story that is being told here to have that visual sense that the isolated, undeveloped nature of this area was so vital for the selection of the site of this camp. Most of our visitors are urbanites. To have an industrial site across the highway would just make this area seem more like what they have down in L.A. or San Diego. The opportunity for visitors to learn here at Manzanar is greatly enhanced by maintaining the undeveloped nature of this greater area.[49]

For Inafuku, replicating a palpable sense of physical isolation and segregation was central to the MNHS visitor experience.

An editorial in the *Los Angeles Times*, however, noted that the project "would be more of a dark glimmer in the distance than a mood-destroying force." While California was obligated to preserve the site as "a reminder of the fragility of civil rights in wartime," the state also needed to reduce its reliance on fossil fuels. The editorial concluded, "California is a changing, developing place where human needs—especially energy needs—and landscapes change. Places that were once considered 'in the middle of nowhere' suddenly find themselves to be somewhere. Accepting that change, while protecting signposts of our history, is an ongoing challenge. This project meets it."[50] For the editorial board, the idea of maintaining an "unchanged" environment, frozen in time, was unrealistic, myopic, and ultimately impossible.

While Manzanar supporters and Inyo County governmental officials had no power to stop the SOVSR, the LADWP, in the spring of 2015, removed the project from its "Priority Queue List," which determined when renewable energy projects gained access to transmission lines. The department, however, reserved the right "to renew exploration into the SOVSR" and would continue to consider its feasibility for commercial operation between 2024 and 2027. With California governor Jerry Brown's 2015 call to expand the state's use of renewable energy to 50 percent by 2030, the agency wanted to keep the project viable.[51] The Manzanar Committee celebrated this move and the withdrawal of a proposal from Northland Power / Independence Solar Farms for another nearby solar project. Still, Bruce Embrey, cochair of the Manzanar Committee, noted that they had to "remain vigilant" against "these massive solar projects."[52]

Indeed, Owens Valley was a desirable place for solar development. This was clear when Inyo County proposed to amend its general plan to provide for solar energy development. Initially, this Renewable Energy General Plan Amendment (REGPA) included the Owens Valley as a "Renewable Energy Development Area" (REDA), which would allow for large-scale energy facilities. In response, the Manzanar Committee joined forces with local and Los Angeles residents, the Owens Valley Committee, a nonprofit organization dedicated to "just and sustainable management of Owens Valley land and water resources," and the Big Pine Paiute Tribe of the Owens Valley, the Bishop Paiute Tribe, and the Lone Pine Paiute-Shoshone Tribe—federally recognized tribes with nearby reservations—to remove the Owens Valley as a REDA. In May 2014, they were successful. Embrey applauded the move, noting, "This is an important first step towards protecting the Manzanar National Historic Site from intrusions into its viewshed. It is also a significant step towards protecting and preserving other priceless cultural sites in the area, and it is a step towards protecting the tourist-based economy of Inyo County."[53]

The next stage of the REGPA process involved drafting a program environmental impact report (PEIR) in accordance with the California Environmental Quality Act. The Manzanar Committee objected to an early version of the report because it noted that MNHS visitors were more engaged with the tourist facilities than the "visual landscape." Embrey countered that this claim was patently false. "Indeed, as one enters the Visitors Center, one is greeted by a quote from a former incarceree describing the majestic, desolate scene that greeted them as they arrived in 1942," he explained. This "tragically beautiful tension" was critical to the experiences of both wartime detainees and present-day visitors.[54]

The final version of the PEIR was amended, but Embrey's letter underscores the extent to which the remembrance of the camp experience hinged on direct links to the natural world.[55] The remains of the built environment—barracks, guard towers, barbed wire—coupled with the surrounding terrain and views were critical to MNHS efforts to encourage visitors to imagine what confinement must have looked and felt like. Without the emptiness of the Owens Valley, Embrey implied, the MNHS could be plopped anywhere. Visitors' experiences would not be nearly as powerful if they did not encounter some approximation of the "majestic, desolate scene" that wartime detainees did. Thus, the "viewshed" was just as worthy of protection as the site itself and its remaining artifacts and structures.

The Inyo County Board of Supervisors approved the REGPA in March 2015, but the status of the Owens Valley with respect to future solar development is still evolving.[56] With a grant from the California Energy Commission, Inyo County planners embarked on the Owens Valley Solar Energy Study in June 2015 in order to evaluate the area for its "appropriateness" for solar facilities.[57] Their draft final report, issued in February 2016, recommended that projects be avoided in the MNHS because "the undeveloped landscape visible from the site can be considered a visually significant resource."[58] The Owens Valley is ever-changing, but local residents have expressed a commitment to ensuring that the environment resembles the one encountered by Japanese Americans in 1942.

* * *

Since the 1960s, former detainees and their families, along with activists, educators, and scholars, have reclaimed and publicized Japanese Americans' wartime memories. Their efforts have been inextricably linked to the environment, whether on the Pacific Coast or in the camps themselves. For some, the injustices of incarceration were inseparable from the landscapes left behind. In confronting the war, they revisited the pain of losing land, trees, and crops and the trauma of abandoning livelihoods in natural resource industries. For others, the injustices of incarceration were inseparable from the landscapes where they were confined. In confronting the war, they relived the hardships of desolate and unhealthful places. They also remembered the beauty that they created and experienced. Their active engagement with the lands and waters surrounding the camps were "acts of grace amidst the profanities of war," in the words of Ketzel Levine.[59]

These stories of remembrance and commemoration further highlight how the history of the Japanese American incarceration "emanates from the soil."[60] Although this federal program was rooted in global war and racial prejudice, its development intertwined with the natural world. Those involved—whether detainees or federal administrators, military guards or neighboring residents—discovered that the environment defined the parameters of human possibility.[61] Indeed, no one person or group had absolute power over the program. They had to negotiate the terms and conditions of confinement with each other and with a dynamic natural world. Moments of resistance and adaptation, triumph and concession, joy and frustration were in constant dialogue with the environment. The natural world, then, shaped understandings of the Japanese American incarceration and transformed the human relationships therein.

Notes

INTRODUCTION

1. Myer succeeded Milton S. Eisenhower, who served as WRA director from March 18, 1942, to June 18, 1942. See Brian Niiya, "Milton Eisenhower," *Densho Encyclopedia*, http://encyclopedia.densho.org/Milton_Eisenhower/ (accessed March 22, 2016).

2. Dillon S. Myer to Herbert B. Maw, July 2, 1942, Box 292/41.030, Entry 16, War Relocation Authority Records, Record Group 210, National Archives and Records and Administration, Washington, DC (hereafter WRA-NARA).

3. Elias J. Strong to D. S. Myer, August 5, 1942, Box 292/41.030, Entry 16, WRA-NARA.

4. Ibid.

5. *Topaz Times*, September 17, 1942; Sandra C. Taylor, *Jewel of the Desert: Japanese American Internment at Topaz* (Berkeley: University of California Press, 1993), 90. For WRA control of camp newspapers, see Lauren Kessler, "Fettered Freedoms: The Journalism of World War II Japanese Internment Camps," *Journalism History* 15, nos. 2–3 (1988): 70–79; Takeya Mizuno, "The Creation of the 'Free' Press in Japanese-American Camps: The War Relocation Authority's Planning and Making of the Camp Newspaper Policy," *Journalism and Mass Communication Quarterly* 78, no. 3 (2001): 503–518.

6. Paul Carter, *The Road to Botany Bay: An Exploration of Landscape and History* (New York: Knopf, 1988); Dolores Hayden, *The Power of Place: Urban Landscapes as Public History*, 2nd ed. (Cambridge, MA: MIT Press, 1997).

7. US War Relocation Authority, *Relocation Communities for Wartime Evacuees* (Washington, DC: Department of the Interior, 1942), 3. For Myer's prewar career, see Richard Drinnon, *Keeper of Concentration Camps: Dillon S. Myer and American Racism* (Berkeley: University of California Press, 1987), 16–20.

8. Yoshiko Uchida, *Desert Exile: The Uprooting of a Japanese American Family*, new ed. (Seattle: University of Washington Press, 1982), 105–106.

9. Kimi Kodani Hill, ed., *Topaz Moon: Chiura Obata's Art of the Internment* (Berkeley, CA: Heyday Books, 2000), 84.

10. Hill, *Topaz Moon*, 77, 81, 83. For an overview of Japanese American art from the camps, see Delphine Hirasuna, *The Art of Gaman: Arts and Crafts from the Japanese American Internment Camps, 1942–1946* (Berkeley, CA: Ten Speed Press, 2005). See also Allen H. Eaton, *Beauty Behind Barbed Wire: The Arts of the Japanese in Our War Relocation Camps* (New York: Harper & Brothers, 1952).

11. Jasmine Alinder, "Camera in Camp: Bill Manbo's Vernacular Scenes of Heart Mountain," in *Colors of Confinement: Rare Kodachrome Photographs of Japanese American Incarceration in World War II*, ed. Eric L. Muller (Chapel Hill: University of North Carolina Press, 2012), 84–86. For photography in the camps more broadly, see Jasmine Alinder, *Moving Images: Photography and the Japanese American Incarceration* (Urbana: University of Illinois Press, 2009).

12. Muller, *Colors of Confinement*, 37, 102; Eric L. Muller, "Outside the Frame: Bill Manbo's Color Photographs in Context," in *Colors of Confinement*, 9, 20.

13. A similar point can be made about the Holocaust, but two recent scholars have started to fill this gap. See Tim Cole, *Holocaust Landscapes* (London: Bloomsbury, 2016) and Timothy Snyder, *Black Earth: The Holocaust as History and Warning* (New York: Tim Duggan Books, 2015).

14. Roger Daniels, *Prisoners Without Trial: Japanese Americans in World War II,* rev. ed. (New York: Hill and Wang, 2004); Tetsuden Kashima, *Judgment Without Trial: Japanese American Imprisonment During World War II* (Seattle: University of Washington Press, 2004); Eric L. Muller, *Free to Die for Their Country: The Story of the Japanese American Draft Resisters* (Chicago: University of Chicago Press, 2003) and *American Inquisition: The Hunt for Japanese American Disloyalty in World War II* (Chapel Hill: University of North Carolina Press, 2007); Brian Masaru Hayashi, *Democratizing the Enemy: The Japanese American Internment* (Princeton, NJ: Princeton University Press, 2008); Greg Robinson, *By Order of the President: FDR and the Internment of Japanese Americans* (Cambridge, MA: Harvard University Press, 2003) and *A Tragedy of Democracy: Japanese Confinement in North America* (New York: Columbia University Press, 2009); Yasuko I. Takezawa, *Breaking the Silence: Redress and Japanese American Ethnicity* (Ithaca, NY: Cornell University Press, 1995); Alice Yang Murray, *Historical Memories of the Japanese American Internment and the Struggle for Redress* (Stanford, CA: Stanford University Press, 2008); Robert Shimabokuro, *Born in Seattle: The Campaign for Japanese American Redress* (Seattle: University of Washington Press, 2001); Cherstin Lyon, *Prisons and Patriots: Japanese American Wartime Citizenship, Civil Disobedience, and Historical Memory* (Philadelphia: Temple University Press, 2011).

15. Thomas James, *Exile Within: The Schooling of Japanese Americans* (Cambridge, MA: Harvard University Press, 1987); Gary Y. Okihiro, *Storied Lives: Japanese American Students and World War II* (Seattle: University of Washington Press, 1999);

Valerie J. Matsumoto, *City Girls: The Nisei Social World in Los Angeles, 1920–1950* (New York: Oxford University Press, 2014); Greg Robinson, *After Camp: Portraits in Midcentury Japanese American Life and Politics* (Berkeley: University of California Press, 2012); Linda Tamura, *Nisei Soldiers Break Their Silence: Coming Home to Hood River* (Seattle: University of Washington Press, 2012).

16. Gordon Chang, ed., *Morning Glory, Evening Shadow: Yamato Ichihashi and His Internment Writings, 1942–1945* (Stanford, CA: Stanford University Press, 1999); Louis Fiset, *Imprisoned Apart: The World War II Correspondence of an Issei Couple* (Seattle: University of Washington Press, 1997); Paul Takemoto, *Nisei Memories: My Parents Talk about the War Years* (Seattle: University of Washington Press, 2006); John Tateishi, *And Justice for All: An Oral History of the Japanese American Detention Camps* (Seattle: University of Washington Press, 1999); Erica Harth, *Last Witnesses: Reflections on the Wartime Internment of Japanese Americans* (New York: Palgrave Macmillan, 2003); Brian Komei Dempster, *From Our Side of the Fence: Growing Up in America's Concentration Camps* (San Francisco: Kearney Street Workshop Press, 2001); Brian Komei Dempster, *Making Home from War: Stories of Japanese American Exile and Resettlement* (Berkeley, CA: Heyday Books, 2010); Heidi Kim, ed., *Taken from the Paradise Isle: The Hoshida Family Story* (Boulder: University Press of Colorado, 2015).

17. Patricia Nelson Limerick, "Disorientation and Reorientation: The American Landscape Discovered from the West," *Journal of American History* 79, no. 3 (December 1992): 1021–1049; Robert Hayashi, *Haunted by Waters: A Journey Through Race and Place in the American West* (Iowa City: University of Iowa Press, 2007), 4, 82; Heather Fryer, *Perimeters of Democracy: Inverse Utopias and the Wartime Social Landscape in the American West* (Lincoln: University of Nebraska Press, 2010), 26, 284; Robert M. Wilson, "Landscapes of Promise and Betrayal: Reclamation, Homesteading, and Japanese American Incarceration," *Annals of the Association of American Geographers* 101, no. 2 (March 2011): 422–444.

18. Louis Fiset, "Thinning, Topping, and Loading: Japanese Americans and Beet Sugar in World War II," *Pacific Northwest Quarterly* 90, no. 3 (Summer 1999): 123–139; Robert C. Sims, " 'You Don't Need to Wait Any Longer to Get Out': Japanese American Evacuees as Farm Laborers During World War II," *Idaho Yesterdays* 44, no. 2 (Summer 2000): 7–13; Robert C. Sims, "The 'Free Zone' Nikkei: Japanese Americans in Idaho and Eastern Oregon in World War II," in *Nikkei in the Pacific Northwest: Japanese Americans and Japanese Canadians in the Twentieth Century*, ed. Louis Fiset and Gail M. Nomura (Seattle: University of Washington Press, 2005), 236–253; Christian Kelly Heimburger, "Life Beyond Barbed Wire: The Significance of Japanese American Labor in the Mountain West, 1942–1944" (PhD diss., University of Colorado at Boulder, 2013); Karl Lillquist, "Farming the Desert: Agriculture in the World War II–Era Japanese-American Relocation Centers," *Agricultural History* 84, no. 1 (Winter 2010): 74–104.

19. Anna Hosticka Tamura, "Gardens Below the Watchtower: Gardens and Meaning in World War II Japanese American Incarceration Camps," *Landscape Journal* 23 (January 2004): 2; Jane E. Dusselier, *Artifacts of Loss: Crafting Survival in Japanese American Concentration Camps* (New Brunswick, NJ: Rutgers University Press, 2008), 51–53, 87; Kenneth Helphand, *Defiant Gardens: Making Gardens in Wartime* (San Antonio, TX: Trinity University Press, 2006), 189–190; Jeffery F. Burton, *Garden Management Plan: Gardens and Gardeners at Manzanar* (Independence, CA: Manzanar National Historic Site, National Park Service, Department of the Interior, 2015) https://www.nps.gov/manz/learn/management/upload/Manzanar-Garden-Management-Plan-2015.pdf (accessed June 9, 2016); Anna Hosticka Tamura, "Gardens Below the Watchtower: Gardens and Meaning in World War II Japanese-American Internment Camps" (master of landscape architecture thesis, University of Washington, 2002); Koji Harris Ozawa, "The Archaeology of Gardens in Japanese American Incarceration Camps" (MA thesis, San Francisco State University, 2016).

20. For the "core tasks" of environmental history, see Paul S. Sutter, "The World with Us: The State of American Environmental History," *Journal of American History* 100, no. 1 (June 2013): 97–99.

21. My approach is certainly not exhaustive. For instance, I do not explore the environmental history of disease or public health, nor do I go into great detail on the waste management and sanitation systems.

22. For the importance of agriculture to environmental history, see Sutter, "The World with Us," 105–109; William Thomas Okie, *The Georgia Peach: Culture, Agriculture, and Environment in the American South* (New York: Cambridge University Press, 2016), 5–7. Three classic studies in environmental history focused on agriculture: Donald Worster, *Dust Bowl: The Southern Plains in the 1930s* (New York: Oxford University Press, 1979); Richard White, *Land Use, Environment, and Social Change: The Shaping of Island County, Washington* (Seattle: University of Washington Press, 1980); William Cronon, *Changes in the Land: Indians, Colonists, and the Ecology of New England* (New York: Hill and Wang, 1983). For other agroenvironmental histories, see Brian Donahue, *The Great Meadow: Farmers and Land in Colonial Concord* (New Haven: Yale University Press, 2004); James C. Giesen, *Boll Weevil Blues: Cotton, Myth, and Power in the American South* (Chicago: University of Chicago Press, 2011); Douglas Cazaux Sackman, *Orange Empire: California and the Fruits of Eden* (Berkeley: University of California Press, 2005); John Soluri, *Banana Cultures: Agriculture, Consumption, and Environmental Change in Honduras and the United States* (Austin: University of Texas Press, 2005); Mart A. Stewart, *"What Nature Suffers to Groe": Life, Labor, and Landscape on the Georgia Coast, 1680–1920* (Athens: University of Georgia Press, 1996).

23. For notable exceptions, see Sucheng Chan, *This Bittersweet Soil: The Chinese in California Agriculture, 1860–1910* (Berkeley: University of California Press,

1986); Connie Y. Chiang, *Shaping the Shoreline: Fisheries and Tourism on the Monterey Coast* (Seattle: University of Washington Press, 2008); Sue Fawn Chung, *In Pursuit of Gold: Chinese American Miners and Merchants in the American West* (Urbana: University of Illinois, 2011); Sue Fawn Chung, *Chinese in the Woods: Logging and Lumbering in the American West* (Urbana: University of Illinois Press, 2015); Valerie J. Matsumoto, *Farming the Home Place: A Japanese American Community in California* (Ithaca, NY: Cornell University Press, 1993); Cecilia Tsu, *Garden of the World: Asian Immigrants and the Making of Agriculture in California's Santa Clara Valley* (New York: Oxford University Press, 2013).

24. For environmental inequalities, see Andrew Hurley, *Environmental Inequalities: Class, Race, and Industrial Pollution in Gary, Indiana, 1945–1980* (Chapel Hill: University of North Carolina Press, 1995); Carl A. Zimring, *Clean and White: A History of Environmental Racism in the United States* (New York: New York University Press, 2016); Karl Jacoby, *Crimes Against Nature: Squatters, Poachers, Thieves, and the Hidden History of American Conservation* (Berkeley: University of California Press, 2014); Colin Fisher, *Urban Green: Nature, Recreation, and the Working Class in Industrial Chicago* (Chapel Hill: University of North Carolina Press, 2015).

25. The role of the state in managing the environment has been a growing topic in environmental history. See Sutter, "The World with Us," 104; Adam Rome, "What Really Matters in History: Environmental Perspectives on Modern America," *Environmental History* 7, no. 2 (April 2002): 304–305; Bruce J. Schulman, "Governing Nature, Nurturing Government: Resource Management and the Development of the American State, 1900–1912," *Journal of Policy History* 17, no. 4 (2005): 375–403.

26. There is a vibrant and growing body of scholarship on the environmental history of war, but these studies tend to focus on the front lines of battle, not the home front. In the case of the Civil War, the war front and home front were one and the same. For the Civil War, see Lisa M. Brady, *War Upon the Land: Military Strategy and the Transformation of Southern Landscapes During the American Civil War* (Athens: University of Georgia Press, 2012) and Megan Kate Nelson, *Ruin Nation: Destruction and the American Civil War* (Athens: University of Georgia Press, 2012). For other studies connecting war and environmental history, see Richard P. Tucker and Edmund Russell, eds., *Natural Enemy, Natural Ally: Toward an Environmental History of War* (Corvallis: Oregon State University Press, 2004); Edmund Russell, *War and Nature: Fighting Humans and Insects with Chemicals from World War I to "Silent Spring"* (New York: Cambridge University Press, 2001); Charles E. Closmann, ed., *War and the Environment: Military Destruction in the Modern Age* (College Station: Texas A&M University Press, 2009).

27. Amy Bentley, *Eating for Victory: Food Rationing and the Politics of Domesticity* (Urbana: University of Illinois Press, 1998); Meg Jacobs, *Pocketbook Politics:*

Economic Citizenship in Twentieth-Century America (Princeton, NJ: Princeton University Press, 2007), 179–220.

28. For the New Deal roots of racial liberalism, see Mark Brilliant, "Re-imagining Racial Liberalism," in *Making the American Century: Essays on the Political Culture of Twentieth Century America*, ed. Bruce J. Schulman (Princeton, NJ: Princeton University Press, 2014), 233. For the war years, see Mark Brilliant, *The Color of America Has Changed: How Racial Diversity Shaped Civil Rights Reform in California, 1941–1978* (New York: Oxford University Press, 2012); Elizabeth R. Escobedo, *From Coveralls to Zoot Suits: The Lives of Mexican American Women on the World War II Homefront* (Chapel Hill: University of North Carolina Press, 2013), 8–9, 34–35.

29. Nikhil Pal Singh, *Black Is a Country: Race and the Unfinished Struggle for Democracy* (Cambridge, MA: Harvard University Press, 2004), 104–105.

30. Jeffery F. Burton, Mary M. Farrell, Florence B. Lord, and Richard W. Lord, *Confinement and Ethnicity: An Overview of World War II Japanese American Relocation Sites* (Seattle: University of Washington Press, 2002), 59–61, 161–163, 203–205, 259; Karen Leong, "Gila River," *Densho Encyclopedia*, http://encyclopedia.densho.org/Gila%20River/ (accessed July 24, 2015); Hanako Wakatsuki, "Minidoka," *Densho Encyclopedia*, http://encyclopedia.densho.org/Minidoka/ (accessed July 24, 2015); Karl Lillquist, *Imprisoned in the Desert: The Geography of World War II–Era, Japanese American Relocation Centers in the Western United States* (Ellensburg: Geography and Land Studies Department, Central Washington University, 2007), 157–158, http://www.cwu.edu/geography/sites/cts.cwu.edu.geography/files/ja_relocation.pdf (accessed July 24, 2015).

31. See, for example, Richard White, *"It's Your Misfortune and None of My Own": A New History of the American West* (Norman: University of Oklahoma Press, 1991); Donald Worster, *Rivers of Empire: Water, Aridity, and Growth in the American West* (New York: Pantheon Books, 1985); Patricia Nelson Limerick, *The Legacy of Conquest: The Unbroken Past of the American West* (New York: Norton, 1987).

32. Burton et al., *Confinement and Ethnicity*, 59–61, 161–163, 203–205, 259, 376–377. See also Lillquist, *Imprisoned in the Desert*.

33. For the Arkansas camps, see John Howard, *Concentration Camps on the Home Front: Japanese Americans in the House of Jim Crow* (Chicago: University of Chicago Press, 2008); Russell Bearden, "Life Inside Arkansas's Japanese American Relocation Centers," *Arkansas Historical Quarterly* 48, no. 2 (Summer 1989): 169–196; Burton et al., *Confinement and Ethnicity*, 149–160, 243–258.

34. Konrad Linke, "Assembly Centers," *Densho Encyclopedia* http://encyclopedia.densho.org/Assembly%20centers/ (accessed June 27, 2017).

35. For the workscape idea, see Thomas G. Andrews, *Killing for Coal: America's Deadliest Labor* (Cambridge, MA: Harvard University Press, 2008), 125. For an overview of scholarship connecting labor and environmental history, see Gunther Peck, "The Nature of Labor: Fault Lines and Common Ground in Environmental and Labor History," *Environmental History* 11, no. 2 (April 2006): 212–238.

36. Greg Robinson, "War Relocation Authority," *Densho Encyclopedia,* http://encyclopedia.densho.org/War%20Relocation%20Authority/ (accessed July 17, 2015).

37. Orin Starn, "Engineering Internment: Anthropologists and the War Relocation Authority," *American Ethnologist* 13, no. 4 (November 1986): 702; Brian Masaru Hayashi, "Community Analysts," *Densho Encyclopedia,* http://encyclopedia.densho.org/Community%20analysts/ (accessed July 20, 2016). For an early description of the Community Analysis Section, John F. Embree, "Community Analysis: An Example of Anthropology in Government," *American Anthropologist,* new ser., 46, no. 3 (July–September 1944): 277–291.

38. Lane Ryo Hirabayashi, *The Politics of Fieldwork: Research in an American Concentration Camp* (Tucson: University of Arizona Press, 1999), 5, 61–66; "Japanese American Evacuation and Resettlement Study," *Densho Encyclopedia,* http://encyclopedia.densho.org/Japanese%20American%20Evacuation%20and%20Resettlement%20Study/ (accessed June 28, 2016); "Dorothy Swaine Thomas," in *Encyclopedia of Japanese American Internment,* ed. Gary Y. Okihiro (Westport, CT: Greenwood, 2013), 179–180. See also Dorothy Swaine Thomas and Richard Nishimoto, *The Spoilage: Japanese American Evacuation and Resettlement* (Berkeley: University of California Press, 1946) and Dorothy Swaine Thomas, *The Salvage: Japanese American Evacuation and Resettlement* (Berkeley: University of California Press, 1952); "Study of the Evacuation and Resettlement of Japanese on the West Coast," 1, no date, Japanese American Evacuation and Resettlement Study Records, Bancroft Library, University of California, Berkeley, BANC MSS 67/14 c, Box 299, Folder W 1.51, http://digitalassets.lib.berkeley.edu/jarda/ucb/text/cubanc6714_b299w01_0051.pdf#page=1 (accessed July 20, 2016).

39. Starn, "Engineering Internment," 702, 706, 710; Karen M. Inouye, "Japanese American Wartime Experience, Tamotsu Shibutani and Methodological Innovation, 1942–1978," *Journal of the History of the Behavioral Sciences* 48, no. 4 (Fall 2012): 326. For other discussions and critiques of JERS and the work of social scientists in the camps more broadly, see Hirabayashi, *The Politics of Fieldwork;* Hayashi, *Democratizing the Enemy,* 19–25; Peter T. Suzuki, "The University of California Japanese Evacuation and Resettlement Study: A Prolegomenon," *Dialectical Anthropology* 10, nos. 3–4 (April 1986): 189–213; Yuji Ichioka, ed., *Views from Within: The Japanese American Evacuation and Resettlement Study* (Los Angeles: Asian American Studies Center, University of California, Los Angeles, 1989); Francis McCollum Feeley, *America's Concentration Camps During World War II: Social Science and the Japanese American Internment* (New Orleans, LA: University Press of the South, 1999); Matthew M. Briones, *Jim and Jap Crow: A Cultural History of 1940s Interracial America* (Princeton, NJ: Princeton University Press, 2012), 113–116. For rejoinders to Orin Starn's critique of the WRA community analysts, see Morris L. Opler, "Comment on 'Engineering Internment,'" *American Ethnologist* 14, no. 2 (May 1987): 383; Rachel Sady, "Comment on 'Engineering Internment,'" *American Ethnologist* 14, no. 3 (August 1987): 560–562.

40. Yuji Ichioka, "JERS Revisited: Introduction," in *Views from Within*, 22–23; Briones, *Jim and Jap Crow*, 116. Ichioka argues that JERS sources should be augmented by other sources. For another positive assessment of JERS, see Arthur A. Hansen, "The Evacuation and Resettlement Study at the Gila River Relocation Center, 1942–1944," *Journal of the West* 38, no. 2 (April 1999): 45–55.

41. For the creation of Little Tokyos, see Paul Spickard, *Japanese Americans: The Formation and Transformation of an Ethnic Group*, rev. ed. (New Brunswick, NJ: Rutgers University Press, 2009), 46. For Los Angeles, see Lon Kurashige, *Japanese American Celebration and Conflict: A History of Ethnic Identity and Festival, 1934–1990* (Berkeley: University of California Press, 2002) and Scott Kurashige, *The Shifting Grounds of Race: Black and Japanese Americans in the Making of Multiethnic Los Angeles* (Princeton, NJ: Princeton University Press, 2008), 13–63. For Seattle's multiethnic Jackson Street neighborhood, see Shelley Sang-Hee Lee, *Claiming the Oriental Gateway: Prewar Seattle and Japanese America* (Philadelphia: Temple University Press, 2010).

42. For prewar ethnic churches, see Anne M. Blankenship, *Christianity, Social Justice, and the Japanese American Incarceration* (Chapel Hill: University of North Carolina Press, 2016), 6–7. For baseball leagues, see Lee, *Claiming the Oriental Gateway*, 142–177. For the urban ethnic economy, see Spickard, *Japanese Americans*, 46–51.

43. The literature on alien land laws is vast. For this discussion, I have drawn on Matsumoto, *Farming the Home Place*, 17, 25, 31, 48; Robinson, *A Tragedy of Democracy*, 11–19; Tsu, *Garden of the World*, 107–138. See also Spickard, *Japanese Americans*, 60–66; Eiichiro Azuma, *Between Two Empires: Race, History, and Transnationalism in Japanese America* (New York: Oxford University Press, 2005), 61–85; Lyon, *Prisons and Patriots*, 27–34; Dudley O. McGovney, "The Anti-Japanese Land Laws of California and Ten Other States," *California Law Review* 35, no. 1 (March 1947): 7–60; Keith Aoki, "No Right to Own? The Early Twentieth-Century 'Alien Land Laws' as a Prelude to Internment," *Boston College Third World Law Journal* 19, no. 1 (December 1998): 37–72.

44. Tsu, *Garden of the World*, 135.

45. Ibid., 7, 71.

46. For Hood River, see Lauren Kessler, *Stubborn Twig: Three Generations in the Life of a Japanese American Family* (Corvallis: Oregon State University Press, 2008). For Livingston, see Matsumoto, *Farming the Home Place*. For strawberry growers, see David A. Neiwert, *Strawberry Days: How Internment Destroyed a Japanese American Community* (New York: Palgrave Macmillan, 2005).

CHAPTER 1

1. Toyo Suyemoto, *I Call to Remembrance: Toyo Suyemoto's Years of Internment*, ed. Susan B. Richardson (New Brunswick, NJ: Rutgers University Press, 2007), 16.

2. Quoted in Lee, *Claiming the Oriental Gateway*, 92.

3. For agriculture, see Yuji Ichioka, *The Issei: The World of the First Generation Japanese Immigrants, 1885–1924* (New York: Free Press, 1988); Matsumoto, *Farming the Home Place*; Spickard, *Japanese Americans*, 40–45. For fisheries, see Arthur F. McEvoy, *The Fisherman's Problem: Ecology and Law in the California Fisheries, 1850–1980* (New York: Cambridge University Press, 1986), 130, 137; Chris Friday, *Organizing Asian American Labor: The Pacific Coast Canned-Salmon Industry, 1870–1942* (Philadelphia: Temple University Press, 1995); Don Estes, "Kondo Masaharu and the Best of All Fisherman," *Journal of San Diego History* 23, no. 1 (September 1977): 1–19.

4. Leonard Bloom and Ruth Riemer, *Removal and Return: The Socioeconomic Effects of the War on Japanese Americans* (Berkeley: University of California Press, 1949), 12.

5. Adon Poli, "Japanese Farm Holdings on the Pacific Coast," Bureau of Agricultural Economics, US Department of Agriculture, December 1944, 20, Japanese Evacuation and Resettlement Study, Bancroft Library, University of California Berkeley (hereafter JERS), Reel 2.

6. Navy secretary Frank Knox, army chief of staff General George C. Marshall, secretary of war Henry Stimson, and President Roosevelt were also in favor of mass removal in Hawaii, but this recommendation was difficult to implement. Moving the Japanese American population to a nearby island was expensive, and Stimson doubted the constitutionality of removing Japanese Americans to the mainland. General Delos Emmons, military governor of Hawaii, eventually persuaded Stimson that removal of more than a few thousands Japanese Americans would harm Hawaii's economy. Ultimately only about seventeen hundred Japanese Americans from Hawaii were confined on the mainland, and another fifteen hundred were confined in Hawaii. See Robinson, *A Tragedy of Democracy*, 113–119.

7. Hayashi, *Democratizing the Enemy*, 76–77.

8. Daniels, *Prisoners Without Trial*, 30–33.

9. Robinson, *A Tragedy of Democracy*, 71–72.

10. John B. Hughes Interview, Hollywood, California, July 19, 1943, JERS, Reel 9. For background on Hughes, see Brian Niiya, "John B. Hughes," *Densho Encyclopedia*, http://encyclopedia.densho.org/John%20B.%20Hughes/ (accessed July 13, 2016).

11. "Portion of the Broadcast, 'News and Views by John by Hughes,'" January 16, 1942, JERS, Reel 9. For dual citizenship, see Lyon, *Prisons and Patriots*, 16–26. After 1924, children of Japanese nationals did not receive automatic Japanese citizenship.

12. "Portion of the Broadcast," January 16, 1942.

13. Long before Pearl Harbor, many people had campaigned for the removal of Japanese immigrants. See Tsu, *Garden of the World*, 107–138.

14. Agnes McAllister to John B. Hughes, January 16, 1942, JERS, Reel 9; Bloom and Riemer, *Removal and Return*, 95–96.

15. Alice Fuller to John B. Hughes, January 22, 1942, JERS, Reel 9. For anti-Semitism in Los Angeles before and during the war, see Shana Bernstein, *Bridges of Reform: Interracial Civil Rights Activism in Twentieth-Century Los Angeles* (New York: Oxford University Press, 2011), 50–55, 96.

16. Mrs. O. Rickeer to John B. Hughes, January 16, 1942, JERS, Reel 9.

17. Edward Jucksch to John B. Hughes, February 7, 1942, JERS, Reel 9. Yellow-peril discourse has generated considerable historical scholarship. For example, see Sucheng Chan, "Asian American Historiography," *Pacific Historical Review* 65, no. 3 (August 1996): 363–400; Erika Lee, "The 'Yellow Peril' and Asian Exclusion in the Americas," *Pacific Historical Review* 76, no. 4 (November 2007): 537–557; Eric Boime, "'Beating Plowshares into Swords': The Colorado River Delta, the Yellow Peril, and the Movement for Federal Reclamation, 1901–1928," *Pacific Historical Review* 78, no. 1 (February 2009): 27–53; Eiichiro Azuma, "Japanese Immigrant Settler Colonialism in the U.S.-Mexican Borderlands and the U.S. Racial-Imperialist Politics of the Hemispheric 'Yellow Peril,'" *Pacific Historical Review* 83, no. 2 (May 2014): 255–276.

18. C. L. Conrow to John B. Hughes, January 20, 1942, JERS, Reel 9. For Japanese cooperatives and associations, see Matsumoto, *Farming the Home Place*, 47–55; Spickard, *Japanese Americans*, 69; Ichioka, *The Issei*, 156–164.

19. Mrs. Paul Hollie to John B. Hughes, January 16, 1942, JERS, Reel 9.

20. Alan Reveil to John B. Hughes, January 16, 1942, JERS, Reel 9.

21. George C. Farnsworth to John B. Hughes, February 3, 1942, JERS, Reel 9.

22. "Japanese Menace Long Seen in Fisheries of the Pacific," *Pacific Fisherman* 40, no. 1 (January 1942): 18–20. For Freeman's long-standing anti-Japanese sentiment, see Neiwert, *Strawberry Days*.

23. "California Sardine Industry Adjusts Self to Wartime Restrictions," *Pacific Fisherman* 40, no. 1 (January 1942): 21.

24. Richard Van Cleve, "Report of the Bureau of Marine Fisheries," California Fish and Game Commission, Thirty-Seventh Biennial Report, 1940–1942, 47.

25. Daniels, *Prisoners Without Trial*, 35–40; Robinson, *A Tragedy of Democracy*, 73–74.

26. Daniels, *Prisoners Without Trial*, 41–46; Robinson, *A Tragedy of Democracy*, 87–93; US Commission on Wartime Relocation and Internment of Civilians, *Personal Justice Denied: Report of the Commission on Wartime Relocation and Internment of Civilians*, with a new foreword by Tetsuden Kashima (Seattle: University of Washington Press, 1997), 83–84.

27. Daniels, *Prisoners Without Trial*, 45–56; US Commission on Wartime Relocation and Internment of Civilians, *Personal Justice Denied*, 84–85. For a thorough analysis of President Franklin Delano Roosevelt's decision to issue Executive Order 9066, see Robinson, *By Order of the President*, 73–124.

28. US Congress, House Select Committee Investigating National Defense Migration, 77th Congress, 2nd session, *National Defense Migration* (hereafter Tolan Committee), Part 29, 11005, 11087–11090. For the rationale of the Tolan Committee, see Robinson, *A Tragedy of Democracy*, 84, 106–107.

29. Tolan Committee, Part 30, 11404.

30. Ibid., 11313.

31. Ibid., 11349–11350.

32. Ibid., Part 29, 11283–11285.

33. Ibid., Part 30, 11413.

34. "White Growers Would Take Up Japanese Acreage, Los Angeles," February 27, 1942, and "No Japs Needed," March–April 1942, JERS, Reel 2.

35. Frank J. Taylor, "The People Nobody Wants," *Saturday Evening Post*, May 9, 1942.

36. Lowell W. Berry to Thomas C. Clark, March 6, 1942, JERS, Reel 2.

37. John Zuckerman to Dave Davidson, March 10, 1942, JERS, Reel 2.

38. John C. Kelley to Dave Davidson, March 11, 1942; W. E. McGillvray to Dave Davidson, March 11, 1942; L. W. or S. T. Moran to Dave Davidson, March 11, 1942; Gordon Lacy to Dave Davidson, March 11, 1942; R. C. Zuckerman to Dave Davidson, March 11, 1942, JERS, Reel 2.

39. John Zuckerman, R. C. Zuckerman, R. E. McGillvray, S. T. Moran, John Kelley to Dave Davidson, March 11, 1942, JERS, Reel 2.

40. Chan, *This Bittersweet Soil*, 160–161, 214–215, 223–224. See also Matthew Morse Booker, *Down by the Bay: San Francisco's History Between the Tides* (Berkeley: University of California Press, 2013), 92, 95–96.

41. John Zuckerman, R. C. Zuckerman, R. E. McGillvray, S. T. Moran, John Kelley to Dave Davidson, March 11, 1942, and R. C. Zuckerman to Dave Davidson, March 11, 1942.

42. Ibid.

43. For the relationship between labor and environmental knowledge, see Richard White, "'Are You an Environmentalist, or Do You Work for a Living?': Work and Nature," in *Uncommon Ground: Rethinking the Human Place in Nature*, ed. William Cronon (New York: Norton, 1996), 171–185. See also Richard White, *The Organic Machine: The Remaking of the Columbia River* (New York: Hill and Wang, 1995), 3–29.

44. John Zuckerman, R. C. Zuckerman, R. E. McGillvray, S. T. Moran, John Kelley to Dave Davidson, March 11, 1942, and R. C. Zuckerman to Dave Davidson, March 11, 1942.

45. Stewart, *What Nature Suffers to Groe*, 63–64; Mart A. Stewart, "'Let Us Begin with the Weather?': Climate, Race, and Cultural Distinctiveness in the American South," in *Nature and Society in Historical Context*, ed. Mikuláš Teich, Roy Porter, and Bo Gustafsson (New York: Cambridge University Press, 1997), 248–249; George M. Fredrickson, *The Black Image in the White Mind: The Debate on Afro-American Character and Destiny, 1817–1914* (New York: Harper & Row, 1971), 71–96.

46. David G. Gutiérrez, *Walls and Mirrors: Mexican Americans, Mexican Immigrants, and the Politics of Ethnicity* (Berkeley: University of California Press, 1995), 46–51.

47. For the connection between Asian immigrants, stoop labor, and strawberry cultivation, see Tsu, *Garden of the World*, 28–36, 59–60. Mexican and Filipino workers were also connected to stoop labor. See Lori A. Flores, *Grounds for Dreaming: Mexican Americans, Mexican Immigrants, and the California Farmworker Movement* (New Haven: Yale University Press, 2016), 21–22, 49–50.

48. E. H. Haack to Dave Davidson, March 12, 1942, JERS, Reel 2.

49. Genevieve Collius to Tom C. Clark, March 14, 1942, JERS, Reel 2.

50. R. F. Malcolm to Truman J. Young, April 3, 1942, JERS, Reel 2.

51. Walter R. Goldschmidt Jr. to Rensis Likert, Bureau of Agricultural Economics, March 11, 1942, JERS, Reel 2. Goldschmidt was an anthropologist who studied two San Joaquin Valley agricultural communities for his doctoral research. See Walter Goldschmidt, *As You Sow: Three Studies in the Social Consequences of Agribusiness* (Montclair, NJ: Allanheld, Osmun, 1947). For crop neglect and damage as an act of disloyalty and sabotage, see US Commission on Wartime Relocation and Internment of Civilians, *Personal Justice Denied*, 126.

52. Daniel Immerwahr, *Thinking Small: The United States and the Lure of Community Development* (Cambridge, MA: Harvard University Press, 2015), 44.

53. Amy Fried, *Pathways to Polling: Crisis, Cooperation, and the Making of Public Opinion Professions* (New York: Routledge, 2011), 60–62.

54. "Memorandum on the Japanese Situation Based on Overall Runs of the First 112 Interviews in Study 40," no date, Records of the Division of Program Surveys, Project Files, 1940–45, Box 5, Entry 207, Records of the Bureau of Agricultural Economics, Record Group 83, National Archives and Records Administration, College Park, Maryland (hereafter BAE Records).

55. Ben L. Owens to Bela Gold, February 19, 1942, BAE Records. For protests concerning the use of family labor in Japanese immigrant farm families, see Tsu, *Garden of the World*, 107–138.

56. US Commission on Wartime Relocation and Internment of Civilians, *Personal Justice Denied*, 107.

57. Executive Order 9102, Establishing the War Relocation Authority, March 18, 1942, The American Presidency Project, University of California, Santa Barbara, http://www.presidency.ucsb.edu/ws/index.php?pid=16239#axzz10yXFVV9p (accessed February 6, 2013).

58. Daniels, *Prisoner Without Trial*, 54; Hayashi, *Democratizing the Enemy*, 87. Civilian Exclusion Order No. 1, http://www.du.edu/behindbarbedwire/ceo_01-01.html (accessed January 31, 2013).

59. Committee for Organization of Non-Profit Farm Corporation, "A Master Plan for Non-profit Farm Corporations," 2, February 13, 1942, JERS, Reel 9; "Cooperative Farm Project for Alien Resettlement," no date, JERS, Reel 9. For Hi Korematsu's relationship with Fred Korematsu, see Peter Irons, *Justice at War: The Story of the Japanese-American Internment Cases* (Berkeley: University of California Press, 1993), 98–99.

60. "Cooperative Farm Project for Alien Resettlement"; "A Master Plan for Non-profit Farm Corporations," 3, 5.

61. "A Master Plan for Non-profit Farm Corporations," 4, 5.

62. Ibid., 6.

63. H. W. Bashore to Charles E. Putnam, February 2, 1942 and Edward W. Torbert to David Weeks, April 6, 1942, JERS, Reel 19.

64. Hideo Hashimoto, "Outline of Cooperative Farm Project for Permanent Resettlement of Japanese Families," March 1942, JERS, Reel 9.

65. Nisei Writers and Artists Mobilization for Democracy, "A Plan for Government Sponsored Farm and Craft Settlement for People of Japanese Parentage," no date, JERS, Reel 9. For Isamu Noguchi's reaction to Japanese American incarceration, see Amy Lyford, *Isamu Noguchi's Modernism: Negotiating Race, Labor, and Nation, 1930–1950* (Berkeley: University of California Press, 2013), 107–129; Masayo Duus, *The Life of Isamu Noguchi: Journey without Borders*, trans. Peter Duus (Princeton, NJ: Princeton University Press, 2006), 162–175; Hayden Herrera, *Listening to Stone: The Art and Life of Isamu Noguchi* (New York: Farrar, Straus, and Giroux, 2015), 173–185. Rather than return to New York City, Noguchi agreed to confinement at Poston, where he arrived in May 1942, to start an arts-and-crafts program. He also developed a parks-and-recreation plan that included extensive gardens and recreational facilities. Embittered and frustrated by the slow progress on his program, he left at the end of August 1942. See "Self-Interned, 1942: Noguchi in Poston Relocation Center," Noguchi Museum, http://www.noguchi.org/programs/exhibitions/self-interned-1942-noguchi-poston-war-relocation-center (accessed October 28, 2017).

66. Nisei Writers and Artists Mobilization for Democracy, "Plan for Government Sponsored Farm," 3.

67. Lyford, *Isamu Noguchi's Modernism*, 112.

68. Taylor, "The People Nobody Wants."

69. Sims, "The Free Zone Nikkei."

70. Senator Ed C. Johnson to Milton Eisenhower, April 4, 1942, JERS, Reel 18. For Governor Carr's support of Japanese Americans, see Adam Schrager, *The Principled Politician: Governor Ralph Carr and the Fight against Japanese American Internment* (New York: Fulcrum, 2010).

71. Milton Eisenhower to E. H. Wiecking, March 26, 1942, JERS, Reel 18.

72. Milton Eisenhower to Elbert D. Thomas, April 23, 1942, JERS, Reel 22.

73. Junkoh Harui Interview, interviewed by Donna Harui, Bainbridge Island, WA, July 31, 1998, demshovh-hjunkoh-01-0012, Densho Visual History Collection, Densho Digital Repository, http://ddr.densho.org (hereafter DVHC-DDR).

74. Tak Yamashita Interview, interviewed by Martha Nakagawa, Oxnard, CA, September 14, 2011, demshovh-ytak-01-0023, DVHC-DDR.

75. Brian Niiya, "Voluntary Evacuation," *Densho Encyclopedia,* http://encyclopedia.densho.org/Voluntary%20evacuation/ (accessed July 31, 2016).

76. US Commission on Wartime Relocation and Internment of Civilians, *Personal Justice Denied,* 103.

77. Daniels, Prisoners Without Trial, 54–55; Civilian Exclusion Orders, nos. 1–108, JERS, Calisphere, https://calisphere.org/item/ark:/28722/bk0014b1k1d/ (accessed May 22, 2017).

78. The WCCA designated the Federal Security Agency to handle preliminary arrangements prior to the storage of property. This included issuing identification

tags for property and preparing lists of property to be placed in storage. The Federal Reserve Bank of San Francisco was responsible for delivering property to warehouses, storing it, and protecting it. See Memorandum from E. F. Cress to Mr. Eisenhower, April 3, 1942, JERS, Reel 1.

79. "Final Report of the Participation of the Farm Security Administration in the Evacuation Program of the Wartime Civil Control Administration, Civil Affairs Division, Western Defense Command and Fourth Army, Covering the Period March 15, 1942 through May 31, 1942," 5, JERS, Reel 1.

80. US War Relocation Authority, *WRA: A Story of Human Conservation* (Washington, DC: US Department of the Interior, War Relocation Authority, 1946), 157–158.

81. "Final Report of the Participation of the Farm Security Administration," 5–6.

82. Ibid., 1.

83. Laurence I. Hewes Jr. to Karl R. Bendetsen, June 5, 1942, in "Final Report of the Participation of the Farm Security Administration."

84. "Final Report of the Participation of the Farm Security Administration," 2.

85. Ibid., 7, 12–14, Table 13, 20.

86. Ibid., Table 7, 31.

87. "The Farm Security Administration's Role in the Disposition of Japanese Land," no date, JERS, Reel 1.

88. "Final Report of the Participation of the Farm Security Administration," 3–4, 14–15.

89. Farm Security Administration press release, March 1942, JERS, Reel 2.

90. "Keeping Up Production on Japanese on Farms," US Department of Agriculture radio broadcast on KGO, March 27, 1942, JERS, Reel 2.

91. US Department of Agriculture, Farm Security Administration, "Notice to All Farmers," no date, JERS, Reel 1.

92. "Mobilization of Farmers on Evacuated Land," Farm Security Administration radio broadcast script, no date, JERS, Reel 2.

93. "Sale or Lease—Large Share of California Flower Industry, Units of One to Twenty Acres, Glass Frame and Field. All Equipment In and Much Acreage Planted. Owners Must Evacuate. Quick Action is Imperative," April 14, 1942, JERS, Reel 2.

94. Farm Security Administration press release, April 1942, JERS, Reel 2.

95. Farm Security Administration press release, April 14, 1942, JERS, Reel 2.

96. Harry Bryant to J. E. Morrish, May 26, 1942, Morrish Collection, Redwood City Library. Transcribed letter in Linda L. Ivey and Kevin W. Kaatz, *Citizen Internees: A Second Look at Race and Citizenship in Japanese American Internment Camps* (Santa Barbara, CA: Praeger, 2017), 193.

97. American Fruit Growers, Inc., "Custodians, Inc.," Newcastle, Loomis, Auburn, California, JERS, Reel 2; "Final Report of the Participation of the Farm Security Administration," Exhibit 9 and Exhibit 10.

98. "Final Report of the Participation of the Farm Security Administration," 3–4, 16, 18–19, 42; US War Relocation Authority, *WRA: A Story of Human Conservation*, 158–159.

99. "Final Report of the Participation of the Farm Security Administration," 32–36.

100. "Supplemental Report of the Participation of the Farm Security Administration in the Evacuation Program of the Wartime Civil Control Administration, Civil Affairs Division, Western Defense Command and Fourth Army in Military Area Number 2, Covering the Period June 1, 1942 through August 9, 1942," JERS Reel 1.

101. "Final Report of the Participation of the Farm Security Administration," 32.

102. Ibid., 29–32.

103. Ibid., 42.

104. Rae V. Vader to John W. Pehle, no date, JERS, Reel 2.

105. Testimony of Yoshihiko Tanabe, Box 2, Folder 70, William Hosokawa Papers, Western History and Genealogy Room, Denver Public Library (hereafter Hosokawa Papers).

106. Statement of Masaru Yamasaki, Box 2, Folder 73, Hosokawa Papers.

107. US War Relocation Authority, *WRA: A Story of Human Conservation*, 159.

108. Victor L. Furth to Edwin C. Arnold, April 21, 1943, and E. L. Schnell, Statement of Northern Farms, Inc., no date, JERS, Reel 2.

109. Victor L. Furth to Edwin C. Arnold, April 21, 1943, JERS, Reel 2.

110. R. W. Hollenberg to Russell T. Robinson, December 11, 1943, JERS, Reel 2. A similar controversy involving payment to Japanese Americans and repayment of WFA loans emerged with Florin Farms. See G. W. Freil to Wayne Phelps, November 25, 1942; Victor L. Furth to Edwin Arnold, April 19, 1943, JERS, Reel 2.

111. For a detailed overview of the WRA-FSA conflict, see also US War Relocation Authority, *The Wartime Handling of Evacuee Property* (Washington, DC: Government Printing Office, 1946), 47–69.

112. Testimony of Robert Sato, July 30, 1981, Box 2, Folder 65, Hosokawa Papers.

113. Washington State Taxpayers Association, "Economic Effects of Japanese Evacuation," June 8, 1943, JERS, Reel 2.

114. Edward M. Joyce to Russell Robinson, August 20, 1942, and Edward M. Joyce to Russell Robinson, August 25, 1942, JERS, Reel 2.

115. Wartime Farm Adjustment Program Bill of Sale, 1942, Columbia River Basin Ethnic History Archive, Washington State University Libraries (hereafter CRBEHA), http://content.libraries.wsu.edu/cdm/compoundobject/collection/imls_2/id/253/rec/5 (accessed July 15, 2016).

116. Lewis Hatch to Dennis Tanaka and the Tanaka Family, September 15, 1942, CRBEHA, http://content.libraries.wsu.edu/cdm/compoundobject/collection/imls_2/id/249/rec/7 (accessed July 15, 2016).

117. Lewis Hatch to Dennis Tanaka, E. Tanaka and family, May 30, 1943, CRBEHA, http://content.libraries.wsu.edu/cdm/compoundobject/collection/imls_2/id/256/rec/2 (accessed July 15, 2016).

118. Letter from Louis Lopez to "To Whom It May Concern," July 13, 1981, part of William Haruo Makabe testimony, August 11, 1981, Box 2, Folder 78, Hosokawa

Papers; Ralph J. Moore to Philip M. Glick, December 29, 1942, and January 19, 1943, Box 261/37.109, Entry 16, WRA-NARA.

119. US War Relocation Authority, *WRA: A Story of Human Conservation*, 159–162; US War Relocation Authority, *Wartime Handling of Evacuee Property*, 45–46.

120. Poli, "Japanese Farm Holdings," 16–18. A farm ownership was defined as agricultural land of one acre or more recorded in the name of a Japanese individual, group of individuals, or organization, in contiguous or noncontiguous parcels.

121. Ibid., 16–18.

122. Ibid., 19.

123. Dave Davidson to R. K. Malcolm, May 1, 1942, JERS, Reel 2.

CHAPTER 2

1. Victor Ikeda Interview, interviewed by Richard Potashin, November 6, 2007, denshovh-ivictor-01-0006 and denshovh-ivictor-01-0033, Manzanar National Historic Site Collection, Densho Digital Repository, http://ddr.densho. org (hereafter MNHS-DDR).

2. C. H. Powers, "Final Report, Engineering Section, Operations Division," 15, JERS Reel 31.

3. There are many studies of New Deal liberalism. See, for example, Alan Brinkley, *The End of Reform: New Deal Liberalism in Recession and War* (New York: Alfred A. Knopf, 1995); William H. Chafe, ed., *The Achievement of American Liberalism: The New Deal and Its Legacies* (New York: Columbia University Press, 2003). For the New Deal "pedigree" of the WRA, see Eric L. Muller, "Of Coercion and Accommodation: Looking at Japanese American Imprisonment through a Law Office Window," *Law and History Review* 35, no. 2 (May 2017): 280–286.

4. Mae M. Ngai, *Impossible Subjects: Illegal Aliens and the Making of Modern America* (Princeton, NJ: Princeton University Press, 2004), 177–180; Daniels, *Prisoners Without Trial*, 56–58; US War Relocation Authority, *Relocation Communities for Wartime Evacuees*, 2. Eisenhower and Myer wrote about their WRA experiences in Milton S. Eisenhower, *The President Is Calling* (Garden City, NY: Doubleday, 1974), 93–127 and Dillon S. Myer, *Uprooted Americans: The Japanese Americans and the War Relocation Authority During World War II* (Tucson: University of Arizona Press, 1971). Myer has been subject to criticism for his work as WRA director. In particular, see Drinnon, *Keeper of Concentration Camps*.

5. M. S. Eisenhower to The Secretary of the Navy, June 1, 1942, Box 310/43.100, Entry 16, WRA-NARA.

6. Jason Scott Smith, "New Deal Public Works at War: The WPA and Japanese American Internment," *Pacific Historical Review* 72, no. 1 (February 2003): 63–92 and *Building New Deal Liberalism: The Political Economy of Public Works, 1933–1956* (New York: Cambridge University Press, 2006), 222–231; Neil M. Maher, "A New Deal Body Politic: Landscape, Labor, and the Civilian Conservation

Corps," *Environmental History* 7, no. 3 (July 2002): 435–461; Neil M. Maher, *Nature's New Deal: The Civilian Conservation Corps and the Roots of the American Environmental Movement* (New York: Oxford University Press, 2007).

7. M. S. Eisenhower to C. E. Rachford, May 4, 1942, JERS, Reel 19.

8. For the importance of environmental factors to the site selection process, see Hayashi, *Democratizing the Enemy*, 16–19.

9. For the McLemore quotation, see US Commission on Wartime Relocation and Internment of Civilians, *Personal Justice Denied*, 71–72.

10. E. J. Utz, "Final Report, Operations Division, March 1946," 2, Box 310/43.110, Entry 16, WRA-NARA; "Establishment of Japanese Relocation Areas," National Reclamation Association Bulletin, May 20, 1942, 9–11, Papers of the National Water Resources Association, Water Resources Archive, Colorado State University, http://hdl.handle.net/10217/31691 (accessed May 22, 2013); Burton et al., *Confinement and Ethnicity*, 38–40; Bureau of Reclamation Press Release, May 26, 1942, Box 307/42.224, Entry 16, WRA-NARA.

11. James T. Nishimura to John L. Dewitt, August 5, 1942, Box 305/42.204, Entry 16, WRA-NARA.

12. James T. Nishimura to President Franklin D. Roosevelt, August 10, 1942, Box 305/42.204, Entry 16, WRA-NARA.

13. E. M. Rowalt to John J. McCloy, August 21, 1942, Box 305/42.204, Entry 16, WRA-NARA.

14. Fred W. Rees to R. B. Cozzens, July 1, 1942, Box 307/42.224, Entry 16, WRA-NARA.

15. G. N. Wells to M. S. Eisenhower, April 28, 1942, Box 307/42.224, Entry 16, WRA-NARA.

16. M. S. Eisenhower to G. N. Wells, May 5, 1942, Box 307/42.224, Entry 16, WRA-NARA.

17. R. B. Cozzens to E. R. Fryer, June 3, 1942, Box 308/42.225, Entry 16, WRA-NARA; E. R. Fryer to Dillon S. Myer, July 15, 1942, Box 307/42.224, Entry 16, WRA-NARA.

18. G. N. Wells to M. S. Eisenhower, April 28, 1942, Box 307/42.224, Entry 16, WRA-NARA.

19. E. F. Cress to US Forestry Regional Office, San Francisco, April 21, 1942, Box 305/42.204, Entry 16, WRA-NARA. For wartime connections between forest fires and fears of enemy subversion, see Jake Kosek, *Understories: The Political Life of Forests in Northern New Mexico* (Durham, NC: Duke University Press, 2006), 191–202.

20. Milton S. Eisenhower to Eugene D. Millikin, June 17, 1942, Box 306/42.205, Entry 16, WRA-NARA.

21. Utz, "Final Report, Operations Division," 3–4.

22. Ira N. Gabrielson, Director, US Fish and Wildlife Service to Director, War Relocation Authority, March 20, 1942, Box 310/43.100, Entry 16, WRA-NARA.

23. A. C. Cooley and C. H. Southworth, "Memorandum for the Commissioner," March 21, 1942, Box 310/43.100, Entry 16, WRA-NARA.

24. Memorandum to Mr. Collier from F. H. Daiker, March 20, 1942, Box 21, Entry 178, Records of the Bureau of Indian Affairs, Record Group 75, National Archives and Records Administration, Washington, DC (hereafter BIA-NARA).

25. Memorandum to Mr. Collier from F. H. Daiker, March 20, 1942, Box 21, Entry 178, BIA-NARA.

26. Jodi A. Byrd, *The Transit of Empire: Indigenous Critiques of Colonialism* (Minneapolis: University of Minnesota Press, 2011), 187, 192, 194.

27. E. M. Rowalt, "Memorandum to the Washington Staff," April 29, 1942, Box 291/41.020, Entry 16, WRA-NARA.

28. John Collier, *From Every Zenith: A Memoir; and Some Essays on Life and Thought* (Denver: Sage Books, 1963), 301–302; Greg Robinson, "John Collier," *Densho Encyclopedia*, http://encyclopedia.densho.org/John%20Collier/ (accessed July 17, 2016); Drinnon, *Keeper of Concentration Camps*, 39–41. For the Indian New Deal, see Graham D. Taylor, *The New Deal and American Indian Tribalism: The Administration of the Indian Reorganization Act, 1934–45* (Lincoln: University of Nebraska Press, 1980); Elmer R. Rusco, *A Fateful Time: The Background and Legislative History of the Indian Reorganization Act* (Reno: University of Nevada Press, 2000).

29. Drinnon, *Keeper of Concentration Camps*, 40–42; Collier, *From Every Zenith*, 301–302; Robinson, "John Collier." For more on John Collier, Poston, and the intersection of Indian and Japanese American lives during World War II, see Byrd, *The Transit of Empire*, 185–194; Hayashi, *Democratizing the Enemy*, 22–24, 88–89.

30. For federal water policy in the American West, see Worster, *Rivers of Empire*; Mark Fiege, *Irrigated Eden: The Making of an Agricultural Landscape in the American West* (Seattle: University of Washington Press, 1999); Donald Pisani, *Water and American Government: The Reclamation Bureau, National Water Policy, and the West, 1902–1935* (Berkeley: University of California Press, 2002). For the Owens Valley battles, see William L. Kahrl, *Water and Power: The Conflict over Los Angeles' Water Supply in the Owens Valley* (Berkeley: University of California Press, 1982); John Walton, *Western Times and Water Wars: State, Culture, and Rebellion in California* (Berkeley: University of California Press, 1992).

31. Untitled, undated WRA report, Box 310/43.100, Entry 16, WRA-NARA; "Announcement of Approved Relocation Centers," Administrative Instruction No. 7, July 6, 1942, Box 310/43.100, Entry 16, WRA-NARA; Burton et al., *Confinement and Ethnicity*, 38–40; US War Relocation Authority, *Relocation Communities for Wartime Evacuees*, 4.

32. E. M. Rowalt, "Memorandum to the Washington Staff," April 29, 1942, Box 291/41.020, Entry 16, WRA-NARA.

33. "Establishment of Japanese Relocation Areas," 15. The one exception was Manzanar. Because of limited agricultural opportunities, the WRA planned to keep the Japanese busy with industrial work instead. See E. M. Rowalt, "Memorandum to the Washington Staff," April 29, 1942, Box 291/41.020, Entry 16, WRA-NARA. For

other WRA site criteria, see Untitled, undated WRA report; US War Relocation Authority, *The War Relocation Work Corps: A Circular of Information for Enlistees and Their Families* (Washington, DC: US Department of the Interior, 1942), 6; Lynne Horiuchi, "Dislocations: The Built Environments of Japanese American Internment," in *Guilt by Association: Essays on Settlement, Internment, and Relocation in the Rocky Mountain West*, ed. Mike Mackey (Powell, WY: Western History Publications, 2001), 258–259; US War Relocation Authority, *WRA: A Story of Human Conservation*, 20–23.

34. D. S. Myer to Secretary of Agriculture, June 23, 1942, Box 310/43.100, Entry 16, WRA-NARA.

35. E. R. Fryer to Milton S. Eisenhower, May 4, 1942, Box 292/41.030, Entry 16, WRA-NARA. For Fryer's previous work with the Navajo, see E. R. Fryer Interview, interviewed by Donald Parman, July 21, 1970, American Indian Oral History Collection, 1967–1972, Center for Southwest Research, University Libraries, University of New Mexico, http://econtent.unm.edu/cdm/ref/collection/navtrans/id/370 (accessed July 18, 2016).

36. "A Self-Liquidating Project," *Millard County Chronicle*, June 25, 1942.

37. S. R. Marean to John C. Page, April 18, 1942, Box 293/41.090, Entry 16, WRA-NARA.

38. E. R. Fryer to M. S. Eisenhower, April 18, 1942, Box 193/41.090, Entry 16, WRA-NARA; Bureau of Reclamation Press Release, May 26, 1942, Box 307/42.224, Entry 16, WRA-NARA.

39. "The War Relocation Authority Has Established . . . ." no date, Box 310/43.100, Entry 16, WRA-NARA. For the arid West as a health destination, see Gregg Mitman, *Breathing Space: How Allergies Shape Our Lives and Landscape* (New Haven: Yale University Press, 2007), 89–129.

40. E. R. Fryer to Milton S. Eisenhower, May 4, 1942, Box 292/41.030, Entry 16, WRA-NARA.

41. Fred W. Ross and Mark W. Radcliffe to R. B. Cozzens, no date, Box 292/41.030, Entry 16, WRA-NARA.

42. Untitled Soil Survey of Central Utah, undated, Box 292/41.030, Entry 16, WRA-NARA.

43. E. J. Utz to D. S. Myer, June 22, 1943, Box 292/41.030, Entry 16, WRA-NARA.

44. "Japanese Will Be Located in New Relocation Area," *Millard County Chronicle*, June 25, 1942; "Sign up Carpenters for Japanese Camp," *Millard County Chronicle*, July 9, 1942.

45. Walton, *Western Times and Water Wars*; Marc Reisner, *Cadillac Desert: The American West and Its Disappearing Water*, rev. ed. (New York: Penguin, 1993); Kahrl, *Water and Power.*

46. Manchester Boddy to Francis Biddle, February 9, 1942, JERS, Reel 1.

47. Tom C. Clark to Ralph P. Merritt, March 7, 1942, Box 21, Folder 6, Manzanar War Relocation Center Records, Collection 122, Special Collections, Charles E. Young

Library, University of California, Los Angeles (hereafter Manzanar-UCLA Records); Robert L. Brown and Ralph P. Merritt, "Project Director's Report," in *Final Report, Manzanar Relocation Center*, Volume 1, Reel 76, Field Basic Documentation of the War Relocation Authority, Records of the War Relocation Authority, Record Group 210, Microfilm C0053, National Archives and Records Administration, Washington, DC (hereafter FBD-WRA).

48. H. A. Van Norman to S. B. Robinson, March 3, 1942, Water Executive Office, Administrative-Executive Files, Manzanar Relocation Center, Correspondence, May 1942–October 1943, WP14-1:3, Los Angeles Department of Water and Power Historical Records Program (hereafter LADWP Records).

49. Proposal: Japanese Alien Problems, Los Angeles County, Submitted by Wayne H. Fisher, Ed F. Williams, and L. A. Hauser, February 16, 1942, Box 52, Fletcher Bowron Collection, Huntington Library, San Marino, CA; Radio Broadcast of Mayor Fletcher Bowron, Station KECA, Thursday, February 19, 1942, 6:30 p.m., Box 52, Bowron Collection. The WRA eventually established one relocation center, Poston (Colorado River), about twelve miles south of Parker.

50. Brown and Merritt, "Project Director's Report"; Harlan D. Unrau, *The Evacuation and Relocation of Persons of Japanese Ancestry During World War II: A Historical Study of the Manzanar Relocation Center*, Volume 1 (Washington, DC: US Department of the Interior, National Park Service, 1996), 128; Press Release, March 7, 1942, FBD-WRA, Reel 75; John L. DeWitt to H. A. Van Norman, March 7, 1942, Water Executive Office, Administrative-Executive Files, Manzanar Relocation Center, Correspondence, May 1942–October 1943, WP14-1:3, LADWP Records.

51. Jeannie Natsuko Shinozuka, "From a 'Contagious' to a 'Poisonous Yellow Peril'? Japanese and Japanese Americans in Public Health and Agriculture, 1890s–1950" (PhD diss., University of Minnesota, 2009), 209–219.

52. T. Blevans to H. A. Van Norman, March 10, 1942, Water Executive Office, Administrative-Executive Files, Manzanar Relocation Center, Correspondence, May 1942–October 1943, WP14-1:3, LADWP Records. See also Kyle Palmer, "Proposed Owens Valley Camp for Japs Opposed," *Los Angeles Times*, March 7, 1942, p. 6.

53. H. L. Ford to Bureau of Power and Water, March 6, 1942, Water Executive Office, Administrative-Executive Files, Manzanar Relocation Center, Correspondence, May 1942–October 1943, WP14-1:3, LADWP Records.

54. Michael Rawson, *Eden on the Charles: The Making of Boston* (Cambridge, MA: Harvard University Press, 2010); David Stradling, *Making Mountains: New York City and the Catskills* (Seattle: University of Washington Press, 2008).

55. Nancy Tomes, *The Gospel of Germs: Men, Women, and the Microbe in American Life* (Cambridge, MA: Harvard University Press, 1998; Charles E. Rosenberg, *The Cholera Years: The United States in 1832, 1849, and 1866* (Chicago: University of Chicago Press, 1987).

56. Natalia Molina, *Fit to Be Citizens? Public Health and Race in Los Angeles, 1879–1939* (Berkeley: University of California Press, 2006), 1–2; William Deverell, *Whitewashed Adobe: The Rise of Los Angeles and the Remaking of Its Mexican Past* (Berkeley: University of California Press, 2004), 172–206.

57. For prewar fears of dangerous Japanese bodies, see Shinozuka, "Poisonous Yellow Peril," 27–206.

58. "Placing Japanese in the Owens Valley," *Los Angeles Times*, March 7, 1942, p. A4.

59. *Inyo Independent*, March 6, 1942, p. 1.

60. Ronald Bishop with Morgan Dudkewitz, Alissa Falcone, and Renee Daggett, *Community Newspapers and the Japanese-American Incarceration Camps: Community, Not Controversy* (Lanham, MD: Lexington Books, 2015), 7–9.

61. H. A. Van Norman to H. L. Ford, March 10, 1942, Water Executive Office, Administrative-Executive Files, Manzanar Relocation Center, Correspondence, May 1942–October 1943, WP14-1:3, LADWP Records.

62. R. F. Goudey to H. A. Van Norman, March 10, 1942, and R. F. Goudey to H. A. Van Norman, March 24, 1942, Water Executive Office, Administrative-Executive Files, Manzanar Relocation Center, Correspondence, May 1942–October 1943, WP14-1:3, LADWP Records. Goudey's recommendations included no more than ten thousand people living at Manzanar unless the sewage treatment plant facilities were enlarged; prohibitions on fishing, wading, swimming, and the disposal of liquid waste in the aqueduct and its tributaries; all garbage hauled below the aqueduct for disposal; no fecal matter or fertilizer made from sewage used on crops draining into the aqueduct; corrals and animals located where they would not contaminate the aqueduct.

63. H. A. Van Norman to Lieutenant General J. L. DeWitt, March 25, 1942, Water Executive Office, Administrative-Executive Files, Manzanar Relocation Center, Correspondence, May 1942–October 1943, WP14-1:3, LADWP Records.

64. "The Silverman Report," in *Final Report, Manzanar Relocation Center*, Volume 1, Appendix 25, FBD-WRA, Reel 76; Unrau, *Evacuation and Relocation*, 227.

65. Ida M. Johnson to the War Relocation Authority, April 30, 1942, Box 293/41.090, Entry 16, WRA-NARA.

66. John C. Page to Board of Directors, American Falls Reservoir District No. 2, May 4, 1942, Box 293/41.090, Entry 16, WRA-NARA.

67. Attorney for American Falls Reservoir District No. 2 to John C. Page, May 23, 1942, Box 293/41.090, Entry 16, WRA-NARA.

68. A. E. Robinson to Commissioner of Indian Affairs, May 2, 1942, Box 3, Entry 180H, BIA-NARA.

69. A. E. Robinson to Commissioner of Indian Affairs, May 5, 1942, Box 3, Entry 180H, BIA-NARA.

70. A. E. Robinson to John Collier, May 5, 1942, Box 3, Entry 180H, BIA-NARA; William Zimmerman Jr. to M. S. Eisenhower, May 21, 1942, Box 3, Entry 180H, BIA-NARA.

71. A. E. Robinson to Commissioner of Indian Affairs, May 2, 1942, Box 3, Entry 180H, BIA-NARA.

72. A. E. Robinson to Commissioner of Indian Affairs, May 5, 1942, Box 3, Entry 180H, BIA-NARA.

73. A. E. Robinson to The Gila River Pima-Maricopa Community Tribal Council, May 5, 1942, Box 3, Entry 180H, BIA-NARA.

74. Memorandum of Understanding between the Director of the War Relocation Authority and the Secretary of the Interior, October 8, 1942, Box 291/41.020, Entry 16, WRA-NARA. The WRA also leased two additional parcels of 850 and 491 acres each to be used for the camp buildings at a cost of one dollar per acre annually.

75. Memorandum of Agreement between the War Department and War Relocation Authority, April 17, 1942, Papers of the US Commission on Wartime Relocation and Internment of Civilians, Part 1, Numerical File Archive, Reel 11; Utz, "Final Report, Operations Division," 16.

76. M. S. Eisenhower to John J. McCloy, June 6, 1942, JERS, Reel 19.

77. "The War Relocation Authority Has Established"; Burton et al., *Confinement and Ethnicity*, 40–43.

78. Utz, "Final Report, Operations Division," 16; Burton et al., *Confinement and Ethnicity*, 40.

79. E. R. Fryer to Colonel Bendetsen, April 25, 1942, JERS, Reel 19; E. R. Fryer to Project Directors, June 16, 1942, JERS, Reel 20.

80. The exceptions were Granada, Heart Mountain, and Gila River. About half of Granada's barracks were sided with Celotex, while all of Gila River's barracks were sided with Sheetrock. Utz, "Final Report, Operations Division," 17.

81. Roscoe E. Bell, "Relocation Center Life, Topaz, Utah, 1942–1945," 9. Special Collections, J. Willard Marriott Library, University of Utah.

82. Burton et al., *Confinement and Ethnicity*, 40–43; Utz, "Final Report, Operations Division," 17; Dr. Carter, "Progress and Organization Report on Manzanar, Japanese Relocation Settlement," June 1, 1942, JERS, Reel 158; "Construction of Buildings Within the Center," undated, JERS, Reel 109. For construction specifications, see War Department, US Army Corps of Engineers, *Specifications for Construction of Abraham Relocation Center at Abraham, Utah*, 69, Box 1, Entry 54, WRA-NARA.

83. George H. Dean, "Conditions at Manzanar Relocation Area, June 1, 1942," Box 293/41.080, Entry 16, WRA-NARA.

84. Toshi Takeda, Block Manager Block 23 to Bob Yeaton, August 11, 1942, Box 142/550, Entry 48, WRA-NARA.

85. Tom Kawaguchi Interview, interviewed by Sandra Taylor, San Francisco, CA, November 5, 1987, Box 1, Folder 5, Topaz Oral Histories, Accession 1002, Special Collections, J. Willard Marriott Library, University of Utah (hereafter Topaz Oral Histories).

86. Utz, "Final Report, Operations Division," 16–17; C. H. Powers, "Final Report, Engineering Section, Operations Division," 7, 15, JERS, Reel 31.

87. Report of meeting held September 3, 1942, Box 129/103, Entry 48, WRA-NARA. JERS analyst Charles Kikuchi wrote frequently about the insect problem and lack of screens during his early days at Gila River. See Charles Kikuchi diary, September 3, 1942, September 4, 1942, September 7, 1942, 653, 655, 664, JERS, Reel 96.

88. Charles F. Ernst to District Engineer, Attention Captain H. F. Dyer, March 25, 1943, Box 103/670, Entry 48, WRA-NARA.

89. "Screening of Barrack and Latrine Buildings, Serial No. 25784," in Report of the Engineering Section, Beginning of Center—September, 1942 to Closing of Center—January, 1946, Central Utah Project, FBD-WRA, Reel 16.

90. "Construction of Buildings Within the Center," undated, JERS, Reel 109.

91. "Japanese Will Be Located in New Relocation Area," *Millard County Chronicle*, June 25, 1942; "Sign Up Carpenters for Japanese Camp," *Millard County Chronicle*, July 9, 1942.

92. "Material Lack Slows Work on Jap Camp," *Millard County Chronicle*, July 23, 1942.

93. Bell, "Relocation Center Life," 9.

94. "Woman Burned by Hot Tar," Topaz Report H73, October 4, 1942, FBD-WRA, Reel 5.

95. "Incomplete Housing Hazard," Topaz Report H82, October 5, 1942, FBD-WRA, Reel 5.

96. Ralph C. Barnhart to Philip M. Glick, May 26, 1943, Box 255/37.105, Entry 16, WRA-NARA.

97. Charles F. Ernst to Charles Welch, June 12, 1943, Box 255/37.105, Entry 16, WRA-NARA.

98. Ralph C. Barnhart to Philip M. Glick, August 21, 1944, Box 256/37.105, Entry 16, WRA-NARA.

99. "Complaint," Topaz Report H104, October 11, 1942, FBD-WRA, Reel 5.

100. Robert Spencer to Robert Lowie, August 22, 1942, JERS, Reel 285. For a description of JERS, see the discussion in the introduction. Spencer was a doctoral student in anthropology at the University of California, Berkeley, when he joined JERS. For more on his work at Gila River, see Arthur A. Hansen, "The Evacuation and Resettlement Study at the Gila River Relocation Center, 1942–1944," *Journal of the West* 38, no. 2 (April 1999): 45–55 and Robert Spencer Interview, interviewed by Arthur Hansen, July 15–17, 1987, O. H. 1958, Japanese American Oral History Project, Oral History Program, California State University, Fullerton, in *Japanese American World War II Evacuation Oral History Project, Part III: Analysts*, ed. Arthur A. Hansen (Munich: K. G. Saur, 1994), 175–340.

101. Robert F. Spencer, "Report No. 2-A, November 2, 1942," 33–35, JERS, Reel 283.

102. Robert F. Spencer, "Report No. 2 on Gila River, November 2, 1942," 20, JERS, Reel 283.

103. Ibid.

104. Burton et al., *Confinement and Ethnicity,* 43.

105. Robert F. Spencer, Field Report No. 1, August 23, 1942, JERS, Reel 283.

106. Minidoka Report No. 21, December 17, 1942, JERS, Reel 332.

107. "Gibson-Thunberg Report on Field Trip to Each of the Ten Relocation Centers," May 27, 1943, Box 310/43.100, Entry 16, WRA-NARA.

108. Edmund Couch Jr., "Report of Sanitary Survey of Water Supply, Minidoka W.R.A. Center," 1944, Box 240/63.400, Entry 48, WRA-NARA.

109. W. Morse Little and Agnes V. Bartlett, "Health Section," *Final Report, Manzanar Relocation Center,* Volume 3, 33, FBD-WRA, Reel 78; Unrau, *Evacuation and Relocation,* 240–242.

110. John F. Baxter to J. A. Harmon, Sanitary Engineer, California State Department of Public Health, February 23, 1943, Box 224/43.120, Entry 48, WRA-NARA.

111. John F. Baxter to Dr. George Shultz, Health Officer, Lone Pine, June 1943, War Relocation Authority Records, RG 210, Box 224/43.120, Entry 48, WRA-NARA.

112. Leland Barrows to Ralph P. Merritt, October 30, 1943, Box 224/43.120, Entry 48, WRA-NARA.

113. The Japanese prefectures sending the largest number of emigrants to Hawaii and the United States were Wakayama, Okayama, Hiroshima, Yamaguchi, Fukuoka, Nagasaki, and Kumamoto. See Spickard, *Japanese Americans,* 15–16; Ichioka, *The Issei,* 40–56.

114. Yukiko Miyahara Interview, interviewed by Kirk Peterson, April 10, 2009, denshovh-myukiko_2-01, MNHS-DDR.

115. Kay Sakai Nakao Interview, interviewed by Debra Grindeland, February 25, 2006, denshovh-nkazuko-01, Bainbridge Island Japanese American Community Collection, Densho Digital Repository, http://ddr.densho.org.

116. Masao Kobayashi to Elizabeth Bayler Willis, no date, Box 3, Folder 18, Elizabeth Bayler Willis Papers, Accession 2583-019, Special Collections, University of Washington Libraries. See also "Harumi Serata," in Dempster, *Making Home from War,* 160–161.

117. Morgan Yamanaka Interview, interviewed by Sandra Taylor, San Francisco, CA, May 11, 1988, Box 1, Folder 6, Topaz Oral Histories.

118. Uchida, *Desert Exile,* 137.

119. "Daisy Uyeda Satoda," in Dempster, *Making Home from War,* 146.

120. Suyemoto, *I Call to Remembrance,* 74, 79, 80. For sensory history, especially the history of sound, see Richard Cullen Rath, "Hearing American History," *Journal of American History* 95, no. 2 (September 2008): 417–431; Peter A. Coates, "The Strange Stillness of the Past: Toward an Environmental History of Sound and Noise," *Environmental History* 10, no. 4 (October 2005): 636–665.

121. Michi Kobi Interview, interviewed by Sandra Taylor, New York, NY, October 6, 1987, Box 1, Folder 13, Topaz Oral Histories.

122. Ishi Morishita to Mrs. Charles Gates, January 26, 1943, ddr-densho-211-9, Gates Family Collection, Densho Digital Repository, http://ddr.densho.org/.

123. Bo T. Sakaguchi Interview, interviewed by John Allen, November 6, 2002, denshovh-sbo-01, MNHS-DDR.

124. Henry Fukuhara Interview, interviewed by John Allen, November 6, 2002, denshovh-fhenry-01, MNHS-DDR.

125. Maya Aikawa Interview, interviewed by Sandra Taylor, Berkeley, CA, November 4, 1987, Box 1, Folder 2, Topaz Oral Histories.

126. Tad Hayashi Interview, interviewed by Sandra Taylor, Berkeley, CA, October 28, 1987, Box 1, Folder 4, Topaz Oral Histories.

127. Warren Watanabe, "First Annual Report: September 1942 through September 1943," 21, Project Reports Division, Historical Section, Box 2, Folder 14, US War Relocation Authority Central Utah Project Papers, Accession 0056-001, Special Collections, University of Washington Libraries (hereafter Central Utah-UW Papers).

128. "State of the City," *Trek* 1, no. 1 (1942): 3, Box 3, Folder 12, Central Utah-UW Papers.

129. Powers, "Final Report, Engineering Section, Operations Division," 6.

130. George H. Dean, "Conditions at Manzanar Relocation Area, June 1, 1942," Box 293/41.080, Entry 16, WRA-NARA.

131. Minidoka Report No. 1, Community Analysis Section, September 19, 1942, JERS, Reel 332.

132. Minidoka War Relocation Project, Report for Quarter Ended September 30, 1942, p. 2, JERS, Reel 332.

133. "Dust, Heat, Lightning, and Rain," *Gila News-Courier*, August 7, 1943, p. 2.

134. Dean, "Conditions at Manzanar Relocation Area, June 1, 1942."

135. Manzanar Project Report No. 11, 29 June 1942, FBD-WRA, Reel 76. See also Report No. 65 submitted to Mr. Bob Brown from the Information Office, June 11, 1942, Box 7, Folder 5, Manzanar-UCLA Records.

136. Karen Piper, *Left in the Dust: How Race and Politics Created a Human and Environmental Tragedy in L.A.* (New York: Palgrave Macmillan, 2006), 127–128. According to Piper, the area continues to be plagued by Owens Lake dust, which is carcinogenic and poses a health hazard to visitors to the Manzanar National Historic Site.

137. Ernest C. Hendrix, "Narrative Report," no date, in "Final Report of Engineering Section," FBD-WRA, Reel 43.

138. Administrative Instruction No. 89, 28 April 1943, Box 312/43.500, Entry 16, WRA-NARA; David A. Rogers to E. R. Smith, 7 May 1942, Box 143/552, Entry 48, WRA-NARA.

139. E. W. Nichols to L. J. Korn, Asst Project Director, October 10, 1942, Box 143/552, Entry 48, WRA-NARA.

140. E. W. Nichols to Lee Noftzger, December 24, 1942, Box 143/552, Entry 48, WRA-NARA.

141. L. H. Bennett to Users of Evaporative Coolers, June 4, 1943, Box 143/563, Entry 48, WRA-NARA. Evaporative coolers were available for sale at the Gila River canteen. See "Why Suffer From Sweltering Heat?" *Gila News-Courier*, February 6, 1943.

142. Arthur Kleinkopf, *Relocation Center Diary*, 117, 165–166. Idaho State Historical Society, Boise, Idaho.

143. Minidoka Relocation Center, Quarterly Report for Period Ended June 30, 1943, p. 18, JERS, Reel 332.

144. For the installation of flooring, see Arthur M. Sandridge and Oliver E. Sisler, "Engineering Section, February 1946," 49–50, FBD-WRA, Reel 78; Manzanar Project Report No. 21, July 13, 1942; Manzanar Project Report No. 23, July 16, 1942; Manzanar Project Report No. 25, July 23, 1942; Manzanar Project Report No. 38, August 22, 1942; Manzanar Project Report No. 45, September 10, 1942; Manzanar Project Report No. 64, October 30, 1942, FBD-WRA, Reel 76. For quote, see E. R. Fryer to Dillon S. Myer, June 29, 1942, Box 310/43.100, Entry 16, WRA-NARA. For trapping of heat, see Letter to a Nisei man (Joe Nagano) from his sister (Masako Nagano), July 13, 1943, ddr-densho-153-67, MNHS-DDR.

145. Residents of Block 4 to Administration, July 24, 1942, Box 129/103, WRA-NARA, Entry 48.

146. Kazumi Yoneyama Interview, interviewed by Martha Makagawa, May 23, 2012, denshovh-ykazumi-01, DVHC-DDR.

147. Yasu Koyamatsu Momii Interview, interviewed by Sharon Yamato, October 25, 2011, denshovh-myasu-01-0001, DVHC-DDR.

148. Robert B. Throckmorton to Philip M. Glick, June 17, 1943, Box 260/37.108, Entry 16, WRA-NARA.

149. Robert B. Throckmorton to Philip M. Glick, July 2, 1943, Box 260/37.108, Entry 16, WRA-NARA.

150. Tom Cameron, "Japanese Get 'Break' in Owens Valley Move," *Los Angeles Times*, March 30, 1942, p. A1.

CHAPTER 3

1. Lewis J. Korn, Acting Project Director to Harvey Hilyard, November 21, 1942, Box 138/515, Entry 48, WRA-NARA.

2. Jack C. Sleathe, MD, Chief Medical Officer to R. B. Cozzens, Acting Project Director, October 31, 1942, Box 143/560, Entry 48, WRA-NARA.

3. Irvin Hull to Charles F. Ernst, Weekly Narrative Report of October 23, 1942, Box 191/24.031, Entry 16, WRA-NARA.

4. Grace Oshita interview, interviewed by Leslie Kellen, February 20, 1985, Box 3, Folder 3, Interviews with Japanese Americans in Utah, Accession 1209, Special Collections, J. Willard Marriott Library, University of Utah (hereafter Utah Interviews-UU).

5. Jean Kariya and Kitty Nakagawa Interview, interviewed by Sandra Taylor, Leonia, NJ, June 14, 1988, Box 2, Folder 6, Topaz Oral Histories.

6. Russell A. Bankson, "Labor Trouble in Topaz," November 5, 1943, Project Reports Division, Historical Section, Central Utah Project, FBD-WRA, Reel 7.

7. For the use of convict labor for public works and agriculture, see Clarence Jefferson Hall Jr., "Prisonland: Environment, Society, and Mass Incarceration on New York's Northern Frontier, 1845–1999" (PhD diss., State University of New York, Stony Brook, 2014); Volker Janssen, "When the 'Jungle' Met the Forest: Public Work, Civil Defense, and Prison Camps in Postwar California," *Journal of American History* 96, no. 3 (December 2009): 702–726; David M. Oshinsky, *"Worse Than Slavery": Parchman Farm and the Ordeal of Jim Crow Justice* (New York: Free Press, 1996); Matthew J. Mancini, *One Dies, Get Another: Convict Leasing in the American South, 1866–1928* (Columbia: University of South Carolina Press, 1996); Rebecca M. McLennan, *Crisis of Imprisonment: Protest, Politics, and the Making of the American Penal State, 1776–1941* (New York: Cambridge University Press, 2008).

8. For western extractive industry workscapes, see Andrews, *Killing for Coal*. For slave workscapes, see Stewart, *What Nature Suffers to Groe,* xii; Mart A. Stewart, "Slavery and the Origins of African American Environmentalism," in *"To Love the Wind and the Rain": African Americans and Environmental History*, ed. Dianne D. Glave and Mark Stoll (Pittsburgh, PA: University of Pittsburgh Press, 2006), 9–20; Joyce E. Chaplin, "Tidal Rice Cultivation and the Problem of Slavery in South Carolina and Georgia, 1760–1815," *William and Mary Quarterly*, 3rd ser., 49, no. 1 (January 1992): 56–57. For other studies that explore how nature shaped labor relations, see Kathryn Morse, *The Nature of Gold: An Environmental History of the Klondike Gold Rush* (Seattle: University of Washington Press, 2003); Chad Montrie, *Making a Living: Work and Environment in the United States* (Chapel Hill: University of North Carolina Press, 2008).

9. Broom and Riemer, *Removal and Return*, 13. The former groups constituted over 32.5 percent of the employed population; the latter groups constituted 18.4 percent.

10. US War Relocation Authority, *The Evacuated People: A Quantitative Description* (Washington, DC: US Department of the Interior, War Relocation Authority, 1946), 61.

11. Executive Order 9102, Establishing the War Relocation Authority, March 18, 1942, The American Presidency Project, University of California, Santa Barbara, http://www.presidency.ucsb.edu/ws/?pid=16239 (accessed June 1, 2017).

12. "Standards and Details—Construction of Japanese Evacuee Reception Centers," June 8, 1942, JERS, Reel 20.

13. Edwin E. Ferguson to Harvey M. Coverley, November 12, 1942, Box 96/471.2, Entry 48, WRA-NARA.

14. *The First Year in the War Program of the Department of the Interior and the Petroleum Administration for War* (Washington, DC: Department of the Interior, 1942), 7.

15. C. E. Needham, ed., *Minerals Yearbook, 1944* (Washington, DC: US Department of the Interior, 1946), 823.

16. Raymond E. Murphy, "Wartime Changes in the Patterns of United States Coal Production," *Annals of the Association of American Geographers* 37, no. 4 (December 1947): 187–190, 193.

17. Edwin E. Ferguson to Harvey M. Coverley, November 12, 1942, Box 96/471.2, Entry 48, WRA-NARA.

18. T. Matsumura, Washington Wood & Coal Co., Seattle, November 9, 1942, Box 233/16.100, Entry 48, WRA-NARA.

19. Minidoka Community Analysis Report No. 1, September 19, 1942, JERS, Reel 332; "An Historical Glimpse of Coal and Coal Division," Field Report No. 42, Community Analysis Section, Minidoka, JERS, Reel 332.

20. Minidoka Report No. 10, November 2, 1942, JERS, Reel 332.

21. Minidoka Report No. 11, November 24, 1942, JERS, Reel 332.

22. Edwin E. Ferguson to Harvey M. Coverley, November 12, 1942, Box 96/471.2, Entry 48, WRA-NARA.

23. "An Historical Glimpse of Coal and Coal Division."

24. "An Historical Glimpse of Coal and Coal Division"; C. T. Takahashi Interview, interviewed by Judith Austin, August 16, 1984, Seattle, WA, OH 1069, Idaho State Historical Society, Boise, Idaho.

25. "An Historical Glimpse of Coal and Coal Division."

26. Gilbert L. Niesse to James F. Hughes, Weekly Narrative Report, October 23, 1942, Box 191/24.031, Entry 16, WRA-NARA.

27. Henry R. Watson to J. F. Hughes, November 6, 1942, Box 102/670, Entry 48, WRA-NARA.

28. Edwin E. Ferguson to Harvey M. Coverley, November 12, 1942, Box 96/471.2, Entry 48, WRA-NARA.

29. "Coal," Topaz Report H197, November 13, 1942, FBD-WRA, Reel 5.

30. Memo to James F. Hughes (Deputy Project Director) from Roy Potter (Supply Officer), October 8, 1943, Box 96/471.2, Entry 48, WRA-NARA.

31. "Coal," Topaz Report H292, December 17, 1942, FBD-WRA, Reel 5.

32. Don Nakahata and Alice Interview, interviewed by Sandra Taylor, Mill Valley, CA, May 12, 1988, Box 1, Folder 7, Topaz Oral Histories.

33. Harry H. L. Kitano Interview, interviewed by Sandra Taylor, Los Angeles, CA, September 20, 1987, Box 2, Folder 7, Topaz Oral Histories.

34. Office Letter No. 31, November 26, 1943, FBD-WRA, Reel 2.

35. "The Following Precautions Should Be Observed When Using Coal Burning Stoves," Minidoka, 1942, FBD-WRA, Reel 87.

36. "Farm Field Crew Walkout, July 15–17, 1943," Field Report No. 143, Community Analysis Section, Minidoka Relocation Center, JERS, Reel 332.

37. "Report on Janitorial Flareup in Minidoka Project," Field Report No. 240, November 20, 1943, Community Analysis Section, Minidoka Relocation Center,

Reel 23, Community Analysis Reports and Community Analysis Trend Reports of the War Relocation Authority, Records of the War Relocation Authority, Record Group 210, Microfilm M1342, National Archives and Records Administration, Washington, DC (hereafter CAR-WRA); Representatives of Maintenance Workers to Harry L. Stafford, November 18, 1943, Harry R. Hatate Papers, Box 1, Folder 2, Accession 4513-001, Special Collections, University of Washington Libraries (hereafter Hatate Papers).

38. "Report on Janitorial Flareup in Minidoka Project"; G. R. Green, Supt. of Construction and Maintenance to All Maintenance Workers, Field Report No. 240, November 8, 1943, Community Analysis Section, Minidoka Relocation Center, CAR-WRA, Reel 23.

39. "Labor Relations in Relocation Centers," 18–20, Community Analysis Report No. 10, October 28, 1944, CAR-WRA, Reel 1; "Report on Janitorial Flareup in Minidoka Project."

40. Representatives of Maintenance Workers to Harry L. Stafford, November 18, 1943.

41. Ibid.

42. "Meeting With Maintenance Group, November 20, 1943," 7, 9, Box 315/43.504, Entry 16, WRA-NARA.

43. For college students, see Okihiro, *Storied Lives*; Allan W. Austin, *From Concentration Camp to Campus: Japanese American Students and World War II* (Urbana: University of Illinois Press, 2007); Daniels, *Prisoners Without Trial*, 72–74. Chapter 5 provides an in-depth discussion of the seasonal work leaves.

44. Dillon S. Myer, "The Truth About Relocation," August 6, 1943, JERS, Reel 22; US War Relocation Authority, *Relocation of Japanese Americans* (Washington, DC: US Department of Interior, 1943), 2–3.

45. Daniels, *Prisoners Without Trial*, 78–80.

46. Myer, "The Truth About Relocation."

47. "Meeting With Maintenance Group, November 20, 1943," 3, 25.

48. Ibid., 10–12, 19–20, 26–27. Since Minidoka had thirty-five blocks, this amounted to 140 people. With the addition of twenty-four relief workers, Minidoka wanted a total of 164 people, over three times the quota of 52 people that the Washington WRA office had allotted Minidoka for janitorial services on the residential blocks.

49. Ibid., 13–15, 21, 27–28. Lignite coal also has a lower energy content. See Donald W. Clements, "Recent Trends in the Geography of Coal," *Annals of the Association of American Geographers* 67, no. 1 (March 1977): 109–125.

50. "Meeting With Maintenance Group, November 20, 1943," 9, 21.

51. Ibid., 9, 19–21, 29, 31–32.

52. "Chronology of Events Connected with Boilermen's Situation," no date, FBD-WRA, Reel 85; "A Preliminary Survey of the Boilermen's Dispute at Minidoka," 4, January 17, 1944, FBD-WRA, Reel 86.

53. G. R. Green to Harry Hatate, December 28, 1943, FBD-WRA, Reel 85; "All Maintenance Workers, Minutes of Meeting," December 29, 1943, FBD-WRA, Reel

85; Harry R. Hatate to Glenn Green, December 30, 1943, FBD-WRA, Reel 85; "A Preliminary Survey of the Boilermen's Dispute at Minidoka," 4–5; "Report on Resident delegation dealing with Janitorial trouble," Field Report No. 257, January 2, 1944, Minidoka Relocation Center, CAR-WRA, Reel 23; "Evacuee Opinion as of Dec. 30, 1943 Regarding Janitorial Situation," Field Report No. 256, December 30, 1943, Community Analysis Section, Minidoka Relocation Center, CAR-WRA, Reel 23.

54. R. S. Davidson to All Boilermen and Janitors in All Residential Blocks, December 31, 1943, FBD-WRA, Reel 85; "Report on Resident Delegation Dealing With Janitorial Trouble"; "Minutes of the Boilermen Meeting," 2, 6, 8, January 4, 1944, FBD-WRA, Reel 85; "Transcript of Staff Meeting, January 5, 1944, 9:30 A.M.," 8–9, JERS, Reel 313.

55. "Effect of Janitorial Walkout, Situation as of Wednesday, January 5, 1944," Field Report No. 258, Community Analysis Section, Minidoka Relocation Center, CAR-WRA, Reel 23; "A Preliminary Survey of the Boilermen's Dispute at Minidoka," 8, 25; "Transcript of Staff Meeting, January 5, 1944," 9.

56. "Transcript of Staff Meeting, January 5, 1944," 11–12, 14.

57. "Meeting of the Administration Officials with Block Manager Representatives, Wednesday, January 5, 1944, 3:00 p.m.," 3, JERS, Reel 313.

58. "Report of Discussion Concerning Lack of Hot Water in the Camp Between Mr. Davison and a Delegation of Women Residents," January 6, 1944, FBD-WRA, Reel 85; Ladies of Hunt Relocation Center to Dillon S. Myer, January 6, 1944, FBD-WRA, Reel 85.

59. D. S. Myer to H. L. Stafford, January 8, 1944, JERS, Reel 313.

60. "Effect of Janitorial Walkout, Situation as of Wednesday, January 5, 1944"; Andrea Geiger, *Subverting Exclusion: Transpacific Encounters with Race, Caste, and Borders, 1885–1928* (New Haven: Yale University Press, 2011), 1–2, 16–17; David Howell, *Geographies of Identity in Nineteenth-Century Japan* (Berkeley: University of California Press, 2005), 28–29, 36. See also Timothy D. Amos, "Portrait of a Tokugawa Outcaste Community," *East Asian History* 32–33 (December 2006–June 2007): 83–108; Gerald Groemer, "The Creation of the Edo Outcaste Order," *Journal of Japanese Studies* 27, no. 2 (Summer 2001): 263–293.

61. Brian Hayashi, "Informants/'inu,'" *Densho Encyclopedia*, http://encyclopedia. densho.org/Informants%20/%20%22inu%22/ (accessed July 21, 2014). See also Hayashi, *Democratizing the Enemy*, 100, 125.

62. "Block Delegates Mediation Meeting with Project Director, Stafford," Field Report No. 261, January 7, 1944, Community Analysis Section, Minidoka Relocation Center, CAR-WRA, Reel 23.

63. "A Preliminary Survey of the Boilermen's Dispute at Minidoka," 27–29.

64. Cherstin Lyon, "Japanese American Citizens League," *Densho Encyclopedia*, http://encyclopedia.densho.org/Japanese%20American%20Citizens%20League/ (accessed June 6, 2017); Hayashi, *Democratizing the Enemy*, 69, 149; Lyon, *Prisons and Patriots*, 20, 45–54.

65. "A Preliminary Survey of the Boilermen's Dispute at Minidoka," 23.

66. "Minutes—Joint Meeting of Boilermen, Janitors and Janitresses, January 10, 1944," in *Life in the Minidoka Relocation Center*, Volume 2, 26–28, Box 1, Yoshito Fujii Papers, Accession 1582, Special Collections, University of Washington Libraries; Block Delegates Mediation Committee to H. L. Stafford, January 10, 1944, FBD-WRA, Reel 85; "Block Delegate Meeting to Discuss Settlement of Boilermen Dispute and to Make Plans for Nominating Convention," Field Report No. 265, January 12, 1944, Community Analysis Section, Minidoka Relocation Center, CAR-WRA, Reel 23; "A Preliminary Survey of the Boilermen's Dispute at Minidoka," 13–14; "Labor Relations in Relocation Centers," 19.

67. "Evacuee Feelings in Block 22 Toward the Voluntary Firing of Utility Building Stoves," Field Report No. 268, January 17, 1944, Community Analysis Section, Minidoka Relocation Center, CAR-WRA, Reel 23. See also, "A Preliminary Survey of the Boilermen's Dispute at Minidoka," 24.

68. "A Preliminary Survey of the Boilermen's Dispute at Minidoka," 31. For the connection between the environment and an Asian American working-class consciousness, see Dorothy Fujita-Rony, "Water and Land: Asian Americans and the U.S. West," *Pacific Historical Review* 76, no. 4 (2007): 573.

69. "Minutes—Joint Meeting of Boilermen, Janitors and Janitresses, January 10, 1944."

70. Bell, "Relocation Center Life," 26–27; Report of the Engineering Section, Beginning of Center—September, 1942 to Closing of Center—January, 1946, Central Utah Project, 142–146, FBD-WRA, Reel 16; Charles F. Ernst to District Engineer, March 20, 1943, Box 103/670, Entry 48, WRA-NARA.

71. Henry R. Watson to Roscoe Bell, September 4, 1943, Box 102/670, Entry 48, WRA-NARA.

72. Frank Iga to Dr. Ochikubo, September 14, 1943, Box 102/670, Entry 48, WRA-NARA. For the Community Council and its role, see Oscar F. Hoffman to Dillon S. Myer, April 3, 1944, CAR-WRA, Reel 8.

73. Henry R. Watson to Roscoe E. Bell, October 22, 1943, Box 102/670, Entry 48, WRA-NARA.

74. Henry R. Watson to Roscoe E. Bell, October 26, 1943, Box 102/670, Entry 48, WRA-NARA.

75. Ibid.

76. *Topaz Times*, October 26, 1943, p. 5. My deepest thanks to Jayanthi Selinger for translating this article for me. A rough translation of this article is also in "Excerpt from Block Managers' Minutes," no date, CAR-WRA, Reel 8.

77. "Excerpt from Block Managers' Minutes"; Charles F. Ernst to Dillon S. Myer, November 3, 1943, CAR-WRA, Reel 8.

78. Robinson, *A Tragedy of Democracy*, 185–186, 192–195. See also Hayashi, *Democratizing the Enemy*, 138–147 and Lyon, *Prisons and Patriots*, 81–104.

79. Charles F. Ernst to Dillon S. Myer, November 3, 1943, CAR-WRA, Reel 8.

80. Zimring, *Clean and White*.

81. Geiger, *Subverting Exclusion*, 1–2, 16–17.

82. "Excerpt from Block Managers' Minutes"; Charles F. Ernst to Dillon S. Myer, November 3, 1943, CAR-WRA, Reel 8.

83. Henry R. Watson to Roscoe E. Bell, October 27, 1943, Box 102/670, Entry 48, WRA-NARA.

84. "One-Third of Pipelines in Center Are Replaced," *Topaz Times*, October 28, 1943, p. 1.

85. Henry R. Watson to Roscoe E. Bell, October 27, 1943, Box 102/670, Entry 48, WRA-NARA; "One-Third of Pipelines in Center Are Replaced."

86. "Trencher Arrives at Project; Now Working Near Hospital," *Topaz Times*, November 20, 1943, p. 1.

87. "Pipeline Work on Jasper Ave to Start Soon," *Topaz Times*, December 7, 1943, p. 1; "Pipe Line Replacement Activity Here Advances," *Topaz Times*, December 18, 1943, p. 1.

88. Eldon McEntire, "Cathodic Protection of Pipe Lines at Topaz, Utah," no date, Box 102/653, Entry 48, WRA-NARA.

89. Henry R. Watson to Roscoe E. Bell, December 8, 1943, Box 102/653, Entry 48, WRA-NARA.

90. Report of the Engineering Section, Beginning of Center—September, 1942 to Closing of Center—January, 1946, Central Utah Project, 142–146.

91. Weekly Narrative Report, May 13, 1944, and July 3, 1944, Central Utah Project, JERS, Reel 109.

92. Second Quarterly Report of the War Relocation Authority, July 1–September 30, 1942, p. 9, Kaoru Ichihara Papers, Box 1, Folder 13, Accession 1839-001, Special Collections, University of Washington Libraries.

93. Henry R. Watson to Roscoe E. Bell, April 7, 1944, Box 102/670, Entry 48, WRA-NARA.

94. Charles F. Ernst to George Ochikubo, April 27, 1944, Box 99/563, Entry 48, WRA-NARA; "Water Service Menaced, More Workers Needed," *Topaz Times*, May 6, 1944, pp. 1–2.

95. New Release from Engineering Section, May 23, 1944, Box 102/670, Entry 48, WRA-NARA; "Volunteers Help Tsugawa Lay 535 Ft of Pipeline," *Topaz Times*, May 31, 1944, p. 2.

96. Oscar Hoffman, "Closing Report of Community Analysis Section," 1945, CAR-WRA, Reel 8; Community Analysis Newsletter No. 7, June 3, 1944, CAR-WRA, Reel 8; Henry R. Watson to Roscoe E. Bell, June 14, 1944, Box 102/670, Entry 48, WRA-NARA; "More Pipes Laid on Opal, Juniper," *Topaz Times*, June 3, 1944, p. 3; "Students Relieve Worker Shortage," *Topaz Times*, June 10, 1944, p. 3.

97. Memo to the Residents of Topaz from L. T. Hoffman, June 19, 1944, JERS, Reel 110.

98. "Pipeline Work on West Opal Avenue Completed," *Topaz Times*, June 21, 1944, p. 1; "Pipelines in 6 Blocks of East Opal Completed," *Topaz Times*, July 19, 1944, p. 1; "Labor Shortage Strikes All Project Sections," *Topaz Times*, September 9, 1944, p. 1.

99. Topaz Project Report No. 47, September 26, 1944, Box 99/549, Entry 48, WRA-NARA.

100. Oscar Hoffman to Dillon Myer, November 24, 1944, CAR-WRA, Reel 8.

101. Hoffman, "Closing Report of Community Analysis Section"; Community Analysis Newsletter No. 13, September 9, 1944, and Community Analysis Newsletter No. 15, October 7, 1944, CAR-WRA, Reel 8.

102. Report of the Engineering Section, Beginning of Center—September, 1942 to Closing of Center—January, 1946, Central Utah Project, 142–146.

103. Hoffman, "Closing Report of Community Analysis Section."

104. Mrs. Minoru Iyaki, "Narrative Report of M & O," in Report of the Engineering Section, Beginning of Center—September, 1942 to Closing of Center—January, 1946, Central Utah Project, 7.

105. O. F. Hoffman to Charles Ernst, November 5, 1943, CAR-WRA, Reel 8.

106. Community Analysis Newsletter No. 20, November 11, 1944, CAR-WRA, Reel 8.

107. Henry R. Watson to Roscoe E. Bell, May 3, 1944, Box 102/670, Entry 48, WRA-NARA.

108. Bell, "Relocation Center Life," 27.

109. George Shimamoto Interview, interviewed by Sandra Taylor, New York, NY, October 5, 1987, Box 1, Folder 12, Topaz Oral Histories.

110. Report of the Engineering Section, Beginning of Center—September, 1942 to Closing of Center—January, 1946, Central Utah Project, 142–146.

111. Community Analysis Newsletter No. 23, December 2, 1944; Community Analysis Newsletter No. 24, December 9, 1944; Community Analysis Newsletter No. 33, February 10, 1945, CAR-WRA, Reel 8; Digest of Minutes of Project Director's Weekly Conference with Division Heads, December 12, 1944, JERS, Reel 109.

112. Report of the Engineering Section, Beginning of Center—September, 1942 to Closing of Center—January, 1946, Central Utah Project, 142–146.

113. "Labor Relations in Relocation Centers," 10.

114. Ibid., 3, 5, 8.

115. Ibid., 4–5.

CHAPTER 4

1. "Unrealized Food Production Capacities at Japanese Relocation Centers," January 7, 1943, Box 21, Part 2, Entry 178, BIA-NARA.

2. Robinson, *By Order of the President*, 132; Drinnon, *Keeper of Concentration Camps*, 40–42. According to Robinson, Eisenhower publicly stated that he resigned to accept a job with the Office of War Information, but he was also "sickened and disheartened by the treatment and predicament of the Japanese-American evacuees."

3. "Unrealized Food Production Capacities at Japanese Relocation Centers."

4. US War Relocation Authority, *WRA: A Story of Human Conservation*, 95.

5. Hayashi, *Haunted by Waters*, 86.

6. Joseph R. Winchester, "Mess Operations Section, February 1946," 6, FBD-WRA, Reel 78.

7. US War Relocation Authority, *WRA: A Story of Human Conservation*, 102; Closing Report, Administrative Management Division, Supply Section, Mess Unit, Box 99/565, Entry 48, WRA-NARA. For a broader discussion of food rationing and the Office of Price Administration during World War II, see Bentley, *Eating for Victory* and Jacobs, *Pocketbook Politics*, 179–220.

8. Winchester, "Mess Operations Section, February 1946," 6, 27–31.

9. "Japanese American Contributions to the War Foods Program," no date, Prepared for Alan Cranston, Office of War Information, for speech on contribution of foreign groups to War Food Program, JERS, Reel 21; D. S. Myer to All Project Directors, April 8, 1943, JERS, Reel 20; E. H. Reed, "The Agricultural Program of the War Relocation Authority, DRAFT, May 31, 1943," JERS, Reel 30; D. S. Myer to The Secretary of Agriculture (Claude Wickard), June 23, 1942, Box 310/43.100, Entry 16, WRA-NARA. For the Lend-Lease program see Warren F. Kimball, *The Most Unsordid Act: Lend-Lease, 1939–1941* (Baltimore: Johns Hopkins University Press, 1969).

10. Dillon S. Myer Interview, interviewed by Helen S. Pryor, Berkeley, CA, July 7, 1970. Regional Oral History Office, Bancroft Library, University of California, Berkeley, https://www.trumanlibrary.org/oralhist/myerds2.htm (accessed June 30, 2016).

11. Sarah T. Phillips, *This Land, This Nation: Conservation, Rural America, and the New Deal* (New York: Cambridge University Press, 2007), 2–3, 9, 126–132, 142. For the work of the Resettlement Administration, see Sara M. Gregg, *Managing the Mountains: Land Use Planning, the New Deal, and the Creation of a Federal Landscape in Appalachia* (New Haven: Yale University Press, 2010), 175–212.

12. Ernest H. Reed, "Termination Report of Ernest H. Reed, Head, Agricultural Section," no date, 18, JERS, Reel 31.

13. "Japanese American Contributions to the War Foods Program"; Reed, "The Agricultural Program of the War Relocation Authority, DRAFT, May 31, 1943"; Reed, "Termination Report of Ernest H. Reed," 2.

14. Reed, "Termination Report of Ernest H. Reed," 5.

15. "Responsibility of the Agricultural Division of W.R.A.—Washington Office," no date, JERS, Reel 30; Reed, "The Agricultural Program of the War Relocation Authority, DRAFT, May 31, 1943," 11–12; Reed, "Termination Report of Ernest H. Reed."

16. D. S. Myer to All Project Directors, April 8, 1943, and 1943 Agricultural Production Schedule, January 6, 1943, JERS, Reel 20; Agricultural Section, Quarterly Report, January 1 to March 31, 1943, JERS, Reel 30; Reed, "The Agricultural Program of the War Relocation Authority, DRAFT, May 31, 1943" 12; Reed, "Termination Report of Ernest H. Reed," 11–14.

17. Agricultural Conference, Gila Project, February 23, 1944, Box 319/51.001, Entry 16, WRA-NARA.

18. 1943 Agricultural Production Schedule, January 6, 1943, JERS, Reel 20.

19. Reed, "Termination Report of Ernest H. Reed," 27–28.

20. Maya Aikawa Interview, interviewed by Sandra Taylor, Berkeley, CA, November 4, 1987, Box 1, Folder 2, Topaz Oral Histories.

21. "Eyes on Tomorrow," *Minidoka Irrigator*, September 10, 1942, p. 2.

22. For WRA control of camp newspapers, see Kessler, "Fettered Freedoms"; Mizuno, "Creation of Free Press." For the frontier and the development of American democracy and character, see Frederick Jackson Turner, "The Significance of the Frontier in American History," in *The Frontier in American History* (New York: Henry Holt, 1921), 1–38. For the subversive potential of the frontier myth, see Richard White, "Frederick Jackson Turner and Buffalo Bill," in *The Frontier in American Culture*, ed. James Grossman (Berkeley: University of California Press, 1994), 7–65. For the links between the frontier and Japanese American incarceration, see Byrd, *The Transit of Empire*, 192.

23. Horace R. McConnell and Henry A. Hill, "Agriculture Section, January 1946," 1, FBD-WRA, Reel 78.

24. McConnell and Hill, "Agriculture Section, January 1946," 6, 15.

25. Agricultural Section, Quarterly Report, January 1 to March 31, 1943, JERS, Reel 30.

26. US War Relocation Authority, *The Evacuated People*, 18.

27. Labor and Employment, Gila River Project, February 25, 1944, Box 319/51.001, Entry 16, WRA-NARA.

28. H. R. McConnell, "Narrative Report, Month of May (1944)," JERS, Reel 157. Minidoka faced a similar labor shortage in the spring of 1944. See Louis E. Rice and Rhuel D. Beebout, "Report of the Agriculture Section, Minidoka Relocation Center, Hunt, Idaho," 61, 88, FBD-WRA, Reel 89.

29. H. R. McConnell, "Narrative Report, Month of June (1944)," JERS, Reel 157.

30. H. R. McConnell, "Narrative Report, Month of September (1944)," JERS, Reel 157.

31. Rice and Beebout, "Report of the Agriculture Section," no date, 34, 36, 68, FBD-WRA, Reel 89. See also Frances E. Haglund, "Behind Barbed Wire," 10, manuscript, ddr-densho-275-76, Frances Haglund Collection, Densho Digital Repository, http://ddr.densho.org/ddr/densho/275/76/.

32. Reed, "Termination Report of Ernest H. Reed," 20–21.

33. Rice and Beebout, "Report of the Agriculture Section," 48.

34. Ibid., 29–30, 48, 54, 56.

35. E. H. Reed to H. L. Stafford, August 4, 1944, Box 320/51.130, Entry 16, RG 210, WRA-NARA.

36. Reed, "Termination Report of Ernest H. Reed," 21–22. For agricultural wages, see Lillquist, "Farming the Desert," 85.

37. Quoted in Briones, *Jim and Jap Crow*, 143.

38. Report on Preliminary Stage of Evacuee Employment (no date), 9, JERS, Reel 279.

39. Charles Kikuchi Diary, October 15, 1942, 919, JERS, Reel 96.

40. Shotaro Hikida, "Monthly Report on the Life of Japanese Evacuees in Gila Relocation Center, October 1942," JERS, Reel 281. For Hikida's background, see

Shotaro Hikida, "The Story of My Life," January 1943, Online Archive of California, http://cdn.calisphere.org/data/28722/27/bk0013c6727/files/bk0013c6727-FID1. pdf (accessed July 1, 2016).

41. David A. Rogers to E. R. Smith, September 1, 1942, Box 146/619.1, Entry 48, WRA-NARA.

42. E. R. Fryer to John C. Henderson, October 8, 1942, in the Kikuchi Diary, 921.

43. W. M. Case and E. H. Reed to LeRoy H. Bennett, June 24, 1943, Box 145/610, Entry 48, WRA-NARA; Final Project Report, Operations Division, Agriculture Section, Gila River Project, 20, FBD-WRA, Reel 43.

44. Final Project Report, 16, 28; Final Project Report (History of Agriculture at Gila), Operations Division, Agricultural Section (no date), 2–3, FBD-WRA, Reel 43.

45. Final Project Report, Operations Division, Agriculture Section, Gila River Project, 14–15; G. Gordon Brown, "Community Analysts Conference: Gila River," Community Analysis Report No. 165, July 29, 1944, CAR-WRA, Reel 5.

46. Seed Production, January 1, 1944, FBD-WRA, Reel 35.

47. Final Project Report, Operations Division, Agriculture Section, Gila River Project, 9–10, 12; E. J. Utz to Leroy H. Bennett, August 24, 1944, Box 314/43.502, Entry 16, WRA-NARA.

48. William M. Case to Charles F. Ernst, June 30, 1943, Box 319/51.001, Entry 16, WRA-NARA.

49. George Sugihara, "The 1943 Farm Program, July 9, 1943," Historical Section, Project Reports Division, Box 1, Folder 24, Central Utah-UW Papers.

50. Bell, "Relocation Center Life," 20.

51. Apprenticeship Training Outline, Agriculture Section, Vegetable Gardening, Central Utah Project, 1944, FBD-WRA, Reel 3. See also Apprenticeship Training Outline, Swine Section, Central Utah Project, 1944; Apprenticeship Training Outline, Agriculture Section-Cattle, Central Utah Project, 1944; Eugene E. Gardner and June Hinckley, "Farm Construction," FBD-WRA, Reel 3.

52. George McColm, "Commercial Vegetable Production," no date, FBD-WRA, Reel 3.

53. George L. McColm Interview, interviewed by Niel M. Johnson, Independence, MO, May 20 and 21, 1991, Harry S. Truman Library, http://www.trumanlibrary. org/oralhist/mccolmgl.htm (accessed June 3, 2016).

54. McColm Interview.

55. Bob Y. Sakata Interview, interviewed by Daryl Maeda, May 14, 2008, denshovh-sbob-01-0012, DVHC-DDR.

56. Reed, "Termination Report of Ernest H. Reed," 21–22, 28–29.

57. Final Project Report, Operations Division, Agriculture Section, Gila River Project, 13, FBD-WRA, Reel 43; Agricultural Conference, Gila Project, February 23, 1944, Box 319/51.001, Entry 16, WRA-NARA.

58. US War Relocation Authority, *Relocation of Japanese Americans*, 2.

59. Bell, "Relocation Center Life," 16–17, 23.

60. George K. Nakano to J. Elmer Morrish, October 5, 1942. Transcribed letter in Ivey and Kaatz, *Citizen Internees*, 222. Ichisaka went on to work on Seabrook Farms in New Jersey. See Frank App and Vernon Ichisaka, *Soil Analysis as a Tool in Crop Production* (Bridgeton, NJ: Seabrook Farms, 1954).

61. W. Wendell Palmer to Roscoe E. Bell, August 30, 1944, Box 100/610, Entry 48, WRA-NARA.

62. E. H. Reed to L. T. Hoffman, August 5, 1944, Box 320/51.130, Entry 16, WRA-NARA.

63. Charles F. Ernst to All Residents, June 23, 1943, JERS, Reel 110.

64. Russell A. Bankson, "The Food Crop Assignment Program at Topaz," 2–3, Historical Section, Project Reports Division, Box 1, Folder 25, Central Utah-UW Papers.

65. "Ag Workers Needed," *Topaz Times*, July 20, 1943, p. 1.

66. "Block System Plan to Begin," *Topaz Times*, July 20, 1943, p. 1.

67. Bankson, "Food Crop Assignment Program," 2–5.

68. For the tense climate at Tule Lake in the wake of segregation, see Robinson, *A Tragedy of Democracy*, 193–194; Barbara Takei, "Tule Lake," *Densho Encyclopedia*, http://encyclopedia.densho.org/Tule_Lake/ (accessed July 1, 2014).

69. Charles Ernst to Dillon Myer, November 6, 1943, Community Analysis Report No. 18a, CAR-WRA, Reel 8.

70. Ibid.

71. Russell A. Bankson, "The Topaz Part in the Tule Lake Harvest," Project Reports Division, Historical Section, Central Utah Project, Box 2, Folder 4, Central Utah-UW Papers.

72. Robinson, *A Tragedy of Democracy*, 194; Burton et al., *Confinement and Ethnicity*, 283; Takei, "Tule Lake."

73. "Agricultural Division Meeting to Discuss Complaints of Farm Workers," August 5, 1943, Community Analysis Section, Minidoka Relocation Center, Field Report No. 160, JERS, Reel 332. See also Hayashi, *Haunted by Waters*, 91–92.

74. "Agricultural Division Meeting."

75. The exceptions were Minidoka, Heart Mountain, and Colorado River. See Lillquist, "Farming the Desert," 78–79.

76. Final Project Report, Operations Division, Agriculture Section, Gila River Project, 20–21.

77. Rice and Beebout, "Report of the Agriculture Section," 6–13, 137.

78. Bell, "Relocation Center Life," 4–5, 21.

79. M. J. Moody, Elmer Fullmer, and Arthur H. Reever, Drainage District Supervisors, "Agricultural and Drainage Needs of Parts of Millard County Drainage District Number 3 in the Abraham Relocation Area," Box 102/670, Entry 48, WRA-NARA.

80. Wendell W. Palmer, "Closing Report, Agriculture Section: Farm Environmental and Land Use Factors-Soil, Drainage, and Irrigation," 3–4, FBD-WRA, Reel 16.

81. Untitled Soil Survey of Central Utah, undated, 22–23, Box 292/41.030, Entry 16, WRA-NARA.

82. Palmer, "Closing Report, Agriculture Section: Farm Environmental and Land Use Factors-Soil, Drainage, and Irrigation," 2–3; Untitled Soil Survey of Central Utah, undated, 1–5, 20, 23–25.

83. Wendell W. Palmer, "Closing Report, Agriculture Section: Agricultural Enterprise, Crops-Vegetables," FBD-WRA, Reel 16.

84. William M. Case to Dillon S. Myer, July 6, 1943, Box 319/51.001, Entry 16, WRA-NARA. For the growing season at Topaz, see Palmer, "Closing Report, Agriculture Section: Farm Environmental and Land Use Factors-Climate," 1.

85. Bankson, "Food Crop Assignment Program," 1.

86. Sugihara, "The 1943 Farm Program."

87. Agricultural Narrative Report for 1944, Central Utah, JERS, Reel 280.

88. Crop Losses Due to Unpreventable Causes, no date, Box 100/610, Entry 48, WRA-NARA.

89. Agricultural Narrative Report for 1944, Central Utah, JERS, Reel 280.

90. "Plenty of Home Grown Vegetables for September–October Assured; Topaz Soil Proven to Be Fertile," *Topaz Times*, August 10, 1943.

91. Bankson, "Food Crop Assignment Program," 5–6.

92. "Agricultural Fair Opens," *Topaz Times*, October 9, 1943, p. 1.

93. Weekly Narrative Report for the Period of September 30 to October 7, 1944, Central Utah Project, JERS, Reel 109.

94. Palmer, "Closing Report, Agriculture Section: Agricultural Enterprise, Crops-Vegetables."

95. Wendell W. Palmer, "Closing Report, Agriculture Section: Agricultural Enterprise, Beef Production," 1-4, FBD-WRA, Reel 16.

96. Wendell W. Palmer, "Closing Report, Agriculture Section: Agricultural Enterprise, Poultry Production," 1–5, FBD-WRA, Reel 16.

97. R. B. Cozzens to Mr. Eisenhower, March 28, 1942, Box 293/41.080, Entry 16, WRA-NARA.

98. R. B. Cozzens to E. R. Fryer, May 11, 1942, Box 293/41.080, Entry 16, WRA-NARA.

99. McConnell and Hill, "Agriculture Section, January 1946," 2–3, 14.

100. McConnell and Hill, "Agriculture Section, January 1946," 2–3.

101. "Quarterly Report from October 1 to December 31," January 29, 1943, JERS, Reel 157; Paul Ohi, "Monthly Report, Farm Project," July 2, 1942, JERS, Reel 157; "Monthly Report, Farm Project," August 1, 1942, JERS, Reel 157; "Manzanar Holds First Rabbit Drive," Manzanar Project Report No. 26, July 24, 1942, FBD-WRA, Reel 76; Yoshi Ohi, "Report of Original Conditions," June 2, 1942, JERS, Reel 157; McConnell and Hill, "Agriculture Section, January 1946," 14, 16.

102. Ned Campbell to Ralph P. Merritt, December 3, 1942, Box 225/52.000, Entry 48, WRA-NARA.

103. H. R. McConnell, "Agricultural Report, Damage to Crops by Wind, June 7, 1943," Box 225/51.000, Entry 48, WRA-NARA; H. R. McConnell, "Agricultural

Division Annual Report, Calendar Year 1943, January 20, 1944," 1, FBD-WRA, Reel 75; Agricultural Division, Monthly Report, June 1, 1943, JERS, Reel 157.

104. McConnell, "Agricultural Report, Damage to Crops by Wind"; McConnell, "Agricultural Division Annual Report," 1; Agricultural Division, Production Report, General Comments, no date (c. June 1943), JERS, Reel 157.

105. McConnell, "Agricultural Report, Damage to Crops by Wind"; McConnell, "Agricultural Division Annual Report," 1–2, 5; Monthly Narrative Report for November 1943, JERS, Reel 157.

106. Monthly Narrative Report, March 1944, JERS, Reel 157.

107. McConnell, "Narrative Report, Month of June (1944)"; H. R. McConnell, "Narrative Report, Month of October 1944" and H. R. McConnell, "Narrative Report, Month of November 1944," JERS, Reel 157.

108. McConnell, "Narrative Report, Month of October 1944" and McConnell, "Narrative Report, Month of November 1944."

109. Arthur M. Sandridge and Oliver E. Sisler, "Engineering Section," 66–67, February 1946, FBD-WRA, Reel 78.

110. McConnell and Hill, "Agriculture Section, January 1946," 7–8.

111. Ibid., 14, 16.

112. "Shortages Sabotage Vegetable Crop," *Gila News-Courier*, December 2, 1942, p. 3.

113. L. H. Bennett to Dillon S. Myer, January 19, 1943, Box 322/54.102, Entry 16, WRA-NARA.

114. Paul G. Robertson to E. J. Utz, December 19, 1942, and E. H. Reed to E. J. Utz, January 20, 1943, Box 322/54.102, Entry 16, WRA-NARA.

115. David A. Rogers to Leroy H. Bennett, May 20, 1943, Box 145/610, Entry 48, WRA-NARA.

116. Monthly Narrative Report for October 1943, JERS Reel 157; Monthly Narrative Report for November 1943, JERS, Reel 157.

117. Narrative Report for December 1943, JERS, Reel 157.

118. McConnell, "Agricultural Division Annual Report," 4–5; H. R. McConnell, "Agricultural Report, Proposed Operations for Calendar Year 1944," December 1, 1943, Box 225/51.100, Entry 48, WRA-NARA.

119. McConnell, "Agricultural Division Annual Report," 1–2.

120. Ralph P. Merritt to D. S. Myer, August 9, 1943, JERS, Reel 157.

121. Winchester, "Mess Operations Section, February 1946," 13.

122. The Manzanar riot and the activism of Harry Ueno have generated many scholarly studies. See Lon Kurashige, "Resistance, Collaboration, and Manzanar Protest," *Pacific Historical Review* 70, no. 3 (August 2001): 387–417; Arthur A. Hansen and David A. Hacker, "The Manzanar Riot: An Ethnic Perspective," *Amerasia Journal* 2, no. 2 (1974): 112–157; Arthur A. Hansen, Betty E. Mitson, and Sue Kunitomi Embrey, "Dissident Harry Ueno," *California History* 64, no. 1 (Winter 1985): 58–64.

123. McConnell and Hill, "Agriculture Section, January 1946," 4.

124. Board of Water and Power Commissioners of the City of Los Angeles to Ralph Merritt, Box 224/43.120, Entry 48, WRA-NARA.

125. D. S. Myer to R. P. Merritt, November 11, 1943, Box 224/43.120, Entry 48, WRA-NARA.

126. H. A. Van Norman to Dillon Myer, January 31, 1944, Water Executive Office, Administrative-Executive Files, Manzanar Relocation Center, Correspondence, January 1944–September 1944, WP14-1:4, LADWP Records.

127. Ralph P. Merritt to Board of Water and Power Commissioners, City of Los Angeles, April 17, 1944, Box 224/43.120, Entry 48, WRA-NARA.

128. H. A. Van Norman to Honorable Board of Water and Power Commissioners, April 24, 1944, Water Executive Office, Administrative-Executive Files, Manzanar Relocation Center, Correspondence, January 1944–September 1944, WP14-1:4, LADWP Records; "Manzanar Hog Ranch Hit as Menace to City's Water," *Los Angeles Times*, May 4, 1944.

129. Statement by Ralph P. Merritt, n.d., Box 224/43.120, Entry 48, WRA-NARA; "Manzanar Hog Ranch Protest Hit as Politics," *Los Angeles Times*, May 5, 1944.

130. Ralph P. Merritt to Gerald E. Kerrin, May 5, 1944, Ralph P. Merritt to C. G. Gillespie, September 22, 1944, Box 224/43.120, Entry 48, WRA-NARA.

131. Floyd M. Hinshaw to W. W. Hurlbut, May 5, 1944, Water Executive Office, Administrative-Executive Files, Manzanar Relocation Center, Correspondence, January 1944–September 1944, WP14-1:4, LADWP Records; "City Asks Inquiry of Hog Ranch Plan," *Los Angeles Times*, May 6, 1944; "Japs Pollute Water, Charge," *Los Angeles Examiner*, May 6, 1944.

132. Charles L. Senn to George M. Uhl, May 18, 1944, Water Executive Office, Administrative-Executive Files, Manzanar Relocation Center, Correspondence, January 1944–September 1944, WP14-1:4, LADWP Records.

133. Ibid.

134. H. A. Van Norman to The Honorable Board of Water and Power Commissioners, May 31, 1944, Water Executive Office, Administrative-Executive Files, Manzanar Relocation Center, Correspondence, January 1944–September 1944, WP14-1:4, LADWP Records.

135. Ralph P. Merritt to C. G. Gillespie, September 22, 1944, Box 224/43.500, Entry 48, WRA-NARA.

136. McConnell and Hill, "Agriculture Section," January 1946, 10.

137. H. R. McConnell, "Proposed Operations, Calendar Year 1945," December 1, 1944, Box 225/51.100, Entry 48, WRA-NARA.

138. Lillquist, "Farming the Desert," 95.

139. Final Project Report, Operations Division, Agriculture Section, Gila River Project, 6–8.

140. Lillquist, "Farming the Desert," 90, 94.

141. Ibid., 95.

142. US War Relocation Authority, *WRA: A Story of Human Conservation*, 97; Reed, "Termination Report of Ernest H. Reed," 28–29.

CHAPTER 5

1. Transcription of a conversation between Mr. James F. Hughes, Assistant Project Director, and Thomas L. Cavett, Investigator of the Dies Committee, no date, Box 103, Entry 48, WRA-NARA.

2. My approach takes cues from Mark Fiege's *The Republic of Nature: An Environmental History of the United States* (Seattle: University of Washington Press, 2012). Fiege argues that the American past cannot be viewed apart from "its natural circumstances." For an earlier version of this chapter, see Connie Y. Chiang, "Winning the War at Manzanar: Environmental Patriotism and the Japanese American Incarceration," in *Rendering Nature: Animals, Bodies, Places, Politics*, ed. Marguerite S. Shaffer and Phoebe S. K. Young (Philadelphia: University of Pennsylvania Press, 2015), 237–262.

3. For wartime propaganda, see William L. Bird Jr. and Harry R. Rubenstein, *Design for Victory: World War II Posters on the American Home Front* (New York: Princeton Architectural Press, 1998); Terrence H. Witkowski, "World War II Poster Campaigns," *Journal of Advertising* 32, no. 1 (Spring 2003): 72; Susan A. Brewer, *Why America Fights: Patriotism and War Propaganda from the Philippines to Iraq* (New York: Oxford University Press, 2009), 87–140. For scrap drives, see Susan Strasser, *Waste and Want: A Social History of Trash* (New York: Henry Holt, 1999), 229–263 and Robert William Kirk, "Getting in the Scrap: The Mobilization of American Children in World War II," *Journal of Popular Culture* 29 (Summer 1995): 223–233. For the conservation of forest resources, see Kosek, *Understories*, 193–202.

4. Hal K. Rothman, *Saving the Planet: The American Response to the Environment in the Twentieth Century* (Chicago: Ivan R. Dee, 2000), 82. For the exploitation of Sitka spruce, see Richard West Sellars, *Preserving Nature in the National Parks: A History* (New Haven: Yale University Press, 1997), 150–155. For wartime oil drilling, see Sarah Elkind, "The Nature and Business of War: Drilling for Oil in Wartime Los Angeles," in *Cities and Nature in the American West*, ed. Char Miller (Reno: University of Nevada Press, 2010), 205–224; Gerald D. Nash, *The American West Transformed; The Impact of the Second World War* (Lincoln: University of Nebraska Press, 1985), 21. For the war's impact on fisheries, see Chiang, *Shaping the Shoreline*, 102–131. For the war's impact on wildlife conservation, see Robert M. Wilson, "Birds on the Home Front: Wildlife Conservation in the Western United States During World War II," in *War and the Environment: Military Destruction in the Modern Age*, ed. Charles E. Closmann (College Station: Texas A&M University Press, 2009), 132–149.

5. Kosek, *Understories*, 202.

6. Quoted in James T. Sparrow, *Warfare State: World War II Americans and the Age of Big Government* (New York: Oxford University Press, 2011), 3.

7. Sparrow, *Warfare State*, 4–12.

8. Mark H. Leff, "The Politics of Sacrifice on the American Home Front in World War II," *Journal of American History* 77, no. 4 (March 1991): 1297; Sparrow, *Warfare State*, 4–12. For another compelling discussion of home front mobilization, see Robert B. Westbrook, *Why We Fought: Forging American Obligations During World War II* (Washington, DC: Smithsonian Institution Press, 2004).

9. For another discussion of the idea of environmental patriotism, see Anne Marie Todd, *Communicating Environmental Patriotism: A Rhetorical History of the American Environmental Movement* (New York: Routledge, 2013).

10. For the national victory garden campaign, see Char Miller, "In the Sweat of Our Brow: Citizenship in American Domestic Practice During WWII—Victory Gardens," *Journal of American Culture* 26, no. 3 (September 2003): 395–409; Cecilia Gowdy-Wygant, *Cultivating Victory: The Women's Land Army and the Victory Garden Movement* (Pittsburgh, PA: University of Pittsburgh Press, 2013), 131–161.

11. Gowdy-Wygant, *Cultivating Victory*, 132. For a broader discussion of the Four Freedoms and the Atlantic Charter, see Elizabeth Borgwardt, *A New Deal for the World: America's Vision for Human Rights* (Cambridge, MA: Harvard University Press, 2005).

12. Gowdy-Wygant, *Cultivating Victory*, 134.

13. US Department of Agriculture in cooperation with the Bureau of Campaigns, Office of War Information, *U.S. Government Campaign to Promote the Production, Sharing, and Proper Use of Food, Book IV: The Victory Gardens Campaign* (Washington, DC: Government Printing Office, 1943), 1–2.

14. US Department of Agriculture, *Book IV: The Victory Gardens Campaign*, 2–4.

15. Ibid., 4.

16. Ibid., 6–10.

17. US Department of Agriculture, *Victory Garden Leader's Handbook* (Washington, DC: Government Printing Office, 1943), 7, 8, 15.

18. "Quarterly Report, April–June 1943," 9–10, Community Activities Section, Manzanar, California, Box 414/67.010, Entry 16, WRA-NARA; Manzanar Project Report No. 21, July 13, 1942, and Manzanar Project Report No. 44, September 2, 1942, FBD-WRA, Reel 76.

19. "Harvest Time for Victory Garden," *Manzanar Free Press*, August 28, 1942, p. 1.

20. Aksel G. Nielsen, "Community Activities Section, Parts I–III," October 1945, FBD-WRA, Reel 78.

21. Memorandum from Community Activities to Lucy Adams, March 20, 1944, Box 225/50.102, Entry 48, WRA-NARA.

22. "Report, Summer Activities Program, 1944," Box 221/18.410, Entry 16, WRA-NARA.

23. Burton, *Garden Management Plan*, 77.

24. W. W. Palmer and Henry R. Watson to Roscoe Bell, December 24, 1943, Box 102/ 670, Entry 48, WRA-NARA.

25. Nielsen, "Community Activities Section, Parts I–III." Char Miller also stresses the personal value of victory gardens for Americans who participated outside the incarceration camps. See Miller, "In the Sweat of Our Brow."

26. "Harvest Time for Victory Garden," *Manzanar Free Press*, August 28, 1942, p. 1.

27. Lucy W. Adams to Bob Brown, March 21, 1944, Box 225/50.102, Entry 48, WRA-NARA.

28. "Minidoka Project Schools," Historical Narrative Report, Community Management Division, Education Section, 15 December 1945, FBD-WRA, Reel 89. For education in the incarceration camps, see James, *Exile Within*, 36–42; Catherine L. Cullen, "The Education of Japanese Americans, 1942–1946: The Fate of Democratic Curriculum Reform," *American Educational History Journal* 38, no. 1 (2011): 197–218. For the origins of nature study in the United States and its connections to progressive education, see Sally Gregory Kohlstedt, " 'A Better Crop of Boys and Girls': The School Gardening Movement, 1890–1920," *History of Education Quarterly* 48, no. 1 (February 2008): 58–93 and "Nature Not Books: Scientific Initiatives and the Origins of the Nature Study Movement in the 1890s," *Isis* 96 (September 2005): 324–352; Peter J. Schmitt, *Back to Nature: The Arcadian Myth in Urban America* (New York: Oxford University Press, 1969), 78, 90–93.

29. Cullen, "Education of Japanese Americans," 203–205.

30. Mitziko Sawada, "After the Camps: Seabrook Farms, New Jersey, and the Resettlement of Japanese Americans, 1944-47," *Amerasia Journal* 13, no. 2 (1986–1987): 117–136. Quotation is on page 130. See also Charles H. Harrison, *Growing a Global Village: Making History at Seabrook Farms* (New York: Holmes & Meier, 2003), 53–71.

31. Fiset, "Thinning, Topping, and Loading"; Hayashi, *Haunted by Waters*, 84–90.

32. Fiset, "Thinning, Topping, and Loading," 124.

33. Ibid., 126.

34. Ibid., 126–127.

35. "Seasonal Work Leave 60.3," *WRA Handbook*, JERS, Reel 21.

36. War Manpower Commission Staff Handbook, Section 7511, JERS, Reel 20.

37. "Farm Workers Sought Here for Sugar Beet Harvest," *Topaz Times*, September 30, 1942.

38. "Sugar Beet Work Starts," *Gila News-Courier*, March 18, 1943, pp. 1–2. See also "Higher Wages to Be Paid," *Gila News-Courier*, April 22, 1943, p. 3.

39. "Sugar Beet Agents Interview Prospective Farmers," *Manzanar Free Press*, February 3, 1943, p. 1. See also "Ten Sugar Beet Prospectors Investigate Rocky Mt. States," *Gila News-Courier*, March 11, 493, p. 1; "Ford Skelly," Topaz Report H397, January 21, 1943, FBD-WRA, Reel 5.

40. *Minidoka Irrigator*, March 6, 1943, pp. 6, 8.

41. Ibid., 8.

42. Quoted in Sims, " 'You Don't Need to Wait Any Longer to Get Out,' " 12.

43. Thomas, *The Salvage*, 253–254, 257.

44. Togo Tanaka Report No. 80, October 26, 1942, FBD-WRA, Reel 75.

45. Thomas, *The Salvage*, 278–279.

46. Togo Tanaka Report No. 80, October 26, 1942, FBD-WRA, Reel 75.

47. "Agricultural Division-Landscape," Topaz Report H154, November 3, 1942, FBD-WRA, Reel 5.

48. Fiset, "Thinning, Topping, and Loading," 127.

49. Minutes, JACL Special Emergency Conference, November 17–24, 1942, Salt Lake City, Utah, Supplement No. 6, "Beet Field Survey," by G. E. Inagaki and Scotty H. Tsuchiya, 4–5, Box 13, Folder 9, James Y. Sakamoto Papers, Accession 1609-001, Special Collections, University of Washington Libraries.

50. Lily C. Hioki Interview, interviewed by Tom Ikeda and Steve Fugita, December 1, 2010, San Jose, California, denshovh-hlily-01-0017, Japanese American Museum of San Jose Collection, Densho Digital Repository, http://ddr.densho.org.

51. Rae Takekawa Interview, interviewed by Alice Ito, May 8, 1998, Vancouver, WA, denshovh-trae-01-0025, DVHC-DDR.

52. Mitsuye May Yamada, Joe Yasutake, Tosh Yasutake Interview, interviewed by Alice Ito and Jeni Yamada, October 8 and 9, 2002, Seattle, WA, denshovh-ymitsuye_g-01-0070, DVHC-DDR; Fiset, "Thinning, Topping, and Loading," 134.

53. Thomas, *The Salvage*, 278–279.

54. Inagaki and Tsuchiya, "Beet Field Survey," 1, 4.

55. Ibid., 1, 3–5.

56. Fiset, "Thinning, Topping, and Loading," 133–135.

57. Ibid., 137.

58. Minidoka War Relocation Project, Report for Quarter Ended December 31, 1942, 4, JERS, Reel 332.

59. "Sugar Beet Crop Needed," Topaz Report H229, November 23, 1942, FBD-WRA, Reel 5.

60. "Letters to the Editor," *Minidoka Irrigator*, December 19, 1942, p. 5.

61. Quoted in Sims, "The Free Zone Nikkei," 248.

62. US Department of Agriculture, Bureau of Agricultural Economics, "Farmers' Attitudes Toward the Use of Japanese Evacuees as Farm Labor, Part I: Sugar Beet and Long Staple Cotton Regions," 1–8, 21, JERS, Reel 20.

63. Ibid., 13–17, 22–23, 26.

64. Inagaki and Tsuchiya, "Beet Field Survey," 5.

65. Monthly Report, Minidoka Relocation Project, October 31, 1942, JERS, Reel 319.

66. Weekly Report, Minidoka Relocation Project, February 27, 1943, JERS, Reel 313.

67. Monthly Report, Minidoka Relocation Project, September 30, 1942, JERS, Reel 319.

68. Memorandum from Joseph G. Beeson to Harry L. Stafford, November 5, 1943, JERS, Reel 313.

69. Mark R. Finlay, *Growing American Rubber: Strategic Plants and the Politics of National Security* (New Brunswick, NJ: Rutgers University Press, 2009), 141, 145, 149.

70. Ibid., 141, 152–153.

71. Mark R. Finlay, "Behind the Barbed Wire of Manzanar: Guayule and the Search for Natural Rubber," *Chemical Heritage Magazine* 29, no. 3 (Fall 2011–Winter 2012), https://www.chemheritage.org/distillations/magazine/behind-the-barbed-wire-of-manzanar-guayule-and-the-search-for-natural-rubber (accessed April 1, 2012); Finlay, *Growing American Rubber*, 152–153.

72. Grace Nichols, "Guayule Research Project," August 1, 1942, JERS, Reel 157. For WRA Administrative Instruction No. 14, see E. H. Reed, "The Agricultural Program of the War Relocation Authority, DRAFT," May 31, 1943, JERS, Reel 30.

73. Robert Emerson to Ralph Merritt, December 10, 1943, Box 14, Folder 6, Manzanar-UCLA Records; Finlay, *Growing American Rubber*, 153.

74. Nichols, "Guayule Research Project"; Finlay, "Behind the Barbed Wire of Manzanar"; Finlay, *Growing American Rubber*, 153.

75. "Manzanar Will Contribute to Rubber Production as Guayule Cuttings Arrive," *Manzanar Free Press*, April 15, 1942, p. 4.

76. "Big Guayule Project Explained," *Manzanar Free Press*, August 10, 1942, pp. 1, 3.

77. For WRA control of camp newspapers, see Kessler, "Fettered Freedoms"; Mizuno, "Creation of Free Press."

78. Nichols, "Guayule Research Project."

79. Neil D. Naiden, "Two Jap Nurserymen Experiment to Solve Rubber Shortage by Guayule Production," *Washington Post*, September 6, 1942.

80. "Report on Guayule Project at the Manzanar Relocation Area, for Submission to the U.S. Forest Service and Bureau of Plant Industry, February, 1943," JERS, Reel 157. This research was later published in scientific journals. See M. S. Nishimura, Robert Emerson, T. Hata, and Akira Kageyama, "The Propagation of Guayule from Cuttings," *American Journal of Botany* 31, no. 7 (July 1944): 412–418; M. S. Nishimura, Frank N. Hirosawa, and Robert Emerson, "Rubber from Guayule," *Industrial and Engineering Chemistry* 39, no. 11 (November 1947): 1477–1485; G. L. Stebbins Jr. and M. Kodani, "Chromosomal Variation in Guayule and Mariola," *Journal of Heredity* 35 (1944): 162–172.

81. Finlay, *Growing American Rubber*, 199–200.

82. John Embree, "Manzanar, Sept. 11–13, 1942," 3–4, FBD-WRA, Reel 75.

83. Finlay, *Growing American Rubber*, 156, 200–201.

84. Ralph P. Merritt to Dillon S. Myer, August 29, 1943, Box 14, Folder 6, Manzanar-UCLA Records.

85. Ibid. For the loyalty questionnaire, see Muller, *Free to Die*, 50–60; Daniels, *Prisoners Without Trial*, 68–70. Nishimura, an Issei, would have applied for repatriation to Japan, whereas Furuya, a Nisei, would have applied for expatriation.

86. Ralph P. Merritt to Dillon S. Myer, August 29, 1943; Vassiliki Betty Smocovitis, "Genetics Behind Barbed Wire: Masuo Kodani, Émigré Geneticists, and Wartime Genetics Research at Manzanar Relocation Center," *Genetics* 187, no. 2 (February 2011): 363–364. Smocovitis notes that Fumi Kodani was declared an illegal immigrant after the war because she had not renewed her student permit and because she was "of a race ineligible to citizenship." With Fumi's uncertain status weighing on him, Masuo Kodani accepted a position with the Atomic Bomb Casualty Commission in 1948 and relocated with his family to Japan.

87. Western Defense Command, Civil Affairs Division, "Persons of Japanese Ancestry Registered at Tule Lake Segregation Center, September 1943 Through 15 July 1944," National Park Service, Tule Lake Unit, https://www.nps.gov/tule/learn/historyculture/wdc-list.htm (accessed June 13, 2017). Nishimura's name does not appear on these lists. According to Mark Finlay, Emerson convinced him not to return to Japan. See Finlay, *Growing American Rubber*, 154.

88. Untitled essay by Ralph Merritt, no date, Box 14, Folder 8, Manzanar-UCLA Records.

89. Murray, *Historical Memories*, 69–71. For WRA paternalism, see also Raymond Okamura, "'The Great White Father': Dillon Myer and Internal Colonialism," *Amerasia Journal* 13, no. 2 (1986–1987): 155–160 and Drinnon, *Keeper of Concentration Camps*.

90. Similarly, Susan Brewer suggests that government depictions of African Americans and Japanese Americans "emphasized loyalty, not freedom and equality." See Brewer, *Why America Fights*, 110.

91. Alinder, *Moving Images*, 48; Ansel Adams, *Born Free and Equal: The Story of Loyal Japanese Americans* (Bishop, CA: Spotted Dog Press, 2001), 13.

92. Alinder, *Moving Images*, 52.

93. I am grateful to Glenn Kageyama, son of Frank Akira Kageyama, a member of the Manzanar research group, for addressing the possible motivations of the guayule scientists and emphasizing this point about their desire to do their share for the war. Glenn Kageyama, email communication with author, August 8, 2016.

94. Finlay, *Growing American Rubber*, 142, 202.

CHAPTER 6

1. Minidoka Report No. 30, January 14, 1943, JERS, Reel 332.

2. Minidoka Report No. 45, February 20, 1943, JERS, Reel 332. For the Minidoka fence, see also Hayashi, *Haunted by Waters*, 99–101.

3. For security procedures, see Office Letter No. 42, Gate Control Procedure, June 16, 1944, Box 57, Folder 1, William C. Carr Papers, Accession 2010, Charles E. Young Research Library, Department of Special Collections, University of California, Los Angeles.

4. Robert L. Brown and Ralph P. Merritt, "Project Director's Report," in *Final Report, Manzanar Relocation Center*, Volume 1, FBD-WRA, Reel 76.

5. Burton et al., *Confinement and Ethnicity*, 59, 203, 259; *Welcome to Topaz: Guidebook of the Center* (Project Reports Division, Historical Section, 1943), 3 in Box 3, Folder 12, Central Utah-UW Papers.

6. Uchida, *Desert Exile*, 112.

7. "Fumi Manabe Hayashi," in Dempster, *Making Home from War*, 69–70.

8. Letter to a Nisei man (Joe Nagano) from his father (Sanezumi Nagano), April 30, 1943, ddr-densho-153-52, MNHS-DDR.

9. "Harumi Serata," in Dempster, *Making Home from War*, 160–161.

10. Charles Kikuchi, "Mr. M of Pasadena," November 10, 1942, JERS, Reel 281.

11. For irrigation in Idaho, see Fiege, *Irrigated Eden*.

12. Kleinkopf, *Relocation Center Diary*, 135, 181.

13. Robert Spencer, Notes on Initial Stay at Gila River, no date, JERS, Reel 283.

14. Gladys K. Bell, "Memories of Topaz: Japanese War Relocation Center, 1942 to 1945," 6. Special Collections, J. Willard Marriott Library, University of Utah; "Fumi Manabe Hayashi," in Dempster, *Making Home from War*, 69–70.

15. "A New Hobby," Community Analysis Newsletter 3, 8 April 1944, CAR-WRA, Reel 8.

16. Bell, "Relocation Center Life," 36–37.

17. Ralph P. Merritt to C. G. Gillespie, October 9, 1944, Box 226/63.020, Entry 48, WRA-NARA.

18. Aksel G. Nielsen, "Community Activities Section, Parts I–III," 30, 34, FBD-WRA, Reel 78. See also Unrau, *Evacuation and Relocation*, 278–279; Burton, *Garden Management Plan*, 63–69.

19. For the WRA's relocation program, see US War Relocation Authority, *Relocation of Japanese-Americans*, 2–3; Daniels, *Prisoners Without Trial*, 78–82; Allan W. Austin, "Eastward Pioneers: Japanese American Resettlement During World War II and the Contested Meaning of Exile and Incarceration," *Journal of American Ethnic History* 26, no. 2 (Winter 2007): 58–84; Robinson, *By Order of the President*, 130–133.

20. Robert Spencer, Notes on Initial Stay at Gila River, no date, JERS, Reel 283. Spencer used the term "moon walking" in his notes, but he was most likely referring to *Tsukimi*, or moon viewing, a Japanese tradition of celebrating the harvest moon. See James Attlee, *Nocturne: A Journey in Search of Moonlight* (Chicago: University of Chicago Press, 2011).

21. Conference of Mr. Roy Nash, Project Director, Manzanar Relocation Area and Mr. Philip J. Webster, Regional Office, September 2, 1942, JERS, Reel 157.

22. P. J. Webster to E. R. Fryer, September 7, 1942, JERS, Reel 157.

23. Conference of Mr. Roy Nash, Project Director, Manzanar Relocation Area and Mr. Philip J. Webster, Regional Office.

24. P. J. Webster to E. R. Fryer, September 7, 1942.

25. Conference of Mr. Roy Nash, Project Director, Manzanar Relocation Area and Mr. Philip J. Webster, Regional Office.

26. Memorandum to Col. Karl R. Bendetsen, August 26, 1942, JERS, Reel 157.

27. Pete Thomas, "At Manzanar, Fishing Was the Great Escape," *Los Angeles Times*, April 24, 2009, p. 1. For fishing at Topaz, see Miné Okubo, *Citizen 13660* (Seattle: University of Washington Press, 1983), 204. For the subversive potential of fishing, see Scott Giltner, "Slave Hunting and Fishing in the Antebellum South," in Glave and Stoll, *To Love the Wind and the Rain*, 21–36; Montrie, *Making a Living*, 35–52.

28. Archie Miyatake Interview, interviewed by Martha Nakagawa, August 31 and September 1, 2010, denshovh-marchie-02, DVHC-DDR.

29. Memorandum to Col. Karl R. Bendetsen, August 26, 1942, JERS, Reel 157.

30. Arthur P. Gough to E. O Sawyer Jr., August 21, 1942, JERS, Reel 157.

31. P. J. Webster to E. R. Fryer, September 7, 1942, JERS, Reel 157.

32. A. G. Nielsen to Roy Nash, September 2, 1942, and P. J. Webster to E. R. Fryer, September 7, 1942, JERS, Reel 157.

33. P. J. Webster to E. R. Fryer, September 7, 1942.

34. Ibid.

35. Ibid.

36. Ibid. Oral histories confirm that detainees went fishing under the guise of other official work, such as working for the survey crew and the garbage crew. See Henry Fukuhara Interview, interviewed by John Allen, November 6, 2002, denshovh-fhenry-01; Henry Nakano Interview, interviewed by Richard Potashin, December 5, 2008, denshovh-nhenry-01, MNHS-DDR.

37. P. J. Webster to E. R. Fryer, September 7, 1942.

38. Ibid.

39. Fred Nagai Interview, interviewed by Richard Potashin, May 10, 2011, denshovh-nfred-01, MNHS-DDR.

40. Mas Okui Interview, interviewed by Martha Nakagawa, April 25, 2012, denshovh-omas-01, Friends of Manzanar Collection, Densho Digital Repository, http://ddr.densho.org.

41. "No More Hikes up to Mountains," *Manzanar Free Press*, February 3, 1943.

42. Hank Umemoto, *Manzanar to Mount Whitney: The Life and Times of a Lost Hiker* (Berkeley, CA: Heyday Books, 2013), xiii, xiv, 88–91.

43. California Statutes and Amendments to the Codes 1943, Volume 1, Chapter 1100.

44. J. Benson Saks to Philip M. Glick, February 28, 1944, Box 260/37.108, Entry 16, WRA-NARA.

45. J. Benson Saks to Philip M. Glick, March 6, 1944, Box 260/37.108, Entry 16, WRA-NARA; J. Benson Saks to Carl Walters, March 3, 1944, Box 260/37.108, Entry 16, WRA-NARA.

46. Notice to All Residents of the City of Topaz from Charles F. Ernst, November 9, 1942, JERS, Reel 110.

47. Minutes, Planning Board, April 14, 1943, JERS, Reel 109.

48. Minidoka Report No. 18, December 1942, JERS, Reel 332.

49. Minidoka War Relocation Project, Report for Quarter Ended December 31, 1942, 2, JERS, Reel 332.

50. Minidoka Report No. 56, March 31, 1943, JERS, Reel 332; H. L. Stafford to Charles Welteroth, March 19, 1943, Box 230/50.300, Entry 48, WRA-NARA.

51. Minidoka Report no. 70, July 10, 1943, JERS, Reel 332.

52. Minidoka Report No. 73, September 3, 1943, JERS, Reel 332.

53. Funeral Services for Yoshio Tamura, Community Analysis Report 191, September 8, 1943, CAR-WRA, Reel 23.

54. For the role of the Spanish Consul, see Hayashi, *Democratizing the Enemy*, 77, 123, 296; Tetsuden Kashima, "American Mistreatment of Internees During World War II: Enemy Alien Japanese," in *Japanese Americans: From Relocation to Redress*, ed. Roger Daniels, Sandra Taylor, and Harry Kitano (Salt Lake City: University of Utah Press, 1986), 52–56.

55. "Analysis of Residents' Report to the Spanish Consul, Part III," General Meeting with a Representative of the Spanish Consul with regard to Project Conditions, Community Analysis Report 252, December 22, 1943, CAR-WRA, Reel 23.

56. "Analysis of Residents' Report to the Spanish Consul, Part II," General Meeting with a Representative of the Spanish Consul with regard to Project Conditions, Community Analysis Report 252, December 22, 1943, CAR-WRA, Reel 23. In reality, one of the drownings had occurred when the pool was in operation.

57. William Maxley Jr., "Canal Operations," June 2, 1944, Box 239/50.3000, Entry 48, WRA-NARA.

58. Minidoka Report No. 76, Camping Activities for the Summer of 1943, FBD-WRA, Reel 88.

59. Harry Stafford to Dillon S. Myer, August 22, 1944, Weekly Report, August 14–19, 1944, JERS, Reel 313; Minidoka Report No. 76, Camping Activities for the Summer of 1943, FBD-WRA, Reel 88.

60. Minutes, Planning Board, December 30, 1942, JERS, Reel 109.

61. Topaz Project Director Report No. 52, October 10, 1944, Box 99/549, Entry 48, WRA-NARA; Grace Oshita Interview, interviewed by Leslie Kellen, February 20, 1985, Box 3, Folder 3, Utah Interviews-UU.

62. Ralph C. Barnhart to Philip M. Glick, May 4, 1943, Box 255/37.105, Entry 16, WRA-NARA.

63. Ralph C. Barnhart to Philip M. Glick, May 26, 1943, Box 255/37.105, Entry 16, WRA-NARA.

64. "Statement of Relationships, Boy Scouts of America and War Relocation Authority," August 12, 1943, Box 325/61.110, Entry 16, WRA-NARA. The Girl Scouts and the WRA signed an almost identical agreement. See "Statement of Relationships, Girl Scouts and War Relocation Authority," January 26, 1944, Box 325/61.109, Entry 16, WRA-NARA.

65. For race and outdoor recreation, see Colin Fisher, "African Americans, Outdoor Recreation, and the 1919 Chicago Race Riot," in Glave and Stoll, *To Love the Wind and the Rain*, 63–76; Fisher, *Urban Green*. For the political implications of outdoor recreation, see Lawrence M. Lipin, *Workers and the Wild: Conservation,*

Consumerism, and Labor in Oregon, 1910–30 (Urbana: University of Illinois Press, 2007).

66. Michael B. Smith, "'The Ego Idea of the Good Camper' and the Nature of Summer Camp," *Environmental History* 11, no. 1 (January 2006): 70–101. See also Schmitt, *Back to Nature*, 96–105.

67. Statement of Joint Policy for Japanese Relocation Centers, Boy Scouts of America–War Relocation Authority, June 8, 1943, Box 324/61.110, Entry 16, WRA-NARA; David I. Macleod, "Act Your Age: Boyhood, Adolescence, and the Rise of the Boy Scouts of America," *Journal of Social History* 16, no. 2 (Winter 1982): 6.

68. Community Analysis Report 157, July 27 to August 7, 1943, CAR-WRA, Reel 23.

69. Ibid.

70. Minidoka Report No. 76, Camping Activities for the Summer of 1943.

71. "1943 Summer Camp of Topaz," Box 1, Folder 7, Central Utah-UW Papers; "Memo of Understanding," June 13, 1943, Box 100/610, Entry 48, WRA-NARA. See also Community Education Section, "Summer Camping Report," October 15, 1943, FBD-WRA, Reel 5.

72. "1943 Summer Camp of Topaz."

73. Meeting of Manzanar District Committee, Boy Scouts of America, June 9, 1943, Box 225/61.110, Entry 48, WRA-NARA; A. G. Nielsen to Lyle Wenter, February 26, 1945, Box 228/67.011, Entry 48, WRA-NARA; Community Activities Report 56, September 1, 1943, CAR-WRA, Reel 20.

74. Summer Camping Program at Gila, November 10, 1943, FBD-WRA, Reel 35.

75. Overnight Outing Regulations for Boy Scouts, March 15, 1944, JERS, Reel 109.

76. Tamura, "Gardens Below the Watchtower," *Landscape Journal*, 9.

77. "Hunt Gets Face-Lifting Treatment; Dustbowl Becomes Desert Oasis," *Minidoka Irrigator*, May 1, 1943, p. 3.

78. The term "survivable places" comes from Dusselier, *Artifacts of Loss*, 51. In addition to Dusselier and Anna Tamura, this section draws on the excellent work of Kenneth I. Helphand, who makes similar arguments about gardens as vehicles for Japanese American empowerment in *Defiant Gardens*. See also Naomi Hirahara, ed., *Green Makers: Japanese American Gardeners in Southern California* (Los Angeles: Southern California Gardeners' Federation, 2000), 53–57; Ronald Tadao Tsukashima, "Politics of Maintenance Gardening and the Formation of the Southern California Gardeners' Federation," in Hirahara, *Green Makers*, 67–93; Ronald Tadao Tsukashima, "Cultural Endowment, Disadvantaged Status and Economic Niche: The Development of an Ethnic Trade," *International Migration Review* 25, no. 1 (Summer 1991): 333–354.

79. Nobuya Tsuchida, "Japanese Gardeners in Southern California, 1900–1941," in *Labor Immigration Under Capitalism: Asian Workers in the United States Before World War II*, ed. Lucie Cheng and Edna Bonacich (Berkeley: University of California Press, 1984), 435–469, quotation on p. 437; Tamura, "Gardens Below the Watchtower," *Landscape Journal*, 5; Hirahara, *Green Makers*, 17–45.

80. Burton, *Garden Management Plan*, 82–84.

81. Ibid., 23–31.

82. Helphand, *Defiant Gardens*, 167. For barrack gardens, see also Burton, *Garden Management Plan*, 18–22.

83. US War Relocation Authority, *Relocation Communities for Wartime Evacuees*, 4. For a fuller discussion of the use of pioneer rhetoric in the context of Minidoka, see Hayashi, *Haunted by Waters*, 70–112.

84. Burton et al., *Confinement and Ethnicity*, 265; Blueprint of Topaz, Box 3, Folder 13, Central Utah-UW Papers.

85. "Residents Urged to Beautify City," *Gila News-Courier*, September 23, 1942, p. 1.

86. Tamura, "Gardens Below the Watchtower," *Landscape Journal*, 7.

87. Quarterly Report on Grounds Section for period of October 1, 1942–December 31, 1942, January 23, 1942, Box 143/552, Entry 48, WRA-NARA. For the extent of the gardens at Gila River, see Ozawa, "Archaeology of Gardens."

88. Quarterly Report on Grounds Section for period of January 1, 1943, to March 31, 1943, April 26, 1943, Box 147/650, Entry 48, WRA-NARA.

89. Nurseries at the Gila River WRA Project, January 1, 1944. FBD-WRA, Reel 35.

90. "Beautification," *Topaz Times*, September 30, 1942, pp. 3–4.

91. "Agricultural Story—Nursery Garden Area," Topaz Report H128, October 23, 1942, FBD-WRA, Reel 5.

92. Minidoka Report No. 56, March 31, 1943, JERS, Reel 332.

93. William Maxey to R. A. Pomeroy, April 27, 1944, Box 239/50.300, Entry 48, WRA-NARA.

94. Henry R. Watson to Clyde Tervort, August 24, 1943, Box 102/670, Entry 48, WRA-NARA.

95. Minutes, Planning Board, August 25, 1943, JERS, Reel 109.

96. "New Offices for Manzanar Personnel Men," *Inyo Register*, August 28, 1942.

97. Roscoe E. Bell to J. Whitney Floyd, Extension Forester, Utah State Agricultural College, October 6, 1942, Box 99/552, Entry 48, WRA-NARA.

98. Roscoe E. Bell to William J. Starley, D. Stevens & Company, May 26, 1943, Box 99/552, Entry 48, WRA-NARA.

99. "Landscaping," Topaz Report H175, November 7, 1942, FBD-WRA, Reel 5.

100. "Gardeners-Ag.," Topaz Report H212, November 17, 1942, FBD-WRA, Reel 5.

101. "City's Arbor Week," Topaz Report H256, December 3, 1942, FBD-WRA, Reel 5.

102. Roscoe E. Bell to Charles F. Ernst, Weekly Narrative Report, November 20, 1942, Box 191/24.031, Entry 16, WRA-NARA.

103. "Arbor Week," Topaz Report H237, November 25, 1942, FBD-WRA, Reel 5.

104. "City's Arbor Week," Topaz Report H256, December 3, 1942, FBD-WRA, Reel 5.

105. Frank S. Twohey to Charles F. Ernst, Weekly Narrative Report of December 4, 1942, Box 191/24.031, Entry 16, WRA-NARA.

106. Manzanar Project Report No. 4, June 16, 1942; Manzanar Project Report No. 25, July 25, 1942; Manzanar Project Report No. 46, September 15, 1942; Manzanar

Project Report No. 64, October 30, 1942, FBD-WRA, Reel 76. See also Burton, *Garden Management Plan*, 69–72.

107. "New Offices for Manzanar Personnel Men," *Inyo Register*, August 28, 1942.

108. Minidoka Report No. 9—Gardens, October 29, 1942, FBD-WRA, Reel 88.

109. Eaton, *Beauty Behind Barbed Wire*, 92–95; Ketzel Levine, "Tending 'Defiant Gardens' During Wartime," National Public Radio, May 29, 2006, http://www.npr.org/templates/story/story.php?storyId=5435131 (accessed January 9, 2008).

110. Tamura, "Gardens Below the Watchtower," *Landscape Journal*, 13.

111. "Transfer of Ownership of Cherry Trees from Francis Miosaku Uyematsu to the WRA Project at Manzanar, California," ca. January 1943 and Francis Miosaku Uyematsu, "Concerning the Wisteria . . . ," no date, Box 215/11.229, Entry 48, WRA-NARA; Lee McCarthy, "The Generations Issue; Roots That Run Deep: Lee McCarthy Traces the Enduring Spirit of Poet Amy Uyematsu's Japanese Grandfather, Whose Generosity and Tenacity Helped Make Descanso Gardens Bloom," *Los Angeles Times*, April 30, 2006, p. W22. Before evacuation, Uyematsu also sold three hundred thousand camellias to Manchester Boddy, the newspaper publisher and advocate of the Manzanar camp. These plants continue to grace his estate, now known as Descanso Gardens. After the war, the cherry trees at Manzanar were transplanted to Inyo County residents' yards.

112. "Creative Beauty," *Topaz Times*, April 24, 1943, p. 4.

113. Suyemoto, *I Call to Remembrance*, 85.

114. Tamura, "Gardens Below the Watchtower," *Landscape Journal*, 2, 10–11.

115. Burton, *Garden Management Plan*, 46–47.

116. Umemoto, *Manzanar to Mount Whitney*, 192.

117. Burton, *Garden Management Plan*, 288–289. For a comprehensive study of Japanese gardens, see Wybe Kuitert, *Themes in the History of Japanese Garden Art* (Honolulu: University of Hawaii Press, 2002).

118. Y. Okuno, "Stones," no date, JERS, Reel 282. See also Robert F. Spencer, Report No. 2 on Gila, November 2, 1942, JERS, Reel 283.

119. Burton, *Garden Management Plan*, 50, 288–289.

120. Quoted in Burton, *Garden Management Plan*, 49. See also Tamura, "Gardens Below the Watchtower," *Landscape Journal*, 16.

121. Administrative Instruction No. 89, April 28, 1943, Box 312/43.500, Entry 16, WRA-NARA. For WRA funding of public landscaping, see Lee Noftzger to John C. Henderson, Employment & Housing Officer, December 31, 1942, Box 143/552 and Meeting of the Landscaping Group, March 29, 1944, Box 240/51.900, Entry 48, WRA-NARA. The WRA also financed nurseries to propagate plants and trees, allowed gardeners to leave the center with government vehicles to collect materials, and employed grounds crews to install and maintain gardens and walks in public areas. See Manzanar Project Report No. 14, July 1, 1942, FBD-WRA, Reel 76; Henry Nishi Oral History, interviewed by Anna Tamura

in Tamura, "Gardens Below the Watchtower," master of landscape architecture thesis, 129–130; Arthur Ogami Interview, interviewed by Alice Ito, March 10, 2004, denshovh-oarthur-01-0007, DVHC-DDR.

122. R. S. Davidson to H. L. Stafford, March 22, 1943, Box 239/50.300, Entry 48, WRA-NARA.

123. Burton, *Garden Management Plan*, 107–108.

124. Helphand, *Defiant Gardens*, 189. Dusselier and Burton make similar points about the subversive nature of gardens. See Dusselier, *Artifacts of Loss*, 87, and Burton, *Garden Management Plan*, 9.

125. Tamura, "Gardens Below the Watchtower," *Landscape Journal*, 11.

126. Y. Okuno, "A Carp," no date, JERS, Reel 282.

CHAPTER 7

1. Visit with Japanese Farmers, October 10, 1946, T. Yatsushiro Daily Reports from Denver Area No. 80, JERS, Reel 107.

2. Abstract of Testimony of K. Mayeda, 1981, Box 2, Folder 73, Hosokawa Papers.

3. Edward H. Spicer, Asael T. Hansen, Katharine Luomala, and Marvin K. Opler, *The Impounded People: Japanese Americans in the Relocation Centers* (Washington, DC: US Department of Interior, 1946), 225.

4. War Relocation Authority, "When You Leave the Relocation Center," no date, Box 1, Folder 5, Hatate Papers.

5. Daniels, *Prisoners Without Trial*, 78–81.

6. "Nisei Farm Lead . . . ," News Release, Columbus, Ohio, no date, JERS, Reel 21.

7. Fiorello H. LaGuardia to Harold L. Ickes, April 11, 1944, JERS, Reel 20.

8. "Incident at Hamburg, Iowa: Digest of Report from Kansas City Relocation Office," no date, JERS, Reel 21.

9. Charlotte Brooks, "In the Twilight Zone between Black and White: Japanese American Resettlement and Community in Chicago, 1942–1943," *Journal of American History* 86 (March 2000): 1655–1687.

10. Hayashi, *Democratizing the Enemy*, 189–190.

11. Press Release, War Relocation Authority, Department of the Interior Information Service, December 18, 1944, JERS, Reel 21.

12. "Secretary Ickes' Message to Center Residents," December 29, 1944, JERS, Reel 20.

13. Memorandum for the Staff of the War Relocation Authority from Harold L. Ickes, December 19, 1944, JERS, Reel 21.

14. Dillon Myer to All Project Directors, December 7, 1944, JERS, Reel 21.

15. Dillon Myer to All Project Directors, December 8, 1944, JERS, Reel 21.

16. "Harumi Serata," in Dempster, *Making Home from War*, 163.

17. Ed Tanaka to Lewis Hatch, February 17, 1945, CRBEHA, http://content.libraries.wsu.edu/cdm/compoundobject/collection/imls_2/id/272/rec/6 (accessed July 15, 2016).

18. Lewis Hatch to Ed Tanaka, February 22, 1945, CRBEHA, http://content.libraries. wsu.edu/cdm/compoundobject/collection/imls_2/id/261/rec/4 (accessed July 15, 2016).

19. Lewis Hatch to Ed Tanaka and family, January 16, 1946, CRBEHA, http://content.libraries.wsu.edu/cdm/compoundobject/collection/imls_2/id/250/rec/2 (accessed July 15, 2016).

20. E. H. Reed, "Report of Farm and Marketing Section for the Month of August," August 31, 1945; E. H. Reed to Frank S. Gumble, September 7, 1945; E. H. Reed to John C. McClendon, September 18, 1945; E. H. Reed to Roy C. Wright, September 18, 1945, Box 320/51/130, Entry 16, WRA-NARA.

21. Myer, *Uprooted Americans*, 195.

22. George Nakagawa Interview, interviewed by Arthur Hansen, January 26, 1988, and June 23, 1988, O. H. 1959, in Hansen, *Japanese American World War II Evacuation Oral History Project*, 66. See also Bloom and Riemer, *Removal and Return*, 125–126.

23. Press Release, War Relocation Authority, Department of the Interior Information Service, February 20, 1945, and February 23, 1945, JERS, Reel 21.

24. A Message from the National Director to the Residents of Relocation Centers, July 12, 1945, JERS, Reel 22.

25. Daniels, *Prisoners Without Trial*, 81, 86; Memorandum, A Message from the Director of the War Relocation Authority [to evacuees resident in relocation centers], c. January 1945, JERS, Reel 22.

26. US War Agency Liquidation Unit, *People in Motion: The Postwar Adjustment of the Evacuated Japanese Americans* (Washington, DC: Department of the Interior, 1947), 72. See also Brighton Community via John Horie and wife, October 24, 1946, T. Yatsushiro Daily Reports from Denver Area No. 115, JERS, Reel 107.

27. The Bureau of Sociological Research was a group of social scientists who studied Poston at the behest of the Office of Indian Affairs. The goal was to create guidelines for administering the camp. Psychiatrist Alexander Leighton was in charge of the study, which led to the publication of Alexander H. Leighton, *The Governing of Men: General Principles and Recommendations Based on Experience at a Japanese Relocation Camp* (Princeton: Princeton University Press, 1945). See also Lane Hirabayashi, "Toshio Yatsushiro," *Densho Encyclopedia*, http://encyclopedia.densho.org/Toshio%20Yatsushiro/ (accessed July 8, 2016) and Hayashi, *Democratizing the Enemy*, 219–222.

28. "Study of Social, Economic Adjustments of Evacuees to Be Continued by Federal Agency," *Pacific Citizen*, July 27, 1946, p. 3. See also Robert M. Cullum, "People in Motion," *Common Ground* (September 1947): 61–68. Many of the fieldworkers were former WRA community analysts. See Katharine Luomala, "Community Analysis by the War Relocation Authority Outside the Relocation Centers," *Applied Anthropology* 6, no. 1 (Winter 1947): 25–31.

29. US War Agency Liquidation Unit, *People in Motion*, 1.

30. Sam Sameshima Family, October 17, 1946, T. Yatsushiro Daily Reports from Denver Area No. 92, JERS, Reel 107.

31. Roy Uyesaka Family, October 17, 1946, T. Yatsushiro Daily Reports from Denver Area No. 95, JERS, Reel 107.

32. K. Sasaki Interview, September 17, 1946, T. Yatsushiro Daily Reports from Denver Area No. 27, JERS, Reel 107.

33. Roy Nakano Interview, August 30, 1946, T. Yatsushiro Daily Reports from Denver Area No. 14, JERS, Reel 107.

34. Colorado Farming Conditions via Mr. S. Kobayashi, Issei, October 24, 1946, T. Yatsushiro Daily Reports from Denver Area No. 55, JERS, Reel 107.

35. George Ohashi Interview, September 21, 1946, T. Yatsushiro Daily Reports from Denver Area No. 36, JERS, Reel 107.

36. Talk with Hitoshige Okabe, October 21, 1946, T. Yatsushiro Daily Reports from Denver Area No. 108, JERS, Reel 107.

37. Colorado Farming Conditions via Mr. S. Kobayashi, Issei, October 24, 1946.

38. Hori Family, November 15, 1946, T. Yatsushiro Daily Reports from Denver Area No. 149, JERS, Reel 107.

39. Fred Mikuni family, October 18, 1946, T. Yatsushiro Daily Reports from Denver Area No. 97, JERS, Reel 107.

40. Mr. Sameshima, November 13, 1946, T. Yatsushiro Daily Reports from Denver Area No. 142, JERS, Reel 107.

41. Mr. Kaihara Interview, October 5, 1946, T. Yatsushiro Daily Reports from Denver Area No. 66, JERS, Reel 107.

42. Mr. J. Horie Interview, October 12, 1946, T. Yatsushiro Daily Reports from Denver Area No. 81, JERS, Reel 107.

43. Nishimura Family, October 25, 1946, T. Yatsushiro Daily Reports from Denver Area No. 119, JERS, Reel 107.

44. Evening with Evacuee Family S. Kobayashi, October 26, 1946, T. Yatsushiro Daily Reports from Denver Area No. 121, JERS, Reel 107.

45. Meeting with Native Nisei, October 16, 1946, T. Yatsushiro Daily Reports from Denver Area No. 90, JERS, Reel 107.

46. Brighton Community via John Horie and wife, October 24, 1946; Spicer et al., *Impounded People*, 219.

47. Nisei Methodist Church Service, October 12, 1946, T. Yatsushiro Daily Reports from Denver Area No. 84, JERS, Reel 107; Spicer et al., *Impounded People*, 219. For Japanese Americans' prewar Colorado farming communities and their relationships with whites, see Eric Walz, *Nikkei in the Interior West: Japanese Immigration and Community Building, 1882–1945* (Tucson: University of Arizona Press, 2012), 73, 168.

48. Meeting with Native Nisei, October 16, 1946; Spicer et al., *Impounded People*, 219.

49. Brighton Community via John Horie and wife, October 24, 1946.

50. Rev. Eizo Sakamoto Interview, October 9, 1946, T. Yatsushiro Daily Reports from Denver Area No. 78, JERS, Reel 107.

51. T. Doisaki, October 24, 1946, T. Yatsushiro Daily Reports from Denver Area No. 98, JERS, Reel 107.

52. Native Issei farmer-Kosuge, October 27, 1946, T. Yatsushiro Daily Reports from Denver Area No. 123, JERS, Reel 107.

53. John Numoto Family, October 17, 1946, T. Yatsushiro Daily Reports from Denver Area No. 91, JERS, Reel 107.

54. Visit with Fred Hisamoto Family, October 18, 1946, T. Yatsushiro Daily Reports from Denver Area No. 98, JERS, Reel 107.

55. Meeting with Native Nisei, October 16, 1946.

56. Visit with Fred Hisamoto Family, October 18, 1946.

57. Mr. Kaihara interview.

58. Meeting of Littleton Nisei Christians, October 22, 1946, T. Yatsushiro Daily Reports from Denver Area No. 109, JERS, Reel 107.

59. Brighton Community via John Horie and wife, October 24, 1946.

60. Elmer R. Smith, "Japanese Resettlement in the Brigham City Area," March 29, 1947, JERS, Reel 108.

61. John deYoung, "Japanese Resettlement in the Boise Valley and Snake River Valley," September 30, 1946, JERS, Reel 107.

62. Ibid.

63. Sawada, "After the Camps," 121, 129–131.

64. Ronald Smothers, "A New Chapter for a Village, Once Barracks," *New York Times*, October 4, 2006, http://www.nytimes.com/2006/10/04/nyregion/04camp.html (accessed June 23, 2017).

65. Elmer R. Smith, "Japanese Resettlement in the Brigham City Area," March 29, 1947, and Elmer R. Smith, "Japanese Resettlement in Utah Lake District, Utah," March 27, 1947, JERS, Reel 108.

66. Sawada, "After the Camps," 131.

67. Elmer R. Smith, "Japanese Resettlement in Utah—Garland and Corrine Areas," February 15, 1947, JERS, Reel 108.

68. US War Relocation Authority, *Wartime Handling of Evacuee Property*, 86.

69. Adon Poli and Warren M. Engstrand, "Japanese Agriculture on the Pacific Coast," *Journal of Land and Public Utility Economics* 21, no. 4 (November 1945): 363–364.

70. Lilian Hoffecker, "Terminal Island, California," *Densho Encyclopedia,* http://encyclopedia.densho.org/Terminal%20Island,%20California/ (accessed July 11, 2016).

71. Robinson, *After Camp*, 208–209; Brilliant, *Color of America*, 49.

72. Walter A. Heath to Mr. Merritt, August 24, 1945, and Mary H. S. Hayes to Mr. Heath, August 23, 1945, Box 296/41.136, Entry 16, WRA-NARA.

73. Bloom and Riemer, *Removal and Return*, 192–193.

74. Asael T. Hansen, "Back Home in Santa Clara Valley," *Pacific Citizen*, December 21, 1946, pp. 10, 14, 15, 16, and Brian Niiya, "Asael T. Hansen," *Densho Encyclopedia,* http://encyclopedia.densho.org/Asael%20T.%20Hansen/ (accessed July 8, 2016). Hansen was also one of the authors of *The Impounded People*. For the experiences of Japanese Americans in the postwar Santa Clara Valley, see Tsu, *Garden of the World*, 211–216.

75. "Economic Adjustment," July 17, 1946, Hansen's Daily Reports from Santa Clara County No. 8, JERS, Reel 108.

76. "Economic Adjustment-Issei Bachelor," August 20, 1946, Hansen's Daily Reports from Santa Clara County No. 30, JERS, Reel 108; US War Agency Liquidation Unit, *People in Motion*, 53.

77. "Farmer-Economic Adjustment," August 2, 1946, Hansen's Daily Reports from Santa Clara County No. 23, JERS, Reel 108.

78. "Economic Adjustment-Yokota's," August 25, 1946, Hansen's Daily Reports from Santa Clara County No. 37, JERS, Reel 108.

79. Arthur Hansen, "Report for July 23 to 29," July 30, 1946, JERS, Reel 108.

80. US War Agency Liquidation Unit, *People in Motion*, 61; Tsu, *Garden of the World*, 29.

81. US War Relocation Authority, *The Evacuated People*, 47.

82. Sasaki was an anthropologist who had also conducted field research for the Bureau of Sociological Research at Poston during the war. See Brian Niiya, "Tom T. Sasaki," *Densho Encyclopedia*, http://encyclopedia.densho.org/Tom%20T.%20Sasaki/ (accessed July 8, 2016).

83. "Economic Adjustment," October 21, 1946, Sasaki's Daily Reports from Los Angeles No. 115, JERS, Reel 108.

84. Fuki Endow Kawaguchi, "On the Brink of Evacuation: The Diary of an Issei Woman," translated from the Japanese and ed. Sanae Kawaguchi Moorehead, with historical notes and introduction by Greg Robinson, *Prospects: An Annual of American Cultural Studies* 28 (October 2004): 378.

85. Bloom and Riemer, *Removal and Return*, 119–120; "Social Organization— Within the Japanese Community," August 22, 1946, Sasaki's Daily Reports from Los Angeles No. 43, JERS, Reel 107. For the postwar demand for Japanese American gardeners in Southern California, see Carla S. Tengen, "Cultivating Communities: Japanese American Gardeners in Southern California, 1910– 1980," (PhD diss., Brown University, 2006), 45–46, 83–89, 135–136; Tsukashima, "Politics of Maintenance Gardening," 77–79.

86. Toshio Whelchel, *From Pearl Harbor to Saigon: Japanese American Soldiers and the Vietnam War* (New York: Verso, 1999), 7–10.

87. "Social Structure—The Less Fortunate People of Los Angeles," September 20, 1946, Sasaki's Daily Reports from Los Angeles No. 54, JERS, Reel 107.

88. "Economic Adjustment-Discrimination," August 15, 1946, Sasaki's Daily Reports from Los Angeles No. 34, JERS, Reel 107.

89. Bloom and Riemer, *Removal and Return*, 84, 87, 92–93, 95.

90. "Economic Adjustment," October 21, 1946, Sasaki's Daily Reports from Los Angeles No. 115, JERS, Reel 108; US War Agency Liquidation Unit, *People in Motion*, 62.

91. Bloom and Riemer, *Removal and Return*, 110–111; Noritaka Yagasaki, "Ethnic Cooperativism and Immigrant Agriculture: A Study of Japanese Floriculture

and Truck Farming in California" (PhD diss., University of California, Berkeley, 1982), 332.

92. Yagasaki, "Ethnic Cooperativism and Immigrant Agriculture," 110–111, 130–131; Gary Kawaguchi, "Race, Ethnicity, Resistance, and Competition: An Historical Analysis of Cooperation in the California Flower Market" (PhD diss.: University of California, Berkeley, 1995), 127–132.

93. Yagasaki, "Ethnic Cooperativism and Immigrant Agriculture," 333–336, 339, 414. See also Naomi Hirahara, *A Scent of Flowers: The History of the Southern California Flower Market, 1912–2004* (Pasadena, CA: Midori Books, 2004).

94. Kurashige, *Shifting Grounds of Race*, 196; "Economic Adjustment—Flower Market," October 15, 1946, Sasaki's Daily Reports from Los Angeles No. 107 and "Economic Adjustment—Flower Market," October 15, 1946, Sasaki's Daily Reports from Los Angeles No. 108, JERS, Reel 108.

95. "Economic Adjustment—Nursery," October 17, 1946, Sasaki's Daily Reports from Los Angeles No. 110, JERS, Reel 108.

96. Ibid.

97. "Southern California Flower Market Incorporated," October 17, 1946, T. Sasaki's Daily Reports from Los Angeles No. 111, JERS, Reel 108.

98. "Economic Adjustment—Flower Market, Grower," October 28, 1946, T. Sasaki's Daily Reports from Los Angeles No. 121, JERS, Reel 108.

99. "Economic Adjustment," November 1, 1946, T. Sasaki's Daily Reports from Los Angeles No. 126, JERS, Reel 108.

100. Testimony of Mitsuo Usui, 1981, Box 2, Folder 63, Hosokawa Papers.

101. "Orange County," November 19, 1946, T. Sasaki's Daily Reports from Los Angeles No. 139, JERS, Reel 108.

102. "Economic Adjustment—Orange County," September 24, 1946, Sasaki's Daily Reports from Los Angeles No. 93, JERS, Reel 108.

103. T. Sasaki, "Coachella-Imperial Valley," October 10, 1946, JERS, Reel 107.

104. "Outgroup Relations in Brawley, California (Imperial Valley)," August 3, 1946, Sasaki's Daily Reports from Los Angeles No. 22, JERS, Reel 107.

105. Kessler, *Stubborn Twig*, 211–217.

106. Ibid., 216.

107. Ibid., 219–225.

108. Myer, *Uprooted Americans*, 199–201. For anti-Japanese violence after the war, see also Kevin Allen Leonard, "'Is That What We Fought For?': Japanese Americans and Racism in California, The Impact of World War II," *Western Historical Quarterly* 21, no. 4 (November 1990): 463–482.

109. Lewis Hatch to Ed Tanaka and family, January 16, 1946.

110. Neiwert, *Strawberry Days*, 208–234.

111. George Nakagawa interview, 66–68.

112. Kessler, *Stubborn Twig*, 213; Harold S. Fisters to Relocation and Legal Divisions, Heart Mountain and Minidoka, Box 238/30.100, Entry 48, WRA-NARA.

113. "House Joint Memorial No. 9," Oregon Legislative Assembly, February 28, 1945. Box 2, Folder 4, Governor Earl Snell Records, Oregon State Archives, http://arcweb.sos.state.or.us/pages/exhibits/ww2/after/pdf/back3.pdf (accessed July 9, 2016).

114. Brilliant, *Color of America*, 36–38; Robinson, *After Camp*, 198.

115. D. S. Myer to Robert Kenny, October 19, 1944, Box 278/39.024, WRA-NARA, Entry 16.

116. Robinson, *After Camp*, 198; US War Agency Liquidation Unit, *People in Motion*, 63–65.

117. For a detailed discussion of Macbeth's career, see Robinson, *After Camp*, 171–182.

118. Robinson, *After Camp*, 199–202. See also Rose Cuison Villazor, "Rediscovering Oyama v. California: At the Intersection of Property, Race, and Citizenship," *Washington University Law Review* 87, no. 5 (2010): 979–1042 and Brilliant, *Color of America*, 30–48.

119. Robinson, *After Camp*, 198; US War Agency Liquidation Unit, *People in Motion*, 63–65.

120. Brilliant, *Color of America*, 53.

121. Robinson, *After Camp*, 208–211; Brilliant, *Color of America*, 49–52.

122. Lilian Takahashi Hoffecker, "A Village Disappeared," *American Heritage* 52, no. 8 (December 2001): 64–71; Susan Moffat, "A Paradise Lost, Never Forgotten," *Los Angeles Times*, January 5, 1994; Bloom and Riemer, *Removal and Return*, 158–197. See also Sandy Lydon, *The Japanese in the Monterey Bay Region: A Brief History* (Capitola, CA: Capitola Book Company, 1997), 120–121.

123. US War Relocation Authority, *Wartime Handling of Evacuee Property*, 92–93.

124. US War Relocation Authority, *WRA: A Story of Human Conservation*, 159–162; US Department of the Interior, War Agency Liquidation Unit, *People in Motion*, 63.

125. US War Relocation Authority, *Wartime Handling of Evacuee Property*, 3–4.

126. Statement of Noriko Bridges, San Francisco, August 11, 1981, Box 2, Folder 76, Hosokawa Papers.

127. Testimony of Thomas T. Shigio, 1981, Box 2, Folder 65, Hosokawa Papers.

128. Robinson, *After Camp*, 4.

129. US War Relocation Authority, *Wartime Handling of Evacuee Property*, 97.

EPILOGUE

1. Frank Finch, "Manzanar, War-Born Jap Town, Dismantled," *Los Angeles Times*, December 2, 1946, p. 2.

2. Ibid.

3. "They've Knocked Down Manzanar and Hauled Away the Pieces," *Los Angeles Times*, December 2, 1946, p. 3.

4. Finch, "Manzanar, War-Born Jap Town, Dismantled"; "They've Knocked Down Manzanar."

5. Wilson, "Landscapes of Promise and Betrayal"; "Minidoka," (Jerome, ID: National Historic Site, National Park Service, US Department of the Interior, no date) http://www.nps.gov/miin/learn/upload/MIIN-Brochure-09.pdf (accessed June 11, 2015); Burton et al., *Confinement and Ethnicity*, 278.

6. Murray, *Historical Memories*, 195–196. See also Tetsuden Kashima, "Japanese American Internees Return, 1945 to 1955: Readjustment and Social Amnesia," *Phylon* 41, no. 2 (Summer 1980): 107–115; Kate Brown, "The Eclipse of History: Japanese America and a Treasure Chest of Forgetting," *Public Culture* 9, no. 1 (Fall 1996): 69–91.

7. Murray, *Historical Memories*, 186. See also Robinson, *After Camp*, 243–246.

8. The findings were published in US Commission on Wartime Relocation and Internment of Civilians, *Personal Justice Denied: Report of the Commission on Wartime Relocation and Internment of Civilians* in 1982 (reprinted by the University of Washington Press in 1997). This report contributed to the passage of the Civil Liberties Act of 1988, which provided a formal federal apology and a one-time payment of $20,000 to each surviving detainee.

9. Murray, *Historical Memories*, 15, 289, 322, 326; Sharon Yamato, "Commission on Wartime Relocation and Internment of Civilians," *Densho Encyclopedia*, http://encyclopedia.densho.org/Commission%20on%20Wartime%20Relocation%20and%20Internment%20of%20Civilians/ (accessed June 13, 2015).

10. Testimony of Haru Isaki, Commission on Wartime Relocation and Internment of Civilians Hearing, Seattle, WA, September 9, 1981, Box 2, Folder 66, Hosokawa Papers.

11. Testimony of Dr. Mary S. Oda, Commission on Wartime Relocation and Internment of Civilians Hearing, Los Angeles, CA, August 4-6, 1981, Box 2, Folder 61, Hosokawa Papers. See also Suyemoto, *I Call to Remembrance*, xxi, 6, 55–61. Suyemoto's son developed respiratory problems while at the Tanforan Assembly Center and died at the age of sixteen.

12. Manzanar Committee, *The Manzanar Pilgrimage: A Time for Sharing* (Los Angeles: Manzanar Committee, 1981), 8–9. See also Karen M. Inouye, *The Long Afterlife of Nikkei Wartime Incarceration* (Stanford, CA: Stanford University Press, 2016), 119–135.

13. Manzanar Committee, *The Manzanar Pilgrimage*, 9.

14. Murray, *Historical Memories*, 210; Manzanar Committee, *The Manzanar Pilgrimage*, 12–13; Stanley O. Williford, "Japanese Group Visits Site of World War II Detention Camp," *Los Angeles Times*, January 2, 1970.

15. About Us, The Manzanar Committee, http://www.manzanarcommittee.org/The_Manzanar_Committee/About_Us.html (accessed June 12, 2015).

16. Jane Naomi Iwamura, "Critical Faith: Japanese Americans and the Birth of a New Civil Religion," *American Quarterly* 59, no. 3 (September 2007): 938, 950–953. See also Elena Tajima-Creef, *Imaging Japanese America: The Visual Construction of Citizenship, Nation, and the Body* (New York: New York University Press, 2004), 135–137.

17. Psyche Pascual, "Japanese-American Group to Revisit Manzanar Camp," *Los Angeles Times*, December 29, 1991.

18. For Manzanar, see Tajima-Creef, *Imaging Japanese America*, 133–143 and Robert Hayashi, "Transfigured Patterns: Contesting Memories at the Manzanar National Historic Site," *Public Historian* 25, no. 4 (Fall 2003): 51–71. For Tule Lake, see World War II Valor in the Pacific National Monument, http://www.nps.gov/valr/index.htm (accessed June 12, 2015). Upon its creation in 2001, Minidoka was called the Minidoka Internment National Monument. Federal legislation changed its name to the Minidoka National Historic Site in 2008. See "Happy 15th Birthday Minidoka National Historic Site," Minidoka National Historic Site Newsletter, January 2016, https://www.nps.gov/miin/learn/news/upload/January-2016-Minidoka-NHS-Newsletter-rev.pdf (accessed June 7, 2016).

19. National Register of Historic Places Program: Research, http://www.nps.gov/nr/research/ (accessed June 12, 2015); National Register of Historic Places Program: Fundamentals, https://www.nps.gov/nr/national_register_fundamentals.htm (accessed June 27, 2017). For background on the National Register of Historic Places and National Historic Landmarks, see "National Register of Historic Places," National Trust for Historic Preservation, http://www.preservationnation.org/information-center/law-and-policy/legal-resources/preservation-law-101/federal-law/national-register.html (accessed July 28, 2015); John M. Fowler, "The Federal Preservation Program," in *Richer Heritage: Historic Preservation in the Twenty-First Century*, ed. Robert E. Stipe (Chapel Hill: University of North Carolina Press, 2003), 41–44.

20. Tajima-Creef, *Imaging Japanese America*, 139–143; Auditorium Restoration, Manzanar National Historic Site, http://www.nps.gov/manz/learn/management/auditorium-restoration.htm (accessed June 12, 2015); Guard Tower, Manzanar National Historic Site, http://www.nps.gov/manz/learn/management/guard-tower.htm (accessed June 12, 2015); Umemoto, *Manzanar to Mount Whitney*, 191; Mess Hall Move, Manzanar National Historic Site, http://www.nps.gov/manz/learn/management/mess-hall-move.htm (accessed June 12, 2015); Manzanar National Historic Site Opens Long-Awaited Barracks Exhibit, April 17, 2015, http://blog.manzanarcommittee.org/2015/04/17/manzanar-national-historic-site-opens-long-awaited-barracks-exhibit/ (accessed June 12, 2015); Outdoor Activities, Manzanar National Historic Site, http://www.nps.gov/manz/planyourvisit/outdooractivities.htm (accessed June 12, 2015); Plan Your Visit, Manzanar National Historic Site, http://www.nps.gov/manz/planyourvisit/index.htm (accessed June 12, 2015).

21. Burton, *Garden Management Plan*, iii–iv.

22. Heart Mountain WWII Japanese American Confinement Site, About the Foundation, http://www.heartmountain.org/thefoundation.html (accessed June 27, 2017)

23. Topaz Museum, Museum Project, http://www.topazmuseum.org/project (accessed June 27, 2017).

24. Topaz Museum, Significant Milestones of the Topaz Museum, http://www. topazmuseum.org/milestones (accessed June 27, 2017).

25. Japanese American Confinement Sites, National Park Service, http://www.nps. gov/jacs/ (accessed June 12, 2015).

26. *Public Law 109-441, Preservation of Japanese American Confinement Sites, Newsletter* 1, no. 1 (Fall 2007), http://www.nps.gov/jacs/downloads/Newsletter1.pdf; *Public Law 109-441, Preservation of Japanese American Confinement Sites, Newsletter* 1, no. 2 (December 2007), http://www.nps.gov/jacs/downloads/Newsletter2. pdf; *Public Law 109-441, Preservation of Japanese American Confinement Sites, Newsletter* 2, no. 1 (June 2008), http://www.nps.gov/jacs/downloads/Newsletter3. pdf (accessed June 12, 2015).

27. Japanese American Confinement Sites, National Park Service; Japanese American Confinement Sites Grant Program, FY 2011 Grant Awards, https://www.nps. gov/jacs/downloads/2011_GrantAwardSummaries_Brief.pdf; Japanese American Confinement Sites Grant Program, FY 2012 Grant Awards, https://www.nps.gov/ jacs/downloads/2012_Grant_Recipients.pdf; *Public Law 109-441, Preservation of Japanese American Confinement Sites, Newsletter* (Fall–Winter 2012), http://www. nps.gov/jacs/downloads/2012_winter_NEWSLETTER.pdf; *Public Law 109-441, Preservation of Japanese American Confinement Sites, Newsletter* (Winter 2014– 2015), http://www.nps.gov/jacs/downloads/newsletter9.pdf; "Japanese American Confinement Sites Grant Program, Fiscal Year 2015 Grants for the Preservation and Interpretation of the Historic Confinement Sites Where Japanese Americans Were Detained during World War II," http://www.nps.gov/jacs/downloads/FINAL_ FY2015ProgramGuidelines_SEPT10.pdf; *Japanese American Confinement Sites Grant Program Newsletter* (Spring 2017), https://www.nps.gov/jacs/downloads/ Newsletter11.pdf; Japanese American Confinement Sites Grant Program, FY 2017 Grant Awards, https://www.nps.gov/jacs/downloads/FY2017ProjectSummaries. pdf (accessed December 15, 2017).

28. Todd Stewart, *Placing Memory: A Photographic Exploration of Japanese American Internment*, essays by Natasha Egan and Karen J. Leong, afterword by John Tateishi (Norman: University of Oklahoma Press, 2008), 3.

29. Junkoh Harui interview.

30. Blaine Newnham, "Junkoh Harui Reclaims His Father's Landmark Gardens on Bainbridge Island," *Seattle Times*, June 17, 1990; Brian Kelly, "Bainbridge 'Treasure' Junkoh Harui's Legacy Will Live On," *Bainbridge Island Review*, October 22, 2008; Junkoh Harui interview.

31. Tristan Baurick, "For 50 Years, Bainbridge Gardens Has Been a Labor of One Man's Love," *Kitsap Sun*, July 19, 2008.

32. Ibid.

33. "Podcast: Who's on Bainbridge: Donna Harui Reflects on Her Family's History on Bainbridge," August 8, 2014, http://bestofbcb.org/ who-002-donna-harui-reflects-on-her-familys-bainbridge-island-history.

34. Tamura, "Gardens Below the Watchtower," master of landscape architecture thesis, 65–68; Levine, "Tending Defiant Gardens."

35. Helphand, *Defiant Gardens*, 210.

36. Levine, "Tending Defiant Gardens."

37. Sharon Yamato, "Toyo Miyatake," *Densho Encyclopedia*, http://encyclopedia. densho.org/Toyo_Miyatake/ (accessed May 29, 2015).

38. Darrell Kunitomi, "All About Trout: The Collector's Edition; Beyond the Barbed Wire, a String of Skinny Goldens," *Los Angeles Times*, April 20, 2004, p. F4.

39. Nancy Matsumoto, "Fishing as a Form of Defiance: Cory Shiozaki and 'The Manzanar Fishing Club,'" Discover Nikkei, April 4, 2013, http://www. discovernikkei.org/en/journal/2013/4/4/manzanar-fishing-club/ (accessed June 16, 2015).

40. Ibid.; Brian Niiya, "Manzanar Fishing Club (film)," *Densho Encyclopedia*, http:// encyclopedia.densho.org/Manzanar_Fishing_Club_%28film%29/ (accessed May 28, 2015).

41. *The Manzanar Fishing Club*, directed by Cory Shiozaki (From Barbed Wire to Barbed Hooks LLC, 2012).

42. *Manzanar Fishing Club*.

43. Phil Willon, "Owens Lake as Solar Power Plant?" *Los Angeles Times*, December 2, 2009.

44. Phil Willon, "L.A. Takes a Shine to Another Owens Valley Product: Sun," *Los Angeles Times*, February 2, 2010.

45. Louis Sahagun, "DWP Is Moving Ahead with Plans for Owens Valley Solar Plant," *Los Angeles Times*, December 25, 2013.

46. Katie Vane, "DWP Solar Proposal Could Have Affects [*sic*] on Manzanar," *The Sheet*, August 14, 2013.

47. Sahagun, "DWP Is Moving Ahead."

48. Brian Black, "The Nature of Preservation: The Rise of Authenticity at Gettysburg," *Civil War History* 58, no. 3 (September 2012): 348–373.

49. Elson Trinidad, "Farewell to Manzanar? A Solar Future Threatens a Sensitive Past," January 7, 2014, http://www.kcet.org/updaily/socal_focus/commentary/ transpacific-routes/farewell-to-manzanar-a-solar-future-threatens-a-sensitive-past. html (accessed May 29, 2015).

50. "A Solar Array Won't Hurt the Mood of Manzanar," *Los Angeles Times*, January 2, 2014.

51. Deb Murphy, "Time Limit Expires on DWP Solar Ranch Request," *Sierra Wave Media*, April 22, 2015, http://www.sierrawave.net/34388/time-limit-expires-on-dwp-solar-ranch-request/ (accessed June 1, 2015); Deb Murphy, "More on LADWP Proposed Solar Ranch," *Sierra Wave Media*, April 27, 2015, http://www.sierrawave. net/34457/more-on-ladwp-proposed-solar-ranch/ (accessed June 1, 2015).

52. "Unified, Grass-Roots Effort Credited with Gaining Indefinite Hold on Industrial-Scale Solar Projects Threatening Manzanar, Owens Valley," press release, Manzanar

Committee, August 3, 2015, https://manzanarcommittee.files.wordpress.com/2015/08/sovsr-corrected-joint-statement-8-3-15.pdf (accessed June 7, 2016).

53. "Manzanar Committee Applauds Inyo County for Taking Important Step Towards Protecting Manzanar, Owens Valley from Large-Scale Renewable Energy Development," press release, May 7, 2014, https://manzanarcommittee.files.wordpress.com/2014/05/inyo-bos-step-statement-5-7-14.pdf (accessed June 1, 2015). For the Owens Valley Committee, see "About Us," Owens Valley Committee website, http://www.ovcweb.org/About%20OVC/AboutOVC.html (accessed August 15, 2016). For the relationship between Japanese Americans and native groups during the solar debate, see Wendi Yamashita, "The Colonial and the Carceral: Building Relationships Between Japanese Americans and Indigenous Groups in the Owens Valley," *Amerasia Journal* 42, no. 1 (2016): 121–138.

54. Bruce Embrey to Planning Department, County of Inyo, January 14, 2015, https://manzanarcommittee.files.wordpress.com/2015/01/inyo-peir-regpa-comments-1-14-15.pdf (accessed July 7, 2017).

55. Renewable Energy General Plan Amendment Final Program Environmental Impact Report, Volume 2, March 2015, 4.1-17, http://www.inyoplanning.org/projects/documents/FinalPEIRVolmeII.pdf (accessed June 2, 2015).

56. Mike Gervais, "REGPA Approved," *Inyo County Register*, March 26, 2015, pp. 1, 3.

57. "Owens Valley Solar Energy Study (OVSES) Project Overview," http://www.inyoplanning.org/OwensValleySolarEnergyStudyOVSES.htm (accessed June 2, 2015).

58. HELIX Environmental Planning, Inc., Owens Valley Solar Energy Study, Draft Final Report, February 2016, Appendix C, http://www.inyoplanning.org/documents/OVSES_Final_Report_DRAFT_160222.pdf (accessed June 6, 2016).

59. Levine, "Tending Defiant Gardens."

60. *Public Law 109-441, Preservation of Japanese American Confinement Sites, Newsletter* 1, no. 2 (December 2007).

61. Fiege, *Republic of Nature*, 11.

Selected Bibliography

MANUSCRIPT COLLECTIONS

Bowron, Fletcher. Papers. Huntington Library, San Marino, California.

Carr, William C. Papers. Special Collections, Charles E. Young Research Library, University of California, Los Angeles.

Columbia River Basin Ethnic History Archive. Washington State University Libraries. https://library.vancouver.wsu.edu/archive/crbeha.

Densho Digital Repository. http://ddr.densho.org.

Fujii, Yoshito. Papers. Special Collections, University of Washington Libraries.

Hatate, Harry R. Papers. Special Collections, University of Washington Libraries.

Hosokawa, William. Papers. Western History and Genealogy Room, Denver Public Library.

Ichihara, Kaoru. Papers. Special Collections, University of Washington Libraries.

Interviews with Japanese Americans in Utah. Special Collections, J. Willard Marriott Library, University of Utah.

Japanese American Evacuation and Resettlement Study. Bancroft Library, University of California, Berkeley, Microfilm.

Los Angeles Department of Water and Power Historical Records Program. Los Angeles, California.

Manzanar War Relocation Records. Special Collections, Charles E. Young Research Library, University of California, Los Angeles.

National Archives and Records Administration, College Park, Maryland.

    Bureau of Agricultural Economics (Record Group 83)

National Archives and Records Administration, Washington, DC.

    Bureau of Indian Affairs (Record Group 75)
    Community Analysis Reports and Community Analysis Trend Reports of the War Relocation Authority, Microfilm M1342
    Field Basic Documentation of the War Relocation Authority, Microfilm C0053
    War Relocation Authority (Record Group 210)

Sakamoto, James Y. Papers. Special Collections, University of Washington Libraries.

Topaz Oral Histories. Special Collections, J. Willard Marriott Library, University of Utah.

US Commission on Wartime Relocation and Internment of Civilians. Papers. Part 1, Numerical File Archive, Microfilm.

US War Relocation Authority Central Utah Project Records. Special Collections, University of Washington Libraries.

Willis, Elizabeth Bayley. Papers. Special Collections, University of Washington Libraries.

PERIODICALS

Gila News-Courier
Inyo Independent
Inyo Register
Los Angeles Times
Manzanar Free Press
Millard County Chronicle
Minidoka Irrigator
Topaz Times

UNPUBLISHED PRIMARY SOURCES

Bell, Gladys K. "Memories of Topaz: Japanese War Relocation Center, 1942 to 1945." Special Collections, J. Willard Marriott Library, University of Utah.

Bell, Roscoe E. "Relocation Center Life, Topaz, Utah, 1942–1945." Special Collections, J. Willard Marriott Library, University of Utah.

Hikida, Shotaro. "The Story of My Life," January 1943. Online Archive of California. http://cdn.calisphere.org/data/28722/27/bk0013c6727/files/bk0013c6727-FID1. pdf.

Kleinkopf, Arthur. *Relocation Center Diary.* Idaho State Historical Society, Boise, Idaho.

McColm, George L. Interviewed by Niel M. Johnson. Independence, MO, May 20 and 21, 1991. Harry S. Truman Library. http://www.trumanlibrary.org/oralhist/ mccolmgl.htm.

Myer, Dillon S. Interviewed by Helen S. Pryor. Berkeley, CA, July 7, 1970. Regional Oral History Office, Bancroft Library, University of California, Berkeley. http:// www.trumanlibrary.org/oralhist/myerds2.htm.

Takahashi, C. T. Interviewed by Judith Austin. Seattle, WA, August 16, 1984. OH 1069, Idaho State Historical Society, Boise, Idaho.

PUBLISHED PRIMARY SOURCES

Adams, Ansel. *Born Free and Equal: The Story of Loyal Japanese Americans*. Bishop, CA: Spotted Dog Press, 2002.

Collier, John. *From Every Zenith: A Memoir; and Some Essays on Life and Thought*. Denver: Sage Books, 1963.

Cullum, Robert M. "People in Motion." *Common Ground* (September 1947): 61–68.

Dempster, Brian Komei. *From Our Side of the Fence: Growing Up in America's Concentration Camps*. San Francisco: Kearney Street Workshop Press, 2001.

Dempster, Brian Komei. *Making Home From War: Stories of Japanese American Exile and Resettlement*. Berkeley, CA: Heyday Books, 2010.

Eaton, Allen H. *Beauty Behind Barbed Wire: The Arts of the Japanese in Our War Relocation Camps*. New York: Harper & Brothers, 1952.

Eisenhower, Milton S. *The President Is Calling*. Garden City, NY: Doubleday & Company, 1974.

Embree, John F. "Community Analysis—an Example of Anthropology in Government." *American Anthropologist*, new ser. 46, no. 3 (July–September 1944): 277–291.

Hansen, Arthur A., ed. *Japanese American World War II Evacuation Oral History Project*. 4 volumes. Munich: K.G. Saur, 1994.

Kawaguchi, Fuki Endow. "On the Brink of Evacuation: The Diary of an Issei Woman." Translated and edited by Sanae Kawaguchi Moorehead, with historical notes and introduction by Greg Robinson. *Prospects: An Annual of American Cultural Studies* 28 (October 2004): 359–382.

Kim, Heidi, ed. *Taken from the Paradise Isle: The Hoshida Family Story*. Boulder: University Press of Colorado, 2015.

Leighton, Alexander H. *The Governing of Men: General Principles and Recommendations Based on Experience at a Japanese Relocation Camp*. Princeton, NJ: Princeton University Press, 1945.

Luomala, Katharine. "Community Analysis by the War Relocation Authority Outside the Relocation Centers." *Applied Anthropology* 6, no. 1 (Winter 1947): 25–31.

Manzanar Committee. *The Manzanar Pilgrimage: A Time for Sharing*. Los Angeles: Manzanar Committee, 1981.

Myer, Dillon S. *Uprooted Americans: The Japanese Americans and the War Relocation Authority During World War II*. Tucson: University of Arizona Press, 1971.

Nishimura, M. S., Robert Emerson, T. Hata, and Akira Kageyama. "The Propagation of Guayule from Cuttings." *American Journal of Botany* 31, no. 7 (July 1944): 412–418.

Okubo, Miné. *Citizen 13660*. Seattle: University of Washington Press, 1983.

Poli, Adon and Warren M. Engstrand. "Japanese Agriculture on the Pacific Coast." *Journal of Land and Public Utility Economics* 21, no. 4 (November 1945): 363–364.

Stebbins, G. L., Jr. and M. Kodani. "Chromosomal Variation in Guayule and Mariola." *Journal of Heredity* 35 (1944): 162–172.

Suyemoto, Toyo. *I Call to Remembrance: Toyo Suyemoto's Years of Internment.* Edited by Susan B. Richardson. New Brunswick, NJ: Rutgers University Press, 2007.

Tateishi, John. *And Justice for All: An Oral History of the Japanese American Detention Camps.* Seattle: University of Washington Press, 1999.

Taylor, Frank J. "The People Nobody Wants." *Saturday Evening Post*, May 9, 1942.

Uchida, Yoshiko. *Desert Exile: The Uprooting of a Japanese American Family.* New ed. Seattle: University of Washington Press, 1982.

Umemoto, Hank. *Manzanar to Mount Whitney: The Life and Times of a Lost Hiker.* Berkeley, CA: Heyday Books, 2013.

GOVERNMENT REPORTS AND HEARINGS

Burton, Jeffery F. *Garden Management Plan: Gardens and Gardeners at Manzanar.* Independence, CA: Manzanar National Historic Site, National Park Service, Department of the Interior, 2015. https://www.nps.gov/manz/learn/management/upload/Manzanar-Garden-Management-Plan-2015.pdf.

Spicer, Edward H., Asael T. Hansen, Katharine Luomala, and Marvin K. Opler. *The Impounded People: Japanese Americans in the Relocation Centers.* Washington, DC: US Department of the Interior, 1946.

United States. Commission on Wartime Relocation and Internment of Civilians. *Personal Justice Denied: Report of the Commission on Wartime Relocation and Internment of Civilians.* With a New Foreword by Tetsuden Kashima. Seattle: University of Washington Press, 1997.

United States. Congress. House. Select Committee Investigating National Defense Migration. *National Defense Migration. Hearings Before the Select Committee Investigating National Defense Migration, House of Representatives, Seventy-Seventh Congress, Second Session.* Washington, DC: US Government Printing Office, 1942.

United States. Department of Agriculture. *Victory Garden Leader's Handbook.* Washington, DC: US Department of Agriculture, 1943.

United States. Department of Agriculture in cooperation with the Bureau of Campaigns, Office of War Information. *U.S. Government Campaign to Promote the Production, Sharing, and Proper Use of Food, Book IV: The Victory Gardens Campaign.* Washington, DC: US Department of Agriculture, 1943.

United States. War Liquidation Unit. *People In Motion: The Postwar Adjustment of the Evacuated Japanese Americans.* Washington DC: US Department of the Interior, 1947.

United States. War Relocation Authority. *The Evacuated People: A Quantitative Description.* Washington, DC: US Department of the Interior, War Relocation Authority, 1946.

United States. War Relocation Authority. *Relocation Communities for Wartime Evacuees.* Washington, DC: US Department of the Interior, 1942.

United States. War Relocation Authority. *Relocation of Japanese-Americans*. Washington, DC: US Department of the Interior, 1943.

United States. War Relocation Authority. *The War Relocation Work Corps: A Circular of Information for Enlistees and Their Families*. Washington, DC: US Department of the Interior, 1942.

United States. War Relocation Authority. *The Wartime Handling of Evacuee Property*. Washington, DC: US Department of the Interior, War Relocation Authority, 1946.

United States. War Relocation Authority. *WRA: A Story of Human Conservation*. Washington, DC: US Department of the Interior, War Relocation Authority, 1946.

Unrau, Harlan D. *The Evacuation and Relocation of Persons of Japanese Ancestry During World War II: A Historical Study of the Manzanar Relocation Center*. 2 vols. Washington DC: US Department of the Interior, National Park Service, 1996.

SECONDARY SOURCES

Alinder, Jasmine. *Moving Images: Photography and the Japanese American Incarceration*. Urbana: University of Illinois Press, 2009.

Andrews, Thomas G. *Killing for Coal: America's Deadliest Labor*. Cambridge, MA: Harvard University Press, 2008.

Aoki, Keith. "No Right to Own? The Early Twentieth-Century 'Alien Land Laws' as a Prelude to Internment." *Boston College Third World Law Journal* 19, no. 1 (December 1998): 37–72.

Austin, Allan W. "Eastward Pioneers: Japanese American Resettlement During World War II and the Contested Meaning of Exile and Incarceration." *Journal of American Ethnic History* 26, no. 2 (Winter 2007): 58–84.

Austin, Allan W. *From Concentration Camp to Campus: Japanese American Students and World War II*. Urbana: University of Illinois Press, 2007.

Azuma, Eiichiro. *Between Two Empires: Race, History, and Transnationalism in Japanese America*. New York: Oxford University Press, 2005.

Bentley, Amy. *Eating for Victory: Food Rationing and the Politics of Domesticity*. Urbana: University of Illinois Press, 1998.

Bernstein, Shana. *Bridges of Reform: Interracial Civil Rights Activism in Twentieth-Century Los Angeles*. New York: Oxford University Press, 2011.

Bishop, Ronald, Morgan Dudkewitz, Alissa Falcone, and Renee Daggett. *Community Newspapers and the Japanese-American Incarceration Camps: Community, Not Controversy*. Lanham, MD: Lexington Books, 2015.

Bloom, Leonard and Ruth Riemer. *Removal and Return: The Socioeconomic Effects of the War on Japanese Americans*. Berkeley: University of California Press, 1949.

Boime, Eric. "'Beating Plowshares into Swords': The Colorado River Delta, the Yellow Peril, and the Movement for Federal Reclamation, 1901–1928." *Pacific Historical Review* 78, no. 1 (February 2009): 27–53.

Booker, Matthew Morse. *Down by the Bay: San Francisco's History Between the Tides.* Berkeley: University of California Press, 2013.

Brady, Lisa M. *War Upon the Land: Military Strategy and the Transformation of Southern Landscapes During the American Civil War.* Athens: University of Georgia Press, 2012.

Brewer, Susan A. *Why American Fights: Patriotism and War Propaganda from the Philippines to Iraq.* New York: Oxford University Press, 2009.

Brilliant, Mark. *The Color of America Has Changed: How Racial Diversity Shaped Civil Rights Reform in California, 1941–1978.* New York: Oxford University Press, 2012.

Brilliant, Mark. "Re-imagining Racial Liberalism." In *Making the American Century: Essays on the Political Culture of Twentieth Century America*, edited by Bruce J. Schulman, 228–250. Princeton, NJ: Princeton University Press, 2014.

Briones, Matthew M. *Jim and Jap Crow: A Cultural History of 1940s Interracial America.* Princeton, NJ: Princeton University Press, 2012.

Brooks, Charlotte. "In the Twilight Zone Between Black and White: Japanese American Resettlement and Community in Chicago, 1942–1943." *Journal of American History* 86 (March 2000): 1655–1687.

Brown, Kate. "The Eclipse of History: Japanese America and a Treasure Chest of Forgetting." *Public Culture* 9, no. 1 (Fall 1996): 69–91.

Burton, Jeffery F., Mary M. Farrell, Florence B. Lord, and Richard W. Lord. *Confinement and Ethnicity: An Overview of World War II Japanese American Relocation Sites.* Seattle: University of Washington Press, 2002.

Chan, Sucheng. "Asian American Historiography." *Pacific Historical Review* 65, no. 3 (August 1996): 363–400.

Chan, Sucheng. *This Bittersweet Soil: The Chinese in California Agriculture, 1860–1910.* Berkeley: University of California Press, 1986.

Chang, Gordon, ed. *Morning Glory, Evening Shadow: Yamato Ichihashi and His Internment Writings, 1942–1945.* Stanford, CA: Stanford University Press, 1999.

Chaplin, Joyce E. "Tidal Rice Cultivation and the Problem of Slavery in South Carolina and Georgia, 1760–1815." *William and Mary Quarterly*, 3rd ser., 49, no. 1 (January 1992): 56–57.

Chiang, Connie Y. "Imprisoned Nature: Toward an Environmental History of the World War II Japanese American Incarceration." *Environmental History* 15, no. 2 (April 2010): 236–267.

Chiang, Connie Y. "Winning the War at Manzanar: Environmental Patriotism and the Japanese American Incarceration." In *Rendering Nature: Animals, Bodies, Places, Politics*, edited by Marguerite S. Shaffer and Phoebe S. K. Young, 237–262. Philadelphia: University of Pennsylvania Press, 2015.

Closmann, Charles E. ed. *War and the Environment: Military Destruction in the Modern Age.* College Station: Texas A&M University Press, 2009.

Coates, Peter A. "The Strange Stillness of the Past: Toward an Environmental History of Sound and Noise." *Environmental History* 10, no. 4 (October 2005): 636–665.

Cole, Tim. *Holocaust Landscapes.* London: Bloomsbury Publishing, 2016.

Cullen, Catherine L. "The Education of Japanese Americans, 1942–1946: The Fate of Democratic Curriculum Reform." *American Educational History Journal* 38, no. 1 (2011): 197–218.

Daniels, Roger. *Prisoners Without Trial: Japanese Americans in World War II.* Rev. ed. New York: Hill and Wang, 2004.

Daniels, Roger. "Words Do Matter: A Note on Inappropriate Terminology and the Incarceration of Japanese Americans." In *Nikkei in the Pacific Northwest: Japanese Americans and Japanese Canadians in the Twentieth Century*, edited by Louis Fiset and Gail M. Nomura, 190–214. Seattle: University of Washington Press, 2005.

Drinnon, Richard. *Keeper of Concentration Camps: Dillon S. Myer and American Racism.* Berkeley: University of California Press, 1987.

Dusselier, Jane E. *Artifacts of Loss: Crafting Survival in Japanese American Concentration Camps.* New Brunswick, NJ: Rutgers University Press, 2008.

Elkind, Sarah. "The Nature and Business of War: Drilling for Oil in Wartime Los Angeles." In *Cities and Nature in the American West*, edited by Char Miller, 205–224. Reno: University of Nevada Press, 2010.

Escobedo, Elizabeth R. *From Coveralls to Zoot Suits: The Lives of Mexican American Women on the World War II Homefront.* Chapel Hill: University of North Carolina Press, 2013.

Feeley, Francis McCollum. *America's Concentration Camps During World War II: Social Science and the Japanese American Internment.* New Orleans, LA: University Press of the South, 1999.

Fiege, Mark. *The Republic of Nature: An Environmental History of the United States.* Seattle: University of Washington Press, 2012.

Finlay, Mark R. *Growing American Rubber: Strategic Plants and the Politics of National Security.* New Brunswick, NJ: Rutgers University Press, 2009.

Fiset, Louis. "Thinning, Topping, and Loading: Japanese Americans and Beet Sugar in World War II." *Pacific Northwest Quarterly* 90, no. 3 (Summer 1999): 123–139.

Fisher, Colin. *Urban Green: Nature, Recreation, and the Working Class in Industrial Chicago.* Chapel Hill: University of North Carolina Press, 2015.

Flores, Lori A. *Grounds for Dreaming: Mexican Americans, Mexican Immigrants, and the California Farmworker Movement.* New Haven: Yale University Press, 2016.

Friday, Chris. *Organizing Asian American Labor: The Pacific Coast Canned-Salmon Industry, 1870–1942.* Philadelphia: Temple University Press, 1994.

Fried, Amy. *Pathways to Polling: Crisis, Cooperation, and the Making of Public Opinion Professions.* New York: Routledge, 2011.

Fryer, Heather. *Perimeters of Democracy: Inverse Utopias and the Wartime Social Landscape in the American West.* Lincoln: University of Nebraska Press, 2010.

Fujita-Rony, Dorothy. "Water and Land: Asian Americans and the U.S. West." *Pacific Historical Review* 76, no. 4 (2007): 563–574.

Geiger, Andrea. *Subverting Exclusion: Transpacific Encounters with Race, Caste, and Borders, 1885–1928.* New Haven: Yale University Press, 2011.

Gordon, Linda and Gary Y. Okihiro, eds. *Impounded: Dorothea Lange and the Censored Images of Japanese American Internment*. New York: Norton, 2006.

Gowdy-Wygant, Cecilia. *Cultivating Victory: The Women's Land Army and the Victory Garden Movement*. Pittsburgh, PA: University of Pittsburgh Press, 2013.

Hall, Clarence Jefferson, Jr. "Prisonland: Environment, Society, and Mass Incarceration on New York's Northern Frontier, 1845–1999." PhD dissertation, State University of New York, Stony Brook, 2014.

Hansen, Arthur A. "The Evacuation and Resettlement Study at the Gila River Relocation Center, 1942–1944." *Journal of the West* 38, no. 2 (April 1999): 45–55.

Hansen, Arthur A., Betty E. Mitson, and Sue Kunitomi Embrey. "Dissident Harry Ueno." *California History* 64, no. 1 (Winter 1985): 58–64.

Harth, Erica, ed. *Last Witnesses: Reflections on the Wartime Internment of Japanese Americans*. New York: Palgrave Macmillan, 2003.

Hayashi, Brian Masaru. *Democratizing the Enemy: The Japanese American Internment*. Princeton, NJ: Princeton University Press, 2008.

Hayashi, Robert. *Haunted by Waters: A Journey Through Race and Place in the American West*. Iowa City: University of Iowa Press, 2007.

Hayashi, Robert. "Transfigured Patterns: Contesting Memories at the Manzanar National Historic Site." *Public Historian* 25, no. 4 (Fall 2003): 51–71

Heimburger, Christian Kelly. "Life Beyond Barbed Wire: The Significance of Japanese American Labor in the Mountain West, 1942–1944." PhD dissertation, University of Colorado at Boulder, 2013.

Helphand, Kenneth. *Defiant Gardens: Making Gardens in Wartime*. San Antonio, TX: Trinity University Press, 2006.

Herrera, Hayden. *Listening to Stone: The Art and Life of Isamu Noguchi*. New York: Farrar, Straus, and Giroux, 2015.

Hill, Kimi Kodani, ed. *Topaz Moon: Chiura Obata's Art of the Internment*. Berkeley, CA: Heyday Books, 2000.

Hirabayashi, Lane Ryo. *The Politics of Fieldwork: Research in an American Concentration Camp*. Tucson: University of Arizona Press, 1999.

Hirahara, Naomi. *A Scent of Flowers: The History of the Southern California Flower Market, 1912–2004*. Pasadena, CA: Midori Books, 2004.

Hirasuna, Delphine. *The Art of Gaman: Arts and Crafts from the Japanese American Internment Camps 1942–1946*. Berkeley, CA: Ten Speed Press, 2005.

Horiuchi, Lynne. "Dislocations: The Built Environments of Japanese American Internment." In *Guilt by Association: Essays on Settlement, Internment, and Relocation in the Rocky Mountain West*, edited by Mike Mackey, 258–59. Powell, WY: Western History Publications, 2001.

Howard, John. *Concentration Camps on the Home Front: Japanese Americans in the House of Jim Crow*. Chicago: University of Chicago Press, 2008.

Hurley, Andrew. *Environmental Inequalities: Class, Race, and Industrial Pollution in Gary, Indiana, 1945–1980*. Chapel Hill: University of North Carolina Press, 1995.

Ichioka, Yuji. *The Issei: The World of the First Generation Japanese Immigrants, 1885–1924*. New York: Free Press, 1988.

Ichioka, Yuji, ed. *Views from Within: The Japanese American Evacuation and Resettlement Study*. Los Angeles: Asian American Studies Center, University of California, Los Angeles, 1989.

Inouye, Karen M. *The Long Afterlife of Nikkei Wartime Incarceration*. Stanford, CA: Stanford University Press, 2016.

Irons, Peter. *Justice at War: The Story of the Japanese-American Internment Cases*. Berkeley: University of California Press, 1993.

Ivey, Linda L. and Kevin W. Kaatz. *Citizen Internees: A Second Look at Race and Citizenship in Japanese American Internment Camps*. Santa Barbara, CA: Praeger, 2017.

Iwamura, Jane Naomi. "Critical Faith: Japanese Americans and the Birth of a New Civil Religion." *American Quarterly* 59, no. 3 (September 2007): 937–968.

Jacoby, Karl. *Crimes Against Nature: Squatters, Poachers, Thieves, and the Hidden History of American Conservation*. Berkeley: University of California Press, 2014.

James, Thomas. *Exile Within: The Schooling of Japanese Americans*. Cambridge, MA: Harvard University Press, 1987.

Janssen, Volker. "When the 'Jungle' Met the Forest: Public Work, Civil Defense, and Prison Camps in Postwar California." *Journal of American History* 96, no. 3 (December 2009): 702–726.

Kahrl, William L. *Water and Power: The Conflict Over Los Angeles' Water Supply in the Owens Valley*. Berkeley: University of California Press, 1982.

Kashima, Tetsuden. "Japanese American Internees Return, 1945 to 1955: Readjustment and Social Amnesia." *Phylon* 41, no. 2 (Summer 1980): 107–115.

Kashima, Tetsuden. *Judgment Without Trial: Japanese American Imprisonment During World War II*. Seattle: University of Washington Press, 2004.

Kawaguchi, Gary. "Race, Ethnicity, Resistance, and Competition: An Historical Analysis of Cooperation in the California Flower Market." PhD dissertation, University of California, Berkeley, 1995.

Kessler, Lauren. "Fettered Freedoms: The Journalism of World War II Japanese Internment Camps." *Journalism History* 15, nos. 2–3 (1988): 70–79.

Kessler, Lauren. *Stubborn Twig: Three Generations in the Life of a Japanese American Family*. Corvallis: Oregon State University Press, 2008.

Kohlstedt, Sally Gregory. "'A Better Crop of Boys and Girls': The School Gardening Movement, 1890–1920." *History of Education Quarterly* 48, no. 1 (February 2008): 58–93.

Kosek, Jake. *Understories: The Political Life of Forests in Northern New Mexico*. Durham, NC: Duke University Press, 2006.

Kurashige, Lon. *Japanese American Celebration and Conflict: A History of Ethnic Identity and Festival, 1934–1990*. Berkeley: University of California Press, 2002.

Kurashige, Lon. "Resistance, Collaboration, and Manzanar Protest." *Pacific Historical Review* 70, no. 3 (August 2001): 387–417.

Kurashige, Scott. *The Shifting Grounds of Race: Black and Japanese Americans in the Making of Multiethnic Los Angeles*. Princeton, NJ: Princeton University Press, 2008.

Lee, Erika. "The 'Yellow Peril' and Asian Exclusion in the Americas." *Pacific Historical Review* 76, no. 4 (November 2007): 537–557.

Lee, Shelley Sang-Hee. *Claiming the Oriental Gateway: Prewar Seattle and Japanese America*. Philadelphia: Temple University Press, 2010.

Leff, Mark. H. "The Politics of Sacrifice on the American Home Front in World War II." *Journal of American History* 77, no. 4 (March 1991): 1297.

Leonard, Kevin Allen. "'Is That What We Fought for?': Japanese Americans and Racism in California, the Impact of World War II." *Western Historical Quarterly* 21, no. 4 (November 1990): 463–482.

Lillquist, Karl. "Farming the Desert: Agriculture in the World War II–Era Japanese-American Relocation Centers." *Agricultural History* 84, no. 1 (Winter 2010): 74–104.

Lillquist, Karl. *Imprisoned in the Desert: The Geography of World War II–Era, Japanese American Relocation Centers in the Western United States*. Ellensburg: Geography and Land Studies Department, Central Washington University, 2007. http://www.cwu.edu/geography/sites/cts.cwu.edu.geography/files/ja_relocation.pdf.

Limerick, Patricia Nelson. "Disorientation and Reorientation: The American Landscape Discovered from the West." *Journal of American History* 79, no. 3 (December 1992): 1021–1049.

Lyford, Amy. *Isamu Noguchi's Modernism: Negotiating Race, Labor, and Nation, 1930–1950*. Berkeley: University of California Press, 2013.

Lyon, Cherstin. *Prisons and Patriots: Japanese American Wartime Citizenship, Civil Disobedience, and Historical Memory*. Philadelphia: Temple University Press, 2011.

Maher, Neil M. *Nature's New Deal: The Civilian Conservation Corps and the Roots of the American Environmental Movement*. New York: Oxford University Press, 2007.

Mancini, Matthew J. *One Dies, Get Another: Convict Leasing in the American South, 1866–1928*. Columbia: University of South Carolina Press, 1996.

Matsumoto, Valerie J. *City Girls: The Nisei Social World in Los Angeles, 1920–1950*. New York: Oxford University Press, 2014.

Matsumoto, Valerie J. *Farming the Home Place: A Japanese American Community in California*. Ithaca, NY: Cornell University Press, 1993.

McEvoy, Arthur F. *The Fisherman's Problem: Ecology and Law in the California Fisheries, 1850–1980*. New York: Cambridge University Press, 1986.

McGovney, Dudley O. "The Anti-Japanese Land Laws of California and Ten Other States." *California Law Review* 35, no. 1 (March 1947): 7–60.

McLennan, Rebecca M. *Crisis of Imprisonment: Protest, Politics, and the Making of the American Penal State, 1776–1941*. New York: Cambridge University Press, 2008.

Miller, Char. "In the Sweat of Our Brow: Citizenship in American Domestic Practice During WWII—Victory Gardens." *Journal of American Culture* 26, no. 3 (September 2003): 395–405.

Mizuno, Takeya. "The Creation of the 'Free' Press in Japanese-American Camps: The War Relocation Authority's Planning and Making of the Camp Newspaper Policy." *Journalism and Mass Communication Quarterly* 78, no. 3 (2001): 503–518.

Molina, Natalia. *Fit to Be Citizens? Public Health and Race in Los Angeles, 1879–1939.* Berkeley: University of California Press, 2006.

Montrie, Chad. *Making a Living: Work and Environment in the United States.* Chapel Hill: University of North Carolina Press, 2008.

Muller, Eric L. *American Inquisition: The Hunt for Japanese American Disloyalty in World War II.* Chapel Hill: University of North Carolina Press, 2007.

Muller, Eric L. *Colors of Confinement: Rare Kodachrome Photographs of Japanese American Incarceration in World War II.* Chapel Hill: University of North Carolina Press, 2012.

Muller, Eric L. *Free to Die for Their Country: The Story of the Japanese American Draft Resisters.* Chicago: University of Chicago Press, 2003.

Murray, Alice Yang. *Historical Memories of the Japanese American Internment and the Struggle for Redress.* Stanford, CA: Stanford University Press, 2008.

Neiwert, David A. *Strawberry Days: How Internment Destroyed a Japanese American Community.* New York: Palgrave Macmillan, 2005.

Ngai, Mae M. *Impossible Subjects: Illegal Aliens and the Making of Modern America.* Princeton, NJ: Princeton University Press, 2004.

Okamura, Raymond. "'The Great White Father': Dillon Myer and Internal Colonialism." *Amerasia Journal* 13, no. 2 (1986–1987): 155–160.

Okihiro, Gary Y., ed. *Encyclopedia of Japanese American Internment.* Westport, CT: Greenwood, 2013.

Okihiro, Gary Y. *Storied Lives: Japanese American Students and World War II.* Seattle: University of Washington Press, 1999.

Ozawa, Koji Harris. "The Archaeology of Gardens in Japanese American Incarceration Camps." MA thesis, San Francisco State University, 2016.

Peck, Gunther. "The Nature of Labor: Fault Lines and Common Ground in Environmental and Labor History." *Environmental History* 11, no. 2 (April 2006): 212–238.

Phillips, Sarah T. *This Land, This Nation: Conservation, Rural America, and the New Deal.* New York: Cambridge University Press, 2007.

Piper, Karen. *Left in the Dust: How Race and Politics Created a Human and Environmental Tragedy in L.A.* New York: Palgrave Macmillan, 2006.

Rawson, Michael. *Eden on the Charles: The Making of Boston.* Cambridge, MA: Harvard University Press, 2010.

Robinson, Greg. *After Camp: Portraits in Midcentury Japanese American Life and Politics.* Berkeley: University of California Press, 2012.

Robinson, Greg. *By Order of the President: FDR and the Internment of Japanese Americans.* Cambridge, MA: Harvard University Press, 2003.

Robinson, Greg. *A Tragedy of Democracy: Japanese Confinement in North America.* New York: Columbia University Press, 2009.

Russell, Edmund. *War and Nature: Fighting Humans and Insects with Chemicals from World War I to Silent Spring*. New York: Cambridge University Press, 2001.

Sawada, Mitziko. "After the Camps: Seabrook Farms, New Jersey, and the Resettlement of Japanese Americans, 1944–47." *Amerasia Journal* 13, no. 2 (1986): 117–136.

Schrager, Adam. *The Principled Politician: Governor Ralph Carr and the Fight Against Japanese American Internment*. New York: Fulcrum Publishing, 2010.

Shimabokuro, Robert. *Born in Seattle: The Campaign for Japanese American Redress*. Seattle: University of Washington Press, 2001.

Shinozuka, Jeannie Natsuko. "From a 'Contagious' to a 'Poisonous Yellow Peril'?: Japanese and Japanese Americans in Public Health and Agriculture, 1890s–1950." PhD dissertation, University of Minnesota, 2009.

Sims, Robert C. "'You Don't Need to Wait Any Longer to Get Out': Japanese American Evacuees as Farm Laborers During World War II." *Idaho Yesterdays* 44, no. 2 (Summer 2000): 7–13.

Singh, Nikhil Pal. *Black Is a Country: Race and the Unfinished Struggle for Democracy*. Cambridge, MA: Harvard University Press, 2004.

Smith, Jason Scott. *Building New Deal Liberalism: The Political Economy of Public Works, 1933–1956*. New York: Cambridge University Press, 2006.

Smith, Michael B. "'The Ego Idea of the Good Camper' and the Nature of Summer Camp." *Environmental History* 11, no. 1 (January 2006): 70–101.

Smocovitis, Vassiliki Betty. "Genetics Behind Barbed Wire: Masuo Kodani, Émigré Geneticists, and Wartime Genetics Research at Manzanar Relocation Center." *Genetics* 187, no. 2 (February 2011): 357–366.

Snyder, Timothy. *Black Earth: The Holocaust as History and Warning*. New York: Tim Duggan Books, 2015.

Sparrow, James T. *Warfare State: World War II Americans and the Age of Big Government*. New York: Oxford University Press, 2011.

Spickard, Paul. *Japanese Americans: The Formation and Transformation of an Ethnic Group*. Rev. ed. New Brunswick, NJ: Rutgers University Press, 2009.

Starn, Orin. "Engineering Internment: Anthropologists and the War Relocation Authority." *American Ethnologist* 13, no. 4 (November 1986): 700–720.

Stewart, Mart A. *"What Nature Suffers to Groe": Life, Labor, and Landscape on the Georgia Coast, 1680–1920*. Athens: University of Georgia Press, 1996.

Stewart, Todd. *Placing Memory: A Photographic Exploration of Japanese American Internment*. Essays by Natasha Egan and Karen J. Leong, afterword by John Tateishi. Norman: University of Oklahoma Press, 2008.

Suzuki, Peter T. "The University of California Japanese Evacuation and Resettlement Study: A Prolegomenon." *Dialectical Anthropology* 10, nos. 3–4 (April 1986): 189–213.

Tajima-Creef, Elena. *Imaging Japanese America: The Visual Construction of Citizenship, Nation, and the Body*. New York: New York University Press, 2004.

Takezawa, Yasuko I. *Breaking the Silence: Redress and Japanese American Ethnicity*. Ithaca, NY: Cornell University Press, 1995.

Tamura, Anna Hosticka. "Gardens Below the Watchtower: Gardens and Meaning in World War II Japanese American Incarceration Camps." *Landscape Journal* 23 (January 2004): 1–21.

Tamura, Anna Hosticka. "Gardens Below the Watchtower: Gardens and Meaning in World War II Japanese-American Internment Camps." Master of Landscape Architecture thesis, University of Washington, 2002.

Tamura, Linda. *Nisei Soldiers Break Their Silence: Coming Home to Hood River.* Seattle: University of Washington Press, 2012.

Taylor, Sandra C. *Jewel of the Desert: Japanese American Internment at Topaz.* Berkeley: University of California Press, 1993.

Tengen, Carla S. "Cultivating Communities: Japanese American Gardeners in Southern California, 1910–1980." PhD dissertation, Brown University, 2006.

Thomas, Dorothy Swaine. *The Salvage: Japanese American Evacuation and Resettlement.* Berkeley: University of California Press, 1952.

Thomas, Dorothy Swaine and Richard Nishimoto. *The Spoilage: Japanese American Evacuation and Resettlement.* Berkeley: University of California Press, 1946.

Todd, Anne Marie. *Communicating Environmental Patriotism: A Rhetorical History of the American Environmental Movement.* New York: Routledge, 2013.

Tomes, Nancy. *The Gospel of Germs: Men, Women, and the Microbe in American Life.* Cambridge, MA: Harvard University Press, 1998.

Tsu, Cecilia M. *Garden of the World: Asian Immigrants and the Making of Agriculture in California's Santa Clara Valley.* New York: Oxford University Press, 2013.

Tsuchida, Nobuya. "Japanese Gardeners in Southern California, 1900–1941." In *Labor Immigration Under Capitalism: Asian Workers in the United States Before World War II*, edited by Lucie Cheng and Edna Bonacich, 435–469. Berkeley: University of California Press, 1984.

Tsukashima, Ronald Tadao. "Politics of Maintenance Gardening and the Formation of the Southern California Gardeners' Federation." In *Green Makers: Japanese American Gardeners in Southern California*, edited by Naomi Hirahara, 67–93. Los Angeles: Southern California Gardeners' Federation, 2000.

Tucker, Richard P. and Edmund Russell, eds. *Natural Enemy, Natural Ally: Toward an Environmental History of War.* Corvallis: Oregon State University Press, 2004.

Villazor, Rose Cuison. "Rediscovering Oyama v. California: At the Intersection of Property, Race, and Citizenship." *Washington University Law Review* 87, no. 5 (2010): 979–1042.

Westbrook, Robert B. *Why We Fought: Forging American Obligations During World War II.* Washington, DC: Smithsonian Institution Press, 2004.

White, Richard. "'Are You an Environmentalist, or Do You Work for a Living?': Work and Nature." In *Uncommon Ground: Rethinking the Human Place in Nature*, edited by William Cronon, 171–185. New York: Norton, 1996.

White, Richard. *The Organic Machine: The Remaking of the Columbia River.* New York: Hill and Wang, 1995.

Wilson, Robert M. "Landscapes of Promise and Betrayal: Reclamation, Homesteading, and Japanese American Incarceration." *Annals of the Association of American Geographers* 101, no. 2 (March 2011): 422–444.

Worster, Donald. *Rivers of Empire: Water, Aridity, and the Growth of the American West*. New York: Pantheon Books, 1985.

Yagasaki, Noritaka. "Ethnic Cooperativism and Immigrant Agriculture: A Study of Japanese Floriculture and Truck Farming in California." PhD dissertation, University of California, Berkeley, 1982.

Yamashita, Wendi. "The Colonial and the Carceral: Building Relationships Between Japanese Americans and Indigenous Groups in the Owens Valley." *Amerasia Journal* 42, no. 1 (2016): 121–138.

Zimring, Carl A. *Clean and White: A History of Environmental Racism in the United States*. New York: New York University Press, 2016.

Index

Printed in the USA/Agawam, MA
December 9, 2019

744520.006